Innovations in Educational Ethnography

Theory, Methods, and Results

Edited by

George Spindler
Lorie Hammond

Ψ Psychology Press
Taylor & Francis Group

New York London

First Published by Lawrence Erlbaum Associates, Inc., Publishers
10 Industrial Avenue
Mahwah, New Jersey 07430

Reprinted 2010 by Psychology Press

Lawrence Erlbaum Associates, Inc., Publishers
10 Industrial Avenue
Mahwah, New Jersey 07430
www.erlbaum.com

Cover design by Kathryn Houghtaling Lacey

Library of Congress Cataloging-in-Publication Data

New horizons in the ethnography of education / [edited by] George Spindler.
    p. cm.
Includes bibliographical references and index.
ISBN 0-8058-4530-5 (cloth : alk. paper)
ISBN 0-8058-4531-3 (pbk. : alk. paper)
1. Educational anthropology. 2. Ethnology. I. Spindler, George Dearborn.

LB45.N49 2005
302.43—dc22

2005040154
CIP

Innovations in Educational Ethnography

Theory, Methods, and Results

Henry (Enrique) T. Trueba
October 29, 1931–July 17, 2004

In memory of our friend and colleague, his words,

"So onward dear friends and colleagues,
beacons of hope, tireless workers,
and leaders all!"

Contents

Preface

If schools are for all children to flourish, then the individual child can be our unit of concern, but not our unit of analysis or reorganization. Why should kids be the focus of change when it is the rest of us—the culture that is acquiring them—that arrange their trouble?
—McDermott and Varenne (chap. 1, this volume).

The above quote, from Ray McDermott and Hervé Varenne, sheds light on the purpose of this book. Herein lies a series of research articles that focus on and/or exemplify how ethnography, a research tool devoted to looking at human interaction as cultural process rather than individual psychology, can shed light on educational processes framed by the complex, internationalized societies we live in today. We invite you to read these pieces not only because each creates a thoughtful and enlightening journey, but also because the issues they raise are important to both educators and ethnographers.

We live in a society and a world in which education has become increasingly pivotal in determining individual opportunity. This has focused the attention of politicians, parents, and other citizens, as well as educators and researchers, on how to achieve equity and quality in education. The uneven school success on the part of various races, classes, and genders challenges the premises of our society, which would view itself as fair and democratic. In addition, both in the United States and abroad, increases in immigration in all countries and in schooling opportunities within third world countries have increased the cultural variation of students who attend schools. Non-Western and traditional world views are being brought into the schooling process, creating classrooms in which cultural brokering becomes an even more essential part of the teaching job than it has always been.

Despite the complexity of these situations, attempts to solve educational problems are often myopically focused on the problems of individual children or groups of children, rather on the larger forces which frame these dilemmas. For example, when we look at the question of "race," we tend to look at how students of various races succeed in or resist schooling, rather than at the structure of schools themselves, their position in a society with a history of racial inequality, or economic factors which require the production of unsuccessful under-classes. Perhaps we avoid this broader view because, as Pollock points out in chapter 4, once we are shown the Indian myth in which the earth rests on a platform on an elephant on top of a turtle, we can see that it is "turtles all the way down." To deconstruct the purposes and outcomes of schooling in modern, complex societies is to look at those societies "all the way down," as well as, as Nader (1974) suggests, "all the way up." In Erickson's eyes (see chapter 7), it is also important to look at turtles "side by side," as researchers working hand in hand with educators immersed in the challenges of modern schooling.

A major issue faced by those who would take on this task is to find that platform, atop elephant or turtle, that yields a clear view. One of the strengths that ethnography has always brought to education is that of "making the familiar strange," thus unearthing surprises in settings previously taken for granted. Since Roger Harker, the award-winning teacher who was only in actuality teaching his White, middle-class students, although no one could see that this was so, and Beth Ann, the model student who suffered psychological damage from the pressures adults placed upon her, ethnographers such as the Spindlers (2000) have used their craft to reveal parts of school culture which were previously invisible. Yet "making the familiar strange" is no easy task when the researcher him/herself is also a member of the society in question, subject to its own blind spots. Explorations concerning the positionality and methodology of the ethnographer play a large role in the included writings. These writings provide vistas on the relationship of researcher to subject, on the meaning of "participation" in participant observation, on ways to give voice to disenfranchised players, and on the complex ways in which all parties experience identities like "race" in the modern world.

This book is a product of both continuity and change. It presents current writings from mentors in the field of ethnography and education, as well as of their students, and of educators engaged in cultural studies of their work. In many ways, it provides fresh, new vistas on the old questions that have always guided ethnographic research, and can be used as a survey both of what ethnography has been and of what it is becoming. Each entry is unique in its approach, in keeping with the ethnographic tradition of unearthing the unexpected. No one philosophy guides the entries, nor were they chosen as exemplary of a particular approach. Yet foundational understandings and principles of ethnography shine through the work, in both predictable and unexpected ways.

While many chapters contain overlapping themes, we have divided the book into two rough categories. Part I contains theoretical chapters about ethnography or examples of innovative ethnography from particular perspectives; the chapters in Part II emphasize the application of ethnographic approaches to educational settings, where researchers, teachers, and students do their work together.

PART I: THEORETICAL AND METHODOLOGICAL EXPLORATIONS IN ETHNOGRAPHY

This section begins with a chapter, by McDermott and Varenne, which challenges researchers to step back from the "diagnostic and remedial preoccupations" of American education, and to ignore the failure of individual children or groups in order to focus on the culture which defines so many children as failing. McDermott and Varenne assert that "culture," rather than the individual or his/her social group, must be the crucial analytic unit for educational research. To understand how the culture which we all share is creating our educational dilemmas is the only way to solve these dilemmas. For "culture is not a past cause to a current self. Culture is the current challenge to possible future selves" (p. 8).

McDermott and Varenne describe three types of analysis which are often applied to social situations: a focus on the individual; a focus on social forces which determine the fate of the individual; and finally, a social transformation which enables individuals to work together to change those forces which surround and define them. In the third, and truly cultural, analysis, the goal is not to solve a problem, or to defend an individual who is its victim, but to reorganize society so that this kind of problem does not come up again. McDermott and Varenne then apply these three ways of thinking to tenacious problems which educators grapple with: school failure, gender, and race, and illustrate how rethinking each of these categories is a far more humane solution than attempting to "help" individual victims of these categories.

The work of McDermott and Varenne demonstrates the way in which an ethnographic approach to educational research can encourage social change through turning conventional understandings on their head. All change, seen in this light, must be reflexive, and must begin in all of us, not in a group "out there" that is having a problem.

> We cannot begin to make change out there until we have made change here, ... with ourselves, with those around us, at the borders than keep us in and others out. . . . The problem of American education is not that we have people divided into too many cultures; the problem is that we have a single culture full of people all too resourceful in dividing its people. (p. 38)

Building on McDermott and Varenne's general call to studying education ethnographically, other authors in Part I analyze various aspects of what this means. In chapters 2 and 3, Kimberly Powell and George Spindler address a central question in ethnography: what does participation mean when one is a "participant observer"? In both cases, these authors use a narrative account of their own experience in ethnography to explore the issue of participation.

In chapter 2, Powell describes her own embodied experience learning and studying Taiko drumming, and reflects upon this experience as both observer and participant. By becoming an apprentice to a performing company, Powell steps out of the role of the observer "on the side" into that of full participant, practicing and performing with a Taiko troupe, and even subjecting herself to rigorous evaluations experienced by apprentices to the troupe. Powell demonstrates that embodied experience yields different understandings than less complete immersion, and questions the often "anaesthetic" experiences, "devoid of heightened sensory experience, grace, purpose, and unity" which typify schooling and alienate so many students.

Powell's discussion provides a stance from which education is rarely viewed, and, in the manner suggested by McDermott and Varenne, challenges common assumptions about the role of the learner in both schooling and in research. It also challenges whether an ethnographer "on the side" can really understand what s/he is seeing, since the experience of participating, with the various risks associated, is significantly different than that of watching. In some ways, Powell's discussion foreshadows Erickson's later argument for co-research, in which he suggests that ethnographers too often live in a distorted "weightless" universe, where they watch Indians lifting canoes without seeing what it is like to lift the weight themselves.

Spindler's chapter addresses a similar theme through a narrative self-study of how being an ethnographer immersed in Native American culture affected his own and his wife's relationship to prior cultural assumptions and to their roles in an academic community. Spindler bases his article upon a definition of three kinds of selves—enduring, situated, and endangered—which emerge in various configurations when people bridge two or more cultural settings. In his own case, rational Western views of how the world works were challenged by Menominee ideas about predictive dreams, witching, and other supernatural phenomena as explanations of events. In describing his own position, caught between cultures, Spindler suggests explanations of how other people, such as Menominee acculturated to American society, manage similarly discrepant belief systems. As in the case of Powell, his work foreshadows some of the applied anthropology in Part II of this book, in which the relationship of schooling to students and teachers who hold multiple world views is addressed by Rosiek and Hammond.

In chapter 4, Mica Pollock carries forth themes from McDermott and Varenne in a way very different from Powell and Spindler. Looking back on several years of ethnographic work in a diverse, urban high school, Pollock traces her own transformation from a stance in which she defined "race" as a problem experienced by students in certain groups, to a broader look at the contradictory and complicated ways in which everyone in society defines race, in and out of school. Pollock defines her work as "race wrestling," in which she considers an important activity for not only educators but also researchers to engage. Like McDermott and Varenne, Pollock asserts that the "problem" of race is often created by the way it becomes defined and reinforced by kids and adults alike. Unfortunately, researchers concerned with questions of racial equity often engage in reinforcing stereotypes about racial identity through their own work. "Rarely do scholars examine the 'institutional choreography' (Fine, 1997) in which students and adults of various 'races', inside and outside of schools, together help produce racialized school patterns of failure or success" (p. 42). "Race wrestling" discourages interventions which reinforce fraudulent racial categories by attempting to "help" members of specific groups in favor of research which engages all of us in reinventing a society in which race as we know it no longer exists. Pollock's work wrestles with a complex taxonomy of the ways in which race is embraced and contradicted within one high school and within the educational research community, like an endless line of turtles, each reinforcing each other.

In chapter 5, Jason Raley also concerns himself with the redefinition of society, through a macro and micro description of a special school and of a classroom within that school in which diverse students living in a "murder capital" are able to find safety and, through this safety, to reconstruct their relationship to mainstream American society as successful participants. Raley's methodology is innovative, in that he not only provides a broad picture of how one high school achieves success in the face of great odds, but also provides a specific example, through linguistic analysis of one discussion, of how the safety created by this school setting enables students to interact in new and creative ways. Raley states that his linguistic analysis of one discussion contains "the most treasure," and we would agree. In this discussion, a group of African American teenagers display multiple identities, using the tools of popular culture and the discourse patterns they share as African Americans, to develop an understanding of a difficult Supreme Court case in which the First Amendment rights of a Ku Klux Klan member are defended. Through one discussion, Raley illustrates how these youth are able to "address the wider system" and forge new ways of trusting each other, creating a model from which we could all learn. As in McDermott and Varenne's theoretical framework, it is not the dilemma of the individual student, nor the admission of systemic guilt, which enabled change to occur. It is a creative remaking of the terms of engagement, molded from but not limited by the shared cultural material which participants bring to the table. A particularly hopeful aspect of Raley's work is that he illustrates how the terms of engagement can be reworked not through large-scale policies or political/social changes, but within a single school and classroom committed to creating a new kind of dialogue.

One beauty of ethnography is the variability of its lenses, and of the rich narratives which different lenses enable researchers to construct. Whereas Powell looked at participation and Raley at language, Ingrid Seyer-Ochi focuses on "place," a concept which has been more commonly applied to indigenous, rural settings, but is in her case focused on an urban neighborhood, San Francisco's Fillmore District. Through interviews with high school students and analysis of how they map their lives, Seyer-Ochi paints a close-grained portrait of race and poverty, danger and safety, within one neighborhood which feeds a diverse high school. Through this portrait, she illustrates the way in which Fillmore students become outsiders within their high school and in relation to opportunities for academic success.

Seyer-Ochi states that she analyzes "lived landscapes, the layered landscapes from which they emerge, and the opportunities they afford for youth." Although the landscape she portrays is hard to define geographically, being intermixed at its borders with other neighborhoods, the "ghetto" which it creates culturally is distinct and unforgettable. In the Fillmore, complex definitions of places perceived to be "inside" and "outside" are negotiated through ownership of "ghetto passes," won through participation in gang activities, and through family and community affiliations. Knowing your place, and hence where it is safe to go, becomes essential for survival. Seyer-Ochi herself obtained "guest passes" by traveling through the neighborhood with a few chosen informants, an activity which enabled her and us to see their world as they see it.

One striking aspect of Seyer-Ochi's work is her comparison of maps drawn by high school students from other parts of the city with those drawn by Fillmore students. Whereas other students draw many parts of the city, including downtown, their high school, tourist attractions, and ethnic neighborhoods, residents of the Fillmore draw only their own neighborhood in detail. Few artifacts could more clearly define "ghetto" than these maps. To Fillmore students, their own high school is not within their territory, which might explain why similar students, in Pollock's work, tend to inhabit the hallways and the outside of a similar school, rather than to be in the classroom. These students, in both cases predominantly African American, tend to see themselves as "outside," and, as Seyer-Ochi's student Anthony states, "you can either be inside or outside, but you can't be both."

This is true, but it is also not that simple. As Seyer-Ochi communicates, through neighborhood tours in which the reader participates, life in the Fillmore involves constant contradictions between inside and out. Residents both complain that the police do not protect them from drug lords, and protest if their neighborhood is raided. Similarly, even a youth who dropped out of school brags to Seyer-Ochi, whom he knows to be a teacher, that he is taking classes at community college. School, like cops, holds status yet must be resisted. While the Fillmore has a "local master identity" which frames the opportunities possible within it, this identity is in constant tension with the rest of the city, and is an artifact which, as McDermott and Varenne state, we all create together.

PART II: STUDYING "SIDE BY SIDE": ETHNOGRAPHIC APPLICATIONS TO EDUCATIONAL SETTINGS

Just as McDermott and Varenne provide a theoretical framework for the studies in Part I, Erickson's essay on "studying side by side" provides guidance for the chapters in Part II. It should be noted that, in keeping with Erickson's suggestions, many of the pieces in this section are produced by researchers who are not ethnographers, per se, but are educational researchers applying ethnographic tools within educational settings. We suggest that one of the biggest current innovations in educational ethnography is its application to a variety of fields outside of anthropology. Although some anthropologists are concerned about the ability of educators and others not trained in anthropology to do good ethnography, we feel that the interest in ethnography currently exhibited in applied settings, such as schools and medical clinics, is playing a major role in making practitioners in various fields aware of how cultural processes determine the success or failure of their efforts. Erickson's suggestion, that we research "side by side" with such practitioners, provides a framework for how ethnographers might apply their expertise to helping practitioners to meet the complex cultural challenges they face.

Erickson traces the evolution of ethnographic research in terms of focus. Traditionally, he states, anthropologists have studied people of lower power and social rank than themselves. In the anthropology of education, most studies have focused on the experience of minority and/or poor children in schools. To balance this trend, Nader (1974) suggests that anthropologists should "study up." In her view, it is only through understanding the politicians, businessmen, testing companies and others who determine school policy, that are we able to see how the structures which disenfranchised children encounter are created in the first place.

In Erickson's view, however, there is a third alternative, and that is to study "side by side," in partnership with educators who are out in schools, dealing with problems on a daily basis. When researchers and practitioners participate in collaborative action research, practitioners are involved not only in data collection and analysis, but also in problem formation and research problem definition. And researchers are involved not only as friendly outsiders, but as insiders engaged in helping to solve problems themselves. In Erickson's terms, they cease to be involved in a "weightless universe," watching a canoe be built, by helping to lift the canoe themselves.

The chapters which follow Erickson's, and make up Part II of this book, are produced by researchers who are engaged in collaborative research within educational settings. These researchers find various ways to partner with teachers and community members. Rosiek and Hammond are teacher educators who partner with teachers and student teachers. Brandt is an instructor in a higher education ethnobotany class, who partnered with her students in reflecting on the relationship between botany and place. And Nichols and Tippins partner with a large team of Filipino teacher educators, teachers, and community members to explore how science and environmental education might be reconstructed to be more relevant to children living in a rural barangay.

The partnerships in research represented by these authors are in science education, but could have happened as easily, or perhaps more easily, in other educational fields. Science is a field which has traditionally considered itself an objective, a-cultural, and a-historical form of discourse. Re-positioning science as a cultural activity, like any other human endeavor, has profound epistemological, pedagogical, and methodological implications. Some of these emerge in the chapters which make up Part II of this book, and which illustrate the kinds of research which an ethnographic approach to education is enabling in a variety of applied fields.

In chapter 8, Jerry Rosiek compares innovations in teacher education with those in cultural anthropology. In teacher education, we must consider whose knowledge defines good teaching, whether or not teachers can produce their own scholarship, how this scholarship should be represented, and what part collaboration might play in the process. In cultural anthropology, people ask similar questions about who should represent the culture of another, how it should be represented, and what role collaboration might play. In Rosiek's view, much might be gained in marrying teacher education with ethnography by making cultural studies "foundational" to teacher education.

The rich possibilities which such a marriage might provide are illustrated by a narrative case study in which Rosiek and Chang, a Hmong high school teacher, collaborated to deconstruct a teaching dilemma which Chang encountered in his biology class. This narrative involves many voices, including that of a female Hmong student who challenged Chang for teaching his students a Western interpretation of disease, Chang's own multivocality in relation to his family's response to illness, and Rosiek's own misinterpretations of the situation. Throughout these narratives, Rosiek illustrates how all players, including the researcher, became caught in culturally conditioned assumptions which their dialogue enabled them to deconstruct. The chapter points out how teachers and researchers alike are blinded as well as enabled by their cultural lenses, and that their own limitations color how they see classroom research. In this situation, Rosiek suggests that all teachers need to learn ethnographic tools so that they might analyze their own reactions reflexively. In a parallel way, Rosiek suggests that the field of anthropology of education can benefit from access to teacher knowledge. Central to Rosiek's work is the notion that education is a cultural rather than a psychological process, and that teachers need to learn tools which enable them to view their work in cultural terms.

In chapter 9, Lorie Hammond, a teacher educator, attempts to "dig deeper" into the ways that pre-service teachers' attitudes toward science are affected by their background culture and experience. Hammond's focus is on cultural dialogues which were integrated into a science methods class for elementary teachers as a kind of "cultural therapy." These dialogues result from a process of planning "standards-based" science lessons for diverse children, then deconstructing how these lessons match or contradict the world views of the diverse pre-service teachers presenting them. Several dialogues are presented as examples of an approach in which science teaching is considered as a cultural process, involving dialogues between the contradictory perspectives which student teachers hold as members of minority communities and as emergent teachers. Central to this chapter are the ideas that (a) science teaching is based on cultural rather than neutral assumptions, (b) the question of "whose" science is taught is a political and historical one, and (c) student teachers' identities as teachers are formed not only in relation to their training, but also in relation to the views which they bring from their own backgrounds. If these premises are true, then teacher education needs to incorporate cultural dialogues such as the ones presented here, even in courses like science which are generally thought to be value neutral.

Like Rosiek, Hammond suggests that both ethnographers and teachers would benefit from research partnerships. If science education is a cultural activity which should be based on a dialogue between various world views, then such dialogue is necessary in the diverse K–12 classroom, and should be built into curriculum reforms. Generally, curriculum reform is viewed as a decontextualized process which can be applied to any situation. However, this chapter suggests that curricula must be able to incorporate and respond to the strengths and weaknesses of local communities. What better partners in inventing and carrying out community-responsive curricula than ethnographers and teachers, and/or teachers schooled in the skills of ethnography?

In chapter 10, Carol Brandt describes how a senior college ethnobotany course is altered through the consideration of how place, "the locations in which we build knowledge in science, is linked to epistemology—the origin, nature, and limits of knowledge." Brandt's approach brings experience of ethnography—participant observation through a day-long field trip, interviews with community members, and an anthropological consideration of place itself—into a college class. The embodied experience which students have in the community of Placitas, exploring the issue of water rights in the arid southwest, served to broaden their dialogue to incorporate both local and global issues and perspectives on social justice. Brandt concludes that "science should never be presented as objective, abstract, or detached, but has a place in students' lives and in the daily lives of people beyond the university walls."

The themes which Brandt's ethnobotany course touches are similar to those of Hammond, in that both transform a science course into an ethnographic experience which involves students in reflexive dialogue about their own relationship to science, the natural world, and culture. Brandt's course is also reminiscent of the work of Powell, who suggests that if embodied experience results in qualitatively different insights on the part of ethnographers, then it is a powerful tool in all kinds of learning. Like Powell, Brandt's students experienced an environment first-hand, rather than reading about it, watching slides or videos, or interacting with speakers at the university. This experience then facilitated a kind of "cultural therapy" in which new insights were evoked.

The final chapter of the book describes a collaborative action research project involving Sharon Nichols, Deborah Tippins, Lourdes Morano, Purita Bilbao, and Tessie Barcenal and the teachers and villagers in a Filipino Barangay called Casay. This research is collaborative at several levels. The purpose of the research, to create a community-based approach to science teacher professional development, is based on the assumption that curricula for a barangay should not be standard, neutral, and international, but should rather be appropriate, contextualized, and responsive to the needs of the people it teaches. The methodology of the research centers around the use of "memory banking" to gather data about community life. "Memory banking" has previously been an agricultural anthropology technique for recording native knowledge about seeds, which was used by Virginia Nazarea, a Filipina researcher. This technique was modified by Nichols et al. to become a tool through which a community can record its collective knowledge of various aspects of life, such as shell fishing, growing buri for baskets, running a local store, and so on. The desire to record community life as experienced by natives, and to use these records as a basis for science education, reveals a deep methodological commitment to collaboration. And finally, the social structure and style of operation of the Casay research team, which involves two American science educators collaborating with three Filipina counterparts, and in turn with teachers and villagers, reflects a deep commitment to an egalitarian, anti-colonial approach to research. Rather than approaching the barangay as "experts," the researchers elicit the expertise of local people, acting as ethnographers, in order to tease out the community's relationship to its environment, the problems it faces, and how science education can be used as a tool to address these problems.

The work of Nichols, Tippins, Morano, Bilbao, and Barcenal not only models Erickson's idea of researching "side by side," but also illustrates the power of such an approach to enable social change. Rather than building a science lab, the community chose to construct a huge palapa hut, without walls, so that as many people as possible could be accommodated for activities, and so that the center could face the outside world without obstruction.

Located on a bluff above the sea, surrounded by a cashew orchard, a net but-terfly house, and a meandering elementary school surrounded by community-tended gardens, the Casay Environmental Education and Indigenous Study Center represents a seamless flow between science, the natural world, and community life. In this site, science and cultural studies are merged in a way which engages community members as ethnographers, children as agents of community improvement, and teachers and researchers as guides and chroni-clers. In Casay, the boundaries which encase traditional research and sepa-rate it from the communities it describes are erased. Both science and cultural studies become the domain of teachers and farmers, children and adults, re-searchers and locals, united in a single purpose: gaining knowledge that will help to improve the life of Casay.

FINAL THOUGHTS

This book is the work of many hands, and provides excellent examples, in our opinion, of trends in both basic and applied ethnography of education. It is clear to us, and will hopefully be clear to the reader, that these two kinds of work augment and reinforce each other. They also represent important cur-rent research directions: in-depth reflection on the process of ethnography, and an application of the insights of ethnography to teaching and learning in schools, universities, and communities.

We particularly want to acknowledge the contributors, whose work is not only insightful and important, but also delightful to read. These are good sto-ries. We hope that you enjoy them as much as we did.

—*Lorie Hammond and George Spindler*
August, 2005

I
Theoretical and Methodological Explorations in Ethnography

1

Reconstructing Culture
in Educational Research

Ray McDermott
Stanford University

Hervé Varenne
Teachers College, Columbia University

Ray McDermott is a cultural anthropologist and a Professor in the School of Education, Stanford University. He has been doing research on theories of political economy and their relation to theories of mind, literacy, learning, ability, disability, and genius. From years of close work at the level of the classroom, his overall take is that American schooling is the unfortunate handmaiden of the divisive social forces that lead a duplicitous life in all the cultural materials available to participants. Recent work includes "A Century of Margaret Mead" and "Estranged ~~Labor~~ Learning" (with Jean Lave).

Hervé Varenne is a cultural anthropologist and a Professor of Education at Teachers College, Columbia University, where he is chair of the Department of International and Transcultural Studies. He is the author of many books and articles on aspects of everyday life and education in the United States and Ireland, including *Americans Together* (1977), *American School Language* (1983), and *Ambiguous Harmony: Family Talk in America* (1992). Most recently, he and Ray McDermott published *Successful Failure* (1998).

> *The word of ambition at the present day is Culture.*
> —Ralph Waldo Emerson (1860)

We concluded our recent book on *Successful Failure* with an unusual call. To improve the fate of children at risk of any labeled failure, "the first and perhaps only step is to turn away from them" (Varenne & McDermott, 1998, p. 217). Counter-intuitive, yes, and surprisingly constructive and respectful to all children. If the only tools available for helping children in trouble are the diagnostic and remedial preoccupations of American education, it might be best to forget individual children and focus instead on how we have created contexts that make some children—about half of them—so problematic. If schools are for all children to flourish, then the individual child can be our unit of concern, but not our unit of analysis or reorganization. Why should kids be the focus of change when it is the rest of us—the culture that is acquiring them—that arranges their trouble? This conclusion was the systematic product of a *cultural* analysis applied to the most pressing issue in American schooling: the attribution of success/failure. In this chapter, we restate our conclusion in order, first, to discuss why culture—and neither the individual nor socializing group—is the crucial analytic unit for educational research and, second, to sketch how a cultural analysis leads to a new articulation of major policy issues, in particular, the failure of students and its complex relation to kinds of person by gender and race.[1]

When we studied children having bad days at school, home, or after-school clubs, we often saw adults rushing to help, but unsure of what to do. Comfort them, protect them, tutor them, these were short-lived possibilities. Helping individual children takes time, and their problems, even at an early age, can seem so deep. Problems continue, and adults run out of time, patience, and know-how. Then, in a fateful shorthand that lasts and lasts, the adults diagnose "the child's problem." Thirty years of researching children with other children, teachers, and parents have led us to doubt any special help that first requires a personal identification or diagnosis and then proceeds with a treatment of the person. To care for the children in trouble, the best action is not to diagnose them, but to reorganize the processes that made adults focus on the children and their received problems rather than on adults themselves. As researchers and policy-makers, and as teachers and parents interested in the best for every individual child, we should not allow isolation, diagnosis, and remediation to be our only recourse. Suppose we focus instead on the institutions that foreground each child's problem, including the institutions that place some of us seemingly in a position to help. Where do these institutions come from historically? What are the grounds of their authority? How are they maintained? How can they be played with, tampered with, and otherwise transformed in unpredictable directions?

Educational institutions must be faced as historical, arbitrary, and artificial, that is, as *cultural* in the best sense of the term. The concept of "culture"

---

[1]We thank Eric Bredo, Shelley Goldman, James Greeno, Mizuko Ito, Rachel Lotan, Mica Pollock, and Ritti Lukose for particularly helpful comments on a much earlier version of this chapter. One paragraph is adapted from McDermott (1999), another from Greeno et al. (1999).

is not new anymore, and no one should use it without respect for its lineage. In the last generation, psychology, sociology, philosophy, and literary criticism have joined anthropology, history, and linguistics in recapturing a sense of collectivity and duration by making culture an indispensable theoretical term. At their best, they have stressed culture as active and constitutive, and so do we—although not without some trepidation. Recently, many in the disciplines most closely involved with culture, fearing what has been done to "culture," have attempted to move beyond the term (e.g., in anthropology, Abu-Lugod, 1991; Ortner, 1999; Rosaldo, 1990; in sociology, Bonnell & Hunt, 1999). We share their concern, but do not think we can ignore whatever it is that anthropologists and others write about "nowadays" when they write about something that is "multi-spatio-ethno-fragmented-scapes/scopes-as-processually-practiced-and-agentively-reinvented-contestatorially" (Boon, 1999, p. 2)—in one word: culture.

American anthropology borrowed the term *culture* from 19th-century German philosophers and transformed it for new purposes. As Boasian anthropologists developed it, culture was used to celebrate what others, far from Europe, produce in their daily round. It was also used, by Franz Boas himself (1940) and more explicitly by the founders of the anthropology of education, Jules Henry (1963) and George Spindler (Spindler & Spindler, 2000), to warn that all cultures are dangerous to their participants, who cannot escape being identified, understood, or explained with the categories used by their significant others. And then something was lost, first in versions of anthropology, and then, even more radically, when the concept was borrowed by other disciplines, and particularly by researchers in education. In the movement from "culture" (as the process driving human adaptations and their products) to "a culture" (as a temporary configuration of institutions, many borrowed from neighbors far and wide) to "a person's culture" (as the internalized property of a grown-up self), the collectivity that was core to earlier theories disappeared. Reconstructing culture in educational research may be part of what has to be done to reconstruct education.

After a section on the misleading use of culture in education, our chapter is in three main parts. First, we make "culture" the central unit of analysis in educational research and propose three requirements of a cultural analysis: a minimal unit of three or more people interpreting each other across time; a goal of moving systematically beyond received categories; and a logic of focusing less on the behavior of isolated persons and more on the work people do to isolate each other as problems independent of their mutuality. Second, we suggest what might be gained by a strict cultural analysis of phenomena one may initially want to address as matters of academic achievement, gender, or race. Third, we note further the consequences of a cultural approach for systematic investigation or research.

CULTURE: FROM PAST CAUSE
TO CURRENT CHALLENGE

Every thought you now have and every act and intention owes its complexion to the acts of your dead and living brothers.

—William James (1868)

The application of the concept of culture to educational issues has been both remarkable and disappointing: remarkable in initially moving theory away from a myopic concern with the properties of individuals, and disappointing when conceptualized as a variable explaining individual behavior. Informed readers of educational research might be confused. Did not anthropologists urge educational researchers to use culture as a key category in the study of individual learning? Yes, as stated, but not much as taken. The initial purpose was to encourage educational researchers to expand the list of things considered in any theory of learning (or any apparent lack of learning), but the deeper purpose, only slowly realized in response to how culture came be popularized in educational writing, was to substitute culture for the individual child as the unit of analysis. Methodologically, anthropologists have always proceeded this way. They have always tried to study what they foolishly called whole cultures—foolishly because they necessarily studied only parts of cultures, parts often borrowed from still other cultures—but behind the rush to wholeness was a sound instinct: the theoretical prize always went to fieldworkers who unpacked the largest and most inclusive forms of constraint on the behavior of individuals. The unit of analysis was the tribe, the region, the economy, the language, the kinship system, and so on, often analyzed in action, fully contested, argued over, worried about, died for, and sometimes rearranged. Individuals and their psychological make-up—good term, *make-up*, for individuals are always made up—were crucial, of course, but never independent of the worlds with which they were in never-relenting interaction.

Consider only the following:

[The culture concept] denotes an historically transmitted pattern of meanings embodied in symbols, a system of inherited conceptions expressed in symbolic forms by means of which men communicate, perpetuate, and develop their knowledge about and attitudes toward life. (Geertz, 1966, p. 89) or that:

> The term culture [refers to] what is learned, . . . the things one needs to know in order to meet the standards of others. . . . If culture is learned, its ultimate locus must be in individuals rather than in groups. (Goodenough, 1971, pp. 19–20)

Both these statements can be, and often are, interpreted to mean that the communicating and learning individual is a privileged unit in cultural analysis. A methodological individualism is more apparent in Goodenough than in Geertz (see the critique by Geertz, 1973, p. 11, of Goodenough for "holding that 'culture [is located] in the minds and hearts of men' "). The differences between them are small once we compare the methods and results of their fieldwork and miniscule if we compare their anthropological approaches to the work of American educational researchers who assume that, if school is not going well, we should try to fix the kids, sometimes their teachers or parents, occasionally the school system, but never those of us who are watching, documenting, diagnosing, researching, and prognosticating. Both Geertz and Goodenough became important anthropologists because they carefully watched people in interaction and listened endlessly not only to interpretations of those interactions but to interpretations of the interpretations, each level being a thread in a knitted portrait eventually brought home in a report (see Geertz, 1960, 1973; Goodenough, 1951). Individuals were their friends, but analytically, we repeat, analytically, they always looked at those persons with a consideration of everyone else in the interpretive networks called Java, Bali, or Truk. Cultural analysis, like school reform, requires we take persons seriously while analytically looking through them—as much as possible in their own terms—to the world with which they are struggling. It is not easy, but it is the best way to see them in their full complexity; anything less delivers a thin portrait of their engagements and leaves them vulnerable to being labeled, classified, diagnosed, blamed, charged, and found lacking without any consideration of how they had been arranged, misheard, unappreciated, set up, and denied by others.

Most anthropologists have emphasized that culture is, above all, about "activities" in relation to a people's "natural environment, to other groups, to members of the group itself and of each individual to himself" (Boas, 1911/ 1938, p. 149). Recently, the same intuition has been recaptured in various theories of "practice" "situated" in "distributed" settings, thereby pointing researchers toward both historical conditions and personal activity (Cole, 1996; Holland et al., 1998; Lave & McDermott, 2002; Lave & Wenger, 1992; Ortner, 1984).

When William James (1868) remarked that "every thought you now have and every act and intention owes its complexion to the acts of your dead and living brothers" (yes, and sisters, of course), he offered a self that is analytically and experientially available only in relation to others, the others actively making something for the self to work with and reorganize. To locate even the most private self, we must focus on its coordination with what has been made by dead and living relatives and neighbors. As John Dewey put it later (1920, p. 200), social institutions are "not a means for obtaining something for individuals, not even happiness. They are the means of creating individuals."[2] Culture is not a consequence of adding up individuals, but of people dealing with each other under both perduring and emergent circumstances. Take a fact from our biographies. Varenne cannot deny he is "French," because all who matter to him know he was born and raised in France. Nor can McDermott deny he is "Irish American" of a kind easily found in New York City. Analytically, we want to resist these commonsensical attributions, because they mask both the processes that make France and America and the activities of all those who must make their life there. To say Varenne is French and just French is to miss how France has been and continues to be a pressing concern for those born in France, Algeria, Canada, and so on. To say McDermott is just Irish American is to miss how definitions of ethnicity, race, social class, religion, and so on, have been a problem, not only for him or those born in the United States, but for the billions of people touched by everything "made in America." *Culture is not a past cause to a current self. Culture is the current challenge to possible future selves.* Specifically, in the context of the United States, America is not what makes Americans. America is the current challenge to the future of all those who cannot escape being caught by the institutions of its State in their many incarnations, wherever, and dare we say whenever, they build their lives.

A focus on culture brings accounts of what has been made for us and what we are now making. Dead and living brothers and sisters have made and continue to make facts for us. Every "fact" is only, as Ralph Waldo Emerson put it (1850/1995), "but some rumor of the fact." Rumors are always open to manipulation, and they are hard to ignore. This child is a success! That child is a failure! "Just the test scores, ma'am." America will have its successes and failures for all to see. It is the American way, the way school is done by often re-

---

[2]In commenting on the above line from Dewey, George Geiger (1939, p. 449) anticipated our own phrasing: "It is only when we turn our backs on the preciously isolated Individual and his changeless nature that anything can be done."

luctant agents.[3] Anything we do or say makes facts for others to accept, reject, and build anew. They do the same for us. Rumors told and retold make the world of today remarkably like the world of yesterday. They reconstitute us. Reconstituted rumors can become small facts in the midst of our families or large facts on a world scale; they can become medium-sized facts on the scale of what we write as anthropologists in Schools of Education, who get read and possibly appropriated for political purposes far beyond us. As social scientists intimately concerned with education, we believe these facts must be faced and culture is the most powerful concept available to catch the action in its full complexity.

WHY CULTURE?

And in this staggering disproportion between man and no-man, there is no place for purely human boasts of grandeur, or for forgetting that men build their cultures by huddling together, nervously loquacious, at the edge of an abyss.
—Kenneth Burke (1935)

Desperately Seeking Units

Let us start with an evocative contrast of disciplinary units of analysis in educational research:

For a psychological inquiry, only one subject is necessary; the minimal unit of analysis is the individual person making a move; and the fundamental cause of the move can be found far in the person's past.

For a social inquiry, two individuals are necessary; the minimal unit of analysis is established in their interaction, and the fundamental cause for either person's move can be found in what the other person did.

---

[3]The word *agent* here is a challenging wink to all those who consider the kind of analysis we present as not paying enough attention to the "agency" of individuals. If paying attention leads back to a concern with the socialized properties of selves, we do not do agency. If paying attention includes a deliberate search for aspects of a person's conditions that the person actually engages, that is, if we approach the person as having become—if only for a moment, or perhaps for a lifetime—the agent "of" the institution that authorizes the performance of specific acts in given contexts, then we are precisely interested in agency. For example, all persons who find themselves in the position of "school teacher" are necessarily, and however reluctantly, "agents of the School."

> For a cultural inquiry, three or more people are necessary; the minimal unit of analysis is established by two of them interacting and the third one interpreting their behavior; and the issue of cause fades into the background as one is led to focus on the consequences of action-as-interpreted (adapted from Arensberg, 1982).

This contrast set is helpful as long as we do not take it literally. It is particularly telling at the level of examples and conclusions where the contrasting evocation of psychological, social, and cultural analyses covers how the disciplines are popularly identified. However psychologists operate on their data, their examples and conclusions are reported as involving individual persons making up their minds. Similarly, social analysts claim to account for the influence of one person (or group) on others. In contrast, cultural analysts should focus on how a wider group of people together act, interpret, and make consequential. Through a cultural analytic lens, people work together, they retell what they just did, and then act again on the basis of what was said to have happened. Cultural analysts are interested in individuals and their interactions, of course, but they are driven to focus, first, on the collective constructions all actors must deal with—whether they personally accept, understand, or even know much about these constructions—and, second, on what others will do, in the future, with what the original actors did.

When applied to schooling, a cultural analysis is less about who is going to succeed, and more about how institutions are built in which so many children can be declared failures. What is it about America that people keep asking of their own children what each child cannot do? How are opportunities organized that so many parents feel relieved when they hear about children from other families doing badly in school? When applied to categories for naming kinds of people, a cultural analysis is less about how people in the different groups can be expected to behave, and more about how people in ever shifting circumstances develop categories for consistently assigning behavioral traits to make up kinds of persons (Frake, 1980, 1998; Michalchik, 2000; Pollock, chapter 4, this volume; Raley, chapter 5, this volume; Rosaldo & Flores, 1997; Seyer-Ochi, 2002, chapter 6, this volume).

In brief, given how units are defined in a study of cultural processes:

> A minimal cultural analysis asks: *What are the resources available to people in a given situation, how and when are they applied, to whom, and with what consequences? Who else is concerned with the people a given situation, and what are the mechanisms that allow them to limit or amplify what is done?*

A minimal cultural analysis in educational research asks: *How can we specify both the promise and the limitations of the resources available to the educating professions? Who else is involved in limiting and expanding what these professions propose, and what are the resources at their disposal?*

A minimal policy analysis based on a cultural analysis then asks: *How can we reorganize resources to construct a world that more closely approximates democratic ideals? Where should we focus our action?*

To give all children equivalent chances, we should spend less time evaluating them, ranking them, and then compensating for the problems said to account for their failure. The problem facing American education is not that we have so many failing children. It is rather that we have so many scales ready to show children failing, a problem made more intractable given the many adults invested in identification and remediation.

The Goal of a Cultural Analysis

One had . . . to come into contact with an alien culture in order to understand that a culture was not a community basket weaving project, nor yet an act of God; was something neither desirable nor undesirable in itself, being inevitable, being nothing more or less than the recorded and visible effects on a body of people of the vicissitudes with which they had been forced to deal.
—James Baldwin (1955)

The following account of culture at work begins, as every story about culture must, in a single place, in what is commonly known as "a culture" or, in this illustrative case, "three" cultures. The story expands quickly across continents and decades as the specifics of the local are grasped in their connections with a wider world. Along the way, an object of concern gets transformed from an unworkable solution to a newly defined problem. This is the way life is, and a cultural analysis should mirror the process.

The adventure begins in 1915 in Tuscany. Three archaeologists reported excavating ancient Etruscan warriors (Culture I) exactly like what experts had imagined. Ancient Etruscans were a high style mystery at the time, and modern Western literati (Culture II) were anxious to locate European origins in the non-Aegean and non-Semitic world of Northern Italy. Despite questions about the archaeologists, the warriors were accepted as genuine, and an Etruscan hall was built at the Metropolitan in 1933. Almost 40 years after their discovery, a curator (Culture III) walked through the hall and suddenly saw a 19th-century work. A faker figured out how to forge a 19th-century version of an ancient Etruscan horse, but not a 20th-century version. By 1953, the 19th century had become apparent, and the forgery was discovered (the details are in von Bothmer & Noble, 1961). Literary critic Hugh Kenner (1985) offers a nice description:

> The faker had worked into [the warriors] every Etruscan mannerism he knew about, and every nineteenth century mannerism he didn't. The style of your own time, it seems, is always invisible. Then time passed, until one fine day an expert registered "nineteenth century!" The stylistic marks of the time in which it was made had, so to speak, worked their way up to visibility; in a few more, presumably, they will have quite overwhelmed all the detail that once looked Etruscan.

One culture, that is, a particular configuration of institutions, political groups and their alliances, people distributed in various positions, discourse styles, and so on, defined a problem: What can we find out about our glorious past, and can we find an ancient Etruscan warrior to fill in the picture? Reason and sentiment produced the need for facts, and a faker in turn produced the artifacts. A culture defined a problem, and a self-conscious member, unfortunately a faker, methodically figured out an acceptable solution and served it up for a handsome profit. Another culture, well, the same culture later by 40 years, recognized the solution as a new and different problem and the Etruscan forgeries were removed.

Many educational professionals, researchers included, have the same status as the museum curators: They are given the authority to place something made up and given to them ("facts" and "data"—both rumors, but precisely organized for the purpose) in a particular place of honor or shame constructed by a complex political world that defines problems and suggests where convincing solutions might be found. Educational researchers often answer to the problems posed by the culture and, worse, they do so both in terms suggested by the culture and without consideration of how the problems and suggested answers came to be so well defined. Educational researchers rarely consider how unlikely it is that a culture formulating a problem of type X could also produce a solution that would not recreate the circumstances that originally brought the problem to attention. In America, generations have given authority to such statements as: "Yes, we continually record unequal school performance across racial, ethnic, class, and gender lines. This is because there is something wrong with either the kids or their schools." Generations have also agreed about the questions to ask: "What is wrong with kids who fail, or what is wrong with their schools?" They point at likely causes: "It must have to do with a lack of genetic intelligence, bad social conditions, irresponsible parents, wrong habits of speech, misunderstanding teachers, incompetent administrators, etc." Any statement by a researcher, critic, or political activist who follows this line of argument will be entertained, discussed, contested, and likely turned into a policy.

We suggest it is the very play of argumentation that may be at fault for producing the particular pains people in education continue to suffer. A cultural analysis inquires into the play of argumentation for signs suggesting how it is anchored in a particular time and place among a people with a shared history. A cultural analysis is not about giving solutions to acknowledged and likely false problems, but about sketching and confronting the conditions that tied problems and apparent solutions together. A cultural analysis should produce more inclusive questions and more comprehensive answers. This is not an easy quest, for cultural analysts are no less embedded in current circumstances than the rest of educational research. It is not easy to do alone and not worth doing haphazardly. In the next section, we offer a procedure—logical and in that sense partial and not uniformly useful, but a procedure nonetheless—for accomplishing the contrarian goal of a cultural analysis.

The Logic of a Cultural Analysis
(Beyond Individual/Social)

> ... individual man, since his separate existence is manifested only by ignorance and error, so far as he is anything apart from his fellows, and from what he and they are to be, is only a negation.
> —Charles Sanders Peirce (1868)

For heuristic purposes, we present the logic of a cultural analysis as a movement in three stages from American commonsense (focus on the individual), to the first versions of the reaction against a simplistic individualism (focus on social forces deterministic of individual behavior), to a transformation of individual and social by emphasizing the activities of persons working together with pre-existing resources that they reconstruct through their interaction. Taking educational problems through these three stages of analysis can deliver a different sense of what is wrong and what can be done.

Stage I. In American public discourse, problems (school failure, gender or race inequalities) are defined often as the problems of individuals (society may be the cause, but it is the individual who is the site of the problem). Although such formulations have intuitive pull, they are undermined by a weak account of the worlds in which individuals develop and/or display and/or get diagnosed as having problems. They also have a long history of blaming the victim. In short: "Those poor people have many problems. Someone should help them."

Stage II.   In the name of being more inclusive, the same problems are often described as the product of overwhelming social forces. This formulation has the advantage of blaming the victim a little less, but leaves the problems intact and, worse, identifiable in the lives of the unfortunate. The problem stays far from those who diagnose and make policy. In short: "Those poor people sure get pushed around. Too bad we can't help them directly."

Stage III.   It takes a crowd of active and intelligent individuals to put together a problem. The person with the problem behavior is only the point of focus. It takes others to set the stage for a problem, to recognize it, document it, worry about it, explain it, remediate it, and still more people to observe, interpret, and comment on the whole process. By the time a school problem gets the attention of government policy, just about everyone has had or is about to have a say on the topic. It takes concerted effort for a people to put together a recognizable problem to acquire a next generation of children. In short: "Let's change the world enough that these problems do not come up anymore."

Stage III has the advantage of taking into account everyone *and* their history *as they continue to make it.* By this way of thinking, problems are not just the result of old causes; rather, they are continually remade under new conditions, even by those who seek specifically to remediate them. This way of thinking seeks what is most powerful among the people observed in the institutional settings where they conduct their lives. What first calls attention to a potential problem, the symptom, so to speak, can often be shown to be linked to other facts even more powerful than the original fact itself. This makes both analysis and change difficult to do. This is most everyone's experience. Education is difficult to make better.

Difficult, yes, but culture is not fate. Institutionalized practices—schools, admission boards, testing companies, and so forth—have been made and can be remade. All of them have taken shape after extensive controversy sensitive to, and symptomatic of, the conditions of the time and depend on constant contributions from each of us. Our common future is not completely determined. New educational researchers, like the museum curator at the Etruscan exhibit in the 1950s, can always notice how a major institution has been fooled; then we can use their authority to demote what others had promoted.

Do all kids have to fall into success and failure boxes once and for all? And why do these boxes overlap so thoroughly with the boxes that separate male from female (and least in math and science) and black from white? In the following discussion, we offer a redefinition of school failure in relation to gender and race. Each example develops the same three stages of analysis. Each one has its own story to tell, but cumulatively, despite their varying data sources, methods, and practical implications, they give a sense of coherence and progress of two kinds: first, a shift from talking about kinds of person (failures, women, and African Americans) to an analysis of the cultural world that conjures up such persons to be talked about and, second, an analytic move beyond the commonsense dichotomies (success/failure, male/female, white/black) that simplify the world without taking into account the principles that organize it.

CULTURE APPLIED

No people come into possession of a culture without having paid a heavy price for it.

—James Baldwin (1955)

Failure's Failure (Beyond Success/Failure)

We start with the identified "problem" of school failure (however defined) and the temptation to look for causes and then solutions that would transform "failure" into "success." We can only summarize the argument from *Successful Failure* in the hope of circumscribing the political and moral issues at stake in a call to understand research on school failure as part of the problem of school failure. Here we go, in three stages: first, an issue, school failure, that moves us; then the realization it is not what it appears to be, for the reason that we seem to be so relentlessly successful at producing, documenting, and consuming failure; and finally an inquiry into what makes it and us tick and how we might reorganize the "us" enough to see the "it" in a new way. In popular discourse, the preferred mode of conversation about school failure is focused on the individual child; the preferred alternative is focused on the school and its society; to these, we add a third stage by focusing on the culture we make available to each other.

Stage I. Isn't it obvious all children are born uniquely different and differentially special, and don't individual differences account for why some do
better in schools than others? As it is always possible to display what people
do not know, anyone claiming that many children fail in school because they
lack skills and capacities certainly has a wealth of data to make the point. By
such an account, if failing kids simply knew more or were at least better able
to learn, school failure would go away. That not being the case, isn't it reasonable to assume some are better than others at certain tasks? Isn't it liberat-
ing and responsible to identify the fit between person and task as early as possible, for the good of both individual and community? Shouldn't people be
treated specially if science has identified a handicap and developed the
means of alleviating it? In short: "The able win; the rest lose. Someone should
give the losers a hand."

There are good reasons to be unconvinced by research that identifies personal characteristics and particular skills as the driving cause of our institutional arrangements. It may be the other way around. Moving on to a more
social analysis:

Stage II. Isn't it also obvious an inadequate social environment prevents
children from achieving their unique potentials? It is always possible to ex-
cuse kids not knowing by blaming their circumstances. They might come
from a different culture. Plus, things are set up against them in any competition against those better prepared. A quick ride through any American city
shows there are few level playing fields. No matter what those on the bottom
know or can learn, Americans will have their winners and losers. In short:
"Some win, because others lose. Too bad there isn't room for everyone."

Yes, but . . . , the scores still speak for themselves, not to mention that dozens of reforms meant to level the field by removing environmental impedi-
ments have not kept 50% of all children from the bottom half of any number
of measured averages. The arguments can go on forever: individual vs. social,
nature vs. nurture. The measurement enterprise can go on forever. Why is it
taken so seriously? Why does learning have to report to psychometric tests
that seem so irrelevant to what young adults need to work? Just how many
people are involved in organizing this mess? And now let's bring everyone together:

Stage III. It takes a whole country of individuals and institutions to put
together the school failure problem. Historically, most modern States have
not produced a failure problem of this kind, and in the strangest way: by assuming that education is only for the few, and not always the elite few, they

have taken the tease from the promise of equal opportunity. In the United States, where everyone has been promised equality, the person with any apparent lack of capacity is the only point of focus (Dumont, 1966/1980; Varenne & McDermott, 1998). Without people to notice, failure to achieve this or that would not make much of a difference.

What is the problem of school failure anyway, and why do we keep reproducing it? It is a big portion of the domestic outlay of funds. Who consumes it? How does it get about? What would happen if it were pulled from the market? What secret investments would be made visible by its threatened disappearance? The glory of human history, that is, the glory of culture, is the continued ability of societies to produce persons who can perform routinely with skills first developed with great difficulty by others in differing circumstances. Cognitive failure does not have to be a focus, but we have turned even the slightest hint of a cognitive lag into the very measure of a child's potential. From hill tribes reading and writing with difficult scripts to contemporary households using the Internet, from traditional peoples in New Guinea dropping stone axes for steel to uneducated revolutionaries manipulating the most complex weaponry, the fact is that most human beings can do just about anything other human beings can do. What is the cultural apparatus that has us so heavily invested in failure that even ways of finding everyone's potential— what a theory of individual differences should be—have been corrupted into another tool for creating inequalities?[4] Every sign suggests we can do without a theory of individual differences. America cannot afford it. For organizing cultural and institutional reform: *Individuals are not special; they are general.*

Gender in the Distribution of Education (Beyond Male/Female)

[The salience of] a distinction between sex and gender . . . depends on a related system of meanings clustered around a family of binary pairs: nature/culture, nature/history, natural/human, resource/product. This interdependence . . . problematizes claims to the universal applicability of the concepts around sex and gender.

—Donna Haraway (1991)

---

[4]Long before psychometrics, Johann Wolfgang Goethe warned us that it was more dangerous to categorize people prematurely than to ignore their differences: "Maybe there are people who are by nature not up to this or that business; precipitation and prejudice are, however, dangerous demons, unfitting the most capable person, blocking all effectiveness and paralysing free progress. This applies to worldly affairs, particularly, too, to scholarship" (1999; this line is from 1823).

If individual differences in aptitude and potential are hard to define, gender differences would appear to be the contrast case. Inter-rater reliability is high, but in a cultural analysis this is suspicious. There is an anthropological rule of thumb:

> Whenever everyone agrees on a set of categories for describing their behavior, there are disagreements systematically obscured.[5]

High certifiability points usually to something else missing and maybe hidden. Varenne is not just French, McDermott not just Irish American, and neither is just male. In cultural analysis, interrater reliability does not deliver results or conclusions, although it is a good way to define problems that should be studied. Faced with a complex visual field, how could everyone get organized to see the same thing, and maybe even the same and exactly wrong thing. Sure, male is male, and female is female, well, uhm, usually, mostly, but how did that get arranged? How is gender defined and hammered home across enough situations that it can be so easily identified, even assumed, while at the same time played with, cross-dressed, operated on (that's literally), protested, and used as a vantage point for critiquing the whole culture? Notice that the putatively obvious signs of gender identification are hidden, clothed over—the primal cover-up—leaving only cultural cues: dress, hairstyles, gestures, smells, neuroses, ad infinitum. What isn't gendered? Boats? The sea? When asked to identify objects as either male or female, why do most Americans say chicken soup is female? Why then beef soup male? It is your call. Not exactly. The call was made long before we gave you the question. The answer is in the air, in the culture, and, just in case, if you did not know that beef soup is male, ask the question about chicken soup first. That will make beef soup male for sure. The air called American culture lives on, because we have just remade it.

In America, great work is performed to ensure that everyone is gendered in accord with the stereotypes of the moment. This propensity can be found in all other cultures, but with the significant caveat that the roles assigned and stereotypes enforced show great variety across cultures and eras of the same

---

[5]Consider Baldwin (1963): "White people in this country will have quite enough to do in learning how to accept and love themselves and each other, and when they have achieved this—which will not be tomorrow and may very well be never—the Negro problem will no longer exist, for it will no longer be needed" (p. 22). Consider also its application to education: White people in this country will have quite enough to teach themselves and learn from each other, and when they have achieved this—which will not be tomorrow and may very well be never—the school failure problem will no longer exist, for it will no longer be needed.

culture. The anthropologist David Schneider (1968/1980, 1984) has even argued that the package of concerns with sexuality is in fact so tightly specific to America that it has vitiated all research into family processes. The correlation between school failure and being female—no, make that being treated as female—can be total in some cultures (a nasty business, but a good example of cultural categories making more of individual differences than is fair). People inside such a culture can easily explain any female's failure in school: "Because she is a female." There has been progress in America on this front. Gender is no longer a publicly acceptable mode of explanation. Even natives see it as an interpretation, a cultural move, and often an inappropriate one. So what of the general absence of women in math, science, and technology fields? The numbers are changing slowly, but this one hasn't gone away yet. So what would a cultural analysis of such a phenomenon look like, and how might it help us to reconstruct the problem?

Stage I.   Time and again, we have reports of girls shying away from mathematics, science, and technology in classrooms. Many of the reports stick close to the gender facts and use assumed characteristics of girls to explain the lack of participation. In short: "Mars wins; Venus loses. Someone should give the girls a hand." Enough said.

Moving on to a more social analysis:

Stage II.   One of the things wrong with little girls is that they have to go through little boys to use computers. Techno-alpha males dominate the early grades, and computers are a perfect local environment for their strong-arm road to cognitive supremacy. Women who become physicists and engineers have to put up with a lifetime of biases; most girls opt out much earlier. In short: "Boys win, because girls lose. Too bad science, math, and technology are so much for the best, brightest, and most competitive that there isn't room for everyone."

And now let's bring everyone together:

Stage III.   Gender is a complex arrangement, and it takes more than little boys to create troubles for computer use in schools. It takes a culture full of people to make such a mess. Yes, boys seem to dominate, but do they really? Are they just arranged to look that way? What is face-to-face domination anyway? Are the utilities and rewards of classroom interaction so well defined that it is easy to tell who is dominant, and how did it get aligned with males and math and not with females and literature? What a strange culture! Who is involved in arranging contexts for math, gender, technology, and domination to be aligned so consistently? In short: "Winning or losing on school tests does not have to be related to success in science, math, and technology. Perhaps we should figure out what this game costs and make attendant alterations."

For a project building computerized math materials for middle school classes, we videotaped children working with our first lessons. Analyses of the tapes enabled us to make informed changes in the curricular materials to fit and transform the demands of real classrooms (Greeno et al., 1999). The boys took more quickly to the materials than the girls and the pattern was resistant to direct intervention by way of, say, rules specifying that girls had to control the mouse. Karen Cole (1995) followed our struggle and reported that male dominance in mouse use is probably the best way for males to accept the directions of females who do not often seek mouse control. The plot thickened as more layers of behavior were considered. Consider the girl who, after expertly telling a mouse-master male what to do across a two-week lesson, reports to the class that she did not help do the work. The girl avoids leadership, takes leadership, then denies leadership. Why was avoidance, and not the guidance, initially described as gendered? When is gender anyway? On what grounds can any piece of behavior be called gendered, with whose help, by way of what interpretative categories, and in what contexts applied? The cultural question is not what do boys and girls do, but *when are the categories male and female made relevant, in what circumstances, by virtue of what work?* Gender is involved, of course, but it is not a reality unto itself. If gender is simply a word we use to notice, regulate, and even distort individual points of order in concerted activities involving millions of others, the cultural contexts in which the word is used are dangerous enough to require constant vigilance. Because "the value of an analytic category is not necessarily annulled by critical consciousness of its historical specificity and cultural limits" (Haraway, 1991, p. 130), gender can sometimes be a powerful analytic category and sometimes not, but never by fiat and only after an analysis of its role in the wider culture.

Race in the Distribution of Education (Beyond White/Black)

Negroes in this country—and Negroes do not, strictly or legally speaking, exist in any other . . .

—James Baldwin (1963)

If it takes a culture full of people to build institutions that can consistently divide a population into categories like successful and unsuccessful, it is efficient perhaps for the same people to make male and female consequential across a wide range of activities, seemingly, and even legally, irrelevant to gender. We should not be surprised that the same people would find other "natural" ways to divide up the population to correlate with division by success and failure hierarchies. Enter race. Race is a fairly new idea which has developed over the past 250 years along with other defining features of modern industrial capitalism: the state, its record keeping and claims to rationality, science, individualism, and colonialism. Groups of people have always found ways to make each other different, but the peculiarity of modern racism—groups making each other not only different, but biologically different right down to individual character and mind, as acclaimed by evolutionarily theory, all of which feeds on colonized populations accounted for and explained—all this is quite new and held together more by institutions that feed on it than by the biological facts of the matter (Dumont, 1966/1980; Hannaford, 1996; Smedley, 1992).

Yes, but, intellectual history aside, aren't people physically different, and haven't such differences always made a difference? Aren't natural differences the product of evolution, and isn't that why there is an overlap between physical history and one's performance in school? Let's use our three stages of cultural analysis to frame answers to these questions.

Stage I. Race is biologically real, and people of different races have different biological endowments that make them systematically strong or weak on certain intellectual tasks. This can be shown on various bell curves. In short: "There is a reason some win and others lose. Someone should give the losers a hand." Enough said.

Moving on to a more social analysis:

Stage II. Race may be biologically real, but racial differences do not extend to the potential to do intellectual work. Under certain economic and political conditions, people of different races get treated differently and consequently might develop negative traits that limit their potentials. Race matters only because we make it matter. Let's try not to do that. It is poverty and lack of opportunity that makes trouble in life. Because more Africans Americans are poor than Whites, race is prominent in the distribution of intelligence and success. We should forget about race when we make educational policy. Let's believe we can forget about race. In short: "Whites win, because

African Americans lose. Even though there isn't room for everyone at the top (or in the middle), race should not be the dividing line."

And now let's bring everyone together:

Stage III.   It takes a whole country of groups and institutions to put together a race problem. Race is a useless category in the biological classification of human diversity, although, by a series of arbitrary distinctions and attention to isolated traits, populations can maintain fairly stable definitions of racial groups. This takes work and requires constant attention to borders and possible moments of integration and access to resources. It is this work we must analyze and reorganize, not the individual black child failing in school. The cultural question is not what do Blacks and Whites do, but *when are the categories black and white made relevant, in what circumstances, by virtue of what work?* Many are involved. Almost 200 years ago, the Abbé Grégoire (1808/ 1996), in writing a defense of the downtrodden of his time, pointed to how the fault rested primarily with those who identify the failures of others:

> Irishmen, Jews, and Negroes, your virtues and talents are your own; your vices are the work of nations who call themselves Christian. The more you are maligned, the more these nations are indicted for their guilt. (p. 39)

People struggling under the conditions of American racism end up often reproducing what they recognize as unfortunate but do not have the tools to reorganize. Racially speaking, how are they to proceed? In her decision to adopt, for the moment—given historical circumstances and present purposes—the descriptively inadequate category of Asian American, Sau-ling Wong made the right call: "Calibration is all" (1993, p. xx). In short: "Differential access to resources by Whites, African Americans, Native Americans, and Asian Americans, may be arbitrary and unfortunate, but it is also well organized by the rest of us. We cannot forget about race until we stop producing and consuming situations that make it matter. We should calculate what this game costs and make attendant alterations."

People in America work hard making sure everyone is raced in accord with the stereotypes of the moment. Racism is American karma. Americans share this propensity with many other cultures, but with the significant caveat that the roles assigned and stereotypes enforced show a variety across cultures and eras of the same culture. School success and failure have become crucial to the articulation and recreation of racial borders and inequalities. If race is only a partial event inside a cultural system, then any correlation between race and measures of school performance can be seen as tautological, a cultural redundancy by which the same interpretive machinery that delivers arbitrary distinctions between kinds of persons also delivers arbitrary measures of learning and techniques for noticing and explaining their correlation. If culture can arrange for that much coherence, and if that coherence can cause us so much trouble, we need a constant cultural analysis to resist the constraints of the categorical coinage of our conversations.

CULTURE INVESTIGATED

A strict cultural approach is necessarily reflexive. We have no choice but to study that which we also make. There is no privileged position from which to escape culture. This general principle holds perhaps more for the sciences of humanity than for the sciences of the physical world. The latter appear much further along in working with the principle that all we claim we know proceeds from particular positions or instruments. This need not lead to radical pessimism about the writing of new statements about the world. "Knowledge" is not disembodied from the texts that codify it, from those who author and authorize it, or from the audiences that support the activities that produce and establish it. But these activities, particularly the processes of "science" embodied in various modes of control, are still extremely useful and well worth continuing. Our goal here is to indicate how these controls are best designed so that we remain consistent within our approach.

For a cultural approach, the core activity involves a search for positions and instruments demonstratably "different" from those that have produced what, at any point in time, is acknowledged as truth. It must be possible to argue that the assumed position allows for the production of statements less directly anchored within the parameters of what would not be controversial. In the social sciences, anthropology may have been most systematic in insisting that those who bend themselves to its discipline must find the alternative vantage points that will make the familiar strange. Repeatedly, anthropologists have transformed settled knowledge into ignorance, and they have shown how further systematic investigation and analysis can transform the identified ignorance into new knowledge. In a process that continues to this day, anthropologists have also criticized each other for not having gone far enough, for not having noticed how the common sense of their time imprisoned them. Like the curators of Etruscan antiquities mentioned earlier, those who bend themselves to a cultural approach (whether in anthropology, sociology, or psychology) must search for that which was not available earlier, at the same time as they destroy the claims of earlier anthropologists by demonstrating how a group of experts can blind themselves to the obvious. This is all the more important that, in most cases, the danger is not that of being taken by a forger. Those whom we observe rarely lie to us. But it is all too easy for an observer not to note that which, later, can be shown as essential for those observed and, reflexively, for the researchers and their own communities.

Methodologically, a fear of common sense, and a corresponding trust in the effectiveness of shifting position, has led anthropologists to seek people who most challenged the political and academic common sense. Initially, they most often traveled across the globe to places like Samoa or Bali. Then they visited systematically hidden neighborhoods in South Chicago or Harlem. More recently they began visiting groups in various centers of authority (classrooms, hospitals, supermarkets) where they used techniques developed in the distant settings to articulate what was so obvious that it went "without saying." These techniques are variously known in the concerned fields as "ethnography," "participant observation," or "naturalistic inquiry," but the labels must not be transformed into new rigidities. They index the continuing quest to find stances that allow for uncovering not only what we know we do not know, but also, and controversially, what until then we did not know we did not know.

We begin with research that starts and ends with obvious categories, proceed to research that attempts to formalize less obvious categories, and finally to research that seeks the processes that make some categories obvious and others hard to see.

Categories, Operations, and Correlations

There is no escaping academic achievement, gender, and race as matters of concern in America. They concern us too, but, for this very reason, we cannot take them as simple categories of the world. We are concerned, for example, when research into gender becomes research into "males" and "females"–whether operationalized on the basis of a box respondents check on a questionnaire, or on the basis of a full genetic analysis. Without a full justification as to why one would wish to relate academic achievement and gender, any demonstration of a correlation, or of no correlation, is unlikely to tell us much that we did not know.

New Categories

Much excellent work has been produced with an awareness that it is dangerous to proceed on the basis of received categories. One could even argue that
the human sciences became the social sciences in the late 19th century precisely when people, from Marx to Durkheim, Weber, Freud, Vygotsky, and
many others, started questioning in detail not only the most common sense
categories of knowledge but the very grounds of the methods for gaining new
knowledge about humanity. The difficulties arose when some were satisfied
with making new common sense categories to be handled as the initial ones
had been. Thus, most irritatingly for us, "culture" gets transformed into a
variable and operationalized as the answer to a few questions about place of
birth or home language. "Race" and "gender" have had a similar fate as they
are brought forth, often under new interesting guises, made into distinct and
independent categories that appear so easily identifiable in our observations
that little further worrying appears necessary.

Cultural Investigations of Culture

One takes a cultural approach only to the extent one remains skeptical of
what is publicly acknowledged. Perhaps the human world is not best understood in terms of gender, race, class, intelligence. Perhaps concern with these
matters hide the very processes our investigations should reveal. This is easy
to say, but first we must face the fundamental difficulty: A cultural approach
must recognize its own grounding in institution and time. This is not only a
call for self-analysis (a dubious task anyway), but a call to use the grounding
against itself. New knowledge, or, better, new statements about the world,
will not come from replication but from the struggle to demonstrate the relevance of the new research to the fields it addresses. New statements will not
be produced from using the same instruments within well-controlled protocols. It will come from the discovery of new instruments that can be used
from different positions and with different populations. Precisely because of
the power of plausibility and common sense, a cultural approach requires that
one move away from plausibility and common sense.

The trick that makes a cultural approach plausible as a practice is the pos-
tulate that human beings do display in their everyday life that which is most
important to them—even when they appear, particularly to a professional observer from a different planet, unaware of these very constraints. In many

ways, our argument has been that people in culture can be made systematically inarticulate about the fundamentals of this culture. In its simplest form this recapitulates a central tenet of American social theorizing at least since the 1920s. It is also a central tenet of much Marxist theorizing, particularly among those interested in hegemony. Our sense is that any statement about apparent unawareness is extremely misleading methodologically if it casts the observer in the role of the magical outsider revealing truths to ignorant participants about themselves. To the extent that all social scientists must claim that their findings were produced by the observation of persons (whatever technique was used, from questionnaires to video analyses), a position that starts with people who are fully unaware actually destroys the very possibility of the enterprise.

Those who wish to take a cultural perspective must take the alternative position: people necessarily reveal the conditions we are interested in, but precisely not in the vocabularies or rhetorical forms of observers. But the ignorance or, better, inarticulateness must be laid with the observers as they struggle to articulate what may in fact not have to be said in the routine of the people's lives. Learning from human beings is akin to reading an alien language: one must assume that what may sound like gibberish is in fact a language, and a translatable one at that. The task of translation, we all know, is not easy, not by any means, precisely because what is most worth translating cannot fit into any of the words (categories, etc.) that initially appeared available. To make the case even more difficult, remember that human culture is not really a text to translate. It is a set of joint practices, a dance or opera say, much of which is not available in discursive form. Thus the analytic task remains even more difficult than usual forms of translation and transformation, because it involves moving the non-textual (that which our informants perform for each other) into the textual (the publications through which we conduct the core of our professional lives).

There are two core problems. The first has been addressed in many interesting ways. The latter is more complex. First, we must find new positions. From the travels of early anthropologists across the globe, to the experiments ethnomethodologists conduct to induce participants to articulate their common sense, many techniques have been developed that do indeed allow for bringing to our professional awareness that which had remained hidden. Second, we must find new ways of saying what we have seen that will both grab the attention of our intended audiences and actually move them away from one common sense to another sense that can be used for further action. Such writing has been difficult to produce, but there is no reason it cannot be produced more effectively than it has so far.

ONWARD

History, despite its wrenching pain,
Cannot be unlived, but if faced
With courage, need not be lived again.

—Maya Angelou (1993)

George Herbert Mead long ago argued that in a democracy, there should be little place for experts like educational researchers to stand apart from the problems they are trying to solve. Every attempt to direct conduct by fixed categories like kinds of person tied to measures of school performance should not only fail, but fail perniciously. For Mead (1899), expert knowledge is better seen as a "working hypothesis" that must enter a community of practice and jostle apparent knowledge until it takes root in a reorganization of what people can do with each other: "Reflective consciousness does not then carry us on to the world that is to be, but puts our own thought and endeavor into the very process of evolution" (p. 371).

Mead's call for knowledge as emergent and subject to circumstance is at the heart of the American pragmatism we have been claiming—with all the trepidation that its own formulation in fact encourages—with quotations from Emerson, Peirce, James, and Dewey (with Kenneth Burke only a little to the side).[6] We have not attempted to stand outside America in these pages, but rather to reveal it to ourselves enough to say something that might make a difference. Cultural analyses that highlight the weight of tradition and structure and only belatedly emphasize change can leave us with either angry desires for revolution or hopeless pangs of social impotence. Both feelings can produce a withdrawal educators cannot countenance. We are working with a different theory of culture. We assume persons are always active and potentially reconstructing received conditions, even when the conditions are overwhelming. The "system" is not set in concrete. It "need not be lived again." The trick is to become most engaged where hostile conditions are fragile and open to breakthrough, as well as where more benign conditions are fragile and must be secured.

Thirty years into studying and confronting school failure, we still have no expert place to stand, no surefire immediate solutions. We get paid to worry about kids who will likely never get paid as well as those who worry about them. We are not in a position to tell everyone how to fix educational problems. What we have is only a renewed place to enter the fray, namely, in the

---

[6]See the nice discussion in Manicas (1998).

middle of things, with an insistence that educational researchers must confront first how their work with the materials of American culture constructs the very problems we think must be solved. This chapter is part of that insistence. In cleaning out our own conceptual house, we have learned to insist on three specific guidelines:

Never accept a problem as stated;
Be particularly wary of problems defined in terms of individuals;
Resist vigorously all problems identified by received categories of kinds of person.

Gender, race, and social class disparities in school performance are lamentable, but need not be made worse by our blaming them on either their victims and their environments independent of, uh oh, us. We are the environments for kinds of kids to be in trouble. So what can we do? Start first by reorganizing the contexts for the problems.

We have worked in, on, and even run educational programs that make a difference to their participants. Each program has offered an existence proof for how everyone can learn; further, if we were careful enough to listen, in each case, the students had something important to teach us about our own position in the system. Educational researchers do not always learn about themselves from the people they study. The title of our book, *Successful Failure*, is as good a name for educational researchers as for the children who fail at school, although opposite: we are treated as successful despite our failures, and the children are treated as failures despite their successes. Reviews of the book have been warm, but some have complained that we do not tell how to fix the problems we identified. We end this chapter as we ended the book: with a refusal to tell everyone what to do. Two conditions threaten the good sense of this move: first, if we wind up being called theorists, standing in opposition to practitioners; and second, if we forget to remind our readers that refusing to tell everyone how to fix American school problems is itself a political move, not as powerful as other moves we can imagine, but a significant step nonetheless; in either case, we will be reduced to having much to say about nothing, and nothing to do about everything.

After Marx and Engels (1846/1947) set down the rules in their *German Ideology*, there has been little reason to think that changing one's mind, or changing everyone's mind, can lead to a changed situation. We are not suffering the illusion that if you agree with us about our ideas you will go forward and change the world. But in our refusal to tell you what to do, we are confronting a core institution in American education. Perhaps the biggest problem facing American education is that we foolishly await a solution, as if some change in the system, some new tool in a fresh bag of tricks, will result in a more egalitarian distribution of school success among kinds of people. Stop it. Now. If we are right, if the problem is not with the kinds of people, but with the rest of us who define, measure, and make policy for their problem, the last thing we want to do is to make recommendations. We cannot begin to make change out there until we have made change in here, under the most local conditions, with ourselves, with those around us, at the borders that keep us in and others out. Do not ask us for a solution. Ask us to help. Ask others to help. Bring down the borders, and everyone will learn to help everyone else, even you, even us. The problem of American education is not that we have people divided into too many cultures; the problem is that we have a single culture full of people all too resourceful in dividing its people. Culture is not a past cause to current divisions. Culture—your culture, our culture, American culture—is the current challenge to any future unity.

REFERENCES

Abu-Lugod, L. (1991). Writing against culture. In R. Fox (Ed.), *Recapturing anthropology* (pp. 137–162). Santa Fe, NM: School of American Research.

Angelou, M. (1993). *Pulse of the morning*. New York: Random House.

Arensberg, C. A. (1982). Generalizing anthropology. In E. A. Hoebel (Ed.), *Crisis in anthropology* (pp. 109–130). New York: Garland.

Baldwin, J. (1955). *Notes of a native son*. Boston: Beacon.

Baldwin, J. (1963). *The fire next time*. New York: Vintage.

Beckett, S. (1955). *Molloy*. New York: Grove.

Boas, F. (1911/1938). *The mind of primitive man*. New York: Macmillan.

Boas, F. (1940). *Race, language, and culture*. New York: Free Press.

Bonnell, V., & Hunt, L. (Eds.). (1999). *Beyond the cultural turn*. Berkeley: University of California Press.

Boon, J. (1999). The Cross-Cultural Kiss: Edwardian and Earlier, Postmodern and Beyond. The David Skomp Lecture. Department of Anthropology, Indiana University.

Bothmer, D. von, & Noble, J. V. (1961), An Inquiry into the Forgery of the Etruscan Terracotta Warriors in The Metropolitan Museum of Art. Papers, Number 11. New York: The Metropolitan Museum of Art.

Burke, K. (1935). *Permanence and change*. Berkeley: University of California Press.

Cole, K. (1995). Equity issues in computer-based collaboration. In J. L. Schnase & E. L. Cunnius (Eds.), *Proceedings of Computer Supported Collaborative Learning '95* (pp. 67–74). Hillsdale, NJ: Lawrence Erlbaum Associates.

Cole, M. (1996). *Cultural psychology*. Cambridge: Harvard University Press.

Dewey, J. (1920). *Reconstruction in philosophy*. New York: Henry Holt.

Dumont, L. (1966/1980). *Homo hierarchus*. Chicago: University of Chicago Press.

Emerson, R. W. (1860). *The conduct of life.* Boston: Ticknor & Fields.

Emerson, R. W. (1850/1995). *Representative men.* New York: Marisilio.

Frake, C. O. (1980). The genesis of kinds of people in the Sulu Archipelago. In A. Dil (Ed.), Language and Cultural Description (pp. 311–332). Stanford: Stanford University Press.

Frake, C. O. (1998). Abu Sayyaf: Displays of violence and the proliferation of contested identities among Philippine Muslims. *American Anthropologist* 100:41–54.

Geertz, C. (1960). *Religion of Java.* New York: Free Press.

Geertz, C. (1966). Religion as a cultural system. In M. Banton (Ed.), *Anthropological approaches to the study of religion* (pp. 1–46). London: Tavistock.

Geertz, C. (1973). *Interpretation of cultures.* New York: Basic Books.

Geiger, G. (1939). Dewey's social and political philosophy. In P. Schilpp (Ed.), *The philosophy of John Dewey* (pp. 337–368). New York: Tutor Publishing.

Goethe, J. W. von. (1999). *Maxims and reflections.* London: Penguin.

Goodenough, W. (1951). *Property, kin, and community on Truk.* New Haven: Yale University Publications in Anthropology.

Goodenough, W. (1971). *Culture, language, and society.* New York: Addison-Wesley.

Greeno, J., McDermott, R., Cole, K., Engle, R., Goldman, S., Knudsen, J., Lauman, B., & Linde, C. (1999). Research, reform and the aims of education. In E. Lagemann & L. Shulman (Eds.), *Issues in education research* (pp. 299–335). San Francisco: Jossey-Bass.

Grégoire, H. (1808/1996). *On the cultural achievements of negroes.* T. Cassirer & J.-F. Briére (Eds.). Amherst: University of Massachusetts Press.

Hannaford, I. (1996). *Race: The history of an idea in the West.* Washington: Woodrow Wilson Center Press.

Haraway, D. (1991). *Simians, cyborgs, and women: The reinvention of nature.* New York: Routledge.

Henry, J. (1963). *Culture against man.* New York: Vintage.

Holland, D., Lachiotte, W., Skinner, D., & Cain, C. (1998). *Identity and agency in cultural worlds.* Cambridge: Harvard University Press.

James, W. (1868/1997). A Letter to Thomas Wren Ward, January 7. In Skrupskelis, I. & Berkeley, E. (Eds.), *The correspondence of William James, Vol. 4, 1854–1877* (pp. 246–251). Charlottesville: University Press of Virginia.

Kenner, H. (1985). *The counterfeiters.* Baltimore, MD: Johns Hopkins University Press.

Lave, J., & McDermott, R. (2002). Estranged labor learning. *Outlines, 4,* 19–48.

Lave, J., & Wenger, E. (1992). *Situated learning.* New York: Cambridge University Press.

Manicas, P. (1998). Dewey and American Social Science. In L. Hickman (Ed.), *Reading Dewey* (pp. 43–62). Bloomington: Indiana University Press.

Marx, K., & Engels, F. (1846/1947). *German ideology.* New York: International.

McDermott, R. (1998). Culture Is Not an Environment of the Mind. *Journal of the Learning Sciences, 8,* 157–169.

McDermott, R. (2005). Situating Genius. In Bekerman, Z., Burbules, N., & Keller, D. (Eds.), *Learning in places.* Bern: Peter Lang.

Mead, G. H. (1899). The working hypothesis in social reform. *American Journal of Sociology, 5,* 369–371.

Michalchik, V. (2000). Knowing Kosrae: The Institutional Organization of Knowledgeability on a Micronesian Island. Unpublished doctoral dissertation, Stanford University.

Ortner, S. (1984). Theory in anthropology since the sixties. *Comparative Study in Society and History, 26,* 126–166.

Ortner, S. (Ed.). (1999). *The fate of culture: Geertz and beyond.* Berkeley: University of California Press.

Peirce, C. S. (1868/1955). Some consequences of four incapacities. In Buchler, J. (Ed.), *Philosophical writings of Peirce* (pp. 228–250). New York: Dover.

Pollock, M. (2004). *Color mute*. Princeton, NJ: Princeton University Press.

Raley, J. (2003). Safe Spaces: A Study or Trust, Risk, and Learning at the Margins. Unpublished doctoral dissertation, Stanford University.

Rosaldo, R. (1990). Celebrating Thompson's heroes: Social analysis in history and anthropology. In H. J. Kaye & K. McClelland (Eds.), *E. P. Thompson: Critical perspectives* (pp. 103–124). Philadelphia, PA: Temple University Press.

Rosaldo, R., & Flores, W. (1997). Identity, conflict, and evolving Latino communities. In Flores, W. & Benmayor, R. (Eds.), *Latino cultural citizenship* (pp. 57–96). Boston: Beacon Press.

Schneider, D. (1968). *American kinship: A cultural account*. Chicago: University of Chicago Press.

Schneider, D. (1984). *A critique of the study of kinship*. Ann Arbor: University of Michigan Press.

Seyer, I. (2002). Smart on the Under, Wise to the Streets: Mapping the Landscapes of Urban Youth. Unpublished doctoral dissertation, Stanford University.

Smedley, A. (1992). *Race in North America*. Boulder, CO: Westview.

Spindler, G., & Spindler, L. (2000). *Fifty years of anthropology and education 1950–2000*. Mahwah, NJ: Lawrence Erlbaum Associates.

Varenne, H. (1977). *Americans together*. New York: Teachers College Press.

Varenne, H. (1983). *American school language*. New York: Irvington.

Varenne, H. (1984). Collective representation in American anthropological conversations about culture. *Current Anthropology, 25*, 281–300.

Varenne, H., & McDermott, R. (1998). *Successful failure: The school America builds*. Boulder, CO: Westview Press.

Wong, S. (1993). *Reading Asian American literature*. Princeton, NJ: Princeton University Press.

2

Inside-Out and Outside-In: Participant Observation in Taiko Drumming

Kimberly Powell
College of Education
The Pennsylvania State University

Kimberly Powell received her Ph.D. from Stanford University in education. Her research focuses on aesthetic foundations of education, youth and community civic engagement, and the cultural contexts of learning. She is currently a senior research associate at The Pennsylvania State University, has taught courses in qualitative methods and art education, and is the managing editor of the *American Journal of Education*.

Participant observation, generally considered the mainstay of ethnographic research, is often at the heart of much debate about the nature of participation, raising epistemological and ontological questions concerning the intent and position of the researcher in relation to knowledge and to those studied. In this chapter, I argue that participatory processes of research offer a valuable contribution to the ethnographer's charge of cultural interpretation, particularly in the examination of tacit and implicit forms of knowledge. I examine my own participation in a Japanese American taiko drumming ensemble and the ways in which my first-hand, subjective experience caused me to challenge conventional wisdom about the concept of embodiment in educational practice. Using examples from my ethnographic study of taiko drumming, I examine the implications that participatory practices have for understanding, challenging, and reshaping educational concepts such as learning.

Participant observation, long regarded as the *sine qua* non of ethnography, is nevertheless an elusive concept, perhaps largely due to the seemingly endless combinations of activities along the continuum of participation and observation. Of the two words that comprise the composite phrase, *participation* appears to be the more hotly contested one, raising epistemological as well as ontological questions regarding ethnography in particular and qualitative research in general. Participation calls into question the role of the researcher, the position of the researcher, and the intent of the researcher in relation to knowledge and what is deemed identifiably real.

It is not surprising, then, to find that many ethnographies employ observational methods more than participatory ones, and that participation has often been defined through activities such as interviews, informal conversations, and limited interactions with those involved in a study. This is particularly true of ethnographies of education, in part due to the limited nature of participatory opportunities in school settings. I believe that this popular conception of participant observation is also indicative of concerns with subjectivity as a form of bias in which the "trustworthiness" (Lincoln & Guba, 1985) of research is at stake.

In this chapter, I recount my participatory experiences in a Japanese American *taiko* drumming ensemble and the ways in which my participation informed me first-hand about the concept of embodied experience, transforming my initial thinking about embodiment as a theoretical construct into a richer, more complex understanding of embodiment as a learning phenomenon. During this 18-month ethnographic study, my participation took many forms, most notably as an apprentice in the ensemble's apprenticeship program. Through describing some of these learning experiences, I address the question of how participant observation can contribute to the ethnographer's charge of cultural interpretation and the implications that participatory practices have for understanding and reconstructing eductional concepts.

In the first section of this chapter, I discuss some of the issues raised by qualitative researchers and ethnographers regarding participant observation and its related conceptual partners, subjectivity and reflexivity. I then describe the cultural and historical context of *taiko*. The last two sections are based on some of my participatory experiences and the impact these had on the construction of a theory of learning that allowed me to question the broader social and cultural practices of schooling.

THE ROLE OF PARTICIPANT
OBSERVATION IN ETHNOGRAPHY

Participant observation has received critical scholarly attention over the recent decades, mostly around the issue of how much participation to include as part of ethnography. Some scholars share ambivalence toward participation as a useful or even appropriate method of study. George and Louise Spindler (1992) warn that participation is not always possible or even desirable, yet George Spindler (1974) did place himself in the position of a third- and fourth-grader in a classroom, following assignments and even receiving unsolicited help from curious children, making him "less threatening and more familiar" to the children (1992, p. 64). Harry Wolcott (1992) signals ambivalence as to whether such involvement is desirable or acceptable; yet at the same time seems to warn of the current trend in ethnography: "We elevate watching to the status of 'participant observation,' which clearly has become the label of choice for much descriptive or naturalistic research" (p. 20), and that most participant observation in education merits the label only in the sense that the researcher is physically present.

Many qualitative researchers, and ethnographers in particular, specify rules or suggestions for delineating *participant observation* from *participation* (e.g., Spindler & Spindler, 1992; Spradley, 1980), for example: experiencing a situation simultaneously as both an insider and an outsider; keeping a record of events, including subjective components such as emotions, personal biases, and how one experiences the situation; becoming explicitly aware of the tacit, implicit knowledge that are taken for granted by those in the culture; and guarding against misinterpretation. Such steps are meant as precautions for the participant observer, to keep researcher bias in check.

Much of this sensitivity toward the participant end of participant observation is fueled by a history of discussion concerning rigor, validity, and truth-claims about qualitative research. Subjectivity versus objectivity has been the focus of many debates in qualitative research, namely, the extent to which subjectivity clouds, disrupts, or hinders the observer from maintaining a professional distance in which he or she can accurately render an observed phenomenon. Subjectivity has been addressed by scholars from a variety of theoretical perspectives such as feminism, critical theory, cultural studies, and autoethnography.[1] These perspectives challenge historically prevalent views of truth and knowledge as an objective reality that exists independently of our own lived experience and has a structure that we can come to know through systematic, empirical investigation. Although subjectivity has been treated differently across different theoretical schools of thought (as objectivity has), there is general agreement across the literature on certain issues. The first is that subjectivity, with its acknowledgement of emotions, biases, and predispositions, can be a useful, personal tool that influences and enhances

---

[1]A substantive review of subjectivity in qualitative research can be found in Jansen and Peshkin (1992).

understanding (e.g., Krieger, 1985; LeCompte, 1987; Peshkin, 1985). Second, knowledge and the perception of reality are socially constructed and are best understood through an interactional approach between researchers and participants (e.g., Eisner, 1991; Guba, 1990), as knowledge of the self and of the "other" mutually inform each other in the co-construction of knowledge (e.g., Fine, 1994; Westcott, 1979). Third, the use of subjectivity in qualitative and ethnographic research addresses issues of authoritative voice, power, and the objectification of the other (e.g., Clifford & Marcus, 1986; Fine, 1994; Marcus & Fischer, 1986; Rosaldo, 1989). This latter point acknowledges the concept of *reflexivity* in qualitative research, a conscious use of reflection to examine one's own personal biases, views, and motivations and to develop self-awareness in interaction with others.

Over the past decade, academic writings on ethnography and participant observation have cast a self-conscious eye on the rhetoric of ethnographic writing in terms of the representation of "self" and "other," ethnography as a literary genre, and the contested place of authorship (Atkinson & Hammersley, 1994; Clifford & Marcus, 1986). James Clifford (1986) argues that participant observation as a method has always recognized the central importance of the researcher's experience, but that the historical conventions dictating ethnography gave authoritative voice to the author through third-person objectivism. Michelle Fine (1994) critiques the authoritative, dispassionate voice of the author, characterized by the use of a collective "they" to suggest some standardized, monolithic mass, an authoritative, imperialist "I" (Rosaldo, 1989), which renders the "other" to the margins of the text. Fine (1994) suggests:

> The project at hand is to unravel, critically, the blurred boundaries in our relation, and in our texts; to understand the political work of our narratives; to decipher how the traditions of social science serve to inscribe; and to imagine how our practice can be transformed to resist, self-consciously, acts of othering. (p. 75)

The goal of reflexivity is not to replace the self for the other, but to understand the ways in which knowledge of self and other mutually inform each other. As a methodology, participant observation potentially connects the researcher and the research subject in a dialogue and in interaction with one another that would not be possible without the type of "common ground" that participation can build (Balsamo, 1990).

These viewpoints on subjectivity and reflexivity are relevant to the ways in which I conceive of my own ethnographic project as a cultural study of learning. One of the goals of an ethnographer is to make explicit the forms of knowledge that are taken-for-granted or might even be unacceptable (Spindler & Spindler, 1992). The sociocultural knowledge that affects behavior, communication, meaning-making and values, for example, is largely implicit, tacitly known to those within a particular social system; yet, at the same time, people are often either unaware or have a vague sense of such knowledge. In the process of uncovering such knowledge, my own lived experience of the phenomena under study contributed to my overall understanding and reconceptualization of a theory of learning. By positioning myself within the text of my ethnography, I depict myself as a learner along with everyone else who was engaged in learning taiko, to "work the hyphen" between Self-Other (Fine, 1994), lessening this distance by engaging in the mutual construction of learning.[2] The reflexive component of my participation, in other words, was essential to my analysis and interpretation of meaning.

METHODOLOGICAL CONSIDERATIONS FOR TAIKO AS A PLACE OF LEARNING

Anthropological ethnography has concerned itself, to a large extent, with the ways in which societies organize the conditions and purposes of learning through its available cultural resources (Spindler & Spindler, 1992). Many ethnographies have largely focused on the learning that occurs in schools; however, the work of Jean Lave, Barbara Rogoff, Dorothy Holland, and other such sociocultural theorists has paved the way for studies of learning outside of school contexts (e.g., Holland et al., 1998; Lave & Wenger, 1991; Rogoff & Lave, 1984; Singleton, 1998). Unquestionably, cultural institutions offer their own forms of learning, curricula, and pedagogy that hold important implications for educational anthropology.

My interest in taiko began when I moved to the West Coast, where it is a prevalent art form, to begin a doctoral program in education. Taiko refers to the contemporary art of Japanese drumming (sometimes referred to as kumidaiko, or harmony drum) as well as to the actual drums used in the art form. After seeing performances of taiko drumming and learning of its historical situatedness in Asian American—and more specifically, Japanese American—politics, I became interested in the ways in which taiko as a curriculum served to educate its members and the larger community in particular forms

---

[2]Elsewhere, this form of writing in which the researcher connects the personal with the cultural has been termed authoethnography or reflexive ethnography (Ellis & Bochner, 2000).

of knowledge, learning, and cultural practice not present in most school-based curricula.

Understanding the ways in which culture is embedded in the organization of a learning requirement requires focused immersion in the practices of those involved. For a study of learning as it unfolds in process, ethnography is a natural methodological choice. Ethnography is a highly descriptive method that offers researchers a chance to investigate the nuances involved in learning as they unfold in everyday practice, capturing a sense of the *emic* language that is specific to a group as well as capturing forms of local knowledge (Geertz, 1973, 1983). What emerged from my ethnographic methods, however, was something completely unexpected at the onset of the study: an opportunity to examine the role of the body in teaching and learning, and to move from material aspects of the body to the concept of embodiment, a methodological field that examines the role of the body in lived experience, cognition, and representation. In short, my participant observation in and of *taiko* required a new theoretical framework that challenges the mind/body dichotomy present in all areas of our society, including our schools.

My participant observation took many forms. Like most ethnographers, I spent an extended period of time in the field—in this case, a period of about eighteen months at San Jose Taiko's rehearsal studio, performance spaces, and San Jose's Japantown. My examination of *taiko* first began with a pilot study of another *taiko* group in the winter of 1998. In total, my research into the history and practice of *taiko* was conducted over a four-year period. I also continued to visit San Jose Taiko months after finishing my data collection in order to follow-up on individual and group progress. Fieldnotes and interviews constituted a considerable part of my research. Documents and artifacts were collected throughout the study, including the San Jose Taiko class reader (a collection of articles and notes for participants in the apprenticeship program), in-house publications of songs, evaluations, performance guidelines, concert programs and newsletters.

Embarking on an ethnography of *taiko* and the ways in which it could be regarded as a sociocultural study of learning required a strong knowledge base in the artistic components of *taiko*. Elliot Eisner's qualitative model of educational connoisseurship and criticism (1991), in which the researcher has a tacit understanding—indeed, first-hand expertise—of the studied phenomena, affected my decision to become a learner of *taiko*. As a trained musician, I had engaged in extensive practice, training, and performances in Western classical music, much of which did not prove useful in understanding *taiko*. North American *taiko* is a hybrid art form, borrowing from such musical forms as jazz, Native American, Latin, and African drumming, and often involves an assortment of percussive instruments such as bells, cymbals, shakers (gourds) as well as traditional Japanese flute and conch shell (the latter of which is used in many traditional Buddhist *taiko* ensembles). In addition to instruments, contemporary *taiko* ensembles use *kata* (form), highly coordinated and synchronized movements, many of which correspond to the type of drum or instrument being used, and often incorporating martial arts principles (e.g., the concept of the *hara*, or center). The effect is an integrated performance that involves both movement and music.

I thus had to learn new rhythmic patterns, sequences, and songs; recognize, understand and distinguish cultural rhythmic markers such as jazz, swing, Japanese rhythms, Afro-Cuban polyrhythms, and other types of rhythm employed by San Jose Taiko as well as the larger community of practice in which SJT was situated. I had to understand the specific performance practices of San Jose Taiko, the uses of choreographed movement (*kata*) and the ways in which they coordinated with drum strikes, a distinguishing marker of *taiko* ensembles. I would learn the notational practices of San Jose Taiko, a system based on an oral tradition of teaching and learning. Before beginning my fieldwork, I participated in a *taiko* course seminar and practicum at my university, as well as workshops with other local *taiko* groups, including those of San Jose Taiko, all of which allowed me to explore the cultural-historical nature of *taiko* drumming, aesthetic features of the art form, Japanese words and concepts involved in *taiko*, and the teaching and learning features that mark *taiko*.

All of this is standard fare in ethnography, and if I had just experienced those activities, I would have been a reasonably competent ethnographer of a *taiko* learning environment. But a curious invitation opened up to me during my negotiations with San Jose Taiko as a site of study, one that would lead me to rethink the role of the body in both methodology and in learning as an educational concept. PJ and Roy Hirabayashi, the directors of San Jose Taiko, insisted that I apprentice in their "Audition Process," a 2-year program in which new members were apprenticed in the art of *taiko*. Perhaps most striking was the fact that they insisted on my participation as part of the "deal." They felt so strongly about my participation that when I suggested that I wished to also study the ensemble *sans* my own participation, they acted genuinely puzzled: If I wanted to study learning, they reiterated, why wouldn't I start with my own, hands-on experience of *taiko*? In other words, why not study learning from the inside-out?

I was, of course, thrilled, if not a bit overwhelmed, by the prospect of actually getting to play *taiko*. Yet at the same time, I was overwhelmed by a sense of anxiety brought on by my training as an ethnographer: How do I explain to the directors of San Jose Taiko the contentious history regarding the ethics of participant observation? How do I explain the dangers of "going native" as a result of one's participation—what every ethnographer is trained to avoid? Quite frankly, I realized that voicing my concerns would perhaps be offensive to the directors. Both PJ and Roy emphasized to me that I would best understand the group through a personal exploration of the meanings of *taiko*. After some degree of internal wrestling and discussion with other colleagues, I worked out a negotiation with San Jose Taiko, in which I would apprentice for a limited amount of time (Phase I of the apprenticeship process, or 4 months), and then step out of my role to become an observer at rehearsals in order to observe from a vantage point that would allow for a holistic perspective on social and musical interaction, from the outside-in.[3] In this respect, my role was as an "active-member-researcher" (Adler & Adler, 1987). The active membership role, defined by Peter and Patricia Adler, describes researchers who become more centrally involved in member activities, assuming responsibilities that advance the group but without a total commitment to members' values and goals. This role contrasts with their concept of the "complete-member-researcher," which includes those who are already or planning to become a full member in the group under study.

The fact that they wanted me to be a participant in their learning process made sense in relation to a larger concern that was raised during our negotiations: reciprocity. They were concerned about what I would give back to the ensemble. Over the several months of my involvement, I learned that they previously had been the subject of ethnomusicological studies. In one case, they felt that the researcher's findings bore little resemblance to the work of San Jose Taiko and reflected more of the researcher's bias toward a particular, political view of *taiko*. With a few exceptions, no effort had been made to interview any of the members in-depth. In another, similar case, a researcher published her work without consulting the ensemble first, and had made no effort to get to know the group, share data with them, or even thank them. Their request, in this context, was perfectly reasonable and reflected their strong desire to create a community of practice—quite literally—among group members, apprenticing members, and the academic researchers.

Moreover, San Jose Taiko's leading role in the establishment of *taiko* as a cultural project for San Jose's Japantown, and the wide recognition they received from the larger *taiko* performance world, places them in a highly visi-

---

[3]This arrangement was mutually beneficial and came about as a request from the ensemble directors and staff, who were concerned about focusing their teaching resources on those who were seriously interested in becoming members of the group.

ble position. Their performance of original repertoire, traditional Japanese costuming fused with American contemporary colors and designs, and dedication to Japanese American political issues through music and through seminars contribute to a carefully constructed identity that balances Japanese traditions with Japanese American traditions, a distinction that arose continuously throughout my study of their practices. Midway through the study, when I had a more informed understanding of San Jose Taiko, I came to understand their concern for my first-hand involvement as one that would give me credibility in their eyes, as someone who might emerge with a complex understanding of what it means to be a participant in such a world, to understand the struggle for an Asian American identity and other political dimensions from within and between the rhythms, movements, and sounds of taiko. In effect, they required virtuosity in the sense of deepening my knowledge and appreciation of the skills and techniques involved in taiko.

LEARNING FROM THE INSIDE-OUT: APPRENTICING WITH SAN JOSE TAIKO

North American taiko is a growing cultural project that aims to connect Japanese Americans with their roots and with their present culture through developing a cultural, artistic expression and positive conception of Japanese Americans (Hayase, 1985; Hirabayashi, 1988; Uyechi, 1995). Currently, there are over 150 taiko ensembles within North America (www.rollingthunder.com, 2002). Taiko scholars generally agree that the first ensembles of taiko, in which different drums play melodic, supporting, and contrasting rhythms together were established in the 1950s in Japan (e.g., Uyechi, 1995). Historical events in the United States have shaped the art form and have imbued it with meaning related to the internment of Japanese Americans during World War II and the ensuing negative conceptions of the Japanese as "other" rather than as American citizens. As one former player with San Jose Taiko writes, "If you can understand the World War II concentration camp experience of Japanese people and the effects that that has had in real, human terms on the Nikkei community to this day, then you can understand the great significance of the upsurge of the American taiko movement" (Hayase, 1985, p. 47).

San Jose Taiko, founded in 1973, is one of the oldest and perhaps most influential taiko groups of North America. The co-founders of San Jose Taiko, Roy and PJ Hirabayashi (Managing and Creative Directors, respectively), have developed their approach to taiko into a forum for social action, community development, cultural preservation, and Asian American identity, characteristics that mark many North American taiko ensembles. Roy articulates their artistic and program goals in the following manner: "Soul and jazz were derived from the Black experience but nothing on the popular market could be referred to as the 'Asian American experience.' . . . We were Japanese Americans who found *taiko* as a connection to our ethnic identity" (*Odaiko,* 1988, p. 2).

Over the years, the organizations' primary goals have been to develop a professional performance ensemble as well as community-based classes that focus on the artistic learning and practice of drumming. Today, San Jose Taiko is a fully established non-profit organization with offices and studio space located in San Jose, California, conducting public workshops, school visits, and other public outreach initiatives. San Jose Taiko has developed a strong, successful performance program as well as a junior program in order to introduce new generations of youth to *taiko*, and continues to provide leadership for others interested in founding their own *taiko* groups, and participate regularly in the community events of Japantown. At the time of this study, their performing group consisted of 12 members, seven of whom are Japanese American, two of whom are of other Asian American descent (Chinese and Filipino), and three of whom are Euro-American descent (the group changed mid-way through the study, as one member left and one came back; however, the ethnic composition remained relatively the same). Half of the ensemble members were women. To stop at these categorizations, however, would oversimplify the composition of the ensemble. The ages of the players ranged from the early 20s to early 50s, with the median age being in the late 20s. Some members have been practicing and performing *taiko* for years, either participating in other *taiko* groups or having played in SJT for years. One member had a Western classical background in piano and voice. Another had training on Western drum sets, read Western notation, and was in the process of learning the Filipino *kulintang* (tonal bells). At least three of the women in the group had formal dance training, from *hula*, to classical Japanese dance, to modern dance. Virtually all of them, regardless of ethnicity, had some experience with Japanese culture either directly (working abroad, or in some cases apprenticing with the professional Japanese *taiko* group, Kodo, in a type of exchange program) or through their spouses or partners.

Over the recent years, San Jose Taiko has established a 2-year apprenticeship they call the Audition Process[4] (often referred to as AP) influenced by

---

[4]San Jose Taiko generally refers to the second year of the Audition Process, as opposed to the first year, as the "apprenticeship" phase. I use the term *apprenticeship* in order to simplify the discussion and also to situate San Jose Taiko's learning environment within the wider academic field of apprenticeship studies, particularly in the tradition of Singleton's edited volume on Japanese apprenticeships (1998) and the work of Lave and Wenger (1991).

their work with the Japanese *taiko* group, *Kodo*. The first year consists of three phases, each lasting about 4 months. At the end of each phase, individuals are given formal evaluations of their progress. If a participant does not meet the required conditions (e.g., the ratings are low and the staff feels that there is little chance for improvement) then they are "cut" from the program. Those who show promise continue to the next phase. After the end of phase III and the subsequent closing of year two of the program, those who successfully pass the evaluation move on to year two of the apprenticeship. This year is not divided into phases; rather, apprentices are now incorporated into the regular performance group, playing in community-related performances and participating in one or two standard songs for the annual spring concert. If apprentices successfully complete this year, they are then gradually incorporated into San Jose Taiko.

During the period of my apprenticeship, there were 12 apprentices (including myself), during which four left the program due to extenuating circumstances. Of the remaining eight, another four were cut from the program due to the individual evaluations administered by the San Jose Taiko staff, leaving four to continue with phase II. During this phase, one participant reinjured her knee during the training and had to drop out, and another participant was cut at this level. This left two remaining apprentices, who successfully passed phase III and entered year two.[5]

As learners, we engaged in multiple activities, many of which involved participating in the cultural expectations of the *dojo* (place of learning) such as bowing at the door of the studio, removing one's shoes, bowing to each other at the beginning and end of each practice, and cleaning the rehearsal space. Maintenance of instruments was also a critical part of our apprenticeship. We learned how to reapply drumheads, tighten the thick ropes of the *shimes* (small drums with hides on either end held in place by a continuous rope tie), sand and paint the wooden percussive instruments, and create our own *bachi* (drumsticks) out of wooden dowels.

---

[5]As previously stated, my apprenticeship occurred during phase I of the Audition Process, the first 4 months of year one, as per agreement with San Jose Taiko. San Jose Taiko wished to focus their resources on those who were planning to seriously continue with the group contingent on their acceptance, and asked if I would become an observer after phase I. This decision also enabled me to observe the complex nature of individual and group learning processes—which my own learning process was obscuring due to the intense amount of concentration needed to learn the elements of drumming. The two apprentices, Marian and Britt, who went on to do the second year of the apprenticeship during the time of my study, are now fully performing members with San Jose Taiko.

An overarching pedagogical framework guides the teaching and learning practices of both the apprenticeship program and the regular performing group's rehearsals, a framework that emerged from a desire to articulate what they were doing as a *taiko* ensemble and its connection to the larger cultural landscape. PJ, the creative director and lead teacher for many of our rehearsals, explains their goals in this way:

> I think it was more like standardizing [the art form]. You know, the question of the day is: "What makes *taiko* *taiko*?" Just pure movement isn't necessarily all-embracive, embraced of *taiko*, you know. So what makes *taiko* in terms of how it's applied, the way we play? And a lot of the way we do things is a lot of philosophical elements, you know. Not necessarily related just to *kata* [form] alone, but just the expression of using *taiko* as an arts expression, a voice. It was definitely something that commanded attention. And, for Asians at that time [the 1970s], it was probably the most dynamic way to feel empowered.

Defining *taiko* has been a central preoccupation of the organization. Their pedagogical framework is anchored by four interdependent principles that illustrate their philosophy about what *taiko* should include: *attitude*, *kata* (form), *musical technique* and *ki* (energy). Throughout my ethnographic study of San Jose Taiko, I witnessed each of these principles in action, either through explicit pedagogical strategies, behaviors, or through both formal and informal evaluations of apprentices and the performers. Each of the four principles is described next and followed with examples of how they were taught and learned during the apprenticeship.

Attitude

For San Jose Taiko, *attitude* is considered an important part of the *taiko* art form: it is seen as necessary for building individual and group confidence. Of general importance are respect and discipline. Respect for the instruments, for one's self, and for other players are considered crucial for the overall betterment of the group and for the practice of *taiko*; discipline of the mind and body through physical and mental training is a necessary building block for artistic competence.

The concept of *attitude* was quite literally embodied through much of our training. Before each rehearsal as well as outside of group practice, members physically train their bodies in order to develop the required stamina and strength for performing, often engaging in a full hour of aerobic exercise and stretching before rehearsing with the drums. Throughout my apprenticeship with San Jose Taiko, we engaged in a pre-set series of physical warmups—side stretches, leg stretches, back stretches, waist twists, neck and hip circles, that are done in unison while we counted to eight in Japanese, so that a chorus of "*ichi, ni, san, chi, go, roku, chichi, hachi!*" would be frequently heard for the first 10 minutes of rehearsal. Calisthenics and running were a regular part of practice; apprentices worked up to 50 pushups and 250 sit-ups, and runs were often conducted around the studio neighborhood or a local park.

Apprentices and performing members nearly always engaged in a brief meditation exercise as part of the practice. Sitting in *sei-za* (legs folded directly beneath you so that upper and lower legs fold against each other), we would close our eyes and focus for a few minutes on the work we have just done and the work we are about to do—or at least this is what is suggested we think about.

What I learned from engaging in these exercises is that these ritualized movements and routinized physical exercises served as a critical transition period from the outside world to the world of *taiko*. It was our first experience in synchronizing our movements as a group. It is no accident that we moved, stretched, and counted together; these group experiences, created by PJ and Roy and based on their own learning of *taiko*, were purposefully designed to help us move and think as a group. Marian, a fellow apprentice, explained the importance of time for "acclimatizing" to *taiko*: "When practicing with the ensemble, you are supposed to be more aware of your surroundings: you know, the peripheral vision and your perspective. . . . There was one time when I was late and I missed the exercising. And I was completely not focused by the time I got there."

As Marian describes, we developed not only an attitude toward learning that involved an inextricable tie between physical and mental preparation, but also a social and cultural system of movement prescribed by our place of learning. These ways of moving our body—the bow at the studio door, removing our shoes, bowing to each other, stretching, running, and counting together—all serve as ways in which we experience a place called *taiko*, in which Japanese-based customs and training fuse with contemporary Western physical training. We learned to perceive the warehouse in which the studio is located as a transformed space, no longer a warehouse but a respected place of learning. We had begun to engage in a process of "interanimation" (Basso, 1996), in which this *taiko* place is integrated into our bodies. A place, philosopher Casey (1996) suggests, has its own "operative intentionality": "Precisely by allowing us to make a diverse entry into a given place—through hands and feet, knees and hips, elbows and shoulders—the body insinuates it-self subtly and multiply into encompassing regions" (p. 21).

It was through these exercises in particular that I began to embody some of the social norms prescribed by San Jose Taiko. Since the cultural project of San Jose Taiko concerns issues such as cultural preservation and social ac-tion, the apprenticeship included activities that encouraged a sense of self as social actor. Each participant was given a class reader, which contained arti-cles on the history of *taiko*, concepts important to learning *taiko*, documents about San Jose Taiko such as performance member guidelines, as well as sev-eral articles about the role of *taiko* in Asian American politics. In addition to the course reader, there were discussions about San Jose Taiko's role in defin-ing the larger field of *taiko*, videotapes of other *taiko* groups and Asian Ameri-can art forms, and "clinics" in which members would discuss an issue con-cerning some aspect of *taiko*, such as the cultural lineage of San Jose Taiko. One of the most notable activities was a walking tour through San Jose's Japantown, which included visits to local businesses, San Jose Taiko's admin-istrative offices, the Japanese American Historical Museum, and the San Jose Buddhist Church Betsuin, a prominent cultural center for the community. One of three left in the country, San Jose's Japantown is marked with placards and signs denoting the internment of many of its residents during World War II. The local museum, in fact, has an exhibit of photographs of lo-cal residents, who author these photos with stories about their internment experience.

San Jose Taiko plays a prominent role in the community of Japantown, performing at all of the local festivals (such as the annual *Obon* festival). A significant part of our education was learning about the ways in which they are involved in the cultural preservation of Japantown, mainly through *taiko* performances but also through community service. Indeed, in one of the let-ters we received for our orientation weekend, PJ had written the following:

> . . . for San Jose Taiko, "taiko" is not just learning how to play the drum. It is a holistic practice of working collectively and also inter-relating and being of ser-vice to the community. That is why we selected the activities for the Retreat that could best exemplify where we place our priorities, philosophically and ar-tistically. (San Jose Taiko, 2000, p. 1)

If the physical training of *taiko* inscribed on and in our bodies a sense of re-spect and discipline for the *playing* of *taiko*, then the cultural-historical prac-tices inscribed an attitude about the *purpose* of *taiko*, an embodied experience of the cultural-historical significance of *taiko* within a broader landscape of meaning.

Kata and Musical Technique

The second and third principles, *kata* (form) and *musical technique*, are integral to each other. *Kata* involves mastery of a coordinated set of movements involving a low, strong, wide-legged stance that helps to center the body and optimize arm and other physical movements required of drumming. Some of these stances derive from martial arts, such as the lowered pelvic stance used for stabilizing the body. Many of the choreographed movements correspond with particular drum strikes. *Kata* is a process, as one member explains, of "making the sound visual." For San Jose Taiko, *kata* is a means through which members can achieve "oneness" with the *taiko*—*kata* literally links the body with the drum (San Jose Taiko, 2001). SJT uses a coordinated set of movements that include a strong, low stance, helping to center the body and optimize the arm and other movements that go along with drumming. Movements are often both fluid yet strong and dynamic. Many derive from Japanese traditions of drumming.[6] Each song has a choreographed set of moves that are learned along with the rhythms that produces a uniform flow of movements and helps to create a visual style that marks not only the song but also the group's ensemble style.

A significant part of our apprenticeship was spent learning and practicing *kata*. Working extensively on the Eastern philosophical concept of the *hara* (the center of the body, located in the lower abdomen), we practiced movements through the pedagogical tools of metaphor, guided imagery, slow-motion movement, repetition, and imitation. More generally, we worked on

---

[6]The dominant style of San Jose Taiko, which involves diagonally-placed drums and drumming on a diagonal plane, is referred to as *Sukeroku* style. O Edo Sukeroku Taiko developed in 1959 at Yushima Tenjin Shrine in Tokyo in order to preserve the heritage of traditional Japanese drumming and to create a new contemporary style (Oedo Sukeroku Taiko, 2002). Prior to their formation, ensemble drumming was mostly found at festivals, such as summer *Obon*. Members were mainly *Obon* drummers, but decided to study basic *taiko* patterns from Japanese classical music in addition to drumming styles from different Japanese prefectures. Unlike many other festival drumming styles, which involve little body movement, the *Sukeroku* style, as it has come to be known, is characterized by identifiable movements that correspond with a slanted drum configuration in which the drum and the drummer's stance are aligned on a diagonal plane. According to the members of this *taiko* group, "Sukeroku" comes from a famous Kabuki character named Sukeroku Hanakawado, a famous war hero who embodied "the essence of Edo (Tokyo, or new East as it translates from the *kanji*) spirit" (Kobayashi, program notes).

developing a heightened awareness of the body and the habitation of space. "With *taiko*, your body is an expression of who you are. . . . Be cognizant of your actions. Challenge yourself to open up; be expansive." In the first few classes, and periodically throughout the apprenticeship, we would be guided through imagery of sites and planes beyond the body. For example, PJ often used the imagery of infinite poles to expand our awareness of our body:

> Be aware of how you see yourself using imagery. Imagine there's a pole going into your head and through the floor, this infinite pole going upwards and downwards. Now, there is another pole. Your center of energy, your *ki* . . . just below your naval; and this pole passes through your body in front of you and behind you. You have this axis to register how you hold your body: your *hara*. The *hara* has infinite expanding lines. Be aware of the infinite dimensions of your body. . . . Measure yourself. Monitor youself. Evaluate.

If poles were a recurring imagery salient to understanding the body in relationship to the *hara*, then rectangles provided an image of the body in relationship to the *hara*, the drum, and the body in motion during *kata*. During one exercise, we were asked to "push" this rectangle from side to side, feeling the resistance in the palms of our hands. While we were engaged in this movement, PJ stated, "This is all about becoming aware of the dimensions of space. Your center's not here," pointing to her lower abdomen; "it's here," drawing an imaginary circle around her waist. "This is awakening parts of our body that we will have to build to make our bodies strong."

Kata is intimately tied to the third principle, *musical technique*, which involves the integration of movement and sound. Aspects of musical technique include learning how to hold the *bachi* (cylindrical drum sticks about 16 inches long), how to strike the drum, and how to coordinate hands to produce rhythmic patterns and produce a consistent tone. Members practice drills to develop and strengthen hands, wrists, and arms to produce the same tone, and also to increase coordination through complicated rhythmic patterns that involve hand and ear coordination. *Taiko* rhythms are taught through a series of syllables called *kuchishoka*, a phonetic system of syllables in which each beat to the drum and its corresponding *kata* are represented by a syllable. Along with telling a player how to hit the drum, the different syllables also signify the timing and rhythm of each drumbeat.

Rhythmic drills are an important and regular component of rehearsals in both the AP classes and in the regular performance ensemble. Drills in *taiko*, as well as most other musical practices, consist of repetitions of some aspect of rhythm, movement, and/or technique, with the idea being that repetition builds muscle memory. Sometimes movements are slowed down in order to break apart complicated patterns or to focus on specific sensory experiences. Weekly practices, especially those with beginners, often included at least an hour of repetitive movements, both slow and fast, to enable *taiko* players to feel exactly where the body needs to be at any given point in a movement, thus building a sense of muscle memory. Hours of practice are devoted to learning how to move the body and think in terms of planes and spaces, to think past the body's borders and toward the embracement of space, instruments, and other players. Both PJ and Roy are conscious of the concept of muscle memory as a critical factor in the ensemble's success and stress this in their training of apprentices. In fact, in the course reader that they distribute to their apprentices during the first year of the Audition Process is an article called "Why Practice Makes Perfect" (Jaret, 1987), which summarizes neurophysiological research into the concept of repetitive practice.

Typically, educators regard such teaching processes as repetition and mimesis as outdated, Draconian pedagogy that yields little more than rote learning, as exemplified in the now common colloquialism, "drill and kill." But dance educators, music educators, and anthropologists conceive of these processes as critical to linking bodily experience to thought and action. Philosopher Suzanne Langer (1957) describes how imitated technique is a transformation rather than simply imitation, a transformation she calls "sense impression." Several of my fellow apprentices as well as the performing members described the importance of muscle memory for mastery. Stuart, a performing member, described it this way:

> I don't think that's something you can just come in on the first day and say, "okay, here's what it is." I mean, it's something that you have to learn, that you have to train your muscles, and get the different [appropriate set of factors] involved so that you don't even have to *know*; you don't have to think about it. . . . Everything has a slightly different feel, maybe a slightly different stance. All of that is for me (and I think for everyone else is) a little bit of muscle memory. You learn something and you basically just have to practice. You can mentally visualize it all, which can go a long way. But until you actually get in there and you practice it over and over and over again it's just not going to stick.

Such automaticity is a necessary precondition for more complex experiences relating to *taiko*, leading to what one professional musician calls the "zone of magic" (e.g., Steinhardt, 1998). The more opportunity one has to practice, the more one encodes movements, sound, and other features into the body, thus freeing a soloist to consider other technical or aesthetic matters. Thus, drilling and "magic" engage in a paradoxical relationship. Although we as apprentices did not necessarily achieve such levels of mastery, those of whom I interviewed in the professional group often spoke of such a quality of experience. Mary, a player who had been with the group for 9 years at the time of my interview with her, described an intangible feeling of "getting something right" that came over time with her growing confidence, a feeling that she describes as "almost mystical." She described a turning point in her learning during a performance of a technically difficult piece that she had been learning for over a year: "When I got to my solo section in that I just sort of took off! And, I don't know, I felt like it was a turning point where I kind of experienced playing with more abandon, you know, of being confident enough in what I'm doing to not think about it so much."

In San Jose Taiko's philosophy of practice, these drills are important in the development of a holistic conception of *taiko* as consisting of drum, player, and space. Learning to think *through* and *with* the body is a learning process that continues well beyond the beginning of an apprenticeship. Over time, and with extensive practice, I developed a keener sense of space around my body and the ways in which my movements traveled through space, shifting my perception of self from bounded entity to a self capable of occupying multiple spatial, temporal, and cultural zones of meaning.

Ki

Beyond leaving a sense impression, there is a connection between drilling and the process of building a relationship between the player and the drum, exemplified in the fourth principle, *ki*. Ki (pronounced "kee") is based in Eastern spiritual and philosophical thought and practice. The Western understanding of this practice has been informed by the Chinese concept of the same principle, *chi*. Ki is defined as "the spiritual unity of the mind and body" (San Jose Taiko, 2001). Ki is an essential principle of martial arts and a basic element of *kata*. Ki is also "the ultimate challenge that each member of SJT must meet." Through *ki*, SJT believes that oneness with the *taiko*, with other members, and even with the audience can be achieved through sound and energy.

Of all of the four principles, *ki* is perhaps the most elusive one to teach and to learn. The embodiment of *ki* concerns a grasping of the holistic relationship that exists among the discrete elements involved in *taiko* playing, often through explicit means such as attending to others' playing; knowing how to support someone's solo; how to convert a mistake into a generative, improvisational moment; and using *kiai* (the conventional shouted syllables of *taiko* playing and martial arts) as a means of keeping tempo, signaling to others, and keeping up the energy required for playing. Because *kiai* involves producing sound, the focus of teaching and learning is on quality of sound as it is produced and felt in the body. One exercise, developed by PJ and another long-time performing and staff member, Yumi, involved "passing" sound back and forth between people. Sounds that were explicitly taught in this manner included "Yoh" and its response, "Hoh." We were instructed to "try to see if you can really feel each other come out and come together." The desired sound is one that is unencumbered, produced with support from the diaphragm muscle and an open, relaxed throat. Metaphoric language was used extensively throughout our training in *kiai* to describe the internal functions required of the bodily production of sound: "Remember the inner tube," PJ explained during one class. "Let's push with your hands and send it along this way. Now, [act as if] your life depended on pushing that wall to me. . . . You can feel your *hara* really push."

In my observations and participation, finding the right moments in which to *kiai* was a critical aspect of understanding the elusive nature of *ki*. While as apprentices we were explicitly taught how to *kiai*, we were never explicitly taught *when* to *kiai*. During each practice, we were encouraged to *kiai* while hitting the drums, accenting the silent moments with syllables like "*Hip!*" or "*sup!*" or "*Yoh!*"

There are also explicit pedagogical strategies that encourage this spiritual and metaphysical aspect of *taiko*. For example, when introducing the *bachi* to beginners, PJ situated its significance in Buddhist practice: "The *bachi* is considered the sacred link between the spirit world and the earth, connecting the body to the sky." The *taiko* drum, drum hide, and the large metal tacks that are used to affix hides to drums all carry cultural significance in Buddhism. While SJT is not a Buddhist *taiko* group, the origins of *taiko* are found in such Eastern spiritual practices as Buddhism and Shintoism; PJ and other members of the group are cognizant of these origins and refer to each of the drum elements as comprising the spirit of *taiko*.

Beyond these more spiritual elements, SJT also takes care to teach its members about the relational aspects of *taiko* playing, brought out by the four principles of *taiko*. During one of our earlier classes, for example, PJ described *taiko* in this way: "[*Taiko*] has its own spirit, and we bring out that spirit with our attitude and [musical] technique. It's not just an instrument. You, too, are the instrument. We, together, are *taiko*." Here, PJ refers to the ways in which attitude and musical technique bring about *ki*, demonstrating the ways in which these component principles are orchestrated into a holistic educational environment that places a premium on a particular disposition toward learning. Through these four principles, attitude, *kata*, musical technique and *ki*, SJT hopes to attain what they call the "ultimate expression of *taiko*, when the art becomes a part of our personality, a way of being and life expression."

Thus far, I have described the philosophical and pedagogical framework of San Jose Taiko, highlighting critical aspects of their pedagogy with examples. I wish to underscore two issues related to methodology that my participation helped bring about. The first is that my direct experience allowed me to embody many of the principles I was observing in others, pushing beyond a conceptual understanding of learning *taiko* to a kind of performative understanding in which learning was experienced and manifested in and through my own body. Embodiment can be analyzed in terms of the ways in which sensory perception is coordinated and gives rise to certain forms of knowledge (e.g., Bresler, 2004; Lakoff & Johnson, 1999) as well as the ways in which the body is culturally inscribed by its surrounding environment and thus gives rise to certain forms of representation (e.g., Bourdieu, 1989; Foucault, 1979). My participation served to organize sensory experience into knowledge of art, self, and self in relation to learning.

The pedagogical emphasis on bodily imagery of spaces, geometric planes, and infinite lines and our repetition of movements in order to embody musical technique and *kata* highlight the relationship between cognition and the corporeal. But a study of *taiko* also highlights the ways in which learning occurs through somatic modes of attention, the "culturally elaborated ways of attending to and with one's body in surroundings that include the embodied presence of others" (Csordas, cited in Bresler, 2004, p. 7). In the case of *taiko*, this also includes an Eastern spiritual principle of mind–body unity as a goal of successful learning. When juxtaposed against Western schooling practices, a cultural study of a learning environment such as *taiko* offers educators a chance to reflect on the cultural organization of modes of attention in schooling and of the ways in which students' surroundings affect the quality of their lived experience, cognition, and learning. Thus, an ethnography of learning in which the body is taken into consideration becomes an opportunity to conceptualize a paradigm and methodology of embodiment, a point on which I elaborate in the conclusion of the chapter.

My second point is an outgrowth of the first. My understanding of *taiko* was co-constructed along with other apprentices and through interaction with the directors and performing members, which thus served to lessen the distance between self and other. In a sense, there is no "other" of which to speak. As a methodology, participation engaged me in a common ground with the participants of *taiko*. In the next section, I develop this point further, inverting the relationship between observer and observed.

DEVELOPING A CRITICAL EYE
AND A CRITICAL "I": WHEN PARTICIPANTS
BECOME OBSERVERS

An essential part of the Audition Process are videotaped and private evaluations, which determine not only a participant's progress, but also whether or not a participant will continue with the apprenticeship and eventually become part of the performing ensemble. Videotaped evaluations are a tool that San Jose Taiko uses so that participants can watch and evaluate their own progress, developing what PJ and many other members of SJT called a "critical eye." These videotaped evaluations were held midway through each of the three phases, in which apprentices would perform songs they had learned so far, watch their performance on tape, and discuss in evaluative terms what they observed about themselves and others.

Along with these videotaped mid-term assessments, individual members are evaluated through an explicit performance rubric—a "report card," PJ calls it—during the middle and toward the end of each phase. Individuals are evaluated on each of the four dimensions. Each of these, in turn, is divided into subcategories. For example, under *kata*, members are evaluated on such aspects as "fluidity," "strength," and "radiating lines from the *hara*." Under *attitude*, members are evaluated on such aspects as "care and respect for equipment," "flexibility and open mind," and "perseverance." For apprentices, songs that are learned during the program are also evaluated.

Individuals generally meet one-on-one, or sometimes with Roy, PJ, and Yumi (a regular staff member and performer with SJT for several years) to discuss these evaluations, reflections, and ultimately whether or not someone is accepted into the next phase of AP. PJ explains that these evaluations are done regularly among the performing members of the group as well as with the newer AP (apprenticing) members and reflect their desire to be conscious of the learning process:

> In the old days [of learning *taiko*], you don't go through this one-on-one, you don't have a "grading system" . . . And what we're trying to kind of cut through is, "well, just tell me what I need to do!" [laughs] You know? And that way we feel it's more the western approach. What are you doing well at? And what can

you improve at? So that you can improve more readily instead of second-guessing. What are *you* looking for? What are *we* looking for?

Although the dimensions on which people are evaluated are the same for beginners as they are for the experienced players with the ensemble, the ranking systems are different: the performing members are evaluated on a scale of 1 to 5 for each dimension, whereas apprentices are evaluated on a scale of 1 to 15, "because we want to show growth, improvement, progress within a certain period of time," reflects PJ. "If one continues through two or three phases [of AP] it's [easy to see progress]: 'Oh, you're really catching up!' A 15 would be exemplary, the model." When asked what a 15 means versus a 12, PJ says that they are able to scan across people to see the high range and the "slower range." She explains that there is a baseline or starting point for someone who has never been exposed to *taiko* or is having a difficult time. "We're also taking into consideration a bit of feelings. We're not going to give them a 1! But let's say just 3 to start with, and that it can show improvement with the weeks following." This rating system has been further developed and used during the AP process than it has for their performing members, fine-tuned "so that we can be a lot more exact as to the kind of individual we're trying to bring in." As for the performing members, they are revisiting this grading system in order to chart their own maintenance and progress. They are also revisiting this system in terms of having members be exemplary role models for incoming members.

These considerations point to a future orientation in their evaluative work—a system that seeks both to establish and improve upon their art as well as historically situate it. In the above quote, in which PJ describes the impetus for establishing an evaluation system, there are two different levels of meaning in her reflection. The first concerns a type of calibration between players. I use the word calibration to refer to the technical assessment of such techniques as *kata* and drumming. Calibration in this sense is almost literal, involving the movement of the body and the visual assessment of that movement in order to understand the "rightness of fit." But I also use it in a more figurative sense. The calibration is between the critical eye of the apprentice and the group itself, a process of fitting in to the social and cultural conventions of the group.

Second, PJ's response, just mentioned, concerns *taiko* as a sociocultural practice, one that "in the old days" consisted of copying the techniques of their *sensei*. By referring to the old days, PJ consciously distinguishes—and, in fact, temporally distances—the practices of San Jose Taiko from those of the other *taiko* ensemble. Furthermore, she aligns SJT's practices with a "more

Western approach" that she characterizes as explicit questioning and articulation of the purposes of learning. Ironically, using this Western approach leads to getting clearer about traditional Japanese aesthetics, such as the principle of *kata*, that comprise *taiko*.

PJ, Roy, and Yumi, a staff member and performer with SJT for several years, met with each of us twice during Phase I to talk about our overall progress: once early on during our training, and once about 2 weeks before the end of Phase I of AP. One by one, auditioning members be called in during our practice to discuss behind closed doors our progress. Although San Jose Taiko and I had a clear understanding that becoming a performer with the ensemble was not a part of my plan (I did not want them to feel that I had ulterior motives for studying them), they nevertheless decided to evaluate me on my potential as a *taiko* player. I was actually unaware of this until they approached me the night of the final evaluation sessions.

When my turn came, I felt my stomach tighten. As a performing musician, I was used to being evaluated; I had gone on numerous auditions, performing for music directors, committees, and music panels comprised of various judges. Although I have learned to distance myself emotionally from these experiences, the feeling of vulnerability has never left me. In addition, I wanted to "prove" to San Jose Taiko that I could *play taiko* as well as I could *research* it. Deep down, I was afraid that they would find me inept and would conclude that I was not a credible player, or—by extension—a credible researcher.

As I walked through the office door that night, a room partitioned off from the rest of the warehouse with walls and a locked door, I headed straight to the back where PJ and Yumi had positioned themselves behind two semi partitions, perhaps for further privacy. The effect however, heightened the tension I felt as I walked toward the back of the room, knowing they were there yet unable to see them. There was something very different about the feel of this meeting in comparison to our normal practices, in which evaluation was open and collaborative among group members and apprenticing members. Everything else we had done in practice had been public and synchronized as a group. This private session felt very secretive. I took a seat across from PJ and Yumi, who handed me my evaluations for mid-phase and the end of phase I.

As I reviewed both of my evaluations, my eyes immediately gravitated to the lower-ranking numbers (the results of my two evaluations are included in Table 2.1). Under the dimension of "musical technique," for example, I had expected much higher scores because of my music training and was somewhat disappointed that I had not received higher "marks." It wasn't until

TABLE 2.1
San Jose Taiko Audition Process Evaluation Form: Author's Evaluation*

Name: Kim Powell		
Date	2/14/01	4/11/01
Kata		
Fluidity/Flexibility/Relaxation	6	7
Center/Balance	5	6
Strength	6	7
Stamina	6	7
Awareness of Form/Control	6	7
Rectangle (shoulders, hips, torso)	5	6
Radiating Lines from Hara	5	6
Stretch/Extension	6	7
Alignment/Carriage/Posture	5	6
Foot/Leg Action/Readiness	5	6
Adaptability, Ability to Adjust	6	7
Renshu	6	7
Matsuri	N/A	5
Yorokobi	N/A	N/A
Oedo (Lines, Circles)	N/A	N/A
Musical Technique		
Coordination	6	7
Adaptability, Ability to Adjust	6	7
Memorization	6	7
Right/Left Hand Balance	6	7
Rhythmic Sense	6	7
Call & Response		5
Control/Speed	6	7
Timing	6	7
Renshu	6	7
Matsuri	N/A	5
Yorokobi	N/A	N/A
Oedo (Lines, Circles)	N/A	N/A
Attitude		
Care & Respect of Equipment	9	10
Teamwork/Respect for Others	9	10
Enthusiasm	9	10
Acceptance of Critique	9	10
Flexibility/Open-mind	9	10
Implementation/Follow-Through	7	8
Positivity	9	10
Focus	9	10
Personal Challenge	9	10
Attendance & Punctuality	7	10
Diligence (Homework)	7	10
Perseverence/Effort	8	9
Patience	9	10

(*Continued*)

TABLE 2.1
(Continued)

Ki		
Projection	5	6
Presence	5	6
Awareness of self & others	5	6
Intensity of Energy/Support w/Ki	5	6
Kiai	5	6

*Written comments by the evaluators have been omitted from this version.

much later that I realized my identity as a musician had always been constructed around musical technique and interpretation. Typically, that is all I have needed in order to be a successful musician. In this educational setting, however, musical technique is just one of four other dimensions involved in *taiko*. The evaluation form reflected a much broader sense of musicianship, one that included energy, attitude and movement. I was not used to receiving comments such as, "In general, you seem to be utilizing more of your entire body versus just your arms. Just maintain all the implementations." I found myself slightly distressed by some of my musical marks; for example, under the subsection, "Call and response," I had received a 5. I thought I had done much better on that, because I know that in general this is a musical strength of mine. I asked what "Call and Response" meant, just to make sure.

"We only did call and response once," Yumi responded, somewhat apologetic in her tone.

I wondered about raising my feelings about my other low scores, but found myself somewhat uncomfortable with the idea. This made me realize that perhaps others felt similarly in terms of bringing up feelings about their "report cards." We had, after all, been raised in a similar educational system in which questioning authority, particularly in terms of grades and other forms of evaluation, was generally discouraged.

An interesting conversation then ensued. Because 1 was the lowest possible score, and 15 the highest, I asked PJ and Yumi what a 7 meant, given that it would indicate the middle of the scale (and because I had a lot of them on my evaluation form). There was a pause as they looked at each other.

"You know, no one's ever asked us that before!" said PJ. She and Yumi laughed.

"PJ and I have different ideas about what a 7 means. So, yeah. We're not exactly sure," Yumi added.

"Okay, so, what does a 15 mean, and what does a 1 mean?" I asked.

"15 is like, Kodo," Yumi said, referring to a professional, internationally known Japanese *taiko* group with whom they have an established professional relationship. Even most of the performing members never achieve a 15, she added.

This interchange struck me as interesting on several levels. First, PJ's response—that no one had ever asked them what their scale numbers meant—could reflect the larger social conventions of privatized report cards and formal evaluations. Because I was in their apprenticeship program for research purposes rather than the goal of becoming a member, I felt that I had less to lose than someone who might feel as if questioning the evaluation system might jeopardize their chances of making the cut.

Second, by setting the standard of 15 outside of the group, San Jose Taiko chooses to situate themselves explicitly within the larger *taiko* community. This system sets up a comparative ranking in terms of assessing individuals and the ensemble as a whole in relation to the larger practice of *taiko*.[7] Aligning their practice with Kodo not only situates them within the *taiko* community; it also legitimizes their practice and goals as a professional *performance* company rather than a *community taiko* group.

Third, and most relevant to methodological inquiry, this incident shifted the gaze of observation, which, in turn, orchestrated different roles and relationships. Renato Rosaldo (1989) has written that "the objects of analysis are also analyzing subjects" (p. 21), and that both ethnographers and participants are positioned in relation to one another in terms of age, gender, race, and other sociocultural factors. The tables turned on me during these evaluative activities. But they also turned for PJ and Yumi, causing each of us to reflect on our assumptions, as when PJ and Yumi realized they weren't clear on their standards of evaluation.

By becoming the object of analysis, this evaluative activity proved to be a critical component in my subjective understanding of the embodied practice of *taiko* as well as an understanding of the emotional experience of evaluation. Although I knew I would not be continuing my training as a potential performing member, this shifted gaze drew me into "reciprocity of perspective" (Schutz,

---

[7]Kodo has an established relationship with San Jose Taiko. SJT stores Kodo's equipment for them for their U.S. tours. They have also established an exchange apprenticeship program in which a few members from San Jose Taiko have gone through Kodo's rigorous 2-year apprenticeship, a model upon which San Jose Taiko's program is loosely based. Kodo is known for their technical, artistic, and innovative performances, performing Japanese regional, folk *taiko* as well as incorporating world music into their compositions. For more information on Kodo, refer to M. Coutts-Smith (1997), *Children of the drum: The life of Japan's Kodo drummers*, a good source of information on Kodo's philosophy, apprenticeship, lifestyle, practice, and performance.

1971)—a type of empathy gained from similar experience that has important implications for the interpretation of meaning. As Alfred Schutz has stated, "observers who place themselves in the same situations as their subjects will thereby gain a deeper existential understanding of the world as the members see and feel it" (Adler & Adler, 1994, paraphrasing Schutz, p. 386). But the goal of participation is not necessarily empathy. I could not directly step into their shoes and into their personal experience of being Japanese American. I could, however, directly step into their world, in the spaces between drums, people, and movements and attempt to understand first-hand the qualities of their learning experiences and the ways in which such embodied knowledge is a critical step—indeed, an act of empowerment—toward achieving the broader social goal of shaping Asian American identity.

CONCLUSION

Throughout this chapter, I have noted the ways in which participant observation, with an emphasis on *participation*, confronts the problematic space between self and other through my own phenomenological experiences that blur these distinctions, and in some cases, invert the relationship between observer and observed. Participation can be in service of a more ethical, responsible, and representative approach to the ethnographic understanding of cultural practices within education (and, most certainly, beyond). In the conclusion of this chapter, I focus on one particular aspect of my research that significantly speaks to ethnographic methods and studies of learning.

My participation in the group informed me first-hand and in an intimate way about the crucial role of embodied experience in learning, transforming my initial thinking about embodiment as an abstract theoretical construct toward a richer, more complex understanding of embodiment as a learning phenomenon. Indeed, my own participation proved critical to my understanding of such internal and often ineffable aspects of learning that are central to the artistic development of the *taiko* apprentices. This understanding enabled me to write more critically and thoroughly about the nature of learning, and also led me to consider more broadly the implications of embodied learning educational research and theory in terms of the ways that knowledge is processed, formed, and stored in our bodies through phenomenological experience of the world.

As an educational concept, embodiment has been a virtually ignored feature in educational research. The arts are educational fields in which the body has been a primary mode of knowing and a field for inquiry (Bresler, 2004). Participatory studies in the arts are a potentially rich source from which to examine the ways in which reason is embodied in educational practice (Powell, 2004), presenting opportunities to question conventionally held theories and practices of both body and mind. Beyond the arts, cultural studies of learning in a variety of settings can offer alternative perspectives on educational theory and practice and lead us, as researchers, to reconceptualize commonly held values and beliefs about schooling.

When treated as educational concepts, *ki* and *kata* offer ways in which to think about a paradigm of embodied knowledge for effective school practices: What, for example, is the *ki* and *kata* of schooling? What qualities of embodiment are orchestrated by local and broader sociocultural meanings, beliefs, and values of American schools? How does a study of *taiko* or another alternative site of learning inform an educational vision of the types of learning experiences we might desire for students?

One of the most significant issues raised by the embodied experience of *taiko* concerns the self in relation to learning, a quality that involves a connection between person, instrument, and other players through the development of a relational identity with learning. Human action and movement are often conceptualized in terms of utility, wherein a person's sense of agency is restricted to utilitarian purposes. *Ki* serves to infuse the experience of learning and playing with intention, a type of embodiment that requires an explicit connection between sensory engagement—the muscle and sinew and sweat of playing, the political performance of Japanese American (and, more broadly, Asian American) identity politics, and a sense of purpose marked by spirituality and transcendence. The concept of *ki* also challenges the body–mind dualism that has dominated traditional Western thought, and, consequently, much of the research into learning, in which cognitive theories often stress internalized, mental processes without critical consideration of the role of the body and sensory engagement. Learning to play *taiko* successfully requires an individual to configure an identity through practice that is infused with the spaces and places between drums, people, and activity. As a philosophical principle, *ki* serves to orchestrate the experience of the body with a sense of agency in which the drummer is aware of how his or her embodied knowledge fits into a larger framework of meaning.

Kata functions as a connective tissue between cultural tools and the self by providing a series of intentional movements that orchestrate certain qualities of meaning. As such, *kata* is instrumental in creating a relationship between the body and the drum. It is also an aesthetic form in which every movement is filled with grace and purpose. There is always a connection between where one has been, where one is, and where one is going. In a sense, *kata* as a concept contests the notion of the utilitarian body by presenting a concept of the body as aesthetic and empowered through physical action.

The *ki* and *kata* of schooling are radically different than that of *taiko*. The embodied experience of schooling might be defined as anaesthetic, as John Dewey might suggest, devoid of heightened sensory experience, grace, purpose, and unity. In schools, bodies perform a primarily utilitarian function, holding our heads up during class, sitting still in desks, raising our hands to be called upon. Add to this the body searches, metal detectors, and surveillance cameras that are now in place at several schools, and Foucault's social analysis of the institutional, disciplined body during the birth of the prison (1979) comes into sharp focus. Implicated in this analysis is the importance of agency in relation to activity. Providing curricular opportunities that are experience-based, that encourage the use of the body, and engage the senses in learning could create a different kind of *kata* for schooling if learners are encouraged to explore connections between learning, self, and the broader social and cultural frameworks of meaning in which they are situated. And, whereas *ki* refers to a quality of spiritual unity within the realm of *taiko*, *ki* refers, in an educational sense, to the purpose, intention, and qualities of experience that connect learners with the purposes of learning. In *taiko*, if players lose the connection between players and drums, then learning becomes technical rather than artistic. In schooling, if students lose (or never have) a connection with the larger purposes, goals, and values of learning or a connection to a larger community of practice, then learning in this setting also becomes technical rather than artistic, inviting legitimate yet too often heard questions from students, such as, "Why are we doing this?" and "Why should I care?" In San Jose Taiko, technical mastery of skills and facts are situated within clearly stated artistic goals and a critical pedagogy of cultural reform. Accounting for the *ki* of schooling would involve providing educational places which encourage students to explore connections between learning and the self and to embody, in the fullest sense, the ways which their own sense of agency stands in relation to knowledge and practice.

Throughout this chapter, I have identified learning as a process of cultural inscription, in which local and broader cultural meanings, beliefs, and values insinuate themselves on, in, and through the body. In doing so, I wish to open up current discussion about learning and the interdependent nature of culture and cognition via sensory and bodily engagement. The ethnographic tradition of participant-observation, with an emphasis on *participation*, can offer an important investigative method of uncovering and illuminating complex educational practices, particularly when ethnographers seek to understand the tacit and implicit knowledge that is taken for granted within an educational setting yet undeniably central to the ways in which participants in a setting construct meaning-making. If, as educational researchers, we are to be accountable for documenting and interpreting the *ki* of educational institutions and their cultural practices, then the corresponding *kata*, or form, of ethnographic methods will have to include an expanded choreography of participatory stances.

REFERENCES

Adler, P., & Adler, P. (1987). *Membership roles in field research.* Newbury Park, CA: Sage.

Atkinson, P., & Hammersley, M. (1994). Ethnography and participant observation. In N. Denzin & Y. Lincoln (Eds.), *The handbook of qualitative research* (pp. 248–261). Thousand Oaks, CA: Sage.

Balsamo, A. (1990). Rethinking ethnography: A work of the feminist imagination. *Studies in Symbolic Interaction, 11,* 75–86.

Basso, K. (1996). *Wisdom sits in places.* Albuquerque: University of New Mexico.

Bresler, L. (Ed.). (2004). *Knowing bodies, moving minds: Embodied knowledge in education.* Dordrecht, The Netherlands: Kluwer Press.

Bourdieu, P. (1989). *The logic of practice.* Stanford: Stanford University Press.

Casey, E. (1996). How to get from space to place in a fairly short stretch of time: Phenomenological prolegomena. In S. Feld & K. Basso (Eds.), *Senses of place.* Santa Fe, NM: School of American Research Press.

Clifford, J., & Marcus, G. (Eds.). (1986). *Writing culture: The poetics and politics of ethnography.* Berkeley: University of California.

Coutts-Smith, M. (1997). *Children of the drum: The life of Japan's Kodo drummers.* Hong Kong: Lightworks Press.

Eisner, E. (1991). *The enlightened eye: Qualitative inquiry and the enhancement of educational practice.* New York: Macmillan.

Ellis, C., & Bochner, A. P. (2000). Autoethnography, personal narrative, reflexivity: Researcher as subject. In N. Denzin & Y. Lincoln (Eds.), *The handbook of qualitative research* (pp. 733–768). Thousand Oaks, CA: Sage.

Fine, M. (1994). Working the hyphens: Reinventing self and other in qualitative research. In N. Denzin & Y. Lincoln (Eds.), *The handbook of qualitative research* (pp. 70–82). Thousand Oaks, CA: Sage.

Foucault, M. (1979). *Discipline and punish: The birth of the prison.* New York: Random House.

Geertz, C. (1973). *Interpretation of cultures.* New York: Basic Books.

Geertz, C. (1983). *Local knowledge.* New York: Basic Books.

Guba, E. (Ed.). (1990). *The paradigm dialogue.* Newbury Park, CA: Sage.

Hayase, S. (1985). Taiko. *East Wind,* Winter/Spring, 46–47.

Hirabayashi, R. (1998). Rhythm journey: Expressions in time 1873–1998. Concert program notes.

Hirabayashi, P. J. (2000). Written communication.

Hirabayashi, P. J. (2001). Interview.

Holland, D., Lachiotte, W., Skinner, D., & Cain, C. (1998). *Identity and agency in cultural worlds.* Cambridge, MA: Harvard University Press.

Jansen, G., & Peshkin, A. (1992). Subjectivity in qualitative research. In LeCompte, M., Millroy, W., & Preissle, J. (Eds.), *The handbook of qualitative research in education* (pp. 681–725). New York: Academic Press.

Jaret, P. (1987). Why practice makes perfect. *Hippocrates.* Nov./Dec.

Krieger, S. (1985). Beyond "subjectivity": The use of self in social science. *Qualitative Sociology,* 8, 309–324.

Lakoff, G., & Johnson, M. (1999). *Philosophy in the flesh: The embodied mind and its challenge to Western thought.* New York: Basic Books.

Langer, S. (1957). The dynamic image: Some philosophical reflections on dance. *Problems of Art.* New York: Scribner's Sons.

Lave, J., & Wenger, E. (1991). *Situated learning: Legitimate peripheral participation.* New York: Cambridge University Press.

LeCompte, M. (1987). Bias in the biography: Bias and subjectivity in ethnographic research. *Anthropology and Education Quarterly,* 18(1), 43–52.

Lincoln, Y., & Guba, E. (1985). *Naturalistic inquiry.* Newbury Park, CA: Sage.

Marcus, G. E., & Fischer, M. M. J. (1986). *Anthropology as cultural critique.* Chicago: University of Chicago Press.

Odaiko. (1988). Newsletter, Vol. 4, No. 3, Fall.

Oedo Sukeroku Taiko. (2002). Web site: http://oedosukerokutaiko.com/english-1.html

Peshkin, A. (1985). Virtuous subjectivity: In the participant-observers 'I's. In Berg, D., & Smith, K. (Eds.), *Exploring clinical methods for social research* (pp. 167–282). Newbury Park, CA: Sage.

Powell, K. (2004). The apprenticeship of embodied knowledge in a *taiko* drumming ensemble. In Bressler, L. (Ed.), *Knowing bodies, moving minds: Embodied knowledge in education.* Dordrecht, The Netherlands: Kluwer Press.

Rogoff, B., & Lave, L. (Eds.). (1984). *Everyday cognition: Its development in social context.* Cambridge, MA: Harvard University Press.

Rosaldo, R. (1989). *Culture and truth: The remaking of social analysis.* Boston: Beacon Press.

San Jose Taiko. (2001). San Jose taiko philosophy. *San Jose taiko class notes and articles.* San Jose, CA: San Jose Taiko.

San Jose Taiko. (2000). Letter to participants.

Schutz, A. (1971). *Phenomenology and social reality: Essays in memory of Alfred Schutz. Collected papers II.* The Hague: Martinus Nijhoff.

Singleton, J. (Ed.). (1998). *Learning in likely places: Varieties of apprenticeship in Japan.* Cambridge, UK: Cambridge University Press.

Spindler, G. (1974). Schooling in Shoenhausen: A study of cultural transmission and instrumental adaptation in an urbanizing German village. In Spindler, G. (Ed.), *Education and cultural process: Toward an anthropology of education.* New York: Holt, Rinehart & Winston.

Spindler, G., & Spindler, L. (1992). Cultural process and ethnography: An anthropological perspective. In LeCompte, M., Millroy, W., & Preissle, J. (Eds.), *The handbook of qualitative research in education* (pp. 53–92). New York: Academic Press.

Spradley, J. (1980). *Participant observation.* New York: Holt, Rinehart & Winston.

Steinhardt, A. (1998). *Indivisible by four.* New York: Farrar, Straus & Giroux.

Uyechi, L. (1995). University taiko: Roots and evolution. Paper presented at the Symposium on North American Taiko, Stanford University.

Varela, F., Thompson, E., & Rosch, E. (1991). *The embodied mind: Cognitive science and human experience.* Cambridge, MA: MIT Press.

Wolcott, H. (1992). Posturing in qualitative research. In LeCompte, M., Millroy, W., & Preissle, J. (Eds.), *The handbook of qualitative research in education* (pp. 3–52). New York: Academic Press.

Westcott, M. (1979). Feminist criticism of the social sciences. *Harvard Educational Review, 49,* 422–430.

3

Living and Writing Ethnography: An Exploration in Self-Adaptation and Its Consequences

George Spindler
Stanford University

George Spindler began his career in the anthropology of education as part of his graduate training in anthropology at the University of Wisconsin, Madison in 1945, immediately after he was mustered out of the army air force. He became an instructor in anthropology for one year in 1947 and transferred to UCLA in the fall of 1948 to work on projective techniques. He pursued there his interests in clinical psychology and sociology, as well as anthropology, as he had at Wisconsin, wrote his dissertation on the Menominee and acquired his Ph.D. there in 1952, after researching and teaching at Stanford for two years. Meanwhile Louise Spindler was acquiring her training in anthropology at Wisconsin, UCLA, and Stanford and acquired her Ph.D. there in 1956, writing her dissertation on Menominee women, the first Ph.D. in anthropology from Stanford. George and Louise worked together in all of their fieldwork with Native Americans and overseas in Germany and in Wisconsin in rural schools. Their big passion in life was to live close to nature, as simply as possible. Louise died in 1997 after seven years of increasing debility from emphysema and congestive heart failure, during which she continued to carry on as a professional anthropologist and collaborated with George in teaching, research, and writing. Their years of collaboration are chronicled in *Fifty Years of Anthropology and Education—1950–2000* (2000, Lawrence Erlbaum Associates). A briefer account is to be found in "The Four Careers of George and Louise Spindler," in *Annual Review of Anthropology* (2000).

This chapter traces the challenges that the Menominee traditional worldview and be-
lief system cast against those of George and Louise Spindler during their fieldwork for

seven seasons, starting in 1948. The effect on the situated selves of the Spindlers and the conflict between their "Stanford" selves and their Menominee selves are analyzed. The consequences for the Spindlers are interpreted. Some advice on writing dissertations is provided.

It is my intention to write about the ways in which intensive fieldwork in anthropology, doing ethnography, can affect the fieldworker, causing a change in self, and perforce, identity. I also discuss, albeit briefly, how to write it up. I try to avoid the politics of ethnographic practice although some of my remarks undoubtedly have political meaning. I also try to be outstandingly personal, rather than to generalize.

My wife, Louise Schaubel Spindler, sadly deceased, and I did 28 field trips, over our 55 years together and on each one we did ethnography, with the Menominee Indians of Wisconsin, the Blood, or Kanai, of Alberta, Canada, the Mistassini Cree of Hudson Bay, the Germans of the Rems Valley in southern Germany, in Roseville, a village in northeast central Wisconsin, and with teachers and children in California schools in three communities near Stanford University, at different times usually, but not infrequently in the same year.

We both started with what we call our "enduring selves." That is a way of thinking of oneself and viewing others that has its roots in childhood. When I look at a portrait of myself at age 15 I can feel, I think, as I felt then, and it is not so much different from the way I feel now, at the age of 84, but there are changes, expansions, conversions, experience of which I had no inkling at 15. But I feel that somehow I anticipated those changes and expansions, not in any specificity, but in very general terms. Be that as it may, my enduring self is quite palpable to me. It may not be for everyone.[1]

But then there is another kind of self of which I am equally aware and it, in contrast to my enduring self, is constantly changing, though some parts stay constant. It is the "situated self," or more appropriately, selves. It is in response to the necessity to make sense in whatever situation one finds oneself in. This situated self may shift and change, within limits that are set by the enduring self, depending on the demands of these situations. I feel that I have a situated self for being a university professor, particularly as a lecturer in large graduate classes. I feel that I have a situated self at dinner parties with friends, another with academic intellectuals, another with working men, especially if

---

[1]The terms I use are from several sources. Though I have modified them to suit my own purposes, I owe the initial inspiration to these sources: Hallowell, 1955; Levine, 1973; Gergen, 1991. A good discussion of these constructs (from our viewpoint) is contained in Spindler & Spindler, 1994 (pp. 13–20).

working with them, and so on. Each situation demands different understandings, gestures, ways of speaking, demeanor. There are common features that
run through all of the situational selves I generate to adapt to these many-
faceted situations. These common features seem to stem from the enduring
self, but that enduring self seems to be adapting, as well, but within certain
limits.

And then there is the "endangered self." This self is engendered by unre-
solvable conflicts between situated selves and the enduring self. These conflicts may be of long duration or of short span. They may be deep or shallow.
They may be entirely conscious or quite murky. One can think of marriages
that become intolerable, of children in schools to which there can be no adaptation, of groups or gangs of people that one cannot abide, of jobs that seem
to suck the life out of one. There is likely to be an element of self conflict in
each, and that conflict is likely to be between the situated self that is demanded and the enduring self that is already there. The ethnographic field
worker is not immune to this conflict. In fact it may be a decisive factor in
whether or not the ethnographic trip is successful.

With the meaning of our terms established, we can turn to the more personal side of these processes that is the subject of this chapter. Although the
outlines of my enduring self were laid down by age 15 there was a lot that was
still to happen. I became a college student, a farmer, a high school teacher, a
married man, an army officer, a father, a graduate student and a teaching assistant, a research associate, a professor, in rapid succession. Each of these situations called for situational self adjustments, and meanwhile my enduring
self was enlarging. But then, along came ethnographic fieldwork. I was 28
when that started in 1948, and for the next 7 years Louise and I did fieldwork
for 3 months each year with the Menominee Indians in northern Wisconsin.
Our daughter, Sue, was with us most of the time. When she wasn't, she was
with one or the other grandmother.

Fieldwork required some phenomenal adjustments on our part. We had to
become different people in order to do good fieldwork. Our situated selves had
to change, and they did. But it was not that simple, and why it wasn't will take
up most of the rest of this chapter. My discussion necessarily focuses on myself.

DOING FIELDWORK

We began reconnaissance on the Menominee reservation in June, 1948. We
did all the usual things . . . went to see the superintendent, tribal board members, officials of the sawmill, proprietors of stores, filling stations, tried to en-

gage people in conversations, visited the Catholic church and talked to the priests, visited the hospital and talked to the medical personnel, for the first 2 weeks, and when we were finished, we knew very little about the Menominee. We were waiting for that big break that every anthropologist has to have before she or he begins to really learn who the people being studied are. And one day it came.

We were driving down highway 47 that bisected the reservation when a lone figure raised a poignant thumb. It was a hot day and she looked hot. We stopped, she got in, and introduced herself as Rose Pochan (*pochan* means deer in Menominee). We knew instantly that she was Bob Deer's half sister. We had met him but didn't know him. We drove on, and she said "Hey, it's hot. Let's stop at Freschette's," which we did. After a few beers and some conversation we got back in the car, went a mile or two and Rose said "Do you guys want to meet a medicine man (shaman)? Turn right here." We did. We went a couple of hundred yards and came to a clearing with a small shingled shack in its middle with a slight old man in front splitting wood. We took our time getting out of the car to give him time to collect himself after this sudden intrusion and Rose introduced us. Our 5-year-old daughter, Sue, was with us and his eyes lit up when he saw her. My beautiful wife and daughter gave our visit a special enhancement and we quickly made friends with each other. I had the wits to give him a handful of tobacco. We conversed in broken English and even more broken Menominee (on my part). That visit was to prove to be of special importance for us.

A couple of weeks later we were traveling down the same highway when we saw the framework for a Medicine Lodge structure being put up several hundred feet from the highway. We noted its location and proceeded to our campsite on nearby Moose Lake and returned the next day. None of the young people hanging around the lodge seemed to know anything about it but there was obviously activity within the lodge. The drumming and singing were driving me crazy—I had to get in! I circled the lodge, found a place where two pieces of canvas did not quite meet and skinned in, only to trip and fall into the center of the lodge where the members were engaged in shooting each other with their medicine bags. In each bag was a small seashell called a megise, which when shot at an uninitiated person was supposed to cause great harm or kill them. Napone, the shaman whom we had met, motioned for me to come sit by him, which I did as quickly as possible. I had no sooner seated myself when a large Winnebago woman dancing past suddenly swung her medicine bag at me and emitted the medicine cry, shooting me in the stomach. After a decent interval I left, thinking my absence might be appreciated more than my presence.

It was getting late so we proceeded to our camp, only about 3 miles away, and prepared supper. Before we had finished our meal I was beginning to feel ill. Louise took my temperature and we were surprised to see that it had reached 101 degrees. I lay down and Louise took over my usual dishwashing job. I slept a bit, but woke up feeling even worse, with a temperature of 103! We decided to go to the hospital in Antigo, some 13 miles distant, for I did not want to be ill at camp.

There the doctor gave me a series of tests to determine the cause of my sudden fever. He finally gave up and put me to bed, with a sign on the end of my bed reading "Fever of Undiagnosed Origin." And it continued to rise, to nearly 104 degrees. I slept fitfully but woke up in the morning virtually fever free and was on my way back to camp by three o'clock in the afternoon. We pondered the event and decided a trip to Napone might be in order. I was impelled by curiosity. What would he make of it? And by the feeling that it would do me some good if I was known as a person who had been witched. I would become human!

Napone was interested. He exclaimed, "I didn't know it would work on a white man." And he promised me an amulet that would protect me from further harm. "Come back in 4 days and bring some whiskey with you. An old man needs some medicine once in a while." I did that and he "installed" the amulet with four songs accompanied by a drum and what I took to be a kind of prayer. I have carried the amulet the rest of my life and I am happy to report that I have not experienced any acts of sorcery.

I did not believe that Suzie Spoon's witchcraft caused my fever, and I do not believe so now, usually, but this was the first happening of many that challenged my airtight Western concepts about the way the world worked. I won't go into more than a very few of them—just enough to make some points relevant to my main theme.

The first happened not long after the witchcraft incident. I woke up one night and saw perched on one of the struts of our umbrella tent a half-dozen little Native Americans, about ten inches tall, dressed in war paint, with sharp little spears poking holes in our tent roof. Since it was raining hard, this was of no small concern. I shouted at them: "Quit that you little guys, you're ruining my tent!" They disappeared. Louise woke up, alarmed by my sudden shout. "What's wrong? What's happening?" "Nothing. Just some little Indians poking holes in our tent!" Of course I had read about the Little God Boys in my preparation for fieldwork. I rolled over and went sound asleep, leaving her in a state of considerable bewilderment.

The next morning we decided not to go into the reservation right away but stay in camp and work on our field notes. Later in the day we went to Zoar (the traditional settlement nearest our camp) and stopped by a truck with the hood up and a gaggle of men around it. I joined them and peered with them at the motor. Because they were engaged in desultory conversation I started to tell them about our experience last night but they left one by one, leaving only Johnson, my good friend. "What was the matter with those guys?" I asked. "You was talking about the 'Little God Boys' and they didn't want no part of that." "Why not?" "They can do a lot of harm. Not really bad things, but they put snarls in your fishing tackle, holes in your tires, sand in your food, but they can do a lot of good, too." "I don't think they'll bother me too much." I ventured. "Just wait!" muttered Johnson.

We returned to our camp and resumed work on our field notes. After a time I got up from the camp chair I was sitting in and walked over to the place where we kept our drinking water with an inch of 5 × 8 note cards in my left hand. I tripped on a root and the notes flew out of my hand and landed in a pail half full of water ten feet away. I couldn't have done that if I had practiced for a week! I spent the rest of the day rescuing the notes and drying them off. The next time I saw Johnson I told him what happened and he said "You was lucky!"

Did I believe that the "Little God Boys" really poked holes in our tent and caused me to throw my notes in the pail of water? Let's take the matter of belief a bit further.

Not long after these incidents we were coming back at about seven o'clock in the evening to our camp when suddenly I had an image of myself opening the refrigerator I had built in the ground with roofing paper and crumpled newspaper and seeing two little green snakes crawl out. I walked to the refrigerator, opened it, and two green snakes did crawl out. The thought occurred to me that they were hallucinations, so I touched one, and indeed, it was real. I believe that happened just as I describe it. What am I to make of this? My rational mind says I had a "flashback," that is, I imagined I had the anticipatory vision after the two green snakes did crawl out of the refrigerator and ascribed it to an earlier moment. But that is not the way it seemed to me then or seems now.

Incidents of the same general kind happened occasionally throughout our fieldwork period. I came to accept them and only question them from the position I am in when I return to Stanford. One may ask, how do the Menominee think of these kind of happenings? Perhaps that can best be answered by describing an event that happened to my trustworthy friend, Johnson. He was young when this happened. He later became one of the major carriers of tradition for the conservative tribal group.

One afternoon I happened to come by his place, a Quonset shaped shelter built of tarpaper spread over a frame of bent saplings, with cardboard insulation inside, and two windows in the front, with a porch extending out from the front. It was a nice combination of whiteman (their phrase) and traditional Menominee structure. It was small, about 15 by 20 feet, and in it lived Johnson, his wife and three children. Other similar and some quite different structures clustered together, scattered throughout the forest. This was Zoar. There was a pop and snack stand by the highway and there were several slot machines of questionable legal status. There was also a Catholic Church of minor dimensions, and a large, old house in which Moon and Jennie Wesoe and their four children lived. Johnson was sitting beside the Dream Dance Drum, a washtub sized, deerskin wrapped drum with beaded decorations representing the origin of the *Nemeh Hetwin* (Dream Dance), smoking what the whiteman called a "peace pipe." Knowing this was a ritual, I stayed a respectful distance away until he was finished. He opened the conversation by saying "Tomorrow I am going hunting." Knowing how to ask the right questions I said, "Why are you going tomorrow?" Then he told me about a dream he had.

"I was out hunting in my dream, that's what you would call it anyhow, and I came to a brushy part and two deer came out of the brush. One of them turned toward me and said 'you can have one of us so that you may live' and with that he jumped into the brush and the other deer stayed. I knew that was my deer so I shot him. I know that's going to happen tomorrow, so I'll go out tonight and rest by that place and wait, so I'll be there first thing in the morning. You know I keep this drum (for Kimeyowan an elder and drum owner) and I ask it to help me for hunting. I believe in that my whole life. I know it's going to happen."

Johnson went out hunting just as he said and returned the next evening with a young buck that he had killed. He said to me, "It happened just as I told you. I got there (where there was a salt lick) and waited and with first light two deer came out of the brush and one jumped right back in the brush and the other just stood there, waiting. I said 'I am going to take your life so I may live' and shot him.' "

There is no doubt in my mind that Johnson believed in the sequence of events that he described. He prayed to the drum with the big pipe. He had the "dream." He waited by the salt lick until the two deer appeared and he shot one of them. Whether the other one disappeared just as he said, or was simply not as good a target as the other is moot. But from Johnson's point of view the original scenario held good.

Louise and I were audience to the telling of such events continuously, once we were accepted by the traditional group. It appeared that its members rarely did anything of much importance unless they had a "dream" or some event occurred that could be interpreted as a sign that a given action should be taken. There is no doubt that this constant exposure had an effect upon us and activated our psyches, or at least mine. But this exposure, and my own activation of the psychic processes, had an effect on my self, and to remain true to our conceptual arrangement, an effect on my situated self.

The psychic activity on my part continued at a steady level. I saw deer before they crossed the road in front of my car. One night I saw two Indians in war paint trying to pull off the old rope trick (running in opposite directions circling our tent with a rope). This was interpreted by Johnson that someone meant to do us harm and we were to be on the alert. One might think all of this would be disturbing but it was not. I have had visual waking hallucinations all my life.

But then something else took place that was not a waking hallucination, or any kind of a hallucination. I was sitting on the edge of our bed working on field notes just taken at a peyote meeting. We had left at midnight rather than staying until dawn. The gas lamp was hissing comfortably and I was quite peaceful and relaxed. Suddenly there was a rustle at the threshold of the tent, which was about six inches high, and a green snake came slithering into the tent and came straight toward me. It stopped about a foot from me and "stood up" (raised the first half of its body nearly straight up), its red eyes (in the reflection of the lamp) shining and its little red tongue flickering in and out. I watched it for a minute or two, then picked it up and put it outside the tent. In a few moments I heard the rustle at the threshold again and in came to the snake. It repeated the behavior and I took it out again. This happened four times. The fourth time I took it some distance from the tent and it didn't return.

As usual, I took the happening to Napone for interpretation. I explained what had taken place in my more than halting Menominee mixed with English and he seemed very interested. He then told me to sit down while he told me something important. What he told me, in Menominee that I somehow understood quite well, was that the snake was probably my guardian spirit. It was an especially important visitation because it had come to me—I did not seek it out by praying and fasting. That it had come four times was important. He then instructed me about what the snake as guardian spirit meant. The snake's power was neither good nor bad, but it was powerful. I needed to "feed it" with tobacco and prayer occasionally. I could ask it for help for really important things, but nothing trivial. I took this seriously and in the circumstance I was in, believed him. Later on, when I was in my own skin, so to speak, I seriously questioned the whole thing, but I found myself questioning it because my preparation had been inadequate, I was a White Man, and so forth, not because guardian spirits are not real. You may ask whether I feed it occasionally, but you won't get an answer. I will say that I think I have had extraordinarily good luck all of my life but it started before this event.

Be that as it may, the events I have described, plus everyday life with the people who lived in the vicinity of Zoar, gave both Louise and me a strong sense of identification with them. To illustrate: the traditionals put on pow-wows for tourists and for a few of the acculturated Menominee at a dance arena, a natural woodland bowl, near Keshena, at the easternmost end of the reservation. We always came with them, or joined them there and sat with them while the performance took place. We had become a part of the group, which one day they acknowledged when they introduced me to the audience as "one of our boys that went west" and Louise as "the reason he went west." We each did a dance, accompanied by their drum group, I a combination of jitterbug and chicken dance, Louise a pipe dance, which was exclusively a man's dance. The Menominee seated on a log nearly laughed themselves off the log. The tourists merely looked puzzled but our performances became a part of the offering. One day we came late, went to the gate to walk in and were stopped by a young woman selling tickets: "That will be one dollar for each of you and 50 cents for your camera." I felt like someone had slapped me with a wet, cold, fish and I stamped off to the car, with Louise accompanying me though her heart wasn't really in it. After I had sat glowering for awhile Johnson came out and said: "That girl didn't know you. I told her to let any-one from Zoar in but she didn't know you." With that we walked back to the entrance and the young lady was nicely apologetic and I felt good. There was no doubt that we considered ourselves members of the group, not Menomi-nee, but bonafide members of the group. Another time when a Warrior's Dance was being held, I joined the line of men dancing behind a leader carry-ing a befeathered lance. The next day our friend Helen told us her "old grand-mother" had said of me, "that's no white man!" This pleased me no end. We weren't just playing Indian. We moved about as more than familiar people—as friends and participants.

Didn't this affect our objectivity? How could we have achieved otherwise the intimacy that makes good ethnography possible? We had plenty of time to exercise objectivity after we returned to Stanford. But it wasn't quite that simple. There had been a permanent alteration in at least our situated selves, and each year for 7 years that alteration became deeper until at least I could say that my situated self had become different, reshaped, permanently. It is still here, in me, 50 years after we finished our last full season of fieldwork with the Menominee. To be sure, we have visited them many times since then. Lorie Hammond, my daughter Sue and her husband, and I returned in 1998, a year after Louise's death. We were surprised and gratified to find the traditionals holding a seasonal summer ritual. We joined them and heard the leader get up at intermission and say "I always read the writing every time we give this dance." And people kept coming up to me and saying "I've read the writing." I was puzzled until it suddenly dawned on me they were referring to Louise's and my book "Dreamers With Power" (Spindler & Spindler, 1971, 1984).

Our total study of the Menominee included five different kinds of Menominee: Native Oriented, Peyote, Transitionals, Lower Status Acculturated, and Elite Acculturated (G. Spindler, 1955; L. Spindler, 1962). Each of these categories required intensive ethnography and no small amount of statistical work, but none of them had the same impact on us as the Native Oriented, or traditionals. The Peyotists came close. We were close to them but never considered ourselves members of their group in the same way we did the traditionals.

We have often pondered the reasons why this would be so. The fact that the traditionals lived in the woods, fished and hunted for a significant part of their subsistence, and carried on rituals that were a part of the traditional schema, were certainly enough to give us a good start in identification with them, because we were "nature buffs" and spent every minute we could in nature, camping, fishing, canoeing. But there was more. We discovered in the second season of fieldwork that the majority of the group were not people who had lived their entire lives in a traditional vein. They were people who had experienced the outside world, who had sickened of it, and had come home to learn the traditional ways from the waning population of elders who had been born into the traditional culture and had lived it all their lives. Most of them, it was true, had been raised by traditional grandparents, or parents, who lived the old culture, but schooling, the great destroyer of traditional identities, had intervened. They grew up, some even went to high school, got jobs, became a part of the lower class of the non-reservation population and after some years, returned to the reservation to learn the old ways and raise their children that way.

We saw in them something of ourselves. We wanted to live a life outside the framework of professional, white-collar culture, for some of the same reasons the traditionals wanted to live outside the framework of white middle-lower culture. The fact that we lived in a tent all summer long attested to the fact that we were looking outside of the box for satisfaction. We lived in tents for 4½ years of our 55 years together. It also made us particularly accessible to the traditionals, and the peyotists, and they could, and did visit us often, without notice.

EXTENSION

We can consider what happened to us as a unique case, or as a process that has some degree of generalizability. We choose the latter. Our problem was, and still is to some extent, that we were living in two quite different and definitely opposed realities. The one the rationalistic, reality-centered, materialistic American culture. The other the non-rational (from our point of view), spiritually-centered, non-materialistic traditional Menominee culture. It was not that the Menominee ignored the material world. They were keen students of nature. They hunted, fished, and gathered. But their explanation for events in that material world was very different than in our culture. I need not belabor this characterization for most of what I have written in this chapter is about that.

We have not settled the question, did we believe the solutions offered by the traditional Menominee culture? Yes and no. We accepted the Menominee view when we were doing fieldwork with them. This is a common anthropological behavior. But in our case the alteration in our worldview that is part of the situated self as well as the enduring self went deeper. Although we never fully accepted the Menominee interpretation in its literal form, we did grant that things may not be as they seem to us, that there is more than one sustainable interpretation of reality. Writing this article has reminded me quite forcibly of our Menominee selves. I feel like feeding my guardian spirit.

The other day I had occasion to be exposed to the struggle that one Hmong student had with her two realities. She is reported by Jerry Rosiek, in a chapter written for this book (Rosiek, this volume). The girl student came in to see her biology teacher, also Hmong. She hesitantly put a question to him, "Do you believe what you are telling us in class?" He put off the question, saying "let me think about this." That satisfied her for the time being. There is a long discussion by Rosiek and he ends by revealing that the student was not asking for herself, but rather about his, the teacher's view. Had he forgotten his Hmongness, his native belief system, in favor of Western interpretations of phenomena? For her, this was cause for concern.

Most immigrants from Asian cultures tend to have this two-reality problem, like immigrants from any non-Western culture. We all have some questions about reality in opposition to what we are taught in school but they are usually not as acute or disturbing. In a multicultural world it behooves we who are charged with the responsibility for teaching to consider this problem. It is real. We have in the United States a whole generation of Native Americans destroyed by forced western style schooling. The two realities they experienced were not merely different, they were opposed. Children were removed from their homes and families, so they had no reinforcement for traditional beliefs or behaviors. In keeping with our guiding constructs, they suffered endangered selves.

Can we justify letting children learn more than one definition of reality? Why not? What's wrong with having two, or more, such definitions? We all relate to such problems in some form. We are composed of situated selves interacting with and affecting our enduring self. We choose to act in conformance with one or another self, depending on circumstances. We know from our Menominee experience that it is possible, and actually enriching, to experience two selves. When we came back from the field each year to Stanford, to teach classes, advise students, monitor dissertations, attend faculty meetings, and do all the things that are a part of being in the academic world in a leading research university, we went through a period of about 2 weeks when we felt thoroughly disoriented, confused, and nothing made sense. It was a dangerous time for us. But then the other reality took over. It all seemed important, imperative, satisfying. But the fieldwork reality remained dormant, only to be activated once again when we returned to the field. We felt, and still feel, enhanced by our experience. Could it be so different for Hmong or Iu Mien, or Laotian, or traditional Mexican, or Chinese?

Our construction of the enduring and situational selves seems useful, but we shouldn't take it too seriously. The concept of self, itself, is adequate, with dimensions of enduring and situated, and even endangered self as necessary for analysis. The danger in the concepts, or in any construct, is that it can become a rigid category into which observations must be forced. This would be fatal to the open, flexible, stance that we think is essential for good ethnography.

WRITING ETHNOGRAPHY

Now it is time to talk about writing the ethnography that is the product of the fieldwork in which all this self adjustment has taken place. I am obviously not discussing the "quick and dirty" kind of research, but rather research that has involved repeated visits to the research site over a substantial amount of time. The usual educational research may not initiate personal adjustment as did our Menominee experience, but all research affects the field worker.

We all have seen, or perhaps have been, one of the avid researchers who comes home and immediately starts collating data, counting occurrences, classifying, coding, doing everything but writing. This phase may last for a month, during which no great harm has been done, or it may last for 6 months, or even a year or more, in which case the dissertation, even more than the dissertator, will likely not recover. The object seems to be to break up the data so that it becomes more manageable in small pieces, unrelated to a whole schema, which has meaning and intent.

That is not the way to go about it. One should do the writing up of the data in the same way that one acquired it, only now the worker has the advantage of having a body of data that will stay still. One should relax, read over one's field notes, ponder photographs, listen to tapes, not once but several times. Take notes if you have to but they are not essential, but do record any summative, or intriguing thoughts you may have. They will be very useful when you actually start writing. Enjoy the experience. After all, they are your data. Remember, no one else knows as much as you do about your topic.

When you have done this for a month or two, even longer, you should have some ideas concerning what your dissertation, or book, is about. Of course you had a field plan before you went to the field but most research does not hew to the preplan. If you are lucky you will also have a clumsy but very useful outline of how you will organize your writing. If you do, start writing, but not necessarily at the beginning—where ever you feel most comfortable—write discursively, not in clipped, decisive sentences. You can clip it up later. But get started. Juices will start flowing and you will be speeding along before you know it.

Now you can start codifying, counting, and so forth thus making your data manipulable, as you come to the parts that require that treatment. This probably seems like improbable advice, but such activities always take longer than one anticipates and the trick is to keep the main current flowing.

Actually, this is all I have to say about writing. I have never thought that writing was the problem. What one does in the field is the problem, and what one did before the field is another problem—did you write? Did you want to write? Has any one in your family ever written? The urge to express yourself in writing about an experience you have had, to share that experience with others, those feelings must be in your heart if you are going to write well. This does not mean that those feelings will not be present if the conditions I stated are not met, but it means that you will have to work harder to get there than someone who has met those conditions.

This account of how to write a dissertation or a book based on work in the field must seem dreadfully inadequate to any reader seeking practical advice on how to do it. But this is what I told the many doctoral students I have monitored through the process of writing their dissertations, and all but one succeeded in doing it. There is plenty of writing about writing. My recommendation would be to read Harry Wolcott's (1994, 1995, 2002) three books on the subject, and Alan Peshkin's (1978, 1982, 1986, 1991, 1997) five case studies of schools in various relations to their communities as examples of the way it should be done.

REFLECTIONS

There is no way I can write a conclusion to this chapter. In this kind of writing the conclusion is in the flow of the text. I can, however, reflect on some of what has been written. It should be obvious that I have not been talking about a collaborative style of research or writing. Certainly Louise and I collaborated, but we did so as a single unit with different facets.

Many anthropologists have worked with the Menominee. One such person remarked, upon reading the manuscript for *Dreamers Without Power* (1971), "These are not the Menominee I know." He was right. He never once visited the native-oriented traditionals. He knew nothing about them. They were to him a vague rumor about "some scruffy people up at Zoar playing Indian."

The native-oriented traditionals were a tiny part of the total reservation population of 3,500 souls. Their whole population could not have consisted of more than 35 adults and 40 children. But various aspects of their culture were widely shared. In truth one could say that for all but the most acculturated to American culture, an even tinier population than the traditionals, the traditional Menominee culture was alive if not well. And one could find traditional persons in unexpected places. For instance, one evening I had an appointment with the foreman of the day shift at the sawmill. This was a large operation and the main source of income for the Menominee. He was a middle-aged Menominee man who spoke perfectly good English and seemed very knowledgeable about the operations of the mill and its economic consequences. "One of the elite acculturated" I said to myself. As he talked, someone came in the back door and my informant said, "Just a moment. Tom Fish has come to visit me." He went out to the kitchen and greeted his visitor in Menominee, and the two proceeded to carry on a conversation in the native language, very fluently. After awhile they parted company and my informant came back into the living room where I sat. I said to him, "You are obviously fluent in Menominee and not only that, but in the old style language form." He was surprised that I recognized the older form.

I asked him if he would take the Rorschach. He said he would and at a later time I collected one from him. I was surprised to find that his protocol would place him in the traditional group. Whatever the Rorschach does or does not do in clinical practice, in our work with the Menominee it was very good at predicting where, in our five categories, an individual would fit, and usually the fit corresponded in all of its dimensions: social, cultural, religious, and so on. In this case it did not. There were two others in our sample who met all of the criteria for elite acculturated placement whose Rorschachs were definitively native-oriented. These people were all excellent speakers of the native language and of English, held high status jobs and appeared in every respect to be elite acculturated. They all had been raised in traditional households in the Kinepoway or Fredenburg areas north and northeast of the center of the reservation. They were operating with the opposed identities of traditional and Western and doing better than most of their brethren. They were exceptional people who could handle the stress of opposed identities. None of them participated in any way in the rituals or social events sponsored by the traditional group.

It is often the exceptions to generalizations that prove informative. These three exceptions raise the possibility that opposed situated identities, in the Menominee situation, can be managed in the adaptive process. It appears, further, that this is done by pursuing one or the other identity. If this is correct that would explain why these three never attended any traditonal events. Social class and areal identification may also determine this adjustment. It is probable that their families of origin were old Menominee with some status. One of the criticisms of the traditional group was that there are so many Potowatami and Chippewa mixed in the group, and so much cultural mixture, that it was not really Menominee culture that was being revived. These are anthropological problems and I cannot resolve them without writing a different kind of chapter.

One matter that calls for more resolution than I have provided is that of our malaise upon returning to Stanford after each of our fieldwork sessions with the Menominee, or for that matter, with the Blood or Cree. But I have to admit, they were most acute with the Menominee. I have said that we were disorganized, purposeless, that our responsibilities seemed irrelevant. This state of being usually lasted at least 2 weeks, and sometimes longer. This is ordinarily termed "culture shock." This terminology treats only with the surface phenomena. What I see is a profound reorientation to the situated selves that are inherent in the Stanford situation, in contrast to the situated selves that we were called on to exhibit in our work with the Menominee, and less so with the Blood or in the comparatively short time we spent with the Cree. I have explored the most important dimensions of these situated selves, so need only to say that the crux of the issues raised had to do with the certainties of realities posed by the two contrastive belief systems. We had grown accustomed to having the certainties of our Western, American worldview challenged by events and voiced beliefs that contradicted it. As I have said, we did not accept them wholeheartedly but our certainties were called into question.

But there was more than that. All summer long we lived in a tent, we cooked our meals under canvas, but not in a tent, and our heat was a campfire, we brushed our teeth at a plank nailed to a tree and rinsed with water from a cooler with a spigot. Our bed, our one luxury, was a double spring mounted on 2×4's and covered by my WWII sleeping bag stuffed with goose down. We found all of this comfortable and pleasant. Not a few of our friends exclaimed: "How could you stand it?" There was no use in trying to explain. We simply smiled. We chose to live that way during all of our fieldwork with Native Americans. Our rationale was that we needed to establish a residence that did not affiliate us with any particular family or institution. Our camp seemed to serve this purpose. After we had established ourselves we were frequently visited by Indians, usually in groups, without notice. But behind all of this rationalization was the fact that we liked being in nature all the way. When we returned to our homes, we found them intolerably stuffy. To the end of our lives together we maintained this love. Life in civilization was a shock after the freedom and security of life in nature.

So our post-fieldwork response to life at Stanford was not simple culture shock. It was a complex of feelings, habits, reorientation of worldview, and nostalgia for the kind of life we most wanted to live.

REFERENCES

Gergen, K. J. (1991). *The saturated self: Dilemmas of identity in contemporary Life*. New York: Basic Books.

Hallowel, A. I. (1955). *Culture and experience*. Philadelphia: University of Pennsylvania Press.

Levine, R. A. (1973). *Culture, behavior, and personality*. Chicago: Aldine Publishing.

Peshkin, A. (1978). *Growing up American: Schooling and the survival of community*. Chicago: University of Chicago Press.

Peshkin, A. (1982). *The imperfect union: School consolidation and community conflict*. Chicago: University of Chicago Press.

Peshkin, A. (1986). *God's choice: The total world of a fundamentalist Christian school*. Chicago: University of Chicago Press.

Peshkin, A. (1991) *The color of strangers: The color of friends: The play of ethnicity in school and community*. Chicago: University of Chicago Press.

Peshkin, A. (1997). *Places of memory: Whiteman's schools and Native American communities*. Chicago: University of Chicago Press.

Spindler, G. D. (1955). *Sociocultural and psychological processes in Menomini acculturation*. Berkeley: University of California Publications in Culture and Society.

Spindler, G. D. (2000). The four careers of George and Louise Spindler: 1948–2000. *Annual Review of Anthropology, 29,* 15–38.

Spindler, L. S. (1962). Menomini women and culture change. Memoir 91. *American Anthropological Association, 64*(1).

Spindler, G., & Spindler, L. (1971). *Dreamers without power: The Menominee Indians.* New York: Holt, Rinehart & Winston.

Spindler, G., & Spindler, L. (1984). *Dreamers with power: The Menominee Indians.* Prospect Heights, IL: Waveland Press.

Spindler, G., & Spindler, L. (1994). *Pathways to cultural awareness: Cultural therapy with teachers and students.* Thousand Oaks, CA: Corwin Press.

Wolcott, H. F. (1994). *Transforming qualitative data: Description, analysis, and interpretation.* Thousand Oaks, CA: Sage.

Wolcott, H. F. (1995). *The art of fieldwork.* Walnut Creek, CA: Altamira Press.

Wolcott, H. F. (2002). *Sneaky kid and its aftermath: Ethics and intimacy in fieldwork.* Walnut Creek, CA: Altamira Press.

4

Race Wrestling: Struggling Strategically with Race in Educational Practice and Research

Mica Pollock

Harvard University

Mica Pollock is an Assistant Professor at the Harvard University Graduate School of Education (mica_pollock@gse.harvard.edu). An anthropologist of education, she studies adults and youth struggling to analyze and address fundamental questions of inequality and difference as a routine part of their everyday lives.

This article introduces a core set of "race talk dilemmas" central to educational practice in the U.S., unearthed in a multi-year ethnographic study of unprompted everyday school and district discourse in California (Pollock, 2004). The author argues that U.S. educational researchers struggle with the very same dilemmas of talking (and thinking) about race. Since both researchers and practitioners often make things more difficult for kids when we do talk about race as well as when we don't, the author suggests that researchers interested in achieving racial equality in education can wrestle more critically and purposefully with race talk and analysis in educational research.

> So, Nat'ralists observe, a Flea
> Hath smaller Fleas that on him prey,
> And these have smaller Fleas to bite 'em,
> And so proceed ad infinitum.
>
> —Jonathan Swift

In *The Interpretation of Cultures*, anthropologist Clifford Geertz paraphrased a myth an informant from India had once told him about the earth: the earth rested on a platform on top of an elephant upon a turtle, and after that, until infinity, it was "turtles all the way down" (1973, p. 29). The world of American education, I argue here, is race dilemmas all the way "down." From researchers to superintendents to teachers to students of all ages, navigating the national system of racialized difference and racial inequality plagues us all in some strikingly shared ways.

My own work suggests that people working in and studying U.S. schools struggle routinely with some basic dilemmas of *talking* (and, relatedly, thinking) about "racial" difference and racial inequality in American education (Pollock 2004). Such dilemmas of race talk, I believe, are *not* "just talk"—they have real ramifications for what we do and don't do about racial inequality. I have found that when researchers and practitioners talk and think clumsily about race in education—and relatedly, when we refuse anxiously to talk and think about race at all—we risk harming the very students many of us set out to assist.

In this article, I introduce a core set of "race talk dilemmas" I claim are central to educational discourse in the U.S., unearthed in a multi-year ethnographic study of unprompted everyday school and district discourse in California (Pollock 2004). I argue here that U.S. educational researchers struggle with the very same dilemmas of talking (and thinking) about race. Since both researchers and practitioners often make things more difficult for kids when we *do* talk about race as well as when we don't, I suggest that those of us who are interested in reducing racial inequality in education might struggle to talk about and analyze race with more critical self-consciousness.

Rather than flailing privately with the dilemmas of race talk and analysis, that is, I believe that both practitioners and educational researchers can assist the field by struggling purposefully and explicitly throughout our work over how most productively to analyze and discuss issues of race in education. I call this project of purposeful struggle "race wrestling." I attempt here to assist such wrestling by first exposing this researcher's journey from more typical race research to more "race wrestling" research (Part 1)—and second, by laying out six specific dilemmas of race talk and analysis that educational researchers, like practitioners, might consider carefully (Part 2).

While my prior work on "race talk dilemmas" in education has hoped particularly to assist practitioners with race talk and analysis (see Pollock 2004), this article speaks to researchers specifically. Throughout this paper, I contend that educational researchers—who get paid, after all, to analyze and talk about educational practice—must wrestle with race in our research on two levels, both of which require rethinking the methodological, analytic, and discursive habits of race research in education. First, I believe that researchers must bring to light the race wrestling already occurring on the ground in schools and districts. That is, we must investigate how *school people themselves* are already arguing about race in their daily lives. Such research requires fortifying a more typical research habit—simplification—with a methodological attention to the ongoing race *disputes* of everyday life. For while race researchers (like all researchers) tend to make race practice appear clear-cut for the purpose of research (thus typically simplifying the social actors responsible for racial orders, the behaviors of racialized actors, and even the very organization of American diversity), race practice in the real world of schools and districts often takes shape as people arguing and struggling over these very things. Real lives are also often far messier than educational research on race suggests: neither kids nor adults consistently exhibit the simple race-group behaviors research expects them to exhibit, many more social actors are responsible in choreography for racial orders than research typically admits, and people argue over categories of racial difference and patterns of racial inequality even as they reproduce them. While we must continue to research the simple ways in which racial inequality gets reproduced (the bluntly unequal distribution of dollars, books, credentialed teachers, science labs or AP courses to racialized groups is one obvious example; see Darling-Hammond 1999, Oakes et al. 1990), it is also a research responsibility to lay out the complex disputes over "racial" difference and racial inequality currently occupying school people. Research on racial inequality and diversity—in education as well as in social science more generally—often masks such crucial everyday struggles, by taking actors out of context to answer simplified questions or by burying the messy arguments of everyday life under abstracted theory. My own suggestion, in contrast, is to investigate and theorize actors' everyday disputes in their full ethnographic complexity—to analyze moments when youth and adults (of all "races") themselves are arguing over how best to understand or navigate their own race issues. Such research on everyday race wrestling has practical as well as intellectual implications. I have found that making familiar disputes, dilemmas, and controversies themselves the phenomena for intellectual examination (Pollock 2001, 2004) assists educators and youth to perceive and address their own racial practices with increased analytic clarity.

Second, I believe that we researchers must wrestle more with our own habits of talking about race in our research. As I will argue here, the six race talk dilemmas I found plaguing practitioners plague race researchers as well; we, too, can consider these dilemmas carefully, and learn to navigate them strategically in a quest to make American education racially equitable. Throughout the paper, then, I discuss lessons from practice (Pollock 2004) that suggest ways in which researchers, too, might wrestle with race more actively in our analyses and writing.

I should state directly that I am claiming here that some basic troubles of race talk and analysis are shared by researchers across "racial" lines. In my work on race talk dilemmas "on the ground" in schools and districts, I have demonstrated that some core problems of talking and *not* talking about race are shared by students and practitioners of all "races," even while white speakers exhibit a subset of particular (and particularly troubling) race talk habits (Bonilla-Silva 2003). Similarly, while white researchers (like myself) exhibit spectacularly a subset of problematic habits of race talk and analysis (Sleeter 1993), I believe that the basic dilemmas of race talk and analysis I present here plague the researcher community writ large.

Before discussing how these race talk dilemmas operate in research, however (Part 2), I want to begin by discussing my own process of learning to see these dilemmas operating in practice. I began my race research asking far more simplifying questions about race in school; my own "race wrestling" process required that I learn instead to attend to the race *struggles* of everyday school life (Part 1).

PART 1: BEYOND SIMPLIFICATION: LEARNING TO RESEARCH EVERYDAY *STRUGGLES* OVER RACE IN SCHOOLS

I taught "Ethnic Literature" and "American Literature" from 1994 to 1995 at "Columbus High School" in "California City" [1], and I conducted two years of almost daily ethnographic research there as a doctoral student in the anthropology of education during 1995–1997. Having arrived at Columbus from the East Coast after a college career spent studying black/white issues in U.S. history, I was, to be honest, fascinated by the school's demographics. District statistics counted Columbus students as roughly 30 percent "Filipino," 30 percent "Latino" or "Hispanic," 20 percent "African-American" or "black," 8 percent "Chinese," 8 percent "Other Non-White" (a bureaucratic category that nobody at the school level really used, but that included the students Columbus people called "Samoan"), and 5 percent "Other White" (a bureaucratic category also typically ignored, but which included the handful of students at Columbus who described themselves as "white"). While the district called these categories "racial/ethnic," Columbus people called these categories the school's "races"—and they regularly used basically the same six categories ("Filipino," "Latino," "black," "Chinese," "Samoan," and "white") to describe and organize their own student and adult diversity in curriculum, public events, and every-day social interactions. Columbus' teaching staff was listed in district docu-ments as roughly 55 percent "Other White" (the group into which I myself fell), 15 percent "African-American," 10 percent "Filipino," 10 percent "La-tino," 5 percent "Other Non-White," and 2 percent "Chinese."

Learning to divide Columbus' student and adult population into this set of groups referred to locally as "races" was one key aspect of becoming a "native" at Columbus, and over my teaching year I learned to talk about students and colleagues matter-of-factly in this set of comparative "racial" terms. Accord-ingly, as a researcher I also set out originally to do research using them. I em-barked initially with two predictable research questions about race and Co-lumbus students: I wanted to know how important "race" categories were to Columbus students' identities, and I wanted to know how race mattered to how students from these groups "got along" socially with one another.

Notably, my interest at the time was not in adult identities or relationships, but rather solely in how Columbus *students* "made each other racial" (Olsen 1997). Research questions about race and schooling (indeed, about race and youth in general) regularly simplify race like this, by framing racial "identity" and race relations as the property of young people (and primarily young people of color) rather than framing race more accurately as a shared practice of orga-nizing diversity and power that involves people of all ages and "races" (for com-ment, see also Payne 1984, Fine et al. 1997). It would take several months for me to learn to listen and watch for how adult players, including the superinten-dent, judge, school board members, and academics *outside* Columbus, were in-tertwined with students in a choreography of racial practice.

It would also take time for me to come to see race categories as things peo-ple at Columbus struggled with rather than simply lived with. Learning grad-ually to listen more closely to the everyday discourse of both students and adults, I would come to recognize that Columbus students were actually argu-ing daily over how accurately their six simple race labels described complex people, and that Columbus adults actually used race labels comfortably to talk about people, patterns and policies only in particular ways at particular times. Listening over time to hundreds of thousands of examples of race label use, I would also come to realize that race labels themselves, ostensibly de-scriptions of "diversity," can never be detached from inherently controversial historic and contemporary orders of *inequality*. As Sanjek (1996) notes, hier-archy is what race is *about*. Indeed, that Columbus people *called* "races" even the groups scholars typically term "ethnic" or "national" (such as "Filipinos," "Chinese," "Latinos," and "Samoans") implied how both student and adult members of these six groups were often engaged in negotiations over social power and resources. Many scholars have defined "race" group systems *as* systems of distributing (and arguing over) power and resources, as opposed to the heritage-connoting, more voluntary systems of "ethnicity" and the geographic "origin"-connoting systems of "nationality." [2]

I began, however, interested not in struggles over racial equality at Columbus, or even in race label use specifically. Rather, I was interested in studying how students organized their identities and social relations racially—and I was not interested in adults as racial beings at all. Luckily, my research on Columbus students was ethnographic, which allowed for redirecting my investigation over its course to pursue deeper understanding of the actual complexity of Columbus racial practice. And early on, for one, listening at length to students talk informally about racial identities and race relations made me realize how much they *debated and struggled* with race categories (and their relevance) as a routine part of their everyday lives.

Having returned to Columbus as an anthropologist in training rather than as a teacher, I now had lots of time to listen to students talk unprompted and at length about race outside of classrooms, conversations for which I had had little time as a teacher and which so-called "qualitative" researchers themselves often eschew in favor of simplifying sit-down interviews or surveys (see Becker 1996). In these impromptu ethnographic conversations, I found that students routinely led the conversation to the topic of racial categorization itself—and that in doing so, they then typically started *debating* the very concept of race-group membership and contesting easy assessments of what everybody "was." Outside the classroom, a number of students who had labeled themselves with one matter of fact "race" category in my classroom now told me stories of how they learned over time to be members of some other group instead, finding out suddenly through familial channels that they "were" one "race" rather than another (as one girl put it to me in an aside during her English class, "I used to be Chinese"). As I spent more time in student-dominated spaces, further, students who were total strangers to me drew me into playing guessing games about their own race group membership, teasing me and student observers to "tell" what everybody present "was." I soon noted that "What are you?" and "What are you mixed with?" were routine informal student questions at Columbus, resulting in lengthy answers like "I'm Samoan, black, Puerto Rican, Filipino, and Indian" as often as single-label answers like "full black." Only *sometimes*, I realized, did students classify themselves into a simple six-group "race" taxonomy—and determining *when* they did so in their everyday school lives became the new goal of my research.

By attending closely to *when* students employed and contested simple race labels, I noted one key pattern of timing organizing such race talk. Columbus

students consistently contested the ability of simple, single race labels to describe complex individuals when they discussed racial classification itself
("What are you mixed with?" "She's not Mexican, she's Samoan!"). Yet they
employed the school's six basic "race" labels to describe themselves and one
another without much question when talking about relations between
groups—and in particular when talking about *equality* in school orders ("I
thought this was supposed to be Latino week!" "The Samoans got hella
time!" "Where're the black people at?!!").

Thinking more about race history and theory, I realized that in alternately
contesting and employing race labels, Columbus students were actually negotiating the basic problem of "race" categories in the United States. Such simple categories (born just centuries ago) have always been inaccurate for describing complex identities, but they are necessary for describing the simple
social orders (and particularly the inequality orders) with which Americans
have come to live. I came to call students' daily wrestling with race categories
"race-bending." For students were neither throwing race categories away, nor
accepting them wholesale—rather, they were alternately challenging the
very idea of such simple categories' ability to describe complex people, *and*
keeping race labels strategically available to describe and analyze social orders
and inequalities in resources (Pollock 2004b). [3]

I was now treating Columbus students' naturally occurring race talk as
complex data—and in doing so, I found more race wrestling in unprompted
Columbus student discourse. Listening carefully to students talk informally
and at length about my second research interest—how race factored in to
how they "got along"—I realized that students also routinely debated *whether
and how race mattered* to their relations with one another. Notably, the direct
research queries I had embarked with first had masked this debate altogether:
Columbus students had turned immediately and comfortably to talk of racial
student-student relations when I asked them how people "got along" at Columbus, saying bluntly that "the Samoans" were currently fighting "the Filipinos," or that "the Latinos" sat separately from "the blacks" in classes, or even
that student race groups were *not* fighting as much as expected these days
(students also routinely insisted to me and to one another that they personally went against the grain by hanging out "with everyone" "regardless of
race"). Columbus adults, too, turned quickly to talk about student "race relations" when asked directly about people "getting along" at Columbus, whether they were asserting or denying race's relevance to those relations. When I
asked one teacher in 1996 generally what she made of "race issues" at Columbus, for example, she replied that among students there usually "weren't
many problems: if there's a fight, it's Mexicans vs. blacks." A new teacher an-

swering the same question in 1997 responded similarly with a classically student-focused answer: "I don't think it's a problem—the kids get along fine." Other teachers complained routinely about how students grouped themselves racially at lunch or in the classroom.

Once again, an ethnographic methodology allowing people to talk unprompted about race and to ruminate at more length on race's relevance to their relations revealed that while Columbus speakers of all ages often turned in scripted ways to note race's relevance to students, the very question of race's relevance to how Columbus kids "got along" was actually a question of routine debate. Looking at student race talk examples across contexts and time, for example, I noted that students routinely denied explicitly that race mattered to them only minutes before speaking matter-of-factly as if race did. I also noted that if allowed to talk in depth about things like student "race riots" at Columbus, students often started arguing over whether student relations *were* purely racial, offering complex arguments about how fights over girlfriends or possessions (often sparked because there was "nowhere to go" after school) *became* racial as groups of friends entered the fray and organized themselves around the available taxonomy of race. Further, students knowingly promoting the pervasive logic that race should *not* really matter to how people in general "got along" often proffered scripted rhetoric about race's *irrelevance* with apparently self-conscious glee: In a practice I came to call "race teasing," Columbus students talking to me, one another, and their teachers about the relevance of race to their friendships and identities often simultaneously suggested smirkingly that race did not matter at all ("no, we're all the same, though!" was a classic example of such a "race teasing" interjection). I began to see that simple talk of student race relations was not always pure description of reality, but rather often a type of scripted simplification—and I began to suspect that the topic of student race relations was simply the most comfortable Columbus script for analyzing race's relevance in school. Indeed, I myself had reproduced this script in my own confident research questions about how race mattered to how kids "got along."

I started to notice something else I had overlooked in my rush to focus on the comfortable topic of how kids got along: students debating race's role in social relations at Columbus were also routinely referencing their relations with *adults*. While my first instinct upon noticing this pattern was to start viewing *all* interactions between students and adults through a racialized research lens, in listening more closely to students talk about race's role in their relationships with Columbus teachers and administrators I noted that students often displayed the same basic ambiguity they displayed when describing how race mattered to their interactions with one another. Students bounced from claiming in one interaction in the principal's office that they "hated white teachers" to claiming in the next interaction in a quiet classroom that white teachers at Columbus weren't "really racist." Students who called pointedly for more "black teachers" during classroom conflicts with non-black teachers complained vigorously in other settings about not "getting along" with black administrators in particular. Students who argued in some moments that Columbus adults (of all "races") treated student race groups differently would argue with shrugs or even indignation at other moments that adults at Columbus didn't "treat people racially" at all. While different contexts indeed seemed to make students differentially comfortable with *stating* race's relevance to student-adult relations, students' ongoing talk also demonstrated that students were often *wrestling* with the very question of when and how race *was* relevant to their relations with Columbus adults, even while at times they also framed these relations confidently in racial terms.

The real story here, I realized finally, was the race wrestling itself. That is, it was a daily activity for students at Columbus to *figure out* and *debate* how race mattered to their own everyday interactions with adults and one another—and to confront listeners of all ages with this very question about race's relevance. Accordingly, this very question of how race mattered to social relations had to be wrestled with similarly in my own research. Any attempt to understand how race mattered in Columbus social relations was going to take many hours of listening to and even participating in impromptu debates about race's role in Columbus life.

Taking direction from students' framing of adults as key players in Columbus "race relations," I also realized I had to listen more carefully to adults talk about how they got along with students. In doing so, I realized that the very question of how race mattered to student-adult relations was also a persistent (though more subterranean) Columbus adult debate. In private, Columbus adults of all "races" sometimes raised the question explicitly of how much their own "race" (often vs. their "class") mattered to how they and students "got along" (one white teacher, for example, wondered to me during a car ride home how much clout she had with students as a "white chick"; a black teacher pointing to her bare arm as she muttered to me in the back of her classroom about "trouble" with various students mused that all students at Columbus had race-based expectations of her teaching). But adults, too, talked racially about student-adult relations at some moments and explicitly denied race's importance to those relations at others. Columbus teachers talking to me and one another in offices or empty classrooms, for example, would often question or even dismiss a reported student accusation of adult "racism," even while mentioning moments later their own or other teachers' repeated conflicts with representatives of particular racial "groups." Administrators, too, would complain with exasperated sighs about district mandates that schools monitor suspensions in racial terms, even while telling me in other private conversations that disciplinary records indeed showed school adults disproportionately suspending "Latinos" or "Samoans" or "blacks." Columbus adults of all "races," then, were quietly debating race's relevance to their relations with students—such that asking adults even informally to provide quick answers to my questions about how race mattered to those relations would inevitably provide me with responses that, like students', oversimplified race's relevance or irrelevance. Quick answers to quick questions about how race mattered to social relationships would never expose the truly complex "logic of everyday life" (Geertz 1973, 17), in which race's relevance to social relations was itself actually a core topic for ongoing debate.

In listening to adults quietly debating race's role in their relations with students, I also realized with a start that this very debate was never publicly engaged. While students sporadically raised the question of how race mattered to student-adult relations by punctuating classroom/deans' office life with joking or angry accusations of teacher "racism," adults in particular were often *deleting* race labels from public talk of this very topic that they quietly (and for many, anxiously) described often as racially charged. Indeed, I realized starkly that school adults were often telling me directly that they were deleting race labels from public talk of various such race-loaded topics. For example, a white teacher wondering to me whether "black" students were statistically overrepresented among students wandering the Columbus hallways would remark simultaneously that he felt it would be inappropriate to ask this question publicly; a black teacher's aide remarking on the overrepresentation of black students in Columbus's "Special Ed" classrooms would whisper that the pattern was something "we don't talk about." A white teacher muttering about administrators' allowance of "Samoan" misbehavior would note that "no one talked about" this racial pattern in public; an Asian American administrator bemoaning "Latino" test scores in private would argue that Columbus reforms should be discussed as serving "all students" rather than particular "groups." Noting the frequency of Columbus people's daily talk *about* race talk, I finally began to work more systematically as an anthropologist to make strange [4] and examine directly this basic act troubling people at Columbus: figuring out when to talk about school people and school life in simple racial terms. [5] I began systematically to seek patterns in *when* people at Columbus used, struggled with, and deleted race labels in their naturalistic everyday discourse.

I soon confirmed that while adults of all "races" indicated in some situations that they saw certain aspects of school life as deeply racialized, they often resisted *describing* these very aspects of school life racially in other locations and in interactions with particular actors. I came to call the shared, adult-dominated practice of deleting race labels from talk "*colormuteness*"— that is, the routine act of knowingly deleting race words from discourse, rather than being truly "color-blind" (Pollock 2004).

Further, noting that quiet Columbus debates over race and race talk often mentioned district, legal, and academic adults *outside* Columbus (people would argue about race when discussing superintendent's policies, or court decrees, or academic research), I expanded my analytic lens to consider the discourse of these players, too. I now observed that the Latino superintendent, too, let race labels wax and wane in his various public pronouncements about school "problems"; that a white judge waffled in using and deleting race labels in discussions of district reform plans; and that even my graduate school professors struggled with talking of "blacks" or "Latinos" or "Asians" or "whites" in their public talk and written research about various charged educational topics. As race talk occurring throughout the world of education became data, I realized that describing people, practices, programs and policies in racial terms seemed to be a problem for every actor I found trying to talk about education.

An ironic twist of fate at Columbus solidified my sense that the patterns of race talk and colormuteness I was finding at Columbus and in California City were actually common American property. Midway through my research, the California City Unified School District replaced the entire Columbus faculty in a reform called "reconstitution," which district representatives described in high-level policy circles as designed to improve the education of "black" and "Latino" students but which they rarely described racially in addresses to school faculties or to the public. Throughout a year of "probation" before Columbus's reconstitution, district leaders instead publicly described the threatened reform almost exclusively as a reform designed to improve the education of "all students." In turn, Columbus adults hoping to avoid reconstitution (some of whom knew of the district's particular interest in "blacks" and "Latinos," and some of whom did not) spoke in public meetings or in documents designed for district readers only of their attempts to improve the education of "all." Columbus' faculty was finally reconstituted without having participated in any sustained school- or district-level conversation about whether Columbus's current programs and reforms *were* sufficiently serving "blacks" and "Latinos"—or about whether the district's "reconstitution" reforms were designed to assist these two populations. And after reconstitution, the same discourse of serving "all students" was reproduced almost immediately with 100 almost complete strangers. Indeed, having been given permission by the new principal to finish my doctoral research at Columbus, I would see the full set of school-level patterns of race talk and colormuteness I had isolated at the pre-reconstruction Columbus get reproduced by a new cast of adults assembled from across the country. Throughout this final year of my research, people at Columbus wrestled with the exact same dilemmas over talking in racial terms about school life.

It was this reproduction of race talk struggles at Columbus that convinced me that the race talk dilemmas I was finding at Columbus actually might be a key issue of racial practice in American education. People working in and on schools in the U.S., I realized, must navigate more directly than many Americans our shared issues of diversity and inequality. And in this navigation, many of us are never quite sure when talking about people or patterns or policies racially makes things better and when it makes things worse. While people in education cannot truly regulate whether we *see* one another in racial terms or *see* racial patterns in schools, then, we struggle all the time in both private conversations and public policies over how and whether we should *talk* racially about one another and about school life. While some people resist race talk out of a simple conviction that race talk is itself "racist" and others resist race talk because they are not particularly concerned about racial inequality, many people resist race talk because they are unsure when talking in racial terms about school people, programs, policies and patterns would be beneficial—either for kids or for our own positions. But such resistance to race talk itself has consequences. Regardless of intention, people in diverse schools and districts are *always* struggling with the consequences of both race talk and colormuteness, whether communities struggle openly, angrily, or only subterraneously (see Fine, Weis, and Powell 1997 for these distinctions). I describe these consequences fully in my book, *Colormute: Race Talk Dilemmas in an American School* (Pollock 2004).

Over my own research journey, thus, I had *learned to see* one subset of everyday race wrestling ongoing in schools—the struggle over talking and not talking in racial terms. I had also come to see it as an educational researcher's responsibility to investigate various such struggles over race, and to and lay them out clearly for analysis. Many scholars have implied that creating racially equitable, or what some have called "truly integrated" schools (Powell 2002), requires that the adults and young people in schools and districts analyze their own ongoing racial practices (see Pollock 2004, Lewis 2003, Dance 2002, Lipman 1998, Tatum 1997, Fine, Weis, and Powell 1997, Delpit 1995). To assist, researchers ourselves can investigate and analyze the daily race struggles of everyday school life. Ethnography, with its detailed attention to the functioning of the everyday and (if done properly) its careful, purposeful refusal to impose simplistic answers from "above," is particularly well-suited to the analytic task of pinpointing and theorizing everyday race struggles in schools. But studying such struggling requires actively learning *to* focus on ongoing controversy over race in schools, rather than just entering schools or communities with familiar racial categories in hand to matter-of-factly do research through.

As we research race wrestling in schools, further, we must simultaneously wrestle with our own dilemmas of race talk and analysis: for many of the race dilemmas of everyday school life are mirrored in educational research. I now want to discuss the six basic "race talk dilemmas" I found operating at Columbus, framing each first briefly as a problem of daily schooling practice and then as an educational research problem. I will spend more time on those dilemmas that particularly plague researchers. I refer readers to Pollock (2004) for a full treatment of how these dilemmas play out in everyday school life.

PART 2: FROM PRACTICE TO THEORY: SIX DILEMMAS OF RACE TALK AND ANALYSIS PLAGUING SCHOOL PEOPLE AND RESEARCHERS

We begin with the most basic dilemma of race talk, one that Columbus youth engaged particularly explicitly (and which they often navigated with far more grace than do researchers). Race categories are social realities built upon biological fictions, and as such they must be engaged inherently paradoxically.

Dilemma 1. We Don't Belong to Simple Race Groups, But We Do

Racialized people are infinitely complex, but racialization itself is and always has been a process of simplification. Racialization is *about* placing complicated people into simple boxes; Americans have practiced this simplification ever since "race" categories were created to separate masters ("white") from slaves ("black") from indigenous populations ("red") in the period of colonial exploration and expansion in the 1400s (Smedley 1999). Over centuries, further, various populations first categorized as members of religious, national-origin, or language groups became "race" group members in a U.S. simple-race taxonomy of power relations (the pan-national, racialized categories

"Asian" and "Hispanic"/"Latino" were gradually simultaneously imposed, chosen, and disputed by the people placed in them). [6] This process of simplification has played out historically, and we replay it in our everyday lives—with fluctuating levels of self-consciousness.

In their everyday discourse, Columbus students attended quite self-consciously to both the complexity of racialized people and the frustrating and often necessary simplicity of racial boxes. A great proportion of Columbus students, for example, often described themselves explicitly as "mixed"—what scholars and census-makers call "multiracial" (Root 1996). Such students describing their personal identities in detail often admitted the nuances of their own parental or ancestral "mixture"; yet analyses of resource distribution always had them comparing (and slotting themselves into) a short list of simple race groups. When articulating their needs for social, educational, and material resources in and out of school, students similarly prioritized simple "race" identifications over the nuances of national origin. Just as a student who listed five "groups" to define her identity often chose just one when assessing the allotment of time in "multicultural" performances at Columbus, for example, Guatemalan- and Salvadoran-descended students united in simply comparing the political clout given U.S. "Latinos" to that given "blacks" or "whites."

As suggested earlier, I came to call students' simultaneous defiance and use of race categories "race-bending": students neither accepted race categories wholesale nor threw race categories away (Pollock 2004b). Rather, they were strategically contesting the very idea of racial categorization, even while keeping race labels available for social analysis and inequality analysis—the very strategy I want to argue here is essential for race research in the 21st century.

Researchers tend to be less good than youth at navigating between contesting the very validity of "race" categories when they oversimplify complex people (or worse, when they reify false notions of biological difference), and *using* these categories for analyzing real social orders built upon them. Some researchers attempt to solve the problem of race-categories-as-simultaneous-fiction-and-reality quickly by simply putting the word "race" in quotation marks (I myself employ this strategy), or with a quick caveat that the researcher does not believe in biological racial difference (indeed proved to be a bogus concept for half a century; see Montagu 1942). Some scholars go so far as to assert that *any* use of the word "race" to imply human difference is itself "racist" (see Patterson 1997). But more typically, education researchers proceed with comparing race groups without ever questioning the foundational premise of "racial" difference at all. As Almaguer and Jung state of so-

cial science writ large, research often "unreflexively" "employs racial categories as if they were biologically given and fixed," a habit that "obscures the
continual ambiguities and contestations over how racial lines have been
drawn historically and are being re-drawn today" (cited in Lewis 2003, 6).
Researchers often compare race group behaviors and race group identities,
too, as if each child or adult has one "group's" grab-bag of traits; as both philosopher Anthony Appiah (1994) and cultural studies/media scholar
Cameron McCarthy (1998) argue, a dangerously oversimplifying account of
"races" often characterizes treatments of "diversity" in scholarship and educational practice.

Of course, leaving race categories unexamined in education analyses also
often serves a strategic equity minded purpose. Since simple categories of race
difference have come to have real consequences in the real world of opportunity, calling these categories continually into question (as Columbus students
themselves hinted) would harm the very populations who now need the most
protection. As titles like *The Education of African-Americans* (Willie et al.,
1991) or *Latino High School Graduation* (Romo and Falbo, 1996) make explicit, analyses calling for racial equality in education rarely interrogate the
theoretical or empirical validity of racial categories themselves. Most researchers commenting on educational opportunity in the U.S. continue to
compare the resources and treatment given simple race groups and the place
of those groups in achievement orders. Scholars worried about how *students*
navigate inequality systems typically proceed as if students fit neatly into simple race groups too.

Yet fully attacking racial inequality, as Columbus students indicated,
seems to require treating simple race categories a bit more paradoxically—
that is, using them to investigate simply ordered inequalities of opportunity
in education, *but also* questioning race categories' very existence as clear-
cut classifications of student or adult diversity. Researchers are far less
skilled at such strategic use than are youth themselves (on youths' strategic
racialization, see Sharma et al 1996, Hall 2002)—we typically leave it to
some researchers to use race categories and other researchers to question
them. Yet education researchers have a particular responsibility to model a
necessarily paradoxical use of race categories. Since we study institutions of
learning, for example, we in particular can say more often that while we do
belong to simple race groups in our inequality orders, we don't belong to
simple race groups in our genes (Fraser 1995). (Anthropologists, whose discipline came into being through a racist 19th-century quest to rank "race"
groups, have a similar responsibility. The American Anthropological Association has thus embarked upon a public information campaign to debunk

public beliefs about race's biology, while also stressing publicly [such as in a usefully explicit disciplinary "Statement on 'Race,' " 1998] that people have built racial orders on "racial" categories for long enough that such categories have *become* real. [7]) As scholars studying the development and identity-formation of the young, we in particular can question too-easy assessments of identities as born (or single) rather than made (and multiple) (Hall 2002, Perry 2002, Root 1996, Cross 1991). Educational researchers can also state more explicitly, as have some lawyers, that strategically using in policy and practice the very biologically bogus race categories central to inequality may for some time remain necessary to make things "fair" (Minow 1990; Guinier and Torres 2002).

Articulating this necessarily paradoxical treatment of race categories more directly in our writing and analysis encourages readers, too, to tackle the 21st century antiracist task of trying alternately to think and *not* think about human beings as members of simple race groups. Authors in the recent *Handbook of Research on Multicultural Education*, for example, help readers to think paradoxically about race categories by warning explicitly that readers should avoid assuming that the group characteristics explored in their papers are simplistically shared by all members of those "groups," *even while* urging educators to teach students from various "groups" in culturally relevant ways (Banks and Banks 1995). Multiculturalist Sonia Nieto (2000) similarly argues that educators must learn about students' "cultural" experiences and heritages *even as* she explicitly mentions the "major pitfall" of such group-based thinking: "the information presented can be overgeneralized to the point that it becomes just another harmful stereotype" of any student "group" (8). Gonzales and Cauce (1995) usefully admit to readers a paradoxical dilemma of "trying to deal effectively with race and ethnicity within the educational system": "How does one recognize ethnic differences and support ethnicity as an important dimension of self-definition without paradoxically encouraging group divisions and intergroup tensions that often result when ethnic categories are emphasized?" (140–141). And in writing about the politics of higher education, Dominguez (1994) helpfully explains explicitly to readers a related paradoxical race task plaguing university professors: professors must try to diversify syllabi and their own faculties without hyper-racializing as "minority intellectuals" the authors or applicants of color involved (335).

As other scholars have suggested, educational researchers too rarely discuss racial categorization with this kind of race-wrestling, explicitly paradoxical stance (Parker et al., 1999; Lee 2003). Rather, we typically land on either side of the fence (racial categories are fixed/racial categories are "unreal"), and in doing so we create real problems for children. The risks of proceeding

in educational research with unproblematized notions of race-group difference will be discussed further later in this paper; let me state for now that
American politics has demonstrated that academic *deconstructions* of racial
categories as "fictions" can also risk dangerous consequences for kids. Around
the same time I was doing my research in California, some California adults
started (mis)using research to imply publicly that since race groups do not biologically exist, monitoring racial inequality itself somehow damages children. Little-known anthropologist Glynn Custred, co-backer (with U.C. re-
gent Ward Connerly) of California's anti-affirmative action "Proposition
209," used the 20th-century anthropological research deconstruction of
race's biology to critique affirmative action policies designed to help children
denied opportunities along these supposedly "false" racial lines ("As an anthropologist," Custred reportedly said at one point in "academic" explanation, "I know that when you've got diversity, you've got a problem"; see
Chavez 1998, 1). Several years later, in another proposed referendum entitled
the "Racial Privacy Initiative," Ward Connerly returned to argue that since
race categories are biologically bogus, race labels should be deleted altogether
from public school data gathered in California. As Connerly told one crowd
of potential voters, he had the state's "mixed" kids in mind: "This initiative is
for the growing population of kids who don't know what box to check—and
shouldn't have to decide. Please give them freedom from race and let them
just be Americans" (see EDITORIAL: Undermining Identity Politics. American Civil Rights Coalition, Friday, April 5, 2002. (http://www.acrc1.org/
editotial.htm) [sic]).

Young Californians wrestling more thoughtfully with race categories, in
contrast, demonstrate that deleting race altogether from educational record-
keeping is a premature proposal—that in fact, negotiating equality in education still requires that we use the discourse of simple race categories to describe educational opportunity and some aspects of social life even as at other
moments we openly defy the very ability of "racial" categories to fully describe complex individuals. By sometimes listing multiple terms to describe
themselves, sometimes creating new racialized words to describe "mixed"
youth accurately ("japapino" was one example), and sometimes applying single, simple race labels to describe their own diversity, Columbus's "mixed"
youth employed race labels strategically to cope with an already racialized, racially hierarchical world—a strategy far more sophisticated than deleting race
categories from educational analysis *or* proceeding matter-of-factly with assumptions about "racial" categories' fixed reality.

Learning to look closely at such everyday ways in which the actual people
in schools *already struggle* with categories of racialized difference within sys-

tems of racial inequality is one key way to produce scholarship that both uti-
lizes and disrupts racial categories. When researchers observe and analyze
people's struggles over drawing lines of racial difference (what anthropologist
Renato Rosaldo (1993) more generally calls negotiations over "borders" of
differentiation, and what anthropologist Frederick Barth (1969) called struggles to draw and maintain "ethnic boundaries"), we show how everyday people remake "racial" difference and racial hierarchy, too, through daily actions
slotting "group" members into expected identities and roles and performances
(and through daily distributions of resources). We also demonstrate how orders of difference and inequality are routinely challenged by everyday people.
Rather than always draw matter-of-fact lines around "racial" communities a
priori in research or refuse altogether to draw such lines, then, education researchers can more often research the everyday analytic struggles *over* racial
categorization ongoing in schools.

Such research is important for assisting school adults, too, to "race-bend,"
for schools are places that rarely take officially sanctioned time to openly
wrestle with the very idea of racial difference. As my own work and other
analyses have demonstrated, however, young people routinely informally debate with one another in and around schools what it means to belong to race
categories, debating, for example, what it means to "act black" or "act white"
(Carter forthcoming, Dance 2002, Perry 2002, Smitherman 2000, Fordham
1996, Rampton 1995), act "Spanish" (Bailey 2000), act "Asian" (Maira 2002,
Hall 2002, Lee 1996), or even act "American" (Suarez-Orozco and Suarez-
Orozco 2001, Olsen 1997), just as they debate other kinds of social categorization and inequality in the margins of school life (Eckert and McConnell-
Ginet 1995, Varenne 1982). Research has also shown that children struggle
informally over racial categories as early as preschool (see Van Ausdale and
Feagin 2001) and elementary school (Hatcher and Troyna 1993), while
"mixed" or "multiracial" students struggle particularly spectacularly over being slotted into (and slotting themselves into) simple U.S. racial orders (see
Root 1996, Pollock 2004b). Student newcomers to the U.S., too, struggle
routinely and usefully over whether detailed national, regional or skin-tone
distinctions from home should be submerged within the new country's simple-race taxonomy (see also Waters 1999, Rumbaut in press).

All such debates are crucial debates to engage more openly in schools, and
highlighting such debate in our research is thus an essential analytic move for
dislodging familiar assumptions among readers and educators not just about
race-group memberships, but also about the identities and behaviors often assumed to go with such memberships. As anthropologist John Jackson (2001)
has said of his own community research in Harlem, for example, document-

ing Harlem African-Americans "constantly theorizing" (and arguing over) notions of "black" and "white" behaviors in their daily lives opened up a space for contesting essentialized notions about fixed "race"-group identity. Noting that "folk theories of racial difference" are daily "refashioned and fought for by the people who hold them dearest," Jackson concluded that, "This jostling over race's falsifiable projection onto the observable data of everyday behavior may serve as the interpretive beginning of the end for some of racial essentialism's most entrenched cliches" (p. 15).

Through analyzing how some people in and around schools already "jostle" daily over categorizing people, identities, and behaviors racially, researchers studying race and schooling can "jostle" other youth and adults' too-easy ideas about race categories and the people in them. Indeed, ethnographic research that has analyzed in detail how some school people already struggle over categorizing children has always itself helped readers rethink the basic categories of schooling. [8]

Dilemma 2: Race Doesn't Matter, But It Does

The second basic dilemma of race talk operating in U.S. schools is that people sometimes want race not to matter to how people are treated in schools and sometimes argue that race should matter very much indeed. For example, students at Columbus wanted to be treated as race group members in curricula recognizing students' heritages, or for the purposes of distributing curricular attention; students did not want to be treated as race group members at moments when deans were considering who to suspend, or when teachers were distributing personal attention.

Since both framing and refusing to frame people racially can alternately be "wrong," debating when race is and *should* be relevant to school life is, if often subterraneously, a core part *of* everyday school life in the U.S. As described earlier, everyday race talk and colormuteness at Columbus itself exposed that people of all ages were themselves debating when race "really mattered" and should matter to how people related to each other at Columbus. Yet only once I allowed such daily debate itself to become central in my research did I realize that debate over race's appropriate and actual relevance was Columbus's daily reality. Further, only once I listened to people debate race's relevance did I realize that I myself had simply focused my research on the most comfortably discussed question about race's relevance at Columbus (how race mattered to relations between Columbus students). As described earlier, the topic of how race mattered to student-*adult* relations was far more submerged in Columbus discourse: Columbus adults, who talked all the time in matter-of-fact racial terms about how students got along, never even used race labels in any public descriptions of relations between students and themselves (Columbus adults would reference "Filipino gangs" or "Samoan/Latino blowouts" at staff meetings or send home letters about conflicts between "Latino" and "African American" students, but when planning together to improve "discipline" schoolwide, adults typically described conflicts with named individuals, "students," or various kinds of "problem student"—never with race group members. Except when quoting students who had spit out race labels in anger, adults discussing discipline almost never described *themselves* publicly as racialized beings, either.) Indeed, this general pattern of colormuteness was mirrored at the district level: district representatives almost never framed school adults in racial terms in public discourse, even though they labeled students racially (albeit sporadically) throughout high-level district statistics and to the city papers.

Researchers, too, often frame students most comfortably in racial terms, often matter-of-factly assuming that race *is* centrally relevant to students and exploring less comfortably the racialized school practices of adults. In an analytic habit I call the "lunchtime cliché," for example, researchers interested in race in schools often march confidently into cafeterias to verify that race matters a lot to students (journalists do the same), surmising that if student "race groups" are not sitting together they are not "getting along." We do this even though research looking at young people debating lunchtime habits reveals instead that the full complexity and depth of race relations cannot simply be surmised by a quick scan of a lunchroom (nor can animosity be assumed; Tatum 1997). We also go straight to lunchrooms to investigate race in student lives despite evidence that race in school involves adults. As I will describe momentarily, researchers also tend to go primarily to students to *ask* them (often too bluntly) about race's relevance. Less often do we frame adults as intertwined racial actors who must be talked to (with care) as well.

This particular habit of student-focus might be particularly common to white researchers, who as adults perhaps are more likely to view students (of color) in racial terms than to view school adults (particularly white adults like themselves) in racial terms (Kincheloe et al 1998, McIntyre 1997, Frankenburg 1993, Sleeter 1993b). [9] Having myself grown up in the extraordinarily homogenous state of Iowa, I must admit, racial categories had always been for me strangely familiar tools for describing *other* people. For me, as for all other Americans, race was "a key component of our 'taken-for-granted valid reference schema' through which we get on in the world" (Outlaw 1990, p. 58), but as a white person I became cognizant of my *own* "whiteness" only while studying race history in college. I turned to teaching as a contemporary antiracist project, but my main goal as a teacher was, unsurprisingly, to interrogate race with *students*. [10] While by the end of my teaching at Columbus I felt "whiter" than I had ever in my life (after countless daily reminders from my students), I still pursued research as a beginning anthropologist that framed students as the school's primary racial beings. I realized that I had to focus on adults as intertwined "racial" actors only once I realized (indeed, remembered from my own teaching experience) that adults were regularly wondering about the relevance of their own and students' "race" to their relations with Columbus kids, even while they spoke of these very relations publicly in de-raced language.

Understanding race's relevance in schools thus requires 1) analyzing the practices of both students and adults, and 2) focusing not just on the topics that adults and students describe matter-of-factly and comfortably in racial terms, but also on the topics causing students and adults to debate (and even delete mention of) race's relevance. Yet allowing the very question of race's relevance to be seen debated by school adults and students is somewhat rare in educational research. Researchers rarely show people in schools wrestling with determining race's relevance in their own lives; instead, researchers typically enter schools to determine race's relevance ourselves. Furthermore, in this quest to prove race's relevance or irrelevance, we often treat both student and adult race talk too simplistically as unproblematic evidence.

As Mertz (1992) argues, the assumption that talk is a purely descriptive "window" on the "real world," rather than a strategic act in itself, actually plagues all research using talk as data. [11] As Hammersley (1998) argues similarly, researchers particularly tend to oversimplify *student* talk by treating it as transparent, unambiguous opinion, rather than as negotiated talk offered to a researcher. Hammersley argues further that while researchers often treat student talk about race as unadulterated "truth," we often *refuse* to take adult talk about race at face value, instead treating it as consistently disingenuous. In so doing, I would add, researchers actually often oversimplify adult talk about race too, "unmasking" racism in such talk as if the researcher alone has access to the "real" thoughts lurking just "underneath the surface." Less often does such research acknowledge that the adults talking might actually be complex people struggling with issues of race and racism themselves (Sears et al., 2000; see also Wetherell and Potter 1992).

Further, while some scholars argue that the goal of anti-racist research is to get past adult denials and discover racism operating as expected in schools (some have suggested that this "uncovering" of adult racism is Critical Race Theory's project; see Parker et al. 1999), such an objective, while very important, risks implying that people in schools just robotically practice racism, never struggle themselves as conflicted human beings to avoid it. Such research also risks being unconvincing to unsympathetic readers who assume the researcher simply found the racism she set out to find. Of course, since some analysts of education prefer to argue simplistically that racism is no longer an issue in schools at all (e.g., Reynolds 1996, McWhorter 2000), researchers who care about racial inequality must also work to prove that race *does* still matter in schools, in order to counter blunt denials of race's relevance (Lewis 2003). How then to navigate between the "race constantly matters in predetermined ways"/"come on, race doesn't matter" poles? I believe that again, analyzing and presenting school people's ongoing disputes *over* race's relevance might actually provide some of the most convincing claims of how race really matters, is known to matter, and is made to matter on the ground in schooling. But this approach is rare. Our surveys and statistics and fieldnotes routinely demonstrate that we enter schools primed not really to see the struggles school people are engaged in regarding race's relevance, but rather to uncover for them more simplistically how race matters (or for some researchers, doesn't matter) in expected ways.

Further, researchers often attempt to solve the problem of determining how race matters to school life by simply asking respondents quickly to tell us (or, if we are so-called "quantitative" researchers, we simply embed the debate in our variables). But in research relying on discourse in particular (interviews, surveys, participant observation), we often forget that summing up race's relevance is anything *but* a straightforward act in the United States. Researchers investigating race in schools *through* talk often appear to forget the particularly strategic nature *of* race talk, which contends always, even when unprompted, with the pervasive American ideology that race should *not* really matter, or matter only at certain times (Sears et al. 2000, Banaji 2001). The assumption that prompted talk about race is a direct representation of informants' attitudes, rather than a strategic response to prompting, runs throughout various methods of race research (Studs Terkel thus confidently titles his collection of interview data *Race: How Blacks and Whites Think and Feel About the American Obsession* [1992, emphasis mine]). But one must question, for example, this classic dismissal of race's importance during an exchange between a researcher and a "black" student interviewee (Grant and Sleeter 1986):

R: Are you going to date just black boys, or what?
Frances: Nope. I'm not just gonna date black ones.

R: Are you going to date just who you want to?

Frances: Yeah, regardless of race. (32)

As seen here, direct queries asking respondents to sum up race's relevance can have respondents obligingly denying that race is relevant at all. In a study of "ethnicity" in a California high school, similarly, Peshkin (1991) proceeded to ask students similarly directly one of his main research questions, which was, "To what extent, if at all, is ethnicity a fact in the students' lives?" (171). While Peshkin acknowledged retrospectively that his other interview questions about student "ethnicity and identity" had not captured the "inconsistencies" of racial identity at his field site (177–178), he continued to treat students' proffered assessments of race's (ir)relevance as uncontroversial. Asked directly about the relevance (and possible irrelevance) of race, Peshkin's interviewees summed up repeatedly that race was unimportant, "not salient," or "not really a big thing." Peshkin, who was himself white, reported receiving similar answers to his direct questions from students of all "ethnicities": "white" students responded that "being white" made little difference at school, while black students he asked "about the importance of being black if someone wanted to know them well . . . did not rank it highly" (191). Interviews with "Filipino" students also suggested that "during their high school years, their ethnicity is not salient" (208). Despite the existence of racial achievement patterns in the school (which Peshkin described elsewhere), Peshkin concluded similarly that:

> At school, non-newcomer Mexicans basically see being Mexican as a fact of little consequence, as I learned when I asked students if being Mexican affected their life in and out of class. Specifically, did being Mexican make a difference regarding the grades they got, how teachers treated them, being popular, getting elected to office, who'd they vote for, what clubs they'd join, success in sports, getting in trouble, getting their share of what the school had to offer? Overwhelmingly, students saw little or no relationship between their ethnicity and any of these points: it was neither helpful nor unhelpful to be Mexican. (184)

Interview questions demanding to know the salience of race in respondents' lives can, of course, also lead respondents to highlight race with expected zeal. In the same study quoted earlier (Grant and Sleeter 1986), interview questions asking students to state the "importance" of "background" could actually lead them to emphasize the salience of group membership just as bluntly:

R: How important do you think a person's background is?

Rakia: It's important.

R: Do you intend to pass down your Egyptian background to your
         kids?

Rakia: Yes. (34)

Since people of all ages often give researchers oversimplified answers
about race's relevance/irrelevance when asked, race research must not only
be wary of simplifying questions, but also pay far more attention to ongoing
contestation over race's relevance. To do so, we can attend both to the subtle
hesitations or stutters within individual interviews (see also Bonilla-Silva
2002), and to the explicit arguments over race's relevance that take shape
during the ongoing life of schools. For such everyday contestation over race's
relevance is itself not just the reality of racial practice, but also the key reason
why various claims about race's role in school can be dismissed so easily (on
such dismissals, see also Lewis 2003). Since people also resist talking in many
situations about the ways in which race matters to them most dangerously, we
can also try to carefully examine the patterned *absence* of race talk in interactions or across institutions, as well as its conspicuous and too-easy presence
(see footnote for further discussion of such methodology [12]).

Dilemma 3: The Deraced Words We Use When Discussing Plans for Racial Equality Can Actually Keep Us From Discussing Ways to Make Opportunities Racially Equal

In Pollock (2004), I discuss at length the paradoxically inequality-increasing
effects of some equity-minded talk of reforms for "all students," which was
rampant at Columbus and in California City. I will say little about this dilemma here, and point readers to the longer treatment in that work. But
there is one core lesson to mention from equity-minded practice for equity-
minded research: the equality discourse of assisting "all students" is both necessary and dangerous. That is, researchers, like practitioners, often proceed as
if demanding that schools serve "all students" itself helps *achieve* equality for
"all"; yet equity-minded calls for assisting "all students" (now routine in U.S.
educational discourse) do not in themselves achieve equality. Further, talk
about "all students" does not precisely analyze *inequality*, either. An over-

reliance in educational discourse on the spirited language of "all students" might, at times, actually make us imagine falsely that we have analyzed and addressed patterns (including racial patterns) of student need.

Dilemma 4: Sometimes the More Complex Inequality Seems to Get, the More Simplistic Inequality Analysis Seems to Become

Every day, Columbus and district speakers embarked upon a daunting task shared with educational researchers: discussing which students are disadvantaged in comparison to whom. Every day, a student population of "low-income minorities" who had weathered years of educational denial walked in to Columbus' run-down building, making Columbus seem to many to be undeniably "disadvantaged" in comparison to the district's more well-off-and-white schools. Yet Columbus also had class patterns, race patterns, language patterns and academic patterns within its own walls. There were other complexities to various school and community inequalities: the Samoans who attended Columbus also lived in predominantly "black" public housing projects, while districtwide, "Chinese" students dominated "academic" schools along with "whites"; "Filipino" test scores topped Columbus charts even while Filipinos demonstrated disappointing levels of English proficiency citywide.

Considering such complexities, speakers at Columbus and citywide argued particularly over how *race* mattered to the economic and educational opportunities afforded students, both within Columbus and districtwide. They argued about whether all racial patterns had exceptions, about how race did and *should* matter to district policies, and how race should accordingly matter to school reforms. They also argued over whether class inequality trumped race inequality or whether "race" dominated "class"; people argued over whether they should "target" student race groups for special assistance as race-group members. And in response to all this analytic confusion about race's role in systems of "disadvantage," many speakers often deleted race labels altogether from vague discussions of "inner city" or "at risk" "disadvantage," both within Columbus and districtwide. In doing so, they often unwittingly avoided thoroughly analyzing the details of how inequalities in educational opportunity actually worked.

Such habits of analytic and discursive murkiness are common to educational research on disadvantage as well. Researchers, like school people, sometimes avoid tackling the full analytic complexity of determining race's role in contemporary inequality systems, either by resorting too often to simple, familiar analyses of racial inequality (for example, favoring easier binary black-white analysis over the substantial complexities of multiracial analysis) or by trumping race analysis simplistically with class analysis (see, e.g., Chavez 1996). Marable (1996, 15) points out that the race/class debate usually ends with the full trumping of race by class, and is thus to some extent a "false debate."

In a demographically complex nation, as we acknowledge not just some class diversity but also the complex "multi-polarity of racial identities (not just black and white, but also red, brown, and yellow)" within many of our communities (Omi and Winant 1994, 158), both researchers and practitioners need to become far more proficient at responding to the complicated question of who exactly is to be called disadvantaged, and in comparison to whom. Once again, researchers can assist practitioners and researchers in training by considering and discussing more explicitly in our analyses how we are analyzing "disadvantage," and particularly how we are analyzing race's relevance to inequality systems. We can explain to readers, for example, when and why we think binary (white/of color, black/white) analyses make the most sense for understanding inequality, and when and why we think analyses must be multiracial. We can explain explicitly when and why we are analyzing the intertwining of race and class, by describing when and how to look within "race groups" for class patterns (Wang and Wu 1996) or within class groups for race ones (Rothstein 2004). Rather than proceeding with a murky language of "risk" ourselves, we also can more often analyze explicitly how racialized denials of opportunity intertwine with patterns of language, immigration, and neighborhood resources. In sum, we can take up the challenge of analyzing and debating *how* race still matters to the complex inequality systems in education, for precise inequality solutions "on the ground" rely perhaps more than ever upon precise inequality analysis. Policymakers wrestling with addressing the distribution of educational opportunity founder upon the same analytic problems as do everyday analysts, and the result is sometimes policy based on inherently imprecise categories of "disadvantage." California's "Proposition 209," which purposefully replaced the complications of race analysis with the murky project of assisting students literally labeled "disadvantaged," quickly helped transform diverse UC campuses into more homogenously white-and-"Asian" spaces—a perfect example of how the triumph of vague analysis on the ground can end up actually making race matter *more* to educational inequality, not less.

Dilemma 5: The Questions We Ask Most About Race Are the Very Questions We Most Suppress

As I have discussed elsewhere (Pollock 2001, 2004), achievement talk is perhaps the kind of race talk that most plagues educational practitioners and researchers in the United States, even though talking racially about student achievement is also one of the most routine acts of U.S. educational discourse. Adults at Columbus, for example, routinely compared in private the presumed achievement motivations and achievement-related behavior of Columbus's "race groups" and their parents; district officials routinely measured the district's race-group achievement patterns in documents kept at district offices, and implied in public talk of teachers with "low expectations" that these patterns were the fault of educators alone. Yet when speaking to one another in public about achievement and how to improve it, school and district people rarely talked about achievement in racial terms at all. The question asked most about race in education ("do racial achievement patterns exist here, and why?") is also the question most often deleted on the ground.

Discussing racial achievement patterns is easy, it seems, if one is far away from the people one holds responsible for that achievement. But when actors in education come together, even *naming* an achievement pattern is often threatening—because naming a pattern always invites an explanation blaming someone for it. Acknowledging that in education talk of racial achievement patterns routinely involves a habit of blaming *other* people, I have urged that practitioners discussing racial achievement patterns might be most productive using an "urgent language of communal responsibility" (Pollock 2001, 2004).

Race researchers, I believe, must also consider carefully how *we* talk about race and achievement from far away. In particular, we must ask whether unproductive blame dynamics are often embedded in our own research. Researchers often seek "achievement gap" causes with zeal, but we more rarely stop to question the effects of our own familiar explanatory habits. For one, researchers, too, regularly isolate (often racialized) groups of players analytically ("Latino parents," "black kids," "white teachers") to stress their responsibility for producing racial achievement patterns. Such analytic isolation is necessary at times to figure out various actors' contributions to creating achievement patterns, but it also encourages a national habit of framing achievement patterns *as* orders produced by isolated sets of players, rather than by multiple intertwined players both inside and outside of schools. As researchers routinely end up "blaming" teachers alone, parents alone, or student race groups themselves for achievement patterns (Pollock 2001), superintendents focus analysis/blame reductively on teachers, teachers focus analysis/blame reductively on students or parents, and everybody blames people in city schools (rather than parents moving to suburbs, for example, or governors, or presidents).

The *tone* in which we researchers discuss racial achievement patterns is also routinely dangerous, even when we mean for the information we present to arouse curiosity in others. Slapping up racial achievement charts and graphs nonchalantly at conferences or rattling off achievement statistics to the newspapers, for example, we often promote a matter-of-fact discussion of racial achievement patterns and their causes—one that helps prime Americans nationwide (and educational researchers in training) to almost expect racial patterns as natural orders. While researchers today are no longer measuring heads to prove the nation's racial inequalities "natural" outcomes of intelligence differentials [13], a research tendency toward naturalizing racial disparities in educational attainment is still uncomfortably strong. Research inquiries often seem to blandly expect racial achievement patterns, setting off to measure academic outcomes with a nonchalance born of familiarity rather than a startled stance of outrage (for a similar argument, see Payne 1984). Far more rarely do we researchers analyze and critique our own matter-of-factness about investigating and describing racial achievement patterns, or frame racial achievement patterns as both unnatural and communally preventable.

Researchers, I would argue, also realize too rarely that particular educational research explanations of racialized achievement gaps have real consequences for the children we describe. For example, Ogbu and Fordham's popular article (1986) arguing that youth of color frame school achievement as undesirably "white" is a prime example of how a feedback loop between research and "real life" reinforces numbing popular assumptions about the nation's "races." As Erickson (1993, p. 42) describes, Ogbu and Fordham's initial claims that black youth resisted academic success were immediately picked up by NPR; radio interviewers confidently set out to grill black "Capitol High" students on *how* (not if) they avoided school achievement for racialized reasons. While Ogbu and Fordham have themselves critiqued the oversimplification of their findings, one popular article after another (see, e.g., Lee 2002) repeatedly cites their work to reinforce the "black and Latino kids don't care" thesis in American race ideology. And as many other scholars have argued, this argument about race-group behavior and attitude has suspiciously been taken as a familiar national fact without sufficient debate (see O'Connor 1997, Conchas 2001). As Carter (forthcoming) argues, for example, those black and Latino youth who resist *social* practices seen as "white" in school have instead been framed by both researchers and their own teachers as rejecting school achievement itself. Such naturalized assumptions have serious consequences for black and Latino students who struggle daily to both achieve *and* "act black" or "act Latino" in school. Further, rarely do popular articles seeking student opinions on "acting white" interrogate the problematic social consequences of analytically assuming achievement motivation to *be* a "white" domain; nor do they typically look within "race groups" for counterexamples. This simplified, familiar framing of "race groups" in school—which blames various groups of color for desiring their own "failure," and in doing so lets everyone around youth in schools off the hook—seems simply too palatable to the American public.

Accordingly, graduate students in U.S. schools of education, too, often seem programmed upon arrival to choose one racialized/ethnic/national-origin group (typically a group of students of color) for their dissertation research (as if this group acts in isolation), and set out to determine how members of that "group" react to the task of achieving in school. Yet having generation after generation of educational researchers lunge forth with ingrained, matter-of-fact assumptions that racialized "kinds of kids" will have racialized attitudes toward schooling (or schooling behaviors) is dangerous business (for a confessional self-analysis of such a research design, see McDermott 1997). It might be far better for kids if we researchers were to more often name and critique shared American assumptions about race and achievement (Steele 1992). We could also promote more often a discourse of communal responsibility pinpointing all the necessary actors that have to be invited to the table to produce solutions (Moses 2001).

Dilemma 6: Though Talking in Racial Terms Can Make Race Matter, Not Talking in Racial Terms Can Make Race Matter Too

Finally, Columbus people were caught, daily, in the most basic dilemma of U.S. racial practice: in a world in which racial inequality already exists, both talking and *not* talking in racial terms can alternately be "racist." This dilemma showed up in the most routine examples of school race talk. For example, Columbus adults regularly privately discussed the racial demographics of an everyday school issue—students wandering in the hallway during classtime. Across Columbus, adults of all "races" whispered anxiously their perceptions that the hall wanderers were predominantly "black." Yet Columbus adults also admitted self-consciously that they deleted the very label "black" from public discussions of the hallway "problem," explaining that openly labeling the hall wanderers as "black" would seem "discriminatory." Simultaneously, they acknowledged that *not* describing the hallway's racial demographics seemed potentially "discriminatory" as well, since black students were effectively allowed to miss class disproportionately and at times to wander through the halls for hours anxiously ignored.

I found further that there was another paradoxical consequence of colormuteness, of which Columbus adults were somewhat less aware. By nervously and self-consciously deleting the very word "black" from their public talk of the hallway, adults actually paradoxically *highlighted* the privately perceived relevance of "blackness" to the hall wandering "problem." Columbus adults quietly whispering about "black students" and then letting them wander in full view actually ended up ignoring black students *in racial terms*—that is, ignoring them precisely "because they were black." Ian Haney Lopez (1996) makes a related argument: "to banish race-words" often "redoubles the hegemony of race," by "leaving race and its effects unchallenged and embedded in society, seemingly natural rather than the product of social choices" (177). Further, in whispering daily about black students' hallwandering behaviors, Columbus adults relentlessly placed black students alone at the center of daily analysis of this school "problem," effectively ignoring their *own* roles in producing the hallways' racial demographics (their own acts of ejecting black students disproportionately from classrooms, for example, or of allowing black students disproportionately to wander). And in doing so, they repeatedly framed black students themselves as "problematic" students whose presence in the hallways could not be openly mentioned—in the process making the "blackness" of students matter more.

A school-level tendency to focus on black students as particular school "problems" (see Noguera 2001, Ferguson 2000) has been shown to be mirrored in the discourse and practice of educational research, even as researchers often *fail* to talk systemically about the obstacles affecting black students and other students of color (see Perry, Steele, and Hilliard 2003). Research focusing on school patterns disproportionately harming black students often focuses analysis on black students' behavior alone, rather than including the various additional actors creating problems harming black students; the strategy often risks reinforcing a notion of black students themselves as particularly problematic. Powell (1997, 3) notes, for example, that research focused obsessively on discovering the role of *black* students in "black underachievement" systematically ignores the role that other people, particularly white people, play in the "knot of minority student failure" (for a more recent example of research framing black youths' behaviors as the primary cause of black underachievement, see Thernstrom and Thernstrom 2003). Sullivan (1996) makes an analogous argument about analytic reduction in the study of impoverished neighborhoods, arguing that, "By focusing on processes internal to a poor community, the researcher continually runs the risk of ascribing the causes of problems within the community entirely to its own members and neglecting processes of disinvestments, exploitation, and exclusion emanating from powerful interests and institutions outside the community" (p. 209). As research on the "model minority" myth shows similarly (Sue and Okazaki 1995), researchers often seem fixated on figuring out what it is about racialized groups' behavior that makes them succeed or fail (one article on "Asian" student achievement puts it classically: "*What is it about Asian students that helps account for their above-average record?*" See Steinberg, 1996, emphasis added). More rarely do we frame student "race groups" as embedded within intergenerational, multiracial systems of schooling opportunity and expectation, systems that both *produce* "group" behaviors and *assume* these behaviors the moment smiling kindergartners arrive.

Such analytic reductions focused on any one "group's" school behavior often have practitioners, too, talking about groups of students as if they naturally *have* group-specific school behaviors or "attitudes" toward schooling (and as if inbred student attitude and actions alone produce achievement outcomes, with "the school" serving primarily as background "context.") As one Columbus adult recently out of graduate school suggested to me in a discussion of the hall wanderers, educational "research" itself often seems to be *about* race group-specific hypotheses implicating the behaviors and attitudes of students and, often, their parents:

> I don't want to say it's *because* they're black—I'm not being prejudiced. I think maybe it's because of other things, and I don't know for sure because I haven't done the research or anything. But something about the socialization of African-Americans—the street culture, and maybe because of the lack of values at home . . .

Research too often muses similarly about the actions of any given such "race group" in isolation, often thus implying to readers that achievement patterns *are* in a sense the result of student "race." Far more rarely do scholars examine the "institutional choreography" (Fine 1997) in which students and adults of various "races," inside and outside of schools, together help produce racialized school patterns of failure or success (one good, short example of systemic research is Valencia's (1991) analysis of "Latino" underachievement, which makes clear that it is not only "Latinos," but also the many actors building the system of opportunities and educational experiences *surrounding* "Latinos," that must be investigated to truly understand "Latino under-achievement"). Thompson (1999) names "colortalk" this kind of talk, which "explicitly names the mechanisms" (implicitly, mechanisms including many actors) by which racialized orders are "maintained" (144).

Achieving sufficiently systemic race talk takes work. Simply talking *more* in practice or research *about kids* as racial beings with racialized behaviors, of course, often does little to challenge preexisting unsystemic analyses that *harm* kids (for a related argument, see Perry in Perry, Steele, and Hilliard 2003). In-deed, every time researchers open our mouths or sit down at our computers to talk about race in education, we risk hurting kids by falling into reductive scripts for talking about them. Again, one tactic for talking systemically in re-search might be to *add up* and *pit against each other* the various everyday analyses of the adults and young people themselves struggling in schools and districts to analyze racial patterns (Pollock forthcoming). At Columbus, for example, while adults routinely talked about the hallwandering "problem" in ways that ended up implicating black students alone, if taken in total ongoing Columbus conversations about the hallways and other school "problems" actually showed that both adults and students were wondering (albeit often in analytically at-omized conversations) about the respective roles of administrators, students, teachers, parents, the district, and various city and national actors in producing racial patterns (as one teacher put it to me, "it just gets too big, trying to *explain* it"). Indeed, in worrying about their own colormuteness re. the hallwandering phenomenon, teachers even indicated at times that they recognized they *them-selves* played roles in producing and allowing this racial pattern ("I don't want to harp on the fact that the hall wanderers are black—I'm not being prejudiced . . . But it needs to be addressed . . . *We're not serving them well enough*"). There is a good deal to be learned from everyday race analyses—if we take the full analysis to be distributed across many actors and treat each individual analysis as partial and flawed.

CONCLUSION: WRESTLING WITH RACE MORE STRATEGICALLY IN EDUCATIONAL RESEARCH

To produce analyses that actually assist educators in dismantling racial in-equalities, I believe, we must analyze the struggles over racial inequality and diversity already occurring on the ground in schools and districts. We must also wrestle with our own habits of talking about and analyzing race in research. Over the course of my own research, I myself had *learned to see* everyday race struggles, rather than simplifying these struggles in a quest to answer my original research questions. I had also countered my beginning research assumptions by reframing racial orders in schools as communally produced, intergenerational, multi-"race" phenomena rather than phenomena specific to kids of color alone. During my research on race at Columbus, I had also realized that as an ethnographer interested in the everyday workings of race and racial inequality, I could simply measure and discuss the experiences of race group members (which race groups had less money? Which ones graduated more? Which ones got suspended more often?). Alternatively, I could make racial practice a strange phenomenon for analysis, by watching people racialize one another, debate race group membership, and mutter anxieties about proceeding racially. My inquiry into race talk "race wrestled" by combining the two approaches. I continued collecting data typically seen as racial "facts"—school demographics, grades, test scores—while listening to (and describing) students and adults struggling over these very facts and what to make of them.

I am concerned that if researchers do not work more to analyze everyday struggles over race, and if we do not struggle more with talking about and analyzing race in our own research itself, we ourselves might continue to rush into dangerously familiar, too-easy analyses of race in education. This article has thus been, in part, a call for employing the ethnographic mantra of "make the familiar strange" when considering our own work. I think that U.S. education researchers, like practitioners, could do far more to debate how we talk about race. We might as well debate this, for we ourselves are already talking about race all the time: any meeting of the American Educational Research Association will always offer hundreds if not thousands of papers referencing and analyzing students in racial terms. Yet while race talk and analysis is typically all over AERA, researchers too rarely make struggling *over* race talk and analysis an explicit part of our communal work.

Fundamentally, we must balance two necessary tasks in our race talk: analyzing adequately the true complexity of human diversity, and analyzing adequately the production of simple orders of racial inequality. It takes much more work, of course, to talk this way in research. It is much harder to talk as if race is not some taken-for-granted system of human difference, but rather a produced system in which lives have and do become actively racialized through "thousands of daily interactions" in and around schools (Johnson in press). It is much harder to talk as if children are not fundamentally different by "race," but as if children's life experiences and opportunities get fundamentally *differentiated* by race. It is much harder to explain that race categories are not at their origins real, but that Americans organize identities and opportunities and life scripts as if they are. And it is much harder to proceed as if race matters a lot at some key moments in schooling and maybe is *not* the central issue in others. But in a country in which shockingly popular contemporary authors discussing education assert blatant falsehoods about race—that race categories should be taken for granted as "genetic" facts, for example (a notion disproved half a century ago [14]), or that serious racialized differences in available life opportunity no longer really exist [15], or that kids of color today really have no interest in achieving in school [16]—researchers and practitioners need to learn to think and talk about race with unprecedented agility. Neither employing race categories too matter-of-factly as natural units of diversity, nor denying the produced social facts of racial inequality, helps children. Accordingly, the more self-consciously researchers struggle with how to talk about and analyze race in education, the better equipped we are to assist the school and district people who are already struggling to do so. We would do well to put such struggle itself at the center of educational research.

ACKNOWLEDGMENTS

The author would like to thank the following thoughtful and generous scholars who read and critiqued this piece: Wendy Luttrell, Heather Harding, Meira Levinson, Maya Beasley, Mia Ong, and Dorinda Carter. Many thanks also to AJE's anonymous reviewers for their helpful critiques.

NOTES

[1] "Columbus" and "California City" are pseudonyms, promised to the second of Columbus's two beleaguered principals. As I now frame Columbus as a place with deeply American dilemmas rather than as a local "case study," naming Columbus also seems unnecessary. Several paragraphs in this paper also appear in Pollock (2004).

[2] For more scholarship framing "racial" systems *as* inequality systems and race categories as categories of power distribution, see Roediger 1991, Espiritu 1992, West 1992, Gilroy 1993, Frankenburg 1993, Omi and Winant 1994, Ignatiev 1995, Harrison 1995, Haney Lopez 1996, Appiah and Gutmann 1996, Sacks 1997, Lipsitz 1998, Kincheloe et al. 1998, Winant 1998, Thompson 1999, Rumbaut in press.

[3] Indeed, everyday people of all ages strategically seize simple categories to deal with simple-category systems of distributing resources (see Omi and Winant 1994 on "racial formation," Spivak 1987 on "strategic essentialism," and Stuart Hall on finding "strategic places from which to speak" [1992; see also Sharma 1996:34]. As Winant (1998:90) writes, the

very concept of "racial" difference serves both to allocate resources *and* to "provid[e] means for challenging that allocation."

[4] As anthropologists George and Louise Spindler have argued (1982), the task of "doing the ethnography of schooling" in familiar places necessitates that researchers "make the familiar strange." For any researcher or practitioner who begins with the familiar—with "home" practices and logics sedimented within her own life—the mantra demands that she work extra hard to make strange the ideas received involuntarily over a lifetime of socialization. But as anthropologists George Marcus and Michael Fischer (1986) admit of American anthropology writ large, "For the most part, anthropologists have taken the job of reflecting back upon ourselves much less seriously than that of probing other cultures" (p. 111).

[5] As I note in Pollock (2004), labeling (or not labeling) each other with race words is of course just one everyday way that Americans make each other racial. We reproduce "racial" difference through the patterned use of particular languages, dialects, styles, or vocabulary; going beyond talk, we make ourselves and each other racial when we make meaning of genetically-insignificant physical characteristics, like skin color or nose shape or eye contour or hair texture. We re-racialize ourselves and one another through the music we listen and dance to, the people we sit down next to, the organizations we belong to, the resources we distribute, and the neighborhoods we choose to live in or not to live in. Racial orders in *school* are also built through the distribution of dollars, through the "tracking" of racialized bodies to designated schools and classrooms, through the false expectations that differential abilities reside in racialized minds, through an "institutional choreography" (Fine 1997) of everyday actions incessantly funneling opportunities to some students and not others. For a full bibliography of these contemporary and historical methods of everyday racialization in the U.S., see Pollock 2004, Introduction and Chapter 1.

[6] On the creation of the U.S. category "white," see Roediger 1991, Ignatiev 1995, Sacks 1997; on "black," see Jordan 1974, Davis 1997; on "Asian," see Espiritu 1992; on "Hispanic" and "Latino," see Delgado and Stefancic 1998, Suarez-Orozco and Paez, 2002.

[7] At the 19th-century origins of the field, anthropologists compared, physically measured, and ranked presumed-different "racial" populations without apparent consciousness about their own culpability in producing these very differences and rankings (see Gould 1981, Baker 1998, Smedley 1999). The core of contemporary anthropological "reflexivity" is a self-consciousness about the ethnographic practice and product (see Wolf 1992, Clifford and Marcus 1986). As Emerson, Fretz, and Shaw (1995) put it, "*What* the ethnographer finds out is inherently connected with *how* she finds it out" (11). The same, of course, can be said for all modes of race research.

[8] Mehan's analysis of mother, psychologist, and teachers arguing over labeling a child "disabled" in a placement meeting (1996), for example, makes readers question the very existence and definition of "disability." Varenne, Goldman, and McDermott's (1997) research (like Spindler's [1987] and Henry's [1963] before them) looks closely at competitive rituals in U.S. schools and has readers rethinking the very process of delineating winners from losers. Looking at children and teachers struggling over defining "English proficiency" in an elementary school classroom, Moll and Diaz (1993) have readers questioning "proficiency" itself. For other analyses making readers rethink definitions of "kinds of kids" in schools, see, e.g., Varenne and McDermott (1998), on disability categories; Fine (1991) on the category "dropout"; Deyhle (1995) and Foley (1996) on the categories "Indian" and "Anglo"; Luttrell (2003) on categories of sexuality; Thorne (1993) on categories of

gender; Page (1991) on the category "low-tracked"; Willis (1977) on class categories. See also Levinson, Foley, and Holland (1996).

[9] Many scholars have pointed out that "whites" have always been central to racial orders in the U.S., even as we are, by this point in history, allowed daily immunity from much race analysis as if "whites" were *not* race group members at all (the greatest privilege given "whites," perhaps, is the privilege of racializing others while seeming un-racial or worse, "normal"). See also Thompson 1999, Lipsitz 1998, Macintosh 1989. On whiteness and schooling, see also Perry 2002, Fine et al. 1997.

[10] I myself, thus, had grown up in an American place where I was almost never explicitly racialized. The homogeneous state of Iowa of the 1970s and 1980s offered no daily personal reminder of my own place in the American racial taxonomy. In the schools in Iowa City at the time, few of us in our almost-completely-all-white schools even sporadically framed ourselves self-consciously *as* "white." (While pride in European immigrant heritage permeates some Iowa associations, national-origin ancestry was not a big concern for my peers either. Iowa today, by the way, appears less homogeneous, as industries attract more migrants from within and outside the U.S. who do not frame themselves as "white.") To say that I was unfamiliar with race, however—or indeed, that any "white" person in the U.S. is—would be only partly true. White people are racialized too, of course; and we too are race-makers (see Roman's aptly titled "White is a Color!", 1993). Indeed, framing *others* racially was a distinctly familiar act of my youth. Further, *questioning* "racial" difference was also on my mind as a young person: as the grandchild of Holocaust survivors persecuted for their racialized group membership (see Fredrickson 2002 on racialized anti-Semitism), I had a fairly skeptical and also fairly negative view of racialization from the beginning, only later in life coming to understand the positive empowerment that could be derived from membership in racialized communities bonded by struggle. West (in Morrison 1992) defines "blackness," for example, as a state of being in which one experiences both a constantly looming system of white supremacy waiting to denigrate one's person, and the joys of belonging a culturally rich community of people empowered through resistance to such denigration.

[11] Mishler (1986) demonstrates more generally that much interview research ignores the effect of the interview situation, often abstracting answers from the context of questions asked and erasing the interviewer entirely from the text presented. See also Briggs 1986.

[12] Prioritizing naturalistic interactions in my research allowed me to recognize that quiet struggles over race and race talk were a key aspect of Columbus people's everyday existence. As described in Pollock (2004), as an ex-teacher, I was given mostly free rein by the principal to walk around the school and talk to people for my research, and I participated in the same casual interactions with students and adults in hallways and classrooms that I had as a teacher, only with more time and with the shared understanding that such conversations *were* my research. I also learned to go looking for race talk in multiple institutional locations: I documented discourse from school board meetings, superintendent's addresses, conversations between teachers held in classrooms, hallways, and happy hours, conversations between teachers, students, parents, and administrators in and out of classrooms, and conversations between students both in and out of school. I also gathered systematically the written artifacts of legal opinions, district and school-level statistics, district pronouncements and press releases, union newsletters, faculty newsletters and memos, student assignments, newspaper articles, and educational research itself. Analyzing such talk eventually helped me discover

the key role of the kind of race talk that simply happens in informal school moments, along with that which happens at the more formalized moments of faculty meetings and public assemblies. As described in Pollock (2004), I chose not to tape record these natural research conversations for a simple self-conscious reason: turning on a tape recorder during a quiet conversation about race seemed likely not only to make people extremely uncomfortable, but indeed, to destroy the very data we were producing. Yet I did not need to capture language at too fine-grained a level of linguistic detail in any case. I came to need instead to capture the basic timing of the appearance of race terms, the topics in connection to which race labels were used, and the worries people expressed about using them. I thus reconstructed conversations immediately after the fact—within minutes or hours—slipping into bathrooms or empty classrooms to scribble them down. Over several years, thousands of speech examples collected through participant observation at Columbus and in its district would reveal that people used, struggled with, and deleted race labels in predictable ways at predictable times.

By making race *talk* my unit of analysis, I had started listening far more carefully to the structure of everyday talk rather than its content alone. Researchers use talk as data most of the time, but we only rarely get self-conscious about using talk as a unit of analysis; most researchers, as Briggs (1996) and Mishler (1986) have pointed out, treat talk captured in the field as simply opinions or "beliefs" to write down. By attending to race talk as a structured social action, I progressed from studying just the presence of race words to studying their patterned absence as well. While collecting data and afterwards, I read repeatedly through my corpus of fieldnotes, attaching a sticky sliver of Post-it to the notes every time race words emerged or were conspicuously absent (e.g., when school speakers who had just spoken to me in private about racial patterns in school discipline spoke haltingly in public of the "problem kids," or when district speakers who had written of "black and Hispanic" students in policy documents spoke with virtuous emphasis of "*all* students" in public). Making lists of such repeated race talk patterns running through my notes (what anthropologist Carol Stack called finding "threads"), I began to see striking patterns in *when* speakers in different institutional locations used race words, and when, in discussing the same topic in another context, they conspicuously did not. After repeatedly culling patterns out of my notes, compiling lists into shorter lists, and coding again, the data finally presented to me three main processes of race talk. People used race labels matter-of-factly, they contested their use, and they deleted them—and two key variables that affected these dynamics were the topic they were talking about and the person(s) to whom they were speaking. (The question of "when" was central to my adviser Ray McDermott, a microethnographer who had spent years looking at the strikingly choreographed timing of classroom activity patterns in several minutes of videotape. Proceeding more often with such "when" questions in race research would help us view racial practice as patterned practice; knowing such patterns, we could also debate better how to reshape our own predictable actions.)

[13] Anthropologists originally (mis)measured the skulls of presumed-distinct race-group members in attempts to naturalize the country's social racial hierarchy as a result of differential "intelligence." Anthropologists passed the 19-century baton to psychologists, who instead purported to measure the inside of racialized heads to prove the U.S. social racial hierarchy "natural"; see Lemann 1999.

[14] For anthropological disproving of race's genetic reality, see Montagu 1997[1942]. See also Fraser, ed., *The Bell Curve Wars*, 1995. For an example of a recent claim of the genetic reality of "races," see, e.g., Hernstein and Murray 1996.

[15] See Reynolds 1996.

[16] See McWhorter 2000. For a counterpoint, see the recent "Tripod" survey research of Ron Ferguson at Harvard, who has found widespread desires for academic achievement among black youth.

REFERENCES

American Anthropological Association. "AAA Statement on 'Race.' " *Anthropology Newsletter* (May 17, 1998): 1.

Appiah, K. Anthony, and Amy Gutmann. *Color Conscious: The Political Morality of Race.* Princeton, NJ: Princeton University Press, 1996.

Bailey, Benjamin. "Language and Negotiation of Ethnic/Racial Identity among Dominican Americans." *Language and Society* 29 (2000): 555–582.

Baker, Lee. *From Savage to Negro: Anthropology and the Construction of Race. 1896–1954.* Berkeley: University of California Press, 1998.

Banaji, Mahzarin. " 'Ordinary Prejudice': Science Briefs." *Psychological Science Agenda*, January/February (2001): 9–11.

Barth, Frederick. *Ethnic Groups and Boundaries.* Boston: Little, Brown and Company, 1969.

Becker, Howard S. "The Epistemology of Qualitative Research." In *Ethnography and Human Development: Context and Meaning in Social Inquiry*, edited by Richard Jessor, Anne Colby, and Richard A. Shweder. Chicago: University of Chicago Press, 1996.

Bonilla-Silva, Eduardo. "The Linguistics of Color Blind Racism: How to Talk Nasty about Blacks without Sounding Racist." *Critical Sociology* 28, Issue 1–2 (2002): 41–64.

Briggs, Charles L. *Learning How to Ask: A Sociolinguistic Appraisal of the Role of the Interview in Social Science Research.* Cambridge: Cambridge University Press, 1986.

Carter, Prudence. *Not in the "White" Way: Aspirations, Achievement and Culture among Low-Income African American and Latino Youth.* Oxford University Press, forthcoming.

Chavez, Lydia. *The Color Bind: California's Battle to End Affirmative Action.* Berkeley: University of California Press, 1998.

Clifford, James, and George E. Marcus. *Writing Culture: The Poetics and Politics of Ethnography.* Berkeley: University of California Press, 1986.

Conchas, Gilberto Q. "Structuring Failure and Success: Understanding the Variability in Latino School Engagement." *Harvard Educational Review*, 71, 3 (2001): 475–504.

Cross, William E. *Shades of Black: Diversity in African-American Identity.* Philadelphia: Temple University Press, 1991.

Dance, L. Jannelle. *Tough Fronts: The Impact of Street Culture on Schooling.* New York and London: Routledge, 2002.

Darling-Hammond, Linda. "Race, Education, and Equal Opportunity." In *The African American Predicament*, edited by C. H. Foreman. Washington, D.C.: Brookings Institution Press, 1999.

Davis, F. J. *Who Is Black? One Nation's Definition.* University Park, PA: The Pennsylvania State University Press, 1997.

Delpit, Lisa. *Other People's Children: Cultural Conflict in the Classroom.* New York: New Press, 1995.

Delgado, Richard, and Jean Stefancic, eds. *The Latino/a Condition: A Critical Reader.* New York: New York University Press, 1998.

Delgado, Richard, and Jean Stefancic, eds. *Critical White Studies: Looking behind the Mirror.* Philadelphia: Temple University Press, 1997.

Delgado, Richard, ed. *Critical Race Theory: The Cutting Edge*. Philadelphia: Temple University Press, 1995.

Deyhle, Donna. "Navajo Youth and Anglo Racism: Cultural Integrity and Resistance." *Harvard Educational Review* 65 (1995): 403–444.

Emerson, Robert M., Rachel I. Fretz, and Linda L. Shaw. *Writing Ethnographic Fieldnotes*. Chicago: University Of Chicago Press, 1995.

Erickson, Frederick. "Transformation and School Success: The Politics and Culture of Educational Achievement." In *Minority Education: Anthropological Perspectives*, edited by Evelyn Jacob and Cathie Jordan. Cincinnati: University of Cincinnati Series, 1993.

Espiritu, Yen Le. *Asian American Panethnicity: Bridging Institutions and Identities*. Philadelphia: Temple University Press, 1992.

Ferguson, Ann Arnett. *Bad Boys: Public Schools in the Making of Black Masculinity*. Ann Arbor: University of Michigan Press, 2000.

Fine, Michelle, Lois Weis, and Linda C. Powell. 1997. "Communities of Difference: A Critical Look at Desegregated Spaces Created for and by Youth." *Harvard Educational Review* 57, 2 (1997): 247–285.

Fine, Michelle, Lois Weis, Linda C. Powell, and L. Mun Wong, eds. *Off-White: Readings on Race, Power, and Society*. New York: Routledge, 1997.

Fine, Michelle. *Framing Dropouts: Notes on the Politics of an Urban Public High School*. Albany: State University of New York Press, 1991.

Foley, Douglas E. "The Silent Indian as a Cultural Production." In *The Cultural Production of the Educated Person: Critical Ethnographies of Schooling and Local Practice*, edited by Bradley A. Levinson, Douglas E. Foley, and Dorothy C. Holland. Albany: SUNY Press, 1996.

Fordham, Signithia. *Blacked out: Dilemmas of Race, Identity, and Success at Capital High*. Chicago: University of Chicago Press, 1996.

Fordham, Signithia, and John U. Ogbu. "Black Students' School Success: Coping with the Burden of 'Acting White.'" *The Urban Review* 18, 3 (1986).

Frankenberg, Ruth. *Women, Race Matters: The Social Construction of Whiteness*. Minneapolis: University of Minnesota Press, 1993.

Fraser, Steven, ed. 1995. *The Bell Curve Wars: Race, Intelligence, and the Future of America*. New York: Basic Books.

Fredrickson, George M. *Racism: A Short History*. Princeton, NJ: Princeton University Press, 2002.

Geertz, Clifford. *The Interpretation of Cultures*. New York: Basic Books, 1973.

Gilroy, Paul. *The Black Atlantic*. Cambridge, MA: Harvard University Press, 1993.

Gould, Stephen Jay. *The Mismeasure of Man*. New York: W. W. Norton and Company, 1981.

Guinier, Lani, and Gerald Torres. *The Miner's Canary: Enlisting Race, Resisting Power, Transforming Democracy*. Cambridge, MA: Harvard University Press, 2002.

Hall, Kathy. *Lives in Translation: Sikh Youth as British Citizens*. Philadelphia: University of Pennsylvania Press, 2002.

Hall, Stuart. "New Ethnicities." In *"Race," Culture and Difference*, edited by James Donald and Ali Rattansi. Newbury Park, CA: Sage Publications in association with the Open University, 1992.

Hammersley, Martyn. "Partisanship and Credibility: The Case of Antiracist Educational Research." In *Researching Racism in Education: Politics, Theory and Practice*, edited by Paul Connolly and Barry Troyna. Buckingham: Open University Press, 1998.

Haney Lopez, Ian F. *White by Law: The Legal Construction of Race*. New York: New York University Press, 1996.

Harrison, Faye V. "The Persistent Power of 'Race' in the Cultural and Political Economy of Racism." *Annual Review of Anthropology* 24 (1995): 47–74.

Hatcher, R., and Barry Troyna. "Racialization and Children." In *Race, Identity and Representation in Education*, edited by Cameron McCarthy and Warren Crichlow. New York: Routledge, 1993.

Heath, Shirley Brice. *Ways with Words: Language, Life and Work in Communities and Classrooms.* Cambridge: Cambridge University Press, 1983.

Henry, Jules. *Culture against Man.* New York: Vintage Books, 1963.

Herrnstein, Richard, and Charles Murray. *The Bell Curve: Intelligence and Class Structure in American Life.* New York: Simon & Schuster, 1996.

Ignatiev, Noel. *How the Irish Became White.* New York: Routledge, 1995.

Johnson, Deborah. The Ecology of Children's Racial Coping: Family, School, and Community Influences. In *Discovering Successful Pathways in Children's Development: New Methods in the Study of Childhood and Family Life*, edited by Thomas S. Weisner. Chicago: University of Chicago Press, in press.

Jordan, Winthrop D. *The White Man's Burden: Historical Origins of Racism in the United States.* London: Oxford University Press, 1974.

Kincheloe, Joe L., Shirley R. Steinberg, Nelson M. Rodriguez, and Ronald E. Chennault, eds. *White Reign: Deploying Whiteness in America.* New York: St. Martin's Press, 1998.

Lee, Carol D. "Why We Need to Re-Think Race and Ethnicity in Educational Research." *Educational Researcher* 32, 5 (2003): 3–5.

Lee, F. R. "Why Are Black Students Lagging?" *New York Times*, November 30, 2002.

Lee, Stacey J. *Unraveling the "Model Minority" Stereotype: Listening to Asian American Youth.* New York: Teachers College Press, 1996.

Lemann, Nicholas. *The Big Test: The Secret History of the American Meritocracy.* New York: Farrar, Strauss and Giroux, 1999.

Levinson, Bradley, Douglas Foley, and Dorothy Holland, eds. *The Cultural Production of the Educated Person: Critical Ethnographies of Schooling and Local Practice.* Albany: State University of New York Press, 1996.

Lewis, Amanda E. *Race in the Schoolyard: Negotiating the Color Line in Classrooms and Communities.* New Brunswick, NJ: Rutgers University Press, 2003.

Lipman, Pauline. *Race, Class, and Power in School Restructuring.* Albany, New York: State University of New York Press, 1998.

Lipsitz, George. *The Possessive Investment in Whiteness: How White People Profit from Identity Politics.* Philadelphia: Temple University Press, 1998.

Luttrell, Wendy. *Pregnant Bodies, Fertile Minds: Race, Gender and the Schooling of Pregnant Teens.* New York: Routledge, 2003.

Maira, Sunaina Marr. *Desis in the House: Indian American Youth Culture in New York City.* Temple University Press, 2002.

Marcus, George E., and Michael M. J. Fisher. *Anthropology as Cultural Critique: An Experimental Moment in the Human Sciences.* Chicago: University of Chicago Press, 1986.

McCarthy, Cameron. *The Uses of Culture: Education and the Limits of Ethnic Affiliation.* New York: Routledge, 1998.

McDermott, Ray. "Achieving School Failure 1972–1997." In *Education and Cultural Process: Anthropological Approaches*, 3d ed., edited by George Spindler. Prospect Heights, IL: Waveland Press, Inc, 1997.

McIntosh, Peggy. "White Privilege: Unpacking the Invisible Knapsack." *Peace and Freedom* (July/August 1989): 10–12.

McIntyre, Alice. *Making Meaning of Whiteness*. Albany: State University of New York Press, 1997.

McWhorter, John. *Losing the Race: Self-Sabotage in Black America*. New York: The Free Press, 2000.

Mehan, Hugh. "Beneath the Skin and between the Ears: A Case Study in the Politics of Representation." In *Understanding Practice: Perspectives on Activity and Context*, edited by Jean Lave and Seth Chaiklin. Cambridge: Cambridge University Press, 1996.

Mertz, Elizabeth. "Language, Law, and Social Meanings." *Law and Society Review* 26, 2 (1992): 413–445.

Minow, Martha. *Making All the Difference: Inclusion, Exclusion, and American Law*. Ithaca: Cornell University Press, 1990.

Mishler, Elliot G. *Research Interviewing: Context and Narrative*. Cambridge, MA: Harvard University Press, 1986.

Moll, Luis C., and Stephen Diaz. "Change as the Goal of Educational Research." In *Minority Education: Anthropological Perspectives*, edited by Evelyn Jacob and Cathie Jordan. Westport, CT: Ablex Publishing, 1993.

Montagu, Ashley. *Man's Most Dangerous Myth: The Fallacy of Race*. Walnut Creek, CA: Altamira Press, 1997 [1942].

Moses, Robert. *Radical Equations: Civil Rights from Mississippi to the Algebra Project*. Boston: Beacon Press, 2001.

Noguera, Pedro. "The Trouble with Black Boys." *Harvard Journal of African Americans and Public Policy* (Fall 2001).

Oakes, Jeannie, with T. Ormseth, R. Bell, and P. Camp. *Multiplying Inequalities: The Effects of Race, Social Class, and Tracking on Opportunities to Learn Mathematics and Science*. Santa Monica, CA: Rand Corporation, 1990.

O'Connor, Carla. "Dispositions toward (Collective) Struggle and Educational Resilience in the Inner City: A Case Analysis of Six African-American High School Students." *American Educational Research Journal* 34 (Winter 1997): 593–629.

Olsen, Laurie. *Made in America: Immigrant Students in Our Public Schools*. New York: The New Press, 1997.

Omi, Michael, and Howard Winant. *Racial Formation in the United States: From the 1960s to the 1990s*. 2d ed. New York: Routledge, 1994.

Outlaw, Lucius. "Toward a Critical Theory of 'Race.' " In *Anatomy of Racism*, edited by David Theo Goldberg. Minneapolis: University of Minnesota Press, 1990.

Page, Reba Neukom. *Lower Track Classrooms: A Curricular and Cultural Perspective*. New York: Teachers College Press, 1991.

Parker, Laurence, Donna Deyhle, and Sofia Villenas, eds. *Race Is-Race Isn't: Critical Race Theory and Qualitative Studies in Education*. Boulder: Westview Press, 1999.

Payne, Charles. *Getting What We Ask for*. Westport, CT: Greenwood, 1984.

Perry, Pamela. *Shades of White: White Kids and Racial Identities in High School*. Duke University Press, 2002.

Perry, Theresa, Claude Steele, and Asa G. Hilliard III. *Young, Gifted, and Black: Promoting High Achievement Among African-American Students*. Boston: Beacon Press, 2003.

Pollock, Mica. *Colormute: Race Talk Dilemmas in an American School*. Princeton, NJ: Princeton University Press, 2004.

Pollock, Mica. "Race Bending: 'Mixed' California Youth Practicing Strategic Racialization in California." *Anthropology and Education Quarterly*, March 2004 (b).

Pollock, Mica. "How the Question We Ask Most about Race in Education Is the Very Question We Most Suppress." *Educational Researcher* (December 2001), pp. 2–12.

Pollock, Mica. *Analyzing Educational Inequality: A Practical Guide.* Forthcoming manuscript.

powell, john. An "integrated" theory of integrated education. www.civilrightsproject.harvard.edu/research/reseg01/powell.pdf 2002.

Powell, Linda C. "The Achievement (K)Not: Whiteness and 'Black Underachievement.' " In *Off-White: Readings on Race, Power, and Society,* edited by Michelle Fine et al. New York: Routledge, 1997.

Rampton, Ben. *Crossing: Language and Ethnicity among Adolescents.* London: Longman Group Ltd., 1995.

Reynolds, W. B. "An Experiment Gone Awry." In *The Affirmative Action* Debate, edited by George E. Curry. Reading, MA: Addison-Wesley, 1996.

Roediger, David R. "What to Make of Wiggers: A Work in Progress." In *Generations of Youth: Youth Cultures and History in Twentieth-Century America,* edited by Joe Austin and Michael N. Willard. New York: New York University Press, 1998.

Roediger, David R. *The Wages of Whiteness: Race and the Making of the American Working Class.* London: Verso, 1991.

Roman, Leslie G. "White Is a Color! White Defensiveness, Post-Modernism, and Anti-Racist Pedagogy." In *Race, Identity, and Representation in Education,* edited by Cameron McCarthy and Warren Crichlow. New York: Routledge, 1993.

Root, Maria P. P., ed. *The Multiracial Experience: Racial Borders as the New Frontier.* Thousand Oaks, CA: Sage Publications, 1996.

Rosaldo, Renato. *Culture and Truth: The Remaking of Social Analysis.* Boston, MA: Beacon Press, 1993.

Rothstein, Richard. *Class and Schools: Using Social, Economic, and Educational Reform to Close the Black-White Achievement Gap.* New York: Teachers College Press, 2004.

Rumbaut, Rubén. "Sites of Belonging: Acculturation, Discrimination, and Ethnic Identity Among Children of Immigrants." In *Discovering Successful Pathways in Children's Development: New Methods in the Study of Childhood and Family Life,* edited by Thomas S. Weisner. Chicago: University of Chicago Press, in press.

Sacks, Karen Brodkin. "How Did Jews Become White Folks?" In *Critical White Studies,* edited by Richard Delgado and Jean Stefancic. Philadelphia: Temple University Press, 1997.

Sanjek, Roger. "The Enduring Inequalities of Race." In *Race,* edited by Steven Gregory and Roger Sanjek. New Brunswick, NJ: Rutgers University Press, 1996.

Schofield, Janet Ward. "The Colorblind Perspective in School: Causes and Consequences." In *Multicultural Education,* 4th ed., edited by James Banks and Cherry A. McGee Banks. Boston: Allyn and Bacon, 1999.

Sears, David O., Jim Sidanius, and Lawrence Bobo, eds. *Racialized Politics: The Debate about Racism in America.* Chicago: University of Chicago Press, 2000.

Sharma, Sanjay, John Hutnyk, and Ashwani Sharma, eds. *Dis-Orienting Rhythms: The Politics of the New Asian Dance Music.* London: Zed Books, 1996.

Sleeter, Christine. "Advancing a White Discourse: A Response to Scheurich." *Educational Researcher* 22, 8 (November 1993): 13–15.

Sleeter, Christine. "How White Teachers Construct Race." In *Race, Identity, and Representation in Education,* edited by Cameron McCarthy and Warren Crichlow. New York: Routledge, 1993 b.

Smedley, Audrey. *Race in North America: Origin and Evolution of a Worldview.* 2d ed. Boulder, CO: Westview Press, 1999.

Smitherman, Geneva. *Talkin That Talk: Language, Culture, and Education in African America.* London and New York: Routledge, 2000.

Spindler, George. "Beth Ann: a Case Study of Culturally Defined Adjustment and Teacher Perceptions." In *Education and Cultural Process: Anthropological Approaches*, Second Edition. Prospect Heights, Illinois: Waveland Press, 1987.

Spindler, George, ed. *Doing the Ethnography of Schooling: Educational Anthropology in Action.* New York: Holt, Rinehart and Winston, 1982.

Spivak, Gayatri Chakravorty. "Subaltern Studies: Deconstructing Historiography." In *In Other Worlds: Essays in Cultural Politics.* New York: Routledge, 1987.

Steele, Claude. "Race and the Schooling of Black Americans." *Atlantic Monthly* (April 1992).

Steinberg, Laurence, with B. Bradford Brown and Sanford M. Dornbusch. "Ethnicity and Adolescent Achievement." *American Educator* 20, 2 (Summer 1996): 28–44.

Suarez-Orozco, Carola, and Marcelo Suarez-Orozco. *Children of Immigration.* Cambridge, MA: Harvard University Press, 2001.

Suarez-Orozco, Marcelo, and Mariela M. Paez, eds. *Latinos: Remaking America.* Berkeley: University of California Press, 2002.

Sue, Stanley, and Sumie Okazaki. Asian-American Educational Achievement: A Phenomenon in Search of an Explanation. In *The Asian American Educational Experience: A Source Book for Teachers and Students*, edited by Don Nakanishi and Tina Yamano Nishida. London: Routledge, 1995.

Sullivan, Mercer L. "Neighborhood Social Organization: A Forgotten Object of Ethnographic Study?" In *Ethnography and Human Development: Context and Meaning in Social Inquiry*, edited by Richard Jessor, Anne Colby, and Richard A. Shweder. Chicago: University of Chicago Press, 1996.

Tatum, Beverly Daniel. "Talking about Race, Learning about Racism: An Application of Racial Identity Development Theory in the Classroom." *Harvard Educational Review* 62, 1 (1992): 1–24.

Tatum, Beverly Daniel. *"Why Are All the Black Kids Sitting Together in the Cafeteria?" and Other Conversations about Race.* New York: Basic Books, 1997.

Thernstrom, Abigail M., and Stephan Thernstrom. *No Excuses: Closing the Racial Gap in Learning.* New York: Simon and Schuster, 2003.

Thompson, Audrey. "Colortalk: Whiteness and *Off-White*." *Educational Studies* 30, 2 (Summer 1999): 141–60.

Thorne, Barrie. *Gender Play: Girls and Boys in School.* New Brunswick, NJ: Rutgers University Press, 1993.

Valencia, Richard. "The Plight of Chicano Students: An Overview of Schooling Conditions and Outcomes." In *Chicano School Failure and Success: Research and Policy Agendas for the 1990s*, edited by Richard Valencia. London and New York: The Falmer Press, 1991.

Van Ausdale, Debra, and Joe R. Feagin. *The First R: How Children Learn Race and Racism.* Lanham, MD: Rowman and Littlefield Publishers, 2001.

Varenne, Herve, and Ray McDermott. *Successful Failure: The School America Builds.* Boulder, CO: Westview Press, 1998.

Varenne, Herve, Shelley Goldman, and Ray McDermott. "Racing in Place: Middle-Class Work in Success/Failure." In *Education and Cultural Process: Anthropological Approaches*, 3d ed., edited by George Spindler. Prospect Heights, IL: Waveland Press, Inc, 1997.

Varenne, Herve. "Jocks and Freaks: The Symbolic Structure of the Expression of Social Interaction Among American Senior High School Students." In *Doing the Ethnography of Schooling*, edited by George Spindler. New York: Holt, Rinehart and Winston, 1982.

Waters, Mary. *Black Identities: West Indian Immigrant Dreams and American Realities.* New York: Russell Sage Foundation; Cambridge, MA: Harvard University Press, 1999.

West, Cornel. "Black Leadership and the Pitfalls of Racial Reasoning." In *Race-Ing Justice, En-Gendering Power: Essays on Anita Hill, Clarence Thomas, and the Construction of Social Reality*, edited by Toni Morrison. New York: Pantheon Books, 1992.

Wetherell, Margaret, and Jonathan Potter. *Mapping the Language of Racism: Discourse and the Legitimation of Exploitation*. New York: Harvester/Wheatsheaf, 1992.

Willis, Paul. *Learning to Labor: How Working-Class Kids Get Working-Class Jobs*. New York: Columbia University Press, 1977.

Winant, Howard. "Racial Dualism at Century's End." In *The House That Race Built*, edited by W. Lubiano. New York: Vintage Books, 1998.

Wolf, Margery. 1992. *A Thrice-Told Tale: Feminism, Postmodernism, and Ethnographic Responsibility*. Stanford, CA: Stanford University Press, 1992.

5

Finding Safety in Dangerous Places: From <u>Micro</u> to <u>Micro</u> and Back Again

Jason Duque Raley
University of California, Santa Barbara

Jason Duque Raley is an assistant professor at University of California, Santa Barbara. He received his doctoral training in Stanford University's Graduate School of Education in the area of Language, Literacy, and Culture, with special training in linguistic anthropology and context analysis. His current work explores the relationship among culture, learning, and social interaction, with focus on the negotiation of trusting relations as a context for learning. His work also examines the epistemology and practice of qualitative research. When not teaching, researching, or writing, Jason is an avocado farmer in the Santa Clara River Valley in Ventura County, California.

The chapter tells two interwoven stories of finding safety in dangerous places. First, one researcher's "discovery" of safety as a concept the students of Pacifica College Prep School use to divide up and organize their cultural landscape. Unlike many other places, including most other schools, Pacifica is a place where they report feeling safe. The second story tells of students finding safety in the interactional contexts they build for each other. In a classroom discussion of one lawyer's choice to defend the First Amendment rights of the Ku Klux Klan, students figure out ways to work with the conventionally dangerous materials of race, history, identity, and the U.S. Constitution. As they proceed to untangle their own claims, students manage to rework these same dangerous materials into increasingly stable contexts of trust, "safe spaces" for genuine argument. In reporting the researcher's and students' discovery of safety, this chapter also reveals something about what is possible when young women (and men) rework the materials that culture provides them. Though students do not turn culture completely on its head, they certainly use it in riskily wonderful ways.

Besides being two interwoven stories, the chapter is also an argument for a rigorous blurring of the distinction between micro and macro in the anthropology of education. Despite the use of a micro–macro distinction to categorize monographs, to delimit a researcher's field of interest, or to describe differences among divisions, the distinction is not a good tool for looking at the world in ways that are responsive to participants' experience. In the study reported here, it was only when the researcher stopped worrying about the distinction between micro and macro, when he followed students as closely as he could across a single conversation, with all his hard-earned ethnographic understandings at stake, that culture and the possibilities for reworking it became visible.

The chapter is organized into four sections. The first section begins with a description of Pacifica College Prep School and the outlines of the research project conducted there from 1998–2001. From there, the chapter describes how the study evolved from a focus on students' multiple worlds to a focus on safety, and also how the analysis moved from wide-angle views of life in and out of classrooms to one 20-minute classroom discussion. The second section is an abridged account of the analysis of "the First Amendment discussion." This is the longest section of the chapter, but one that contains the most treasure. The fourth and final section summarizes research findings, returning to reconsider the idea of safety and the value of blurring distinctions.

INTRODUCTION

I stop for a cup of coffee at the cart outside my department. A sunny day—there are lots of those in this stretch of the California coast—with blossoms and birds and foot traffic. A prospective graduate student waves from some distance off, quickens pace and arrives to face me. We have talked before about his interest in education and indigenous peoples. A handshake and warm greetings. Then something like this: *I asked around after our meeting last week*, he starts. *People say you do _micro_ stuff. I think I'm interested in more _macro_ issues, so . . . I don't know. Are you _micro_? Or _macro_?* Although unusually rushed, my response still managed to be opaque in all the usual ways. How does one say, *Yes, neither one, both?*[1] This chapter is an effort to improve my reply.

---

[1] In their wonderful book *Successful Failure*, Hervé Varenne and Ray McDermott rely on a neologism from James Joyce (1939), "who preferred to confront all dichotomies by taking *one aneither*" (Varenne & McDermott, 1998, p. 163). That seems just right, but still too obscure to be a satisfactory answer to my student's question.

The chapter tells two interwoven stories of finding safety in dangerous places. First, the story of this researcher's finding safety as a concept one group of "natives" uses to divide up and organize a cultural landscape. When the students of Pacifica College Prep School describe their school experience, they contrast it with their experience in other schools, with visits to the city on the other side of the freeway, with "hot spots" in their neighborhood. Pacifica is a place where they report feeling *safe*. The second story tells of students finding safety in the interactional contexts they build for each other. In a classroom discussion of one African American lawyer's choice to defend the First Amendment rights of the Ku Klux Klan, students figure out ways to work with the conventionally hazardous materials of race, history, identity, and the U.S. Constitution. As they proceed to untangle their own points-of-view, students manage to rework these same dangerous materials into increasingly stable contexts of trusting social relations.

Besides being two interwoven stories, this chapter is also an argument for the rigorous blurring of the distinction between *micro* and *macro* in the anthropology of education.[2] The work is rooted in a tradition that has gotten very good at describing how, and when, culture works *against* man (and woman).[3] Because we can only ever work with what is *always already there* (Varenne & McDermott, 1998), we most often get what *always already is*. The opportunities for hope are too rare. In reporting my and students' discovery of safety, this chapter reveals something about what is possible when young women (and men) *rework* the materials that culture provides them. Although students do not turn culture completely on its head, they certainly

---

[2]The chapter's claims could be read as fitting into an ongoing defense of attention to the *micro* world of social interaction over and against *macro* approaches (cf. Schegloff, 1987; etc.). My intent here is not to argue for a *microanalytic* approach, but to argue instead for a method that is *responsible* to the actual lives of the persons we research, lives in which our distinctions between *macro* and *micro* are blurred, lives that are lived from one *micro* moment to another. Though the research I report here is original, the argument is hardly new. The work of Bateson and Mead (1942) surely makes the point regarding the usefulness of scrutinizing small moments of interaction for understanding broader cultural patterns. Twenty-five years ago, McDermott and Roth (1978) reviewed a broad collection of like-minded efforts. Since then, technological and methodological advances have secured a place for the analysis of small pieces of everyday life, including for educational research (see, e.g., the recent special issue of *Journal of Applied Linguistics*, 23[3]). This chapter, then, is less an example of an innovative method than an renovation of an old point, sensitive to the innovated present.

[3]Henry's (1963) *Culture Against Man* is the most obvious specific reference, but Henry is certainly not alone in his anthropologically informed critique of schooling. Other scholars whose work might be cited here include Concha Delgado-Gaitan, Perry Gilmore, Shirley Brice Heath, Ray McDermott, Alan Peshkin, David Smith, Enrique "Henry" Trueba, and Hervé Varenne.

use it in riskily wonderful ways. It was only when I stopped worrying about the distinction between *micro* and *macro*, when I followed students as closely as I could across a single conversation, with all my hard-earned ethnographic understandings at stake, that culture and the possibilities for reworking it became visible.

The rest of the chapter is organized into four sections. The first section begins with a description of Pacifica College Prep School and the outlines of the research I conducted there from 1998 to 2001. From there, I tell how the study evolved from a focus on students' multiple worlds to a focus on *safety*, and also how the analysis moved from wide-angle views of life in and out of classrooms to one 20-minute classroom discussion. The second section is an abridged account of the analysis of "the First Amendment discussion." This is the longest section of the chapter, but one that I hope contains the most treasure. If we pay close enough attention, we will learn something about safety as a *possibility* and, even better, how students and their teacher act responsibly to accomplish it. If we are careful enough, we may even get permission to think about ourselves as responsible actors, and how safety is within our grasp. The third section summarizes research findings, returning to reconsider the idea of *safety* and the value of blurring distinctions. The chapter concludes with a coda that considers implications beyond the boundaries of a school or classroom.

PACIFICA COLLEGE PREP AND THE FIRST AMENDMENT DISCUSSION

By 1998, the word about Pacifica College Prep School was starting to make its way out.[4] Most early reports in newspapers and magazines focused on the school's surprisingly successful basketball program. Barely enough players to field a squad, they were unexpected champions. When all the students in the school's first graduating class were admitted to four-year colleges and universities, the public focus shifted. At the time of the research reported here, Pacifica was the only high school, public or private, located in Bayview, a city of 25,000 wedged between a major commuter freeway and the San Francisco Bay. The overwhelming majority of Bayview's residents are African American, Latino, Pacific Islander, and South Asian.[5] Bayview's two most widely

---

[4]All names of places and persons are pseudonyms.

[5]State of California, Demographic Unit, Department of Finance, Sacramento, "Population Estimates for Cities & Counties," May 1997.

cited qualities seem to be the one-time highest per capita murder rate in the nation, and a 65% high school dropout rate. Bayview's residents bear the burden of stigma with amazing grace, but the burden still weighs heavily on Bayview's youth. To all but the school's founders and ardent supporters, the academic success of Pacifica's students was a new surprise. In newspapers and magazines, Pacifica College Prep was a *story*.

"In this community of unrealized dreams and limited resources stands Pacifica Prep, a small oasis of academic excellence and opportunity for those students willing to take advantage of it."

"At night, tiny Pacifica College Prep's basketball gym glows like an oasis in a city that has been rocked by poverty, violence, and drugs."

"When your home is Bayview, where Pacifica Prep is located, it's not hard to see why you would want to spend more time at school."

"When it's sweltering in Silicon Valley, no breeze blows in Bayview."

"A school of dreams."

Naturally enough, the good story of Pacifica College Prep begged for explanations that could be carried to other towns and other schools where "at-risk" students lived. The students and their school were "beating the odds," "making a difference," and, in perhaps the clearest research-based articulation of Pacifica's mystique, "[bridging] gaps in academic achievement, gaps rooted in ethnicity and class." The questions came easily: *How was such a school possible?* and *How could its lessons be carried to other places?* For some, Pacifica's formula for success was not all that complicated. One news article proposed that, "At the core of Pacifica is a simple principle: press students to achieve and then help them attain their ambitions." In his university's alumni magazine, the school's founder and director was quoted: "My educational philosophy is pretty basic: Set expectations high and provide the proper support so students can be successful in meeting those goals." Words and phrases like "hard work," "dedication," "aiming high," "pushing students," and "demanding and asking for the best" echoed this core belief.

From Fall 1998 until Spring 2001, I spent nearly 3 years in field research at Pacifica College Prep. I began before very many people had taken notice of Pacifica's success, intrigued as the rest of the world would soon be by Pacifica's impressive record. I figured to work against the tide of research on academic failure by studying an example of school success. Although skeptical of disparaging claims made about Bayview, my research did confirm many of the claims made about Pacifica College Prep. Pacifica's students, and especially its teachers, worked very hard. Expectations were indeed high, and there was a super-saturation of support. Students often remained at school until long past dark, some working on school projects, many just "hanging out." All of Pacifica's students went to college.

It became clear early on that thinking of Pacifica Prep as an island of hope in Bayview's sea of despair was, at best, an oversimplification of a much more complicated historical, economic, and political situation. Bayview's only public high school closed in 1976. The closing was justified as a response to declining enrollment in the six high schools in the larger school district, but was historically situated in the racist "blockbusting" practices of unscrupulous investors and poorly conceived desegregation policies. For two decades, the vacant school stood as a grim reminder of battles lost on issues of public services, political representation, and basic civil rights. Despair is hardly ever the whole picture, and it is certainly not the whole picture of Bayview. Yes, Bayview was once labeled "the nation's murder capital," but it is also the home of generations of vibrant, active working-class families who grow fruits and vegetables in backyard gardens, who attend church on Sundays, who wake up early to make breakfast for children before heading to work, who run small businesses and work in startup technology companies. And while Bayview grapples with its history of political and economic disenfranchisement, new immigrants continue to flow into the city from Mexico, Central America, and Southeast Asia, along with young professionals attracted by the relatively low cost of housing. About the same time as my fieldwork, a building (and demolition) boom in Bayview had begun, taking special advantage of the historically agricultural land that had so far avoided residential and commercial development. Bayview continues to evolve, and survive.

About midway through the fieldwork, questions and theories that oriented the study—*What is the recipe for these students' success?* and especially the theory-driven question, *How are students able to navigate the boundaries among their "multiple worlds"?*—gave way to the pressures of evolving findings. Trying to see students lives through the conceptual lens of "multiple worlds" was leaving much of the texture of their lives out of focus. Shadowing students in and out of school, listening to their talk during "ethnographic drives" around the neighborhood, acting and interacting with them across a range of settings, I kept stubbing my toe on the hard surfaces of their everyday lives, surfaces often mapped in shades of *safety*. Bayview is mostly safe; the affluent, low-crime city across the freeway is mostly not. The neighborhood gym is safe if you are a basketball-playing male, not so much if you are not. The barber shop is safe, unless you are driving around town with a White guy (forget that he is also Latino—it matters that he looks White). The new Starbucks, on the other hand, frequented by commuters crossing the Bay on their way to jobs in Silicon Valley, is decidedly unsafe. Quietly, and often amid long explanations of the value of hard work and dedication, students were also telling me about *what mattered* to them in their lives at Pacifica. Over and over again, the young people of Pacifica Prep define their school as a place that is *safe*. Unless you are with the same White guy.[6] Safety was a dimension of local cultural structure, a concept students used to "divide up and organize their own cultural worlds" (Frake, 1977, p. 5), including that part of the world occupied by schools.

The study that had started out as a study of school success and the navigation of multiple worlds evolved into a study of safety. Though the evolution was responsible to student accounts of their experience, I was uncomfortable with the term "safety" from the start. It was a porcelain phrase for me, sanitized and sterile. Not responsible to the warp and weave of students everyday lives, either in school or out of school, and, frankly, not very interesting as a context for learning. Boostrom (1998) captures my discomfort.

> The tendency of 'safe space' talk to censor critical reflection turns sympathy into sentimentality, open-mindedness into empty-headedness. That we need to hear other voices in order to grow is certainly true, but we also need to be able to respond to those voices, to criticize them, to challenge them, to sharpen our own perspectives through the friction of dialogue. A person can learn, says Socrates, 'if he is brave and does not tire of the search' (Plato, p. 81d). We have to be brave because along the way we are going to be 'vulnerable and exposed'; we are going to encounter images that are 'alienating and shocking'. We are going to be very unsafe. (p. 407)

I carried both *safety* and my uneasiness with the term into writing the ethnography of the school, anticipating that I would report both phenomena as equally relevant findings. That the ethnography of the school was soon consumed by the analysis of the recording of a single classroom discussion was something of an accident.

What I learned to see through the lens of the First Amendment discussion was that safety is not a feature of the place, nor something individual students got to explore for their own Self-flexibility. Safety is something students and their teachers have to work at, all the time, as they navigate a landscape already crisscrossed by the fault lines of race, language, history, politics, and school achievement. But I had little idea of these eventual findings when I

---

[6]Gender and race, of course, are just two resources with which safety (and danger) get built. The point is that, from students' point of view, what gets built with them is safety or danger.

started. I knew only that the discussion started to burn a hole in my pocket the minute I walked out of the classroom.

ANALYZING THE FIRST AMENDMENT DISCUSSION

Valentine's Day, 2001. On this morning I would shadow a student, Andrew, across his various settings and interactions. *Safety* was prominent in my conceptual toolkit. Over the more than 2 years of interviews and observations that preceded this day, "safety" had emerged as a powerful way to think about kids' experience of Pacifica. A pervading sense of safety seemed connected to students' claims that, unlike in other settings, at Pacifica they could "be themselves." And rather than the full occupation of some essential "self," "being yourself" at Pacifica described students' feeling that they were not confined to any particular "self" but could "try on" various selves without fear of censure. I was interested in capturing the specific phenomenon of students' "trying on" various ways of being, including especially ways of speaking.

I sit in a chair near the classroom door, a few feet from Andrew's seat, not more than a few feet from several other students in the small classroom. The class starts in typical fashion. It's 8:00 and these are high school juniors. The teacher wanders around the room, collecting papers from one place and putting them down in another, writing some words down on the board, being busy. Peet sits in the teacher's chair, other students are scattered about the room's small, two-person tables. Small talk about the challenge of waking up and getting moving, disbelief from one student that there is no teachers' lounge at the school where they might be able to get some coffee. A class trip to Starbucks is suggested but smilingly vetoed.

Students sing the birthday song to Sally. Andrew adds a solo verse, and I wonder if the microphone I've asked him to wear will pick up others' talk as well as his own. The teacher distributes enrollment forms for the upcoming Advanced Placement Economics exam. What seems like universal dismay is at least partly mitigated when the teacher explains that even if a student gets the lowest score, it "looks good" to college admissions officers that the student has taken the risk of taking the test. Many, including Andrew, say they will take the test.

The activity for the day involves discussing the issues of Constitutional law, outlined in several essays students were to have read for homework. The teacher assigns each essay to a pair of students whose job is to create three discussion questions. The teacher conducts a short lesson on the qualities of an "effective discussion question." The teacher's example lesson generates questions for one of the essays, so she must reorganize the groups. A few pairs of students become groups of three. Students spend the next twenty minutes or so generating candidate discussion questions. The teacher moves from group to group giving evaluative feedback and probing students. The teacher concludes this small group activity by introducing the next activity: a whole group discussion.

For the whole group discussion, the teacher and several students rearrange the desks and chairs into a rough circle (Fig. 5.1, "Physical Layout for First Amendment Discussion," depicts the organization of persons and furniture for the discussion). The teacher describes the activity again—"kind of a college sort of discussion"—including some instructions on finding and presenting evidence for a point-of-view, as well as a requirement that everyone speak at least twice. This requirement is neither followed nor mentioned again. The class then discusses the following topics in order: (1) equal rights for women and men; (2) the separation of church and state; and (3) the Ku Klux Klan's first amendment rights to assembly and free speech.

The last discussion is organized around an essay written by Anthony P. Griffin, an African American civil rights lawyer who accepted an invitation by the Texas American Civil Liberties Union to represent the Ku Klux Klan and Michael Lowe, the Grand Dragon of the Texas Realm of the Klan. The case centered on a contempt citation brought by a Texas state prosecutor against Lowe. As part of an effort to stall the Klan's campaign of terror against the few Black residents of a public housing project, the citation required Lowe to disclose the Klan's membership list. As a result of his decision to represent Lowe and the Klan, Griffin was dismissed as Texas general counsel for the National Association for the Advancement of Colored People (NAACP). Ironically, the First Amendment right to withhold organization membership lists was first recognized in 1958 by a unanimous U.S. Supreme Court decision in NAACP v. Alabama, which held that forcing an organization to turn over its membership lists violated its members' First Amendment right to freedom of association. On June 6, 1994, the Texas high court dismissed the contempt citation against Lowe, citing many of the First Amendment principles argued by Mr. Griffin.[7]

This "First Amendment" discussion is heated, although for much of the discussion it only hovers above the surface of Griffin's claims. Griffin's essay is not merely about defending the Klan's First Amendment rights; it is most centrally about his special obligation *as an African American* to defend those

---

[7]The facts of this case can be found in Wilkins (1995).

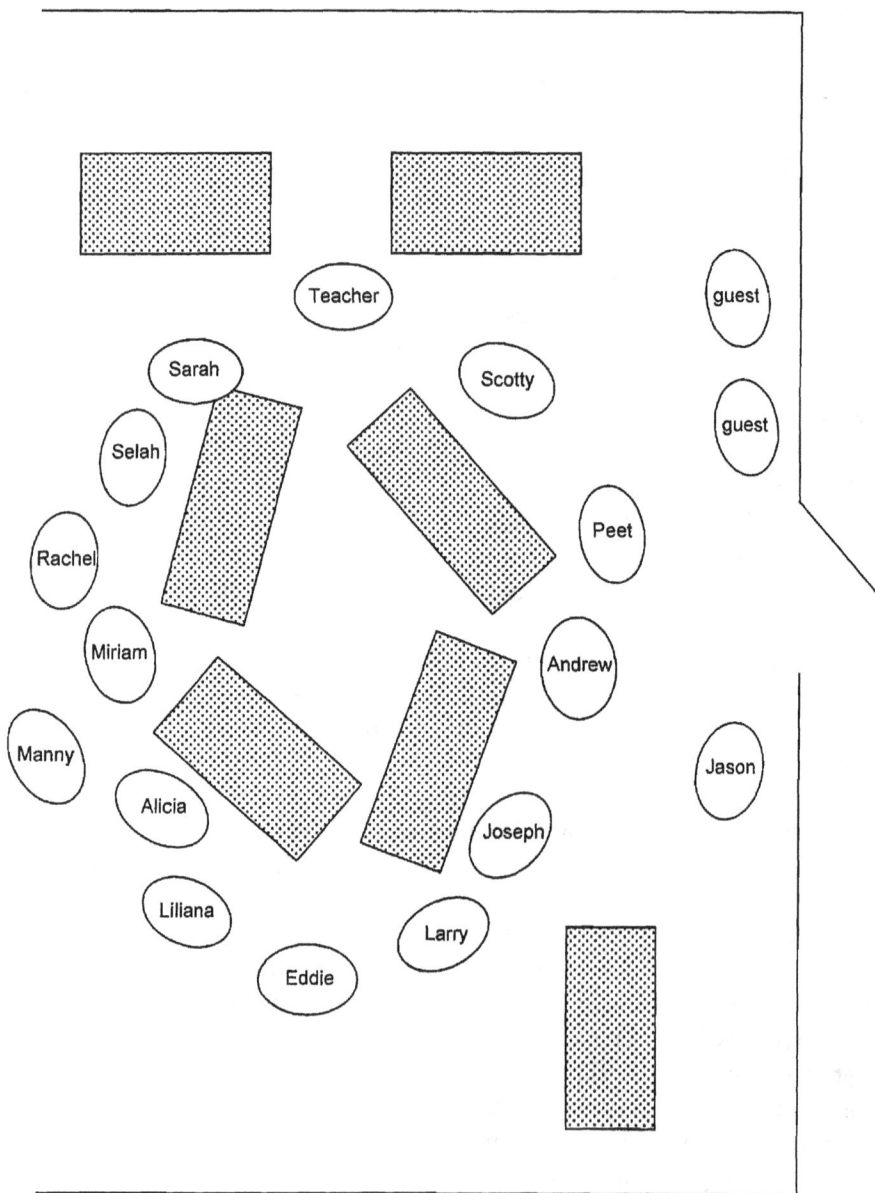

FIG. 5.1. Physical layout for First Amendment discussion.

rights. Race is not a new topic for these students. They talk about race frequently, joke about it, argue over it, celebrate and complain about their experience with it. Yet after they review the basic features of Griffin's argument, they manage to spend more than two-thirds of the discussion without significantly mentioning race. They get to race and everything else, eventually, without shifting their breakneck pace. But it does take some time.

I have to remind myself to take notes, feeling drawn as an observer into the rapids of this discussion. Students laugh and tussle and work to make sense of the topic and of each other. Over its 20 minutes, the activity evolves from a report of Griffin's argument, through students' asserting and arranging available claims, to finally achieve a committed, deliberative discussion involving questions about race, identity, and the distribution of rights and opportunity.[8] The talk extends past the scheduled end of class. Class ends abruptly, with the promise that "we will return to this on Friday." The last comment on the tape recording is Joseph, walking out of the classroom: "Now *that* was fun."

After I followed Andrew out of the classroom, I returned to the car and scribbled a few lines of notes: *Something happened during the [First Amendment] discussion. I think it matters for safety—I know it does—but I'm not sure how. I'm going to have to look harder at this. Were the different [points-of-view] the same as different selves? And what about it looking like a fight but [feeling like] laughter?* Hours of subsequent transcription and analysis complicated my overall view.[9] (See Appendix A for more details on transcription conventions.) I also worried as I transcribed, fearful that somebody, somewhere, would read it and write about these "angry" kids, who bullied each other and the teacher, who did not follow rules most people could recognize, who talked loud and fast and in each other's way.

As it happened, the transcription and its analysis unleashed an altogether fresh understanding of safety. Ultimately, I found safety in the spaces between people, in their ongoing production of trusting relations. On the way, I

---

[8]That participants were able to achieve a conversation about race at all remains exceptional (cf. Pollock, 2004), even in the setting of this school, where the successful achievement of such conversations was probably more common than in other places. For the analysis of a less successful "talk about race" in this same school, one that ended with hard feelings and unresolved claims to authority, see Raley (forthcoming).

[9]As Edelsky (1981) puts it, "transcribing data is at once problematic, intuition-producing, and fraught with often unreported yet important decisions" (p. 384; see also Ochs, 1979). Transcriptions of the First Amendment discussion in earlier reports (see Raley, 2003) met most of the requirements for conversation analysis (cf. Jefferson, 1985; Sacks et al., 1974) and enabled a very close analysis of the sequential organization of the discussion. For the purposes of this report, the guidelines set forth by Gumperz and Berenz (1990) are better.

saw that safety could look dangerous, play could look like fighting, and no-body seemed to be doing much of anything without the incidental coopera-tion of everyone else. Safety turned out to be contingent, interactional *achievement*. Safety was not a fixed attribute of the school at all, but a joint project strung across persons, constituting the context of their social rela-tions.

A Close Analysis

The First Amendment discussion is organized, in the first place, by Anthony P. Griffin's essay. The details of Griffin's case are not vital to the discussion, or are anyway mostly ignored by students. The central issue is the controversy that flows from Griffin's central claim, that he is *especially* obligated by the fact of his being an *African American*. The relationship between Griffin's *race* or *racial identity* and his choice to defend the Klan's rights is the heart of the present matter. The world is not arranged to make a conversation about race and civil rights easy. In spite of any expectations we might have about it be-ing easier for this group of students—African American, Latino, South Asian, and Pacific Islander students who at least share in common the con-ventional category "persons-of-color"—it can be hard work.

The analysis of the First Amendment discussion reveals the hard work that goes into finding workable solutions to two interactional problems. The first problem involves answering the question, *What will our talk be about?* Re-porting the relevant content of Griffin's essay is relatively straightforward, but determining the various positions in the argument around Griffin's claims is more challenging. I think of this problem as one of *building a text*. The sec-ond problem involves answering the questions, *What is going on here? How will we talk about this?* In this specific case, the question might be phrased, *How will we build a house that race and history and identity and learning and we can live in?* I think of this problem as a problem of *building contexts*. Like all of us, stu-dents and their teacher only have the resources and materials that are always already available to them. Their problem is our problem, and their materials are our same materials.

I describe the details of the analysis selectively. I dedicate the most detail to the early parts of the discussion. This is where interactional problems of *text* and *context* come into focus and the materials for addressing those prob-lems are first made available. I provide somewhat less detail in describing the analysis of two short segments of the ensuing discussion, concentrating on the way *text* and *context* problems are addressed. The final section describes the results of participants' hard work. This final section offers the least amount of detail, though perhaps the most satisfaction to the reader.

Locating the Problems and Gathering the Materials

At the start of the discussion, no one is quite sure which essay they will discuss next. Students and Teacher *negotiate the topic*. In this opening episode, students also wrestle to avoid the primary responsibility for leading the discussion. This much is already clear: these students and their teacher are in territory they recognize to be dangerous, and the territory lies not far from home. In fact, that this is dangerous territory is the reason the teacher gives for heading this way (23).

```
→  23  Teacher  =sh::: because this one is: the most controversial?
                 I do wanna jump to the first amendment=
   24  Liliana   thank you
   25  Teacher  as a consistent right.
   26  Peet     °thas not our ⌐(section:)°
   27  Teacher             ⌊u::m an if we have time
                 then we can ⌐go to number 2.
   28  Andrew              ⌊°I ain't ⌐read this yet rogue.°
   29  Joseph                       ⌊thas not our ⌐section
   30  Peet                                        ⌊(we still be reading ⌐it)
→  31  Teacher                                                           ⌊but u::h
                 I think this one kind of (.2)
                 hits ⌐ho:me⌐a little bit?
→  32  Liliana      ⌊ye:s  |
→  33  Selah               ⌊that one (   ) (trippin)
```

Once the topic is fixed and responsibilities determined, students proceed to represent the details of Griffin's argument, that as a Black man he is especially obligated to defend the First Amendment Rights of the Ku Klux Klan. Rachel is especially tentative, speaking haltingly and with long pauses (66, 69). Students express their dismay that such a thing could be possible (33, 68, 75), openly citing Griffin's race (70).

```
   58  Teacher  =wha was this about
                 just to set the ⌐sta:ge remind everyone what this is about
   59  Liliana              ⌊free speech?
   60             (.4)
   61  Liliana   we didn have all the same number two?
```

```
62  Eddie      where we at?
63  Liliana    wasn that person arguing about that?
64  Rachel     mm yea:h (.6)
               and ho:w:
65  Liliana    and stuff.
66  Rachel     how he: (.9)
               u:h (.2)
               he did- (1.7)
               like he:: (1.4)
               fought for: (1.2)
               like the Klu Klux Klan?
               even though he didn really like
67  Teacher         ⌈⌈mm-hm
68  Eddie           ⌊⌊he defended ⌈the (    )?
69  Rachel                        ⌊and so he still hafta do that
               if he wants to: u:m (1.5)
               m::: (.8)
               choose for ⌈himself and (    )
70  Eddie                 ⌊wha::t? he black?
71  Liliana    ye:p. and he had a
72  Teacher    and-
73  Liliana    ⌈⌈and
74  Eddie      ⌊⌊he work with the Klu ⌈Klux Klan?
75  (    )                            ⌊(he just) stu:pid
```

The group eventually determines that no one *forced* Griffin to defend the Klan's First Amendment rights, but that Griffin felt a special *obligation* to do so. Joseph steps forward to clarify the details of Griffin's position.

```
91  Joseph     if you can't (.3)
               honor the free speech and the rights
               of your- of your worst enemy,
               then you have no right to honor the free speech
               of those you care about.
92  Eddie      where it say dat?
93  Andrew     mm tru:⌈::e
94  Joseph             ⌊it's really what he's suggesting,
               it's like if you- (.2)
95  (    )     °he said wha⌈:t?°
96  Joseph                 ⌊the point
```

		of the whole first ⌐amendment is tha:t if y-=
97	Alicia	└he's I(h)n it for the <u>mo(h)ney</u>=
98	Selah	=enh henh- ⌐heh-<u>heh</u>
99	Joseph	└if yo:u are gonna sup<u>port</u> it

for those that share your <u>view</u>,
you hafta support for <u>every</u>body.
you hafta support it for those who <u>don't</u> share your view,
you have to support it f- .hh for those who <u>hate</u> you,
those who are <u>against</u> you,
those .hh who have views that you don't (.) <u>agree</u> with=

100	Andrew	=°m:: ⌐I bet he charged them a lotta money°
101	Joseph	└you've still got to support their right to free speech

they still have a right to <u>do</u> that
regardless of how you feel about it.

After a few exchanges, Larry asserts the first clear alternative to Griffin's claim. Joseph asserts Griffin's position more forcefully. Using the first person pronoun /we/, Joseph also begins to make Griffin's position look like a position he—or the group—might own.

123	Larry	when you just see

what the heck they did in the <u>pa:st</u> (.8)
nothing just depends on their-
their fre- freedom of speech.

124		(2.3)
125	Joseph	(tight)=
126	( )	=true
127	Andrew	°tru:::e°
128	Joseph	cuz when we try and <u>silence</u>

those who don't <u>agree</u> with us
or d- have views that we don't (1.1) <u>like</u> (.8)
that leads to op<u>pressions</u>:
<u>h</u>olocausts.

129	( )	(what holocaust?)
130	Joseph	thas pretty much what the holocaust <u>wa:s</u>

it was Hitler tryin to op<u>press</u> and <u>silence</u>
those people that <u>he</u> didn like. (1.5)
we can't <u>do</u> that.

After some rumbling, the teacher solicits "other views" (135). In response, Selah turns to Joseph.

```
135  Teacher  any (.) other (.) views?
136  Andrew   good ⌜point good point.
137  Selah         ⌞yeah.
138  Teacher  let it out ⌜go ahead
139  Selah              ⌞okay. are you just trying to- (.3) like (.2)
              argue //for this point? or do you really feel like that.
```

By changing the topic from the content of Griffin's argument to the nature of Joseph's commitment to his position, Selah foregrounds a tension that pervades most of the rest of the discussion: *Is this how you really feel?* The talk that immediately followed set my ethnographic antennae twitching. Listening and typing, I laughed and remembered faces and stories and conversations and field trips and hours spent with students in and out of school. The sequence touched a primary nerve, electric, connected to so much of my thinking.[10] The talk became the first major topographical feature of the First Amendment discussion, both for the analysis and, as the analysis revealed, for participants themselves. The effort and space required by the original analysis of these exchanges earned them their own title: "the *bidness* episode."

Recall that there are two main interactional problems participants are working on in the First Amendment discussion. First, participants work to figure out what the argument will be about. More specifically, they work to determine the configuration of positions that will be available for students around Griffin's central claim of his special obligation to defend the First Amendment rights of the Ku Klux Klan. This first problem is one of building a *text* for their talk. The second problem has to do with building a *context* for their talk.[11] This at least includes defining their situation, defining their relations with each other, and defining the relation between their local project and non-local, social, and cultural matters. The sequences that constitute what I call "the *bidness* episode"—starting with Selah's question to Joseph and ending with Selah's assertion of her own position vis-à-vis Griffin's argument—provide some raw materials for dealing with these problems, and provide details both to the participants and to the analysis.

---

[10]In the original analysis (Raley, 2003), I spent a lot of energy (and space) identifying the broad range of analytic possibilities contained within the boundaries of a single turn, Andrew's /*why y'all in my man bidness?*/. That effort forced me back out to the discussion, which organized the analysis briefly reported here.

[11]Also recall that the boundary between text and context is blurry. *Text* and *context* are mutually constitutive.

The *Bidness* Episode

Figure 5.2 describes the analysis of the *bidness* episode. Because so much of the talk in the *bidness* episode reaches across turn, sequences, and episode boundaries, the analysis is displayed immediately alongside the transcript.

What do participants achieve in the *bidness* episode? What does the *bidness* episode offer them? First, both teacher and students confirm a group norm: It is not all right to ask what a person "really feels." This is an important achievement, and seems to make it possible for students to argue for positions without having to worry about being held personally accountable for them. Second, students achieve a game of complex play, built not around the metacommunicative statement, *This is play*, but rather built around the metacommunicative question, *Is this play?* (Bateson, 1972). This is no small feat, given the apparent seriousness of much of the talk in the episode.

Students have to work hard to keep *Is this play?* on the table. Keeping the question on the table, moreover, also keeps an answer relevant. This is an important point vis-à-vis the risky topics these students are figuring out how to talk about. With Griffin's essay as the seed of the text students are building, it is hard to avoid the risk altogether. Selah's question to Joseph—/*are you just trying to . . . argue for this point? or do you really feel like that*/—makes avoidance practically impossible. In the first place, Selah's question *localizes* the risks. They no longer reside inside the topic of the discussion but are, abruptly, right here, right now. Her question also *personalizes* the risk associated with these newly local tensions, placing Joseph on the proverbial hot seat. Whatever answer Joseph gives next matters *to* Selah, but may matter more *for* Joseph. The risk is that Selah and Joseph could push each other apart, or even that Joseph could be forced out of the conversation on personal grounds. In the rush of talk that follows, beginning with Andrew's /*why y'all in my man bidness?*/, the world of the discussion stays dangerous but the local, personal risk is *distributed*. Joseph's answer to Selah's /*. . . do you really feel like that*/ no longer matters so much. What matters instead is everybody's answers to the question *Is this play?* The immediate risk is that the group will fall apart over this. Of course, things work out. When the conversation gets serious again, quickly, Larry introduces new material for the group to work on. The group ends up laughing together, and Joseph walks out of class saying /*now that was fun*/. By making an answer to the question, *Is this play?* the appropriate next move, students redistribute the situational risk from the individual, who would bear the responsibility for his or her position, across the members of the group, who jointly bear the responsibility for deciding whether or not they will be playing or fighting.

135 **Teacher** any (.) other (.) views?

136 **Andrew** good ⌈point good point.

137 **Selah** ⌊yeah.

138 **Teacher** let it out ⌈go ahead

139 **Selah** ⌊okay. are you just trying to- (.3) like (.2)
       argue ⌈for this point? or do you really feel like that.

140 **Larry** ⌊°I'd drop a little bomb°

- - - - - - - ➤

141 **Andrew** why y'all in my man bidness?

142 **Selah** wai-⌈w- wai- w- WAIT no:=

143 **Joseph** ⌊enh henh-heh

144 **Andrew** =why you all in my man ⌈bidness?
                                    ⌊I a(h)m not up in

145 **Selah** h(h)i ⌊b(h)is

146 **Rachel** ⌈he-heh-heh-heh-⌈heh

147 **Liliana** ⌊he-HAH-⌈HAH-HAH-HAH

148 **Andrew** ⌊why you all in
       my man ⌈bidness?

149 **Teacher** .⌊n(h)- n- n(hh)

150 **Andrew** why you all in my man bidness?

- - - - - - - ➤

In direct response to the teacher's soliciting "other views," Selah asks Joseph if he "really feels" the position he has just outlined in support of Griffin's defense of the Klan's First Amendment rights. Selah's question foregrounds a tension around public accountability for personal positions that will pervade the rest of the First Amendment discussion.

Andrew confronts Selah. Andrew is not asking as much as he is *telling* Selah to get out of Joseph's "bidness." In rescuing – perhaps even *preventing* – Joseph from having to answer Selah's question, Andrew may also be enforcing a social norm against asking directly what any person "really feels."

Andrew's talk has all the features of a <u>tease</u> (Drew, 1987). Not only is it in a sequential environment where teases typically occurs, but it is also *exaggerated, formulaic,* and set *in direct contrast* to Selah's content and style. As a tease, it has both a serious aspect and grounds for its own interpretation as <u>nonserious</u>. In spite of Selah's initial strong denial, Selah treats Andrew's talk as an accusation deserving a <u>serious</u> response. Joseph laughs. Laughter builds across Andrew's three repetitions, so that by the end Selah, Rachel, Liliana, and even the teacher have laughed or are laughing. In the absence of any strong competing claims, we may argue that Andrew's repetitions are designed with this laughter in mind.

Whether it *responds to* the available nonseriousness of Andrew's talk or *works on* Andrew's talk to make it nonserious, all this laughter helps to build a <u>nonserious</u> or "play" <u>frame</u> around the interaction.

FIG. 5.2. (Continued).

In an elaboration of the serious aspect of Andrew's prior turns, the Teacher describes a formal rule for conduct in "effective discussions." Liliana and Selah treat the Teacher's talk as "serious," invoking a serious, not-play frame for their talk. Teacher, Liliana, and Selah dispute the definition of Selah's question as an attack. They do not dispute the content of the norm, only its application.

At the same time, Larry and Andrew produce a "split" or "schism," building a neighboring line of talk. Pointing to a photo of Griffin on the first page of the essay, Larry proposes that Joseph and Griffin look alike. Larry's utterance is explicitly additive; that is, not only might Joseph share Griffin's personal position (Selah's question), but Joseph may look like Griffin too. The idea that Griffin and Joseph look alike is laughable. In this way, Larry's utterance reaches back to propose a "play" frame for Selah's initial question.

Teacher and Selah argue the application of the norm. Selah withdraws, begrudgingly.

In spite of what might have been closure of the earlier sequence, Larry replays the sequence, using the first part of a question-answer pair to effectively demand Andrew's attention. Besides keeping Andrew temporarily engaged, the timing of the sequences between Larry and Andrew invite a reframing of the whole activity as play by reaching across to the neighboring talk. As before, laughter helps to ratify their activity as play.

Andrew's last utterance to Selah is an unambiguous directive, though it exaggerates the application of the norm by extending it beyond the bounds of this "effective discussion."

151-
159

→ Teacher   wait a minute wait a minute
             effective discussion is not
             attacking the person
             it's talking

Larry   ((pointing to photo))
         that look a little bit
         like Joseph too

Liliana   she's asking a question though

Andrew   a(h)(h)::w

Selah   tha- thas why I asked him

Group   (loud laughter)

Teacher   I know but-
           it- it's about talking about
           the issues.

Andrew   thas crucial

- - - - - - →

158-
169

→ Teacher   I know but-
             it- it's about talking about
             the issues.
             so whether or not Joseph (2)
             actually believes this or not

Selah   okay okay fine

Larry   don it?

Teacher [is not important. (.)
         then tha-

Andrew   oh: [hhh

Selah   thas beside the point the:n

Larry   [heh-heh

Teacher   it's about talking about

Andrew   don be tryin
          to ask him [after class neither

Teacher   [the issues that are::

( )   [(   )

Teacher   (   )

( )   [yeah right

- - - - - - →

145

170 **Larry**: [[don be ( )
171 **Selah**: [my [thing is::
172 **Joseph**:   [hunh hunh heh hh
173 **Liliana**:   (I be talkin. aright?)
174 **Selah**: my thing is that,
in the history of the United States (.4)
the Klu Klux Klan has ha:d (.7)
a negative impact (.7)
and it's been more than just freedom of speech.
they- they've carried out (.3)
actions of killing? (.3)
and torturing people. so:- (1.4)
I see your point that we need to:o support or-
he would feel like he needed to support
everybody's freedom of speech,
but when they have (.6)
things like that behind in the past like that?
of- of violence? and negativity? and oppressing? (.6)
African-Americans? (.7)
then it- it turns into a different story.
it's- it's different then.

The talk that follows, especially Joseph's laughter, appears to reassert the nonserious or "play" frame of Andrew's earlier teasing sequence.

Selah returns to the work of configuring an argument. The group follows, but now with the following local resources:

a) a norm for conduct that says that it is not appropriate to publicly identify or challenge someone's "real" beliefs

b) the possibility that whatever they are doing, they are playing

FIG. 5.2. Analysis of the *bidness* episode.

Building *Texts* and *Contexts*

From the bidness episode, participants continue working on both interactional problems, text and context. Just as the problems of text and context are not independent of one another, so participants' work on these problems is hard to isolate. The work weaves in and out, and any single utterance often works on both problems at the same time.[12] In what follows, I analyze two different segments of talk from the middle of the discussion, places where work on the text is explicit and simultaneous work on the context can be sorted out. Both segments begin with a student proposing a new position for the emerging configuration of positions in the unfolding argument. In both segments, the proposed position is rejected by other students. Both segments, then, are observably consequential for the *text* of the discussion. Both segments are also places where the context of the discussion is shaped, though in ways the analysis must strive to identify.

Although his proposed position is soundly and pointedly rejected, Andrew does not give up easily. In the next piece of the segment, Andrew uses a novel set of tactics. Here, he publicly declares his personal view as a kind of *retreat* from the configuration of positions. By defining his proposal as what he would do, he effectively removes it from group consideration.

```
205- Liliana    he wouldn-
210  Andrew     I would u:se it to bust em up
     Selah      from within?
     Andrew     I would use it
                you know what I'm sayin
                to find ⌜sumpn else out
     Selah              ⌞( ) they're also like, you know,
                threatening and stuff.
     Andrew     thas what I would do.
```

If Andrew is retreating with his claim, then Joseph's next utterance appears to take his retreat seriously. Joseph's "so::" proposes a firm transition into a new line of talk. Simultaneous with the start of Joseph's talk, Eddie makes a statement that keeps Andrew's proposal alive. No one follows Joseph's lead, and for the next several turns the group continues to work on Andrew's position.

---

[12]The mutually constitutive relation between text and context, as between culture and social interaction, has been explored at length and with great care by many social scientists, including especially anthropologists. See Bateson (1972), Birdwhistell (1970), Frake (1980), Garfinkel (1967), Gumperz (1977), McDermott (1977), Mehan and Wood (1975), Varenne and McDermott (1998).

179-
204

Andrew I mean if you de<u>fen</u>d em
Larry jes leave em alo:ne
Andrew if you de<u>fen</u>d em
 you know what m sayin
 you get to know em on a more personal <u>lev</u>el
 you |might (.) be able to find sumpn about

Selah what- what (GET)
Peet that's <u>cold</u>

((*lots of overlapping talk*))

Andrew n-n-n-n-N-NO
 NO-NO LOOK.
 NAH-N-NAH| LOOK.

Alicia (that's <u>BULL</u>.)

Andrew you might be able to find sumpn about (.)
 the |Ku Klux Klan
 that you might not have been able
 to <u>find</u> about.
 you might have |been able to use that
 in a different situa

Peet (that's <u>cold</u>)

Peet whatchyu gon find? (..)
Liliana how would you (tell me that)
Peet HUH whatchu gon find?

Andrew YOU CAN FIND
 you can |find out a flaw
 in the Ku Klux Klan
 that you can probably <u>use</u> |in- later
 to bust them up though

Selah thas not what Joseph was
Peet now <u>what</u> would you find?
Manny <u>nah</u>
Liliana but if- I don think he wouldn want
Manny no:o
Miriam <u>he:ll</u> no.

211-
234

Eddie   (you) could use it against their own

( )   they find out ⌈they gon kill you?
Andrew   ⌊ba- know what m sayin?
Peet   (I'm not with y'all) on that one

Joseph   so:o it's not that they're- (always so   )
         they also have like (   )
         um:::m

Joseph   (   ) already threatened their life

Larry   y'all both ⌈smoke some crack
Selah   ⌊shut up Eddie
Rachel   henh heh-hunh-⌈heh heh
Eddie   ⌊I feel Andrew ⌈(   )
Peet   ⌊all three of 'em

Andrew   you feelin me E ro:gue?
         you feelin me ro:gue?
Selah   thas not cool

Joseph   the reason he would want to do this is tha:t (.6)
         if he can sho::w
         if he shows that-

Larry   ((accusingly))
         °y'all not going to do that Black-on-Black crime°
Peet   ⌈henh-heh
Rachel   ⌊HENH-heh-⌈heh
Sarah   ⌊hah-henh-heh-henh
Peet   ⌊HAH-heh-heh-heh
Eddie   hah-heh-hah

FIG. 5.3.

Although the group does continues to discuss Andrew's proposal in this last piece of the segment, the nature of the present talk is different from the prior talk. Here, the transition that would leave Andrew's proposal behind is imminent, or at least possible. Andrew has begun a retreat into a personal perspective, a region the group has already marked effectively off-limits (see Fig. 5.2). Joseph's talk is headed in a different direction. In the language of this chapter, Andrew's proposal does not look like it will be part of the *text* the group is building. So what is going on in the group's continued talk about Andrew's perspective?

I propose that the group's later talk in this segment is primarily responsive to their problem of *context*. In the first part of this segment, Andrew was challenged directly and forcefully by several members of the group, including Manny, who is otherwise practically silent. (Remembering Andrew's earlier confrontation with Selah, we might see this as a case of tables being turned.) From there, Eddie commits and Andrew confirms Eddie's personal support, all in a highly marked local vernacular. Among these youth, to say that you *feel* another person may or may not signal total agreement with that person's ideas or actions, but it at least communicates *empathy*. And Andrew's use of *"rogue"* is even more notably marked. Where "man," "dude," "brother" (or "bruh"), and other personal nouns are often used as tag-referents, "rogue" may be used uniquely by young people in Bayview.[13]

In addition to the public show of support, the group manages to build their activity around the question, *Is this play?* As in the *bidness* episode, Larry is near the center of the action. Larry's first turn, *"y'all both smoke some crack,"* is a teasing way to reject Andrew and Larry, comparing them to habitual drug users. In his second turn—*"y'all not going to do that Black-on-Black crime"*—Larry redefines the local confrontation (over Andrew's proposal) as a member of a commonly referred-to class of criminal behavior (crimes committed by African Americans against other African Americans). Larry hardly owns the label "Black-on-Black crime." On the contrary, it is a widely used label for a commonly recognized kind of problem, a label one might read in a newspaper headline or legislative policy report. It is also the label most frequently used by residents to condemn crime when it occurs in Bayview. Larry not only exaggerates the confrontation, he does so

---

[13]My own time in Bayview revealed that youth tend to be aware of "*rogue's*" distinctiveness, citing it as one clear way to know whom you are talking to (a person *from* Bayview) and where you might be standing (*in* Bayview). In fact, students were generally as aware about ideologies of language (cf. Schieffelin et al., 1998) as they were aware of ideologies of race, class, and geography.

with a creative turn to the "outside" world.[14] The laughter that follows answers the question: *Yes, this is play.*

Over this last set of turns, participants manage to re-confirm their relations as mutually supportive and re-orient their activity around the question of play. Moreover, they achieve all of this with many of the same resources (and persons) used in the earlier *bidness* episode. In their use of non-local resources (e.g., the label "Black-on-Black crime"), participants begin to sort out their relationships to the social and cultural world outside the school. Students again treat the world outside the classroom, including that part of the world where race is a dangerous material, more as a building material than a house they must inhabit.

In another segment from further along in the discussion, the group goes through many of the same motions. Again, they manage to assert a "play" frame, and they manage to distribute risk across persons. At the beginning of the segment, Larry re-asserts a position that the group had earlier considered but not incorporated into their building *text*. If we take Selah's utterance seriously (342), there appears to be some enthusiasm for the position this time. As we might now expect, Joseph offers a rebuttal (343).

```
340  Larry            we not- silencing them
                   we just ┌not supportin them.
341  Selah               └henh-heh
342  Selah    (   ) o:::oh ┌true da:t
343  Joseph              └no:: but look-
             if you refuse to defend their free speech
             thas sayin- thas like saying I want to silence them.
             if we try- if we tried to do something like that
             to like silence ┌someone that we didn li:ke
344  Alicia               └.hh hhhhhh
```

Larry hardly concedes the point, instead repeating it as if it were a brand new idea (345). Over the short course of just a few turns, highlighted by a joking exchange between Andrew and Larry, the group once again proves impossible to transcribe, laughing and overlapping in several side sequences.

---

[14]Bakhtin (1981, 1986) and Volosinov (1978) write at length about the sources and functions of reported speech. The following quote is of the sort one is likely to find.

> At any moment in the development of the dialogue there are immense, boundless masses of forgotten contextual meanings, but at certain moments . . . they are recalled and invigorated in renewed form (in a new context). Nothing is absolutely dead: every meaning will have its homecoming festival. (Bakhtin, 1986, p. 170)

345 Larry   how bout ⌈we jes leave em alo:ne and go on with they <u>day</u>?
346 Joseph   ⌊that would be just
347 Andrew   let em go on about they bidness?
348 Larry   <u>ye:ah</u>=
349 Andrew   =have a Coke and a smile?
350 Larry   ye⌈(h)ah
351 Joseph   ⌊henh
352 Peet   hhhh
353 Rachel   why- why why ⌈was they tryin to get more (   )
354 Larry   ⌊burn some more crosses if you like
355 Andrew   hhh heh heh henh je(h)s don bring it in <u>my</u> la:(h)wn
356 Scotty   <u>yea:h</u>
357 Teacher the whole issue is surrounding
358 (   )   (don bother me)
359 (   )   ((overlapping talk))
360 Teacher the u:mm (1.8)
361 Manny   <u>I</u> wou:⌈:ldn
362 Joseph   ⌊°m:: y'all <u>trippin</u> °

Over the next few turns, the Teacher does finally succeeds in her efforts to get the group back on track, but Larry's position that a person can *respect* without *acting to defend* the First Amendment rights of the Klan is preserved as one of three positions the group will eventually deliberate.

What about the *contexts* that participants are always working on, that are always mutually constitutive with the group's *texts*? Andrew's question (347) looks like a request for clarification from Larry, perhaps notable for the way /bidness/ echoes his earlier confrontation with Selah in the *bidness* episode. In this segment, while Andrew's question accelerates the tempo of the group's talk so that it eventually becomes impossible to transcribe, it also slows the discussion down, giving the group some time to consider the implications of Larry's claim. Larry had asserted the same position much earlier, with identical wording:

178 Larry   u:m:: (1.2)
              so why would you (I couldn)
              why would you defend somebody
              with so much <u>hate</u> that <u>kill</u> people (.4)
              burn <u>crosses</u> in people's <u>lawns</u> (.4)
              um:: (.4)
              <u>lynch</u> (.2) people of <u>color</u>? (1.7)

why would you wanna de<u>fend</u> somebody like that,
wouldn you wanna: (.8)

179 **Andrew** I mean if you ⌜de<u>fend</u> em
180 **Larry**   ⌞jes leave em alo:ne
181   (1.8)

This earlier iteration of the position may have been buried as the group turned to rejecting Andrew's position that *"if you defend em . . . you might be able to find sumpn . . . to bust them up."* In the segment at hand, Andrew's question reserves some space for Larry's position in the group's emerging text. In this way, Andrew supports Larry's work.

But it is the second utterance of the segment—*/have a Coke and a smile?/* (349)—that makes it one of the most analytically challenging (and entertaining) of the whole discussion. "Have a Coke and a smile" was a famous slogan for Coca-Cola, first appearing as a song lyric in television commercials in 1979. So what is it doing here, in this discussion, used (and evidently understood) by kids who were not yet born by the time the ad campaign was phased out? The original intent of the slogan was probably straightforward: connect Coke with pleasure, and do so with a tune that people will keep humming. Despite its original use, I understood the phrase, and may even have used it myself, as an ambiguously insincere wish-you-well, a pat-you-on-the-back-while-I-push-you-down-the-stairs kind of comment. Of course, such understandings do not constitute an analysis. Here is how an actual analysis could go.

Some part of me recalled having heard the phrase from a comedian, perhaps Eddie Murphy. Because the students were not close at hand during the analysis, I asked my brother-in-law what he thought. A hip-hop aficionado, he was able to name several musical artists who had included the phrase in rap lyrics. He didn't remember any comedian. I turned to the World Wide Web and searched for the phrase. Websites for Coke fan clubs and Coca-Cola memorabilia—as well as some "remember the 1980s" websites—were easy to spot. My brother-in-law was right about the rap songs; the search also turned up more than a few websites with transcribed rap lyrics. Several websites, and more than a few chatrooms, used the phrase in ways that resonated with my basic sense of its double meaning. And several websites attributed the first use of the phrase to an African American comedian, though about half credited Eddie Murphy and half Richard Pryor. From the clues, and after a drive to the video rental store, I reconstructed the following.

During the 1980s, Eddie Murphy starred in two feature-length film productions of his standup comedy: *Delirious* (Gowers, 1983), and its follow-up,

Raw (Townsend, 1987). Like many comedians before him, African American and otherwise, Murphy was criticized for his obscenity, especially for his use of the "n-word," his apparent homophobia, and his crude, explicit talk of sex. Among his most public critics was Bill Cosby, the acclaimed African American comedian and onetime spokesperson for Coca-Cola. According to Murphy's account in *Raw*, Cosby called Murphy and scolded him for his use of profanity. Murphy later recounted his conversation with Cosby to Richard Pryor, another African American comedian, famous in the 1970s for his genre-transforming, (for some, frighteningly) obscene comedy. As Murphy retells it, Pryor recommended that Murphy "tell Bill (Cosby) to have a Coke and smile and shut the fuck up."

What's so funny about that? Murphy (and Pryor) transformed "have a Coke and a smile" into a masterfully double-edged sword of a phrase. As such, the phrase has since found its way into more common usage, including contemporary rap music. It has also, evidently, found its way into the U.S. History class at Pacifica College Prep. Here, "have a Coke and a smile" is the beginning of a playful sequence involving Andrew, Larry, Joseph, and Peet, where they play-act the position of permitting but not defending the Klan's First Amendment rights. Students again manage to ask and answer the question, *Is this play?*, and they do so using whatever materials are available.

Arguing, Finally

Eventually, students configure three distinct positions. The first of these positions is most forcefully presented by Joseph, though others soon join in. It is a position based on a person's right to a point-of-view. Underlying the local position is a philosophical stance that one's rights are inviolable. It may be summarized:

> *Defending the Klan's First Amendment rights is a matter of moral principle. The First Amendment rights of the Klan are inviolable, no matter how we feel about the Klan or their activities.*

The second position, offered in a rough form by Selah early on and expanded by Selah and others over the course of the discussion, rejects Griffin's claim regarding the defense of the Klan's rights by denying those rights altogether. It is a position explicitly built with history and race. Underlying this local position is a philosophical stance that one's rights are dependent, in this case on one's prior actions. It goes something like this:

> *No one should defend the Klan's First Amendment rights because the Klan doesn't deserve them. The Klan forfeited those rights by committing hateful—and illegal— crimes against people of color.*

A third position supports the Klan's rights, but opposes Griffin's argument about the defense of those rights. This argument rests on a distinction between *defending* and *respecting* the Klan's rights, worrying that paying so much attention to the Klan is likely to give them more credibility than they deserve. Although it references history and race, the position is built with everyday materials of front lawns and neighborhoods. Any underlying philosophical stance is hard to make out, but could be inferred as more or less utilitarian.

> *No one should defend the Klan's First Amendment rights, at least not in public, because to do so lends credibility to their cause. It is possible to respect the Klan's First Amendment rights without publicly defending or supporting these rights.*

The two most prominent positions, the first and second of the three just described, are most fully articulated by Joseph and Selah in the following segment. Here, with a quick nod to the preceding topics of hate crimes and marches, Joseph provides the basic outline of the position he has been developing all along: the Klan's First Amendment rights are inviolable, no matter what we think of their activities (414, 416).

```
414  Joseph                                                unfortunately
               what it comes down to is tha:t
415  (    )     (insane)
416  Joseph    the lawyer recognized the fact tha:t (.4)
               no they don't have the right to do hate crimes
               but when they do things like marches against (.4)
               minorities or marches against (.2)
               homosexuals or whatever (.6)
               sadly enough according to the constitution
               they have a right to do that. (.4)
               they have every right to do that if they choose to.
               they have the right to assemble
               they have the right to free speech.
               and regardless if those views disagree with us
               or the fact tha:t (1.4)
               we do:: not (.) in any way care for their: (.) actions
               or: (.) their pa:st (.8)
```

they have a right to <u>do</u> things like that
an if- and

Selah interjects (417), and after the beginnings of a question from Joseph
(418), Selah articulates the basic thrust of the position she has been developing.

417 **Selah**   so why they wouldn say no (   )?
418 **Joseph**   that's the same <u>thing</u> it's like (.3)
                  how c'we validate our ow-
                  how could <u>we</u>: say ⌐that
419 **Selah**   ⌐cuz we were <u>oppressed</u> and we didn <u>have</u>
                  we didn have the same <u>rights</u> as everybody else
420 **Peet**   <u>yeah</u>
421 **Selah**   it was <u>obvious</u>.
                  people were gettin: (.) beaten up and thrown out of p- places
                  jus because they were <u>Black</u>.
422   (.8)
423 **Larry**   then why would ⌐you de- WHY why
424 **Alicia**   ⌐it had the (   )
425 **Andrew**   b- bu- bu- but but ⌐<u>look</u> tho:ugh.
426 **Larry**   ⌐why would you defend <u>them</u>?

At least two facts of Joseph's and Selah's utterances are worth mentioning.
The first is the shrinking distance between the students and the positions
they have been working to articulate, most clearly evident in the use of pro-
nouns. For the first time, students use /we/ and /us/ to refer to both those who
would defend the Klan's First Amendment rights and the victims of the
Klan's—and others'—racism. The latter use is especially notable in Selah's
clear, repeated substitution of /we/ for the historical *they* who were dispos-
sessed of basic civil rights (419).

The second fact involves the local construction of race. Not only are *they*
now /we/, but *they[we] /were gettin: beaten up and thrown out of places just because they[we] were black/*. That these students are Black/African American/
People-of-color is now an inescapably relevant fact, not just for these stu-
dents-as-young-people-in-Bayview but for these students-as-holders-of-
positions in *this* discussion. Race may be, after all, a thing students have been
talking about all along. Up to this point, anyway, race has been relatively
mute, or at least distanced from students' selves. Now publicly connected to
how these students view themselves, race is a fact newly present for the

group.[15] Any risk that might be attached to race, to the defense of civil rights, to historical experience, is unavoidably personal.

Joseph, Selah, and Larry are not alone in grappling with race and responsibility, at least not for very long. From this point forward, for all but the last minute or so when the teacher and students bring the day to a close, students argue from personal, fully engaged positions and race remains in the visible (or audible) foreground. The following selection is representative of the rest of the First Amendment discussion (emphasis added).

```
      478  Teacher  =who's going to determine the ⌐validity?
      479  Alicia                              └Selah's just ⌐arg(h)uing=
  → 480  Selah                                            └ME:e.
      481  Alicia   =⌐⌐that it has to be something done to you.=
      482  Teacher  =└└heh-  heh-hah heh-hah
  → 483  Selah              me. right her:e,
      484  Joseph           thas true
      485  Joseph   who determines the ⌐va-
      486  Selah                        └thank you.
      487           hey. who determines which one is valid?
      488  Teacher  lemme tell ⌐you guys-
      489  Selah               └wait a minute of course its valid.
               I mean it- it's- it's- it's written on the wall.
      490  Teacher  so what if ⌐(there are other people who)
      491  Andrew              └whether it's right or not you know what m sayin=
      492  Teacher  =⌐⌐think the other group is valid?
      493  Andrew   =└└is a whole nuther issu:e.
      494  Selah    what you me-? hhh
  → 495  Joseph    cuz then we tried to=
      496  Selah    =why- why are they marching though?
               look at- look at the basis. look-
               look at the root of why they're marching
  → 497  Joseph    that's what they believe. we believe-
               when we (.) march we believe that we deserve the rights,
               the same rights as everyone else deserves.
               we ⌐believe that we deserve
      498  Alicia      └Selah's saying that there are actions that are taken
```

─────────────────

[15]Becker (1984) might call this a move from a contextual relation of *silencing* (i.e., not really making this about race, at least not in a personal way) to *personalizing* (i.e., making it clear that this is at the same time about race and also about everyone involved).

→ 499   Andrew   some people said
                 we weren't even ⌐people
    500 Joseph   ⌐(here's) what they believe.
                 we might not agree with that
    501 Alicia   the other group was jus marching ⌐just to march to say ( )
→ 502 Joseph   ⌐just as the rest of America
                 ⌐may not agree with us.
    503 Larry   ⌐we had a cause
→ 504 Andrew   hold on in- when we were marchin
    505   ((lots of overlapping talk))
→ 506 Andrew   HOLD ON HOLD ON HOLD ON HOLD ON (.2)
                 HOLD ON hold on.
                 when white people- I mean when we were marchin
                 and white people didn believe we had the right to march
                 and we weren't people?
                 jes because they didn believe in the same thing we believe in,
                 do we still have the right to march?
    507 Selah   yeah. but you kno:w (.) y-
                 they stepped in and they stopped a lot of it. (.4)
                 and people were killed (.2)
                 and people were ⌐beaten
    508 Andrew   ⌐we- were they right?
    509 Selah   what?
    510 Andrew   were they right for steppin in and killin people?
    511 Selah   NO:oo.
    512   (.8)
    513 Selah   but ⌐st- in in
    514 Andrew   ⌐then when- how could we ⌐say that we c-
→ 515 Selah   ⌐in those actions
                 they weren't allowing us to free speech
→ 516 Andrew   EXACTLY
                 we're fightin for free speech
                 why not let (.) another man that we don't-
                 we don't agree wid his opinion why- (..)
                 why we takin-

The discussion is now about what we may do and about what has happened to us, where we are not White people, and where we marched for civil
rights. The move to a fully engaged, personal argument may also be understood as a re-organization of materials for the construction of identities. Al-

though no person is required to take up Selah's call, the individual identity of Black/African American/Person-of-Color is at least publicly *available*, along with a collective identity that is evidently organized around the experience of race and history. In short, at least part of what this discussion becomes is the negotiation of who (or what) I/we are allowed to be.

The discussion ends abruptly, as Alicia notices me glance at my watch and word spreads that the discussion has extended past the scheduled end of class. The teacher promises that the group will return to the argument and tempts the group with the promise of a personal story. Andrew, apparently unable to stop arguing with whatever talk comes his way, challenges the teacher (874).

```
651  Teacher                         we're only two minutes after
                      an I jus wanna ⌈tell you
652  Peet                            ⌊class been over?=
653  Liliana    =FIVE ⌈minutes after
654  Alicia            ⌊FIVE minutes
655  Teacher    no- no no
656  Scotty     why you didn stop it?
657  Joseph     it's nine thirty ⌈three.
658  Alicia                       ⌊this clock is wrong.
659  Peet       hey I'd ra- it's ⌈(   ) let's blow.
660  Joseph                      ⌊it's nine thirty three
                it's only three    minutes over
661  Scotty                      sh:: h
662  Rachel                      its three minutes after
663  Teacher    we will:
664  Peet       yes, that is (   )
665  Teacher    we will return to this
666  Alicia     thank ⌈you, Jason
667  Teacher          ⌊on Frida:ay
                henh-heh and um: (.4)
                I have a s- (.5)
                I'll tell you my story on Friday
668  Andrew     why we couldn get the story today?
```

Joseph's final comment, the last transcribable utterance in the recording of the First Amendment discussion, is one I missed hearing that day and did not notice until I finished transcribing. In retrospect, it is the best explanation for my intuitive interest in this discussion.

669 Joseph   now that was fun.

DISCUSSION

> We do not, of course, have in mind anything like a conclusive definition of
> these concepts. Such a definition (insofar as any scientific definition may be
> called conclusive) might come at the end of a study, but not at its beginning.
> (Volosinov, 1973, p. 45)

If the only important achievement of the First Amendment Discussion were
the definition and enforcement of a norm for social behavior, we could proceed with a more or less conventional understanding of safety. We might say
that the norm prohibiting participants from challenging each other's "real"
beliefs *shelters* students from the scorn of their colleagues, making it easier for
them to try out potentially volatile perspectives and identities. The support
students offer each other, often loudly, and the ongoing achievement of a
"play" frame would expand, but ultimately support, this conventional view of
safety-as-shelter. Whatever these folks are doing, they manage to be playing,
so students are sheltered from things ever getting too serious. Stretching the
idea: Not only are students "safe" to "try out" perspectives and identities, but
are "safe" to "play with" their underlying tensions. Ultimately, any of these
could also resonate with the idea that "being safe" at Pacifica means "being
able to be yourself" (or selves).

Looking more carefully, we get permission to think about another version
of safety, one located closer to the edge of the group's forward motion, in the
many moments when whatever comes next will matter for whether this discussion ends as *fun*. In "A Theory of Play and Fantasy," Gregory Bateson
(1972) recognized a "complex form of play, the game which is constructed
not upon the premise 'this is play' but rather around the question 'Is this
play?'" (p. 182). Across the First Amendment discussion, participants do not
merely propose and accept that what is going on is "play," but rather play
with the "exuberances" of their language (Becker, 1984), inviting each other
to help decide if what they are doing is fighting or playing or both. The pattern recurs again and again. The risks that reside in the First Amendment discussion get localized and personalized, until the group creates circumstances
of uncertainty—*Is this play?*—they must work together to resolve.

In this class on this day, students not only have to worry that what they are
doing could be fighting, but they appear to introduce opportunities for such
worry. Participation in any social scene requires that participants achieve

some "working consensus" about what they are up to (Goffman, 1976; Kendon, 1990; McDermott & Roth, 1978). This "more complex form of play" operates as a direct challenge to consensus. Twisting a phrase, we might call it "working *uncertainty*." Unlike the natural, everyday uncertainty that is "normatively residual" for social interactions (Goffman, 1976), the ambiguities underlying much of the talk in the First Amendment discussion cannot be resolved by recourse to the internal features of an utterance, nor can they be resolved by reference to the "activity frame" (Frake, 1977; Goffman, 1974; Tannen & Wallat, 1993).[16] The surface form of students' talk does not provide the grounds for its definitive interpretation, and knowing whether this is an "effective discussion," a lecture, a therapy session, or a round of the "dozens" will not ultimately determine whether any of this talk is an invitation to fight or to laugh together. To be sure, both the individual utterance and the activity frame nudge participants in some general direction, but neither provide participants with enough materials to finally decide exactly *how* to interpret whatever it is they are doing.

Faced with "working uncertainty," where do participants turn? Without easy recourse to language or to larger activity frames, participants can only turn toward probabilistic beliefs about who they are and what they can expect from each other when they are together. In this way, the introduction of *working uncertainty* compels distinctive questions about whether and how participants <u>trust</u> each other. In their actions and next actions, participants not only ask the question "Can <u>I</u> trust <u>you</u> [i.e., to treat my action as playful]?" but also implicitly ask "Do <u>you</u> trust <u>me</u> [i.e., to play and not fight with you]?" *Working uncertainty* momentarily untangles the knotted threads of everyday social relations so that they can be seen and shared as trusting. This is the achievement of <u>trusting relations</u>, most clearly conceived by McDermott (1977, p. 199):

> I am talking about trust as a quality of the relations among people, as a product of the work they do to achieve a shared focus. Trust is achieved and managed through interaction (Garfinkel 1963; McDermott & Church 1976). It takes

---

[16]This use of "frame" is distinct from the way I use "frame" to describe the definition of this situation as "play." The concept of "activity frame" is meant to capture the reportable definition of a situation, much like the "what's going on" that defines Edelsky's (1981) "floor." College students will attend *lectures*, many adults in the United States spend an hour or more *in therapy* each week, and some African American males, among many others, will *play the dozens*. Each of these is an example of an "activity frame" that helps participants (and observers) understand what is going on at any specific moment. What I mean by frame owes more to Bateson (1972) and is akin to Goffman's "key" (1974).

constant effort for two or more people to achieve trusting relations, and the slightest lag in that work can demand extensive remedial efforts. . . . Trust is not a property of persons but a product of the work people do to achieve trusting relations, given particular institutional products.

Answers to these trust-focused questions may be grounded in probabilistic beliefs, but the talk itself contains clues that make trust more readily available and recognizable. Specifically, the same utterances that introduce "working uncertainty" may also contain clues that remind students that they share some things in common. Andrew's /why y'all in my man bidness?/ may be uncertainly playful, but it is unmistakably a language known and spoken in this place, by these young people when they are together. Larry's suggestion that the picture of Griffin /look like Joseph too/ may also be an offer of shared knowledge. In drawing the comparison, Larry may be drawing from a commonplace joke among Pacifica's students, in which they parody well-known racist claims to ignorance, that "all [Blacks, Latinos, Asians, etc.] look alike," to make a joke that fits the tense local environment.[17] So with Larry's later comments about "Black on Black crime" and the suggestion that the Klan "have a Coke and a smile." In any event, offers of shared knowledge may invite participants to trust each other as people with something in common (cf. Erickson & Shultz, 1982, on comembership).

Yet even as "working uncertainty" creates a special focus for trust, and offers of shared knowledge urge participants to see each other as persons with something in common, it is only when participants laugh together that they finally confirm their trust and trustworthiness.[18] By laughing together, partic-

---

[17]Pacifica's students frequently poked fun at presumed similarities among members of a racial or ethnic group, and often in students' interactions with me. For an entire academic year, we shared a running joke in which students claimed that I looked "just like Tom Green," a young, white, male talk show host known for his gross-out humor and juvenile behavior. If I disputed the claim, students typically shrugged and explained with a laugh that "all you white folks look alike." On the one hand, this was funny because students knew that I "look White" but that I identify as both White and Latino. It was also funny because it appropriated and transformed the idea that "all [Blacks, Latinos, etc.] look alike." These encounters occasionally led to longer, playful teasing exchanges, where the comparisons would grow increasingly impossible— "all you Bayview kids look alike," "[Jason] looks just like [a female teacher]," etc.—not unlike the ritual insult exchanges Labov (1974) describes in detail. The point is that Larry could be doing much more than the surface form of his utterance, or even the available responses of his colleagues suggests.

[18]For more on "laughing-together" as a social phenomenon, see Glenn (2002), Jefferson et al. (1976), Jefferson (1985).

ipants display their answers to questions of trust: Yes, we can—and do—trust each other. Yet it is never easy. "Working uncertainty" is something that participants introduce and sustain, against the gravitational pull toward minimal consensus. And offers of shared knowledge partly work because they are subtle, available only to those who have something genuinely in common. Laughing-together may finally be a kind of celebration of the hard work of achieving trusting relations.

What we end up with is an understanding of *safety-as-possibility*. I intend a double meaning. In the first case, *safety-as-possibility* captures the experience of security and freedom to take risk. In the second case, *safety-as-possibility* captures the idea that safety itself is always *only* a possibility, a local, situated achievement of real people talking about real topics in real time. Safety is not a thing, inert, that we can locate in a design feature of a school. It is not a machine that we can design, build, and set running. Safety is, rather, a possibility that must get negotiated again and again.

CODA

The First Amendment discussion reveals something about Pacifica that does not make it into brochures or newspaper articles. Pacifica provides, or at least makes possible, some small experiences of democracy. David Tyack (1993), renowned historian of education, helps us to think about this point.

> [I]nequalities are often reproduced in schools, but schools can also become, as Dewey said, a microcosm of a just future society. Mere celebration of difference—making people feel better about themselves and less judgmental about others—evades the crucial issue of power. Dewey showed how schools might create an experience of democracy that would teach the young a process for shaping a common civic culture. In a socially diverse society, this pluralistic public culture needs constantly to be renegotiated. (p. 29)

But nobody gets to make democracy from scratch. The work, and ours, is fundamentally cultural.

> Human beings do not *adapt to* culture; they *work with* and they *make* culture. They do not create out of nothing, and what they make always exhibits the traces of the materials they borrow and how it was used in earlier interactions. (Varenne & McDermott, 1998, p. 215)

The materials that these children and adults have to work with in the First Amendment discussion—race, class, achievement, identity, and so on—are the same materials they have to work with in the rest of their lives at Pacifica College Prep. Pacifica's students and teachers can instruct us in this regard, for the materials they have to work with are the same materials that all of us in the wider society have to work with, no matter what we are doing. What's more, Pacifica's students and teachers must put together these materials in response to the same tensions that cut across the school, the community, and society. In the way they arrange these materials, then, students and teachers provide us ways of *addressing the wider system*. You see, children and adults *can* do public, critical thinking. They *can* negotiate the terms of authority. They *can* talk about race. And they *can* forge ways of trusting each other.

The end, now: What is possible for them, is possible for us.

REFERENCES

Bakhtin, M. M. (1981). *The dialogic imagination* (M. Holquist, Ed., and C. Emerson & M. Holquist, Trans.). Austin: University of Texas Press.

Bakhtin, M. M. (1986). *Speech genres and other late essays* (V. W. McGee, Trans.). Austin: University of Texas Press.

Bateson, G. (1972). A theory of play and fantasy. In *Steps to an ecology of mind* (pp. 177–193). San Francisco: Chandler Publishing Company. (Originally published 1955)

Bateson, G., & Mead, M. (1942). *Balinese character: A photographic analysis.* New York: The New York Academy of Sciences.

Becker, A. L. (1984). Biography of a sentence: A Burmese proverb. In E. M. Bruner (Ed.), *Text, play and story: The construction and reconstruction of self and society* (pp. 135–155). Prospect Heights, IL: Waveland Press.

Boostrom, R. (1998). 'Safe spaces': Reflections on an educational metaphor. *Journal of Curriculum Studies, 30*(4), 397–408.

Drew, P. (1987). Po-faced receipts of teases. *Linguistics, 25,* 219–253.

Edelsky, C. (1981). Who's got the floor? *Language in Society, 10,* 383–421.

Erickson, F., & Shultz, J. (1982). *The counselor as gatekeeper: Social interaction in interviews.* New York: Academic Press.

Frake, C. O. (1977). Plying frames can be dangerous: Some reflections on methodology in cognitive anthropology. *The Quarterly Newsletter of the Institute for Comparative Human Development, 1*(3), 1–7.

Goffman, E. (1974). *Frame analysis: An essay on the organization of experience.* London: Harper & Row.

Goffman, E. (1976). *Relations in public: Microstudies of the public order.* New York: Harper & Row.

Gowers, B. (1983). *Eddie Murphy Delirious* [Motion picture]. Hollywood: Paramount.

Gumperz, J. J., & Berenz, N. (1990). *Transcribing conversational exchanges.* Berkeley Cognitive Science Report No. 63. Berkeley, CA: Institute of Cognitive Studies.

Henry, J. (1963). *Culture against man.* New York: Vintage Books.

Jefferson, G. (1972). Side sequences. In D. Sudnow (Ed.), *Studies in social interaction* (pp. 294–338). New York: Free Press.

Jefferson, G. (1985). An exercise in the transcription and analysis of laughter. In T. van Dijk (Ed.), *Handbook of discourse analysis: Vol. 3. Discourse and dialogue* (pp. 25–34). London: Academic Press.

Kendon, A. (1990). *Conducting interaction: Patterns of behavior in focused encounters.* Cambridge: Cambridge University Press.

Labov, W. (1974). The art of sounding and signifying. In W. W. Gage (Ed.), *Language in its social setting* (pp. 84–116). Washington, DC: The Anthropological Society of Washington.

McDermott, R. P. (1977). Social relations as contexts for learning in school. *Harvard Educational Review, 47*(2), 198–213.

McDermott, R. P., & Roth, D. (1978). The social organization of behavior: Interactional approaches. *Annual Review of Anthropology, 7,* 321–345.

Mehan, H., & Wood, H. (1975). *The reality of ethnomethodology.* New York: Wiley.

Merton, R. K. (1987). Three fragments from a sociologist's notebooks: Establishing the phenomenon, specified ignorance, and strategic research materials. *Annual Review of Sociology, 13,* 1–28.

Ochs, E. (1979). Transcription as theory. In E. Ochs & B. Schiefflin (Eds.), *Developmental pragmatics* (pp. 43–72). New York: Academic Press.

Peshkin, A. (2001). *Permissible advantage?: The moral consequences of elite schooling.* Mahwah, NJ: Lawrence Erlbaum Associates.

Pollock, M. (2004). Race wrestling: Struggling strategically with race in educational practice and research. *American Journal of Education, 111,* 25–65.

Raley, J. D. (2003). *Safe spaces? A study of risk, trust, and learning at the margins.* Unpublished doctoral dissertation, Stanford University.

Sacks, H., Schegloff, E. A., & Jefferson, G. (1974). A simplest systematics for the organization of turn-taking for conversation. *Language, 50*(4), 696–735.

Schegloff, E. (1987). Between macro and micro: Contexts and other connections. In J. C. Alexander, B. Giesen, R. Münch, & N. J. Smelser (Eds.), *The micro–macro link* (pp. 207–234). Berkeley: University of California Press.

Schieffelin, B. B., Woolard, K. A., & Kroskrity, P. V. (1998). *Language ideologies: Practice and theory.* New York: Oxford University Press.

Tannen, D., & Wallat, C. (1993). Interactive frames and knowledge schemas in interaction. In D. Tannen (Ed.), *Framing in discourse* (pp. 57–76). New York: Oxford University Press.

Townsend, R. (1987). *Eddie Murphy Raw* [Motion picture]. Hollywood, CA: Paramount.

Varenne, H., & McDermott, R. (1998). *Successful failure: The school America builds.* Boulder, CO: Westview Press.

Volosinov, V. N. (1978). Reported speech. In L. Matejka & K. Pomorska (Eds.), *Readings in Russian poetics: Formalist and structuralist views* (pp. 149–175). (Translated by L. Matejka & I. R. Titunik). Ann Arbor, MI: Michigan Slavic Publications. (Work originally published 1930)

Wilkins, D. B. (1995). Race, ethics, and the First Amendment: Should a Black lawyer represent the Ku Klux Klan? *George Washington Law Review, 63,* 1030.

APPENDIX

Conventions Used for Transcribing Spoken Behavior

word ⌈word] ⌊word wo-]	**Overlaps:** Left brackets mark the point where current talk is overlapped by other talk. Generally, overlapping talk is indented to the point of initial overlap. Right brackets mark the point where overlapping talk ends.
⌈⌈word wor-] ⌊⌊word] word	**Simultaneous utterances:** Where two utterances begin simultaneously, *two* left brackets occur at the beginning of the lines. Right brackets mark the point where overlapping talk ends.
word= =word	**Turn latching:** The equals sign indicates "latching"—i.e., no interval between the end of a prior and the start of a next piece of talk. It is used for the relationship of a next speaker's talk to a prior speaker's, for the relationship of two parts of a same speaker's talk, and as a transcript convenience for managing long utterances which are overlapped at various points.
word(..)word word(#)word	**Pauses:** Each period within parentheses indicates a pause of about a tenth of a second. Each pound sign within parentheses indicates a pause of about a second.
(1.2)	**Timed pause:** Numbers in parentheses indicate elapsed time in tenths of seconds.
wo::rd	**Lengthening:** Colon(s) indicate that the immediately prior sound is lengthened.
wor- -henh-	**Cutoffs:** A short dash indicates an abrupt termination of a word or syllable, often a glottal stop. Can also be used at the beginning of words or syllables (particularly laughter particles) to indicate the release of a glottal stop.
w-w-w-word	**Stuttering:** Within a word, short dashes indicate stuttering.
?	**Rising pitch:** A question mark indicates rising pitch.
.	**Falling pitch:** A period indicates falling pitch.
,	**Continuing intonation:** A comma indicates continuing intonation, typically a falling–rising pitch.
word	**Stressing:** Underlining indicates some form of stressing, and may involve pitch and/or volume.

WORD	**Loud volume:** Capital letters indicate substantially increased volume.
°word°	**Low volume:** Degree signs indicate that the talk they enclose is low in volume.
hhh	**Exhalation:** A series of h's indicates audible exhalation.
.hhh	**Inhalation:** A series of h's preceded by a period indicates audible inhalation.
wo(h)rd	**Breathiness, laughter:** A single h in parentheses indicates plosive aspiration which could result from breathiness, laughter, or crying.
huh henh hunh	**Laughter particles**
( )	**Unintelligible or unheard speech:** Empty parentheses indicate that no hearing was achieved.
(word)	**Problematic hearing:** Material in parentheses indicates a hearing that the transcriber was uncertain about.
((*chanting*)) ((cough))	**Descriptions and comments:** Double parentheses enclose material that is not part of the talk being transcribed (e.g., a comment by the transcriber that the talk was being spoken in some special way) or verbalizations that are not transcribed. For additional clarity, transcriber comments are italicized.
♦	**Episode boundary:** The diamond-shaped symbol indicates the start of a new episode of talk within a longer speech event. Often made up of several sequences, episodes are like scenes in a play or stanzas in a poem, fitting into a larger and longer narrative structure.

6

Lived Landscapes
of the Fillmore

Ingrid Seyer-Ochi
University of California, Berkeley

Ingrid Seyer-Ochi (Stanford University, Ph.D., Education; M.A., History) is an Assistant Professor in Social and Cultural Studies at the University of California's Graduate School of Education. A common equation underlies all of her research: an interest in the experiences of socially-constructed and marginalized groups as they interact with multiple institutions across structured and segregated landscapes. Her interest in the spatial organization of learning opportunities emerges in part from a childhood spent moving (via truck, camper, and sailboat) from place to place. She brings her experiences as an anthropologist, historian, and urban high school teacher to all of her research and teaching. She lives in Oakland with her husband, daughter, and Pug.

Focusing on the San Francisco neighborhood of the Fillmore, "The Lived Landscapes of the Fillmore" analyzes the relationship between the lives of local youth and various aspects of their built and social environment. Drawing upon over 500 maps composed by 281 San Francisco students, I tease out the defining characteristics of the Fillmore's public image and master identity. Using these maps in conjunction with my observations of and conversations with Fillmore residents, I argue that the neighborhood's local master identity is defined by a core set of characteristics, including: extensive social knowledge and shared histories; an expansive faith-based network; a conflictual sense of communal belonging and anomie; a perceived sense of chaos; an ambivalent, often combative relationship with the police force; drug dealing and its myriad social, economic and emotional influences; organized "gangs"; organized vio-

lence (predominant); a sense of random violence (less common), and a related high frequency of homicides (specifically among young Black males); high unemployment, the "hanging out" (and "outside") that accompanies it and the frequently evolving "street corner" landscape evolving from both. I conclude with an analysis of the "ghetto pass," a social tool whose many uses highlight the social nature and borders of the lived landscape.

> *It is not on any map; true places never are.*
>
> —Herman Melville

Our sense of place is shaped through our experiences directly with it, our understanding of the history it embodies, and our interactions across its changing social and structural landscape. Sense of place is the geographic component of our need to belong, the "Lure of the Local," as Lucy Lippard calls it in her aptly titled book of the same name. From early childhood our connections to place begin to develop; we come to know places via all our senses: sight, sounds, tastes, and smells interact with our emotions to shape our "sense of place." It is these same senses that later serve to evoke and inspire our memories of places and times past. These evolving senses of place develop alongside, in fact are mutually constitutive of, our social relationships. Residents of all places "make due" with the natural, built, and social resources available to shape the local master identity of a neighborhood. These resources are produced within and distributed across *layered landscapes*: the built and historic layers draw from and transform the natural landscape. What people make of these conditions and materials and the lives that are thus made possible are embedded in what I term *lived landscapes*. Architect and planner James Rojas has studied the way spaces are created and used by locals, coining the term *enacted environment* (1993). I use the term *lived landscapes* to refer to a similar concept.

In this chapter I analyze these lived landscapes, the layered landscapes from which they emerge, and the opportunities they afford for youth. Lived landscapes are intertwined with the specifics of the layers preceding them: the conditions embedded in the natural, historic, and built landscape lay out the conditions facing the residents of any place. This study is drawn from a multi-year ethnography of San Francisco's Fillmore neighborhood, its youth, and the high school serving them. The people of the Fillmore experience their social landscape not only as that which is located in the Fillmore, but in terms of the relationship of themselves and their place to the wider city, region, and nation. I employ Gerald Suttles' (1968) concept of *public images* to make sense of the relationship of the Fillmore to the city of San Francisco.

Suttles argues that, despite the many variations and contradictions *across* in-dividuals and groups, people's senses of neighborhoods and cities—of all places—are united by *shared* images: *common* characteristics uniting the ma-jority's conception of a given place. Using maps drawn by over 250 San Fran-cisco youth, I tease out the construction of the varied, often conflictual, pub-lic images of the city as a whole, its neighborhoods and, specifically, the Fillmore. Using community-level maps drawn by Fillmore youth, I argue that key aspects of these public images are intensified and drawn upon in the con-stant re-creation of the neighborhood's *local master identity*. This master iden-tity is constructed on a daily basis in relation to surrounding neighborhoods (and their residents), drawing on its public images and key forces embedded in the natural, historic, and built landscape. This "master" public image of the Fillmore is further developed through the maintenance of a complex net-work of social and spatial borders. Age, race, peer (e.g., church or gang mem-bership), and gender boundaries are all critical to the organization and func-tioning of the Fillmore's lived landscapes. After analyzing the defining characteristics of the Fillmore's social identity, I conclude with an analysis of the "ghetto pass," a social tool whose many uses highlight the social nature and borders of the lived landscape.

A CITY, A NEIGHBORHOOD, AND ITS PEOPLE

San Francisco is a city of neighborhoods, over 20 (depending on how you count). If you ask a San Franciscan where they live, they will almost always begin their description with their neighborhood, perhaps guiding you closer to their actual address with the addition of cross streets or a well-known land-mark. Located almost in the exact center of the city is the district of the Western Addition, an approximately 16 by 12 block area, bordered by Van Ness, Fell, Divisadero, and California Streets. The District is roughly divided into four quadrants by the intersection of six-lane Geary Boulevard and Fill-more Street. Centered along nine blocks of Fillmore Street (from Ellis to Fell), roughly six to 10 blocks to each side (Divisadero to the West, Laguna to the East) is the Fillmore, the heart of the African American community in San Francisco and home to my three research participants: Sky, Anthony, and Caprisha. Fillmore Street, which extends beyond the Western Addition to the North and South, runs through the heart of the Western Addition. The street has defined the community for African Americans since the 1930s. Youth who refer to "the Fillmore" (or "the Fillmoe" or "the 'Moe") are thus referring to *their* neighborhood. The Western Addition is a formal district, closely aligned with census tracts and a current supervisor's district. The Fillmore is considered by its residents to be its "own" neighborhood, although official maps and documents subsume it within the Western Addition. Precise statistics on the Fillmore are nearly impossible to gather, as the area shares census tracts with the surrounding neighborhoods of Pacific Heights, Hayes Valley, Haight-Ashbury, and Civic Center. Although outsiders will often sugarcoat their descriptions, referring to it as a "public housing area" or "the Black neighborhood," the youth I worked with were far more blunt. They are proud of "the Fillmoe" but they also call things as they see them. They call the Fillmore a ghetto.

At first glance, neither "ghetto" nor its more subtle kin, "inner-city," seem to fit the Fillmore. There are no high-rise projects reminiscent of Cabrini Green. Although low-income housing complexes abound, most are owned by local organizations, churches, or outside corporations and are governed by resident committees. This variation in ownership and distance from the homogenizing effect of the Public Housing Authority gives each complex an individual look and feel. The paint may be faded, but the pink, red and green colors are still apparent. Many residents plant flowers around their unit, and, as the Fillmore is one of the sunnier parts of the city, the colorful plants thrive. San Francisco is a city of parks as well as neighborhoods and the Fillmore is no exception. Three major parks dominate the community, with numerous mini-parks and benches scattered about. Trees abound, particularly along Webster Street and the aptly named Grove.

Lined with trees on both sides, Grove Street is fully shaded, dappled sunlight sneaking through the leafy coverage in rare spots. Walking along Grove one almost feels they've left the city for a brief while. That is, if they aren't looking around. Crossing Webster and Buchanan Streets in the heart of the Fillmore, Grove Street is one of several major hang-outs for local drug dealers and their customers from within and beyond the neighborhood. The trees provide shade, but not much peace. Anthony grew up one block from Grove and spent most of his middle and high school years hanging "outside," on the corner of Grove and Buchanan. Five young men (all African American, all younger than twenty) were killed in the Fillmore between 1998–2000, all of them within a three-block radius of this corner. Walking through the Fillmore one afternoon in the spring of 2001, I stopped to visit a makeshift memorial to the area's most recent victim, a 17-year-old. Half-empty bottles of VO brandy, their dark green glass muted in the bright light, surround the base of the stop sign at the corner of Buchanan and Hayes, wilted balloons and dried flowers adding some color. Though most Fillmore residents are not involved in the neighborhood's gang or drug world, all of them must deal with their powerful influence on a daily basis. These influences are at their most powerful with high-school-aged teenagers.

Located in San Francisco's Outer Richmond, Thomas Jefferson High School is the Fillmore's physically distant "neighborhood school." The student body, like the city's population, is extremely diverse, representing over 40 nationalities and 35 languages. Graduating seniors pursue a wide range of pathways, including four-year colleges, junior colleges, vocational schools, and work. Traditional high schools such as Jefferson are increasingly rare, unable to meet the needs of so many different students under one roof. "We're a dinosaur," Jefferson's principal used to say. "I believe in schools like this, but I know it, we're on our way out."

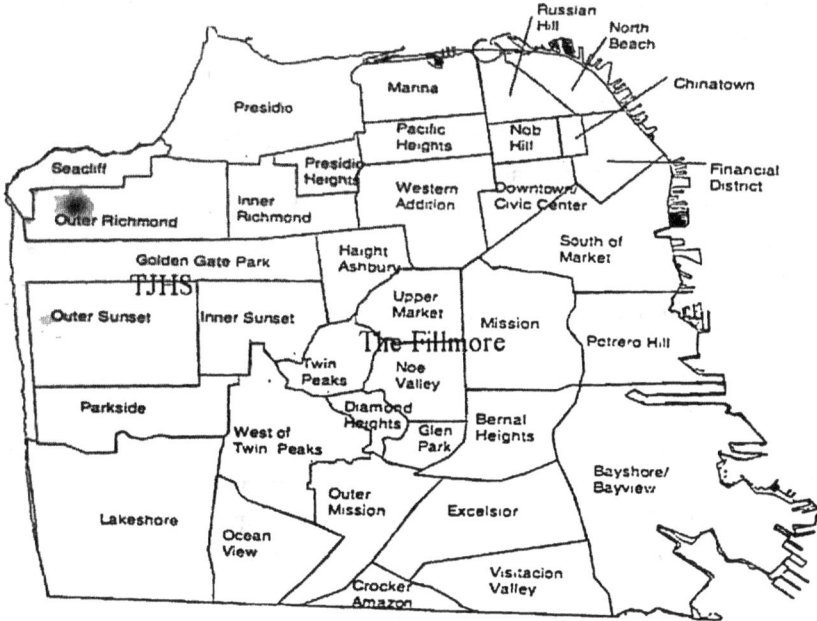

Traditional high schools revel in their ability to "provide something for everyone" but it was not clear to me, as I began my teaching career there in 1993, that Jefferson was fulfilling that promise. Although touted by many as the district's "flagship school" in terms of diversity, average GPAs, AP test scores and college acceptance rates, Jefferson High has a side that is rarely publicized: high drop-out, failure, and disciplinary transfer rates for African

Americans and Latinos, whispered teacher complaints about the increasing numbers of Black kids in the halls, arrests of Latino and Vietnamese gang-bangers that are kept hush-hush; the list goes on. Jefferson mirrors its home city in terms of diversity, yet it also exemplifies San Francisco's less publicized side: its history of racial and ethnic residential segregation, increasing gentri-fication, diminishing numbers of working-class residents, and increasing eco-nomic inequality. Although Jefferson is diverse by any standard, a quick glance into any classroom belies the numbers. Over 40% of the students are Chinese American. As the majority of the "other non-White" students (16.4%) at Jefferson are of Vietnamese or Southeast Asian descent, and 9% are "other Asian," the student population is over 65% Asian American. Walking into any random class, a visitor is likely to find only two or three La-tino or African American students in the average class of 37. The school may be diverse, but it does not always feel that way to students. Like San Fran-cisco, what diversity the school can claim is highly segregated, with Asian American students filling most of the honors and AP courses and African Americans composing 35% of the Special Education enrollment (though they are only 11% of the student body). In 1998–1999, the Institute, Jeffer-son's "at-risk" program, was almost 66% African American and Latino (com-pared to school-wide numbers of only 16%). This disparity is rarely talked about among Jefferson staff, at least not openly. Like San Francisco as a whole, the school prides itself on a tradition of excellence and diversity. School traditions, like city histories, are not easily changed.

In order to understand the relationship of my students' "lived landscapes" to their lives at school, I knew I would have to participate in their lives within and beyond Jefferson's walls. During the 1998–1999 school year I co-taught the American Government/Economics class (required for all seniors) of Jefferson's Institute program. The majority of our students lived in the Fill-more. As I was teaching and for months after their graduation, I also shad-owed three of my students as they traveled to and from home and among work, the Fillmore streets, school, church, Upward Bound meetings, and bas-ketball practices. In addition to my work with these three (Anthony Taylor, Caprisha Shaw, and Sky Jones), I also spent extensive time with their fami-lies, close friends, and neighborhood peers. All research methods have their drawbacks and shadowing certainly comes with its share. My primary concern was the method's inherent focus on the individual. Given that I set out to document the forces which structure, constrain, and enable individual lives, I feared my own methodological focus on individuals would perpetuate na-tional, cultural, and disciplinary traditions of focusing on (and blaming) per-sons rather than the forces shaping and determining their lives. In this study I sought that elusive balance, striving to document the structuring of the *conditions* as well as *individuals'* experiences and negotiations of them.

MAPPING THE LIVED LANDSCAPE

Lived landscapes can be thought of as maps, specific to individuals though based on common conceptual maps shared across groups. These maps change over time. Sky's 18-year-old sense of the Fillmore today is very different from that of the seven-year-old walking for the first time from her home to her school six blocks away. Many of us have experienced the shock of returning to a place from our childhood only to be surprised by how much smaller it is than our memory had led us to believe. The difference between Sky's seven- and 18-year-old senses of the blocks between Raphael Weill Elementary (now Rosa Parks) and the corner of Golden Gate and Steiner Streets is far more than a matter of size or distance. When Sky left for her first day of kindergarten with excitement, fear and awe, she knew little about Raphael Weill Elementary, first grade, the educational system, or her relationship to society's institutions and her place within them. She had yet to hear at least once a week (if not per day) that her mother needed to get her to school on time, needed to feed her breakfast before she arrived, needed to check her homework, and needed to read to her more often. She had yet to see the looks her teachers gave her mother when she did enter the hallways and offices of Raphael Weill. She had yet to see her mother, and herself, as a "problem." As Sky's perception of herself and her mother changed, so also did her sense of her home, peers, neighbors and their physical and social relationship to the world beyond the Fillmore.

Sky's maps of the Fillmore, San Francisco, and the world beyond them are cumulative and individually distinct but they are far from solitary. They are, in fact, inseparable from her interactions with others across the social and institutional landscape that makes up their shared world. These senses of place are difficult to capture in words or visuals. I thus employed a range of methods in my effort to understand the sense-making my participants made of their worlds. I asked them to draw maps, I asked their peers and schoolmates to draw maps, and I asked them to guide me through the Fillmore. Mostly, I watched and I listened as I accompanied them through their daily navigations. I then tried to make sense of what they had shown me.

> "A map is a composite of places, and like a place, it hides as much as it reveals. It is also a composite of times, blandly laying out on a single surface the results of billions of years of activity by nature and humanity."
>
> Lucy Lippard, *Senses of Place* (1997, p. 82)

During my time with youth, I asked them to draw a variety of maps. The materials I collected from these exercises display an amazing array of information and creativity and are open to endless hours of interpretation. Making sense of the mapmakers' sense-making is a challenging and potentially dangerous task, however. Norms of what officially constitutes a "map" are narrowly defined and, as the maps drawn indicate, are shared by many. When asking youth to draw maps, I made every attempt to distance my request from these norms, asking students "not to draw the maps you see every day, like the city maps you see posted at Muni stops" but to capture "your own mental maps, including the people, places, spaces, and things that are important to you, indicating however you can the relationship among these." In all, I collected over 500 student maps from 281 different students. Most of these maps were given as classroom-based assignments in my classroom and those of four colleagues. I also gleaned a range of maps from my participants in non-school, informal settings: on a napkin while eating lunch, while walking through the Fillmore, or sitting in Caprisha's church.

Although I was asking individual youth to construct maps, I sought a understanding of what Kevin Lynch (1960) calls *public images*, the common mental images of place and space shared by groups of people. Applying Lynch's concepts of cognitive mapping and public images to my own work has allowed me to reconstruct San Francisco and the Western Addition according to residents' experiences and understandings, rather than by arbitrary political or economic divisions.

One of the first things I noted in my map analysis was the sheer *range* of maps students constructed. Some students sketched relatively accurate maps of the entire city whereas others focused on key neighborhoods or tourist attractions. Some included locations critical to them personally and others included the transportation routes they most frequently followed. A number of students centered their maps on their own homes, connecting all other places to that personal center. Whereas most students connected the many places they drew, a few students presented locations as distinct and disconnected, almost floating. I was interested in the *public image* of the city shared by large numbers of Jefferson students. In particularly, I was interested in how students located and identified neighborhoods, specifically the Western Addition and the Richmond (Jefferson's two primary "feeder" neighborhoods). Given my interest in the relationship between the Fillmore and Jefferson High School, I began by comparing the maps of students from the Fillmore with those from other neighborhoods. I compared two sets of maps, those of the entire city and those of the student's "community" from these two groups of students.

Two key differences quickly emerged, with the most striking variations between Fillmore residents and those from the Richmond and Sunset districts.[1] The first major difference was among the city maps. Youth who lived in the Richmond and Sunset tended to sketch maps indicating a general knowledge of the entire city with numerous neighborhoods, tourist sites, and transportation routes included. Over 87% of the non-Fillmore students I worked with drew city maps that included at least six of the city's neighborhoods with 94% including Jefferson High School. Raisa's map is both representative and particular in several ways. Like many Richmond students, Raisa sketches a rough outline of the entire city, including five neighborhoods, her home, and Jefferson High School. Like many of the maps I analyzed, this one is oriented with street grids, though few streets are actually named. Many students, unfamiliar with particular parts of the city, identified some areas as "unknown" or "undiscovered." Raisa indicates that she had little knowledge of the outer Sunset and labeled a bordering neighborhood, "the other side." Over 50% of the non-Fillmore students identified key neighborhoods with symbols, for example, a pagoda for Japantown and a high rise for Downtown. Some captured their ethnic associations of neighborhoods, with a Mexican flag in the Mission being the most common. Raisa makes no particular comments on the Richmond and Sunset, though she captures the residential aspect of the outer Sunset in her written commentary. The traffic and congestion of Downtown are also highlighted. She characterizes the remaining three neighborhoods in terms of social class (and perhaps race, though this is not explicitly identified). She comments on the wealth and privilege of Pacific Heights ("Looking @ life through rose colored glasses" accompanied by several large homes and lawns). Along Mission Street, the main thoroughfare of the city's Latino district, she depicts a hold-up ("Give me your money" says one stick figure, "OK, just don't shoot," replies the victim). Finally, Raisa identifies the Bayview/Hunters Point as the "Ghetto," using stick figures to mime a planned drive-by shooting ("Hey, lets do a drive by today." "OK"). Although Raisa does not include the Fillmore on her map, she does hit on defining characteristics of several other neighborhoods. Her association of the Pacific Heights with privilege, the Mission District with a hold-up, and the Bayview with a drive-by resonate with some aspects of those neighborhoods' public

---

[1]The majority of Jefferson's students live in the Richmond and the Sunset. A small number of the map drawers lived in Chinatown, the Mission, Hunters Point/BayView, the Tenderloin and the Presidio. Some interesting variations are revealed in the maps drawn by these students. Students from the Mission, Hunters Point/Bayview and Tenderloin tended to draw maps more similar to those of Fillmore youth, whereas the Chinatown and the Presidio youth's maps more closely resembled those of Sunset and Richmond youth.

images. Raisa's map was the among the more direct of those depicting the public images of different neighborhoods, but her inclusion of several neighborhoods city-wide was typical.

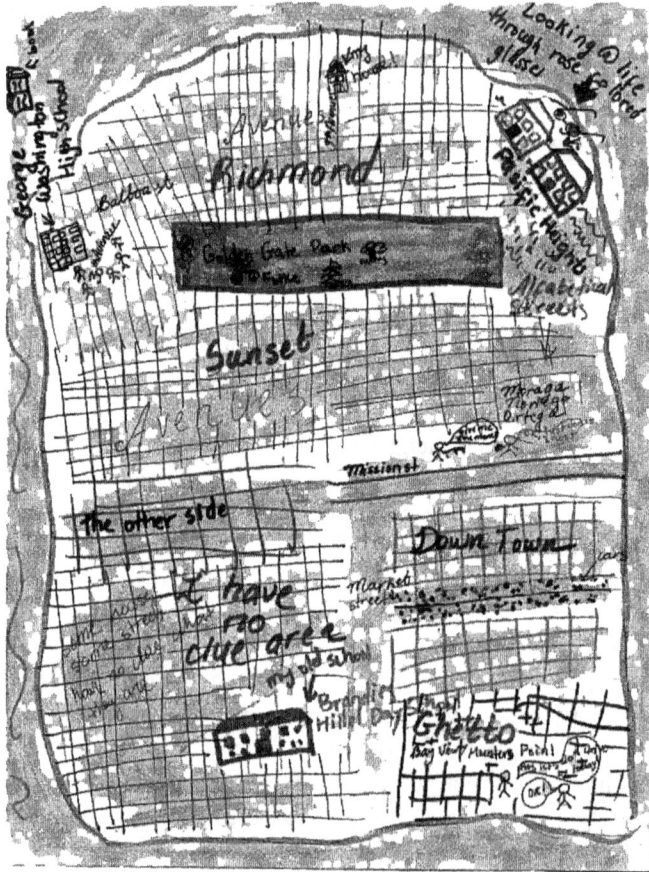

In contrast to the broad city-maps of Richmond youth, Fillmore youth presented with the same task drew maps more narrowly focused on their geographic community, often a five or six block area. Of the 25 city maps I analyzed from Fillmore youth, less than half included Jefferson High School. Sky's map of San Francisco was representative of these maps. After the students had drawn their maps I asked a few students to share and explain what they had included. Sky volunteered to describe her map. She stood up confidently, displayed her map with a flourish and began, almost chanting as she mimed her walk through the Fillmore.

My map is of my community, it shows the surfaces I touch every day, the places I survive on. I start off at home, I walk down the street, I take a few cuts (class laughs), I pass the senior citizen center—so that's why I drew a little heart there (points)—'cause they make me feel good (smiles and hugs herself), and then I go by my friends, maybe I cut over to the Ella Hill Hutch Center and play a little ball (feigns a jump shot). If I'm hungry I swing by the McD's. I might take the Muni out someplace (points to bus stop). And here (pauses for emphasis) in the center (pause) is a heart, my heart, the heart of the 'Moe.

The class erupts, a "You go, girl" and "Alright, alright" punctuating the general applause and laughter. After class as Sky and I discuss her map, I ask her if Jefferson is one of the surfaces she touches. She dwells on this question for some time, starting several explanations but never finishing, pausing to think further. After several minutes, a look of clarity crosses her face. "No, this place doesn't touch me because . . . 'cause I won't let it. I'm not gonna let that happen. (pause) . . . 'cause it won't reach back. Maybe, but I'm not counting on it, ya know?"

Sky's map is representative of many of the Fillmore students' city maps in its clear focus on the Fillmore. Although asked to draw a map of the city, she, along with most of her peers, represented "San Francisco" as the Fillmore. In typical Sky fashion, she has added a creative flair to her map, sketching a light red heart over the center of her map, a small pink one at the senior citizen center. Amanda Watts' (quite hastily drawn) map, while less artistic, did include some locations beyond the Fillmore. Amanda focuses her map on the Fillmore and her personal connections to the rest of the city. She highlights her home, her brother's store and Jefferson High School. Fillmore Street is proudly labeled "Filmoe." Critically, she highlights the two main transportation routes she uses to get to and from school (i.e., the 5 Fulton and the 38 Geary bus lines). The only other institution she includes in the Fillmore is the Kabuki theater. This choice was somewhat of an anomaly as Amanda, like most of her friends, rarely went to movies there. She does place the theater, accurately, on the "other side" of Geary. Amanda conveyed that she knows little about the Richmond, to which she buses five days a week for school, noting "never been ? ? not past Clement" in the lower right corner. Although Amanda's map represents a wider range of the city's neighborhoods than Sky's, her focus remains more narrow than the majority of non-Fillmore students.

Whereas many of the maps I gathered did address differences *across* neighborhoods (with Raisa's map being the most obvious in its social commentary), Anthony's map of San Francisco did so most directly: his map is *centered around* differences—critical inequalities, in fact—among neighbor-

ocean

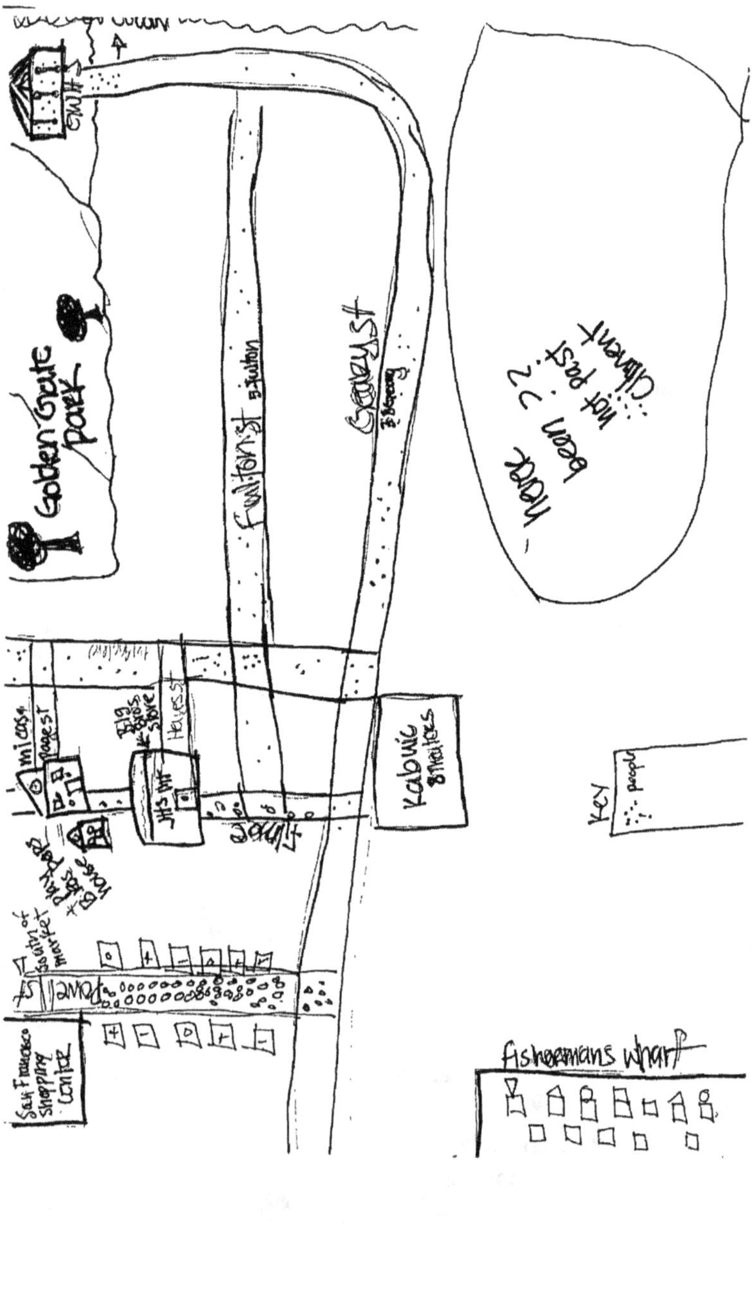

swim

Golden Gate Park

Fulton St

Market St

Geary St

Broadway

have
been 2x
not past
Clement

Macys
Ross St

Big
Boss
Store

Hayes St

JHS Inn

Gough

Ross
Store
+ place

South of
Market

Powell

San Francisco
Shopping
Center

Kabuki
8 theaters

Key
people

fishermans wharf

hoods. He identifies the three neighborhoods in his life at the time: his places of residence, study, and work (the Fillmore, Richmond, and Marina Districts, respectively). He represents the differences among the three neighborhoods through his inclusion of four key characteristics: housing (quality and quantity), eating establishments (quality and quantity), liquor stores (quantity) and candy stores (quantity). In the Fillmore, he locates two institutions associated with the Japanese community, the Miyako candy store and the Kabuki theater. The eating establishments are limited to a Taco Bell and McDonald's and the residences to low-income housing. (Although he locates schools in each of the other neighborhoods, he does not include Ben Franklin Middle School or any of the Fillmore's elementary schools in his map.) He writes "liquor stores" across the middle of the Fillmore and later told me this meant "more than ten, at least. I mean, if you count all them corner stores, there's hundreds." Anthony's almost interchangeable use of corner stores and liquor stores was the first of many clues I gleaned regarding these critical Fillmore institutions. In contrast to the Fillmore, he depicts the Richmond as a land of residential homes, pizza parlors, restaurants and candy stores. And Jefferson High School. Liquor stores, fast-food joints, and low-income housing are noticeably absent. The third neighborhood, one of San Francisco's wealthiest and most White, the Marina, he portrays as an area of restaurants, candystores, one liquor store, and Marina Middle School. Notably, he locates this neighborhood "between" the other realms of his life, a choice I found puzzling until I talked with him further.

Anthony worked at the Marina Safeway for almost two years. During this time, he frequently expressed anger and frustration with his fellow employees, the management, and the customers. One day when he seemed particularly sullen he explained he was "out of it" because he had been told (not asked) to carry a young woman's half-full bag of groceries to her car.

> It was some BMW or something and can you believe, we get there and she's left the car unlocked, cell phone sitting right on the front seat for anyone to see? I just couldn't believe that, now. She sure didn't seem to be worried about losing it, that's for sure.

Despite the anger and frustration developing as he encountered these monumental economic disparities on a daily basis, Anthony said he really *liked* the Marina. "Everyone thinks I hate it, just like you, but I don't. I like it there. It's peaceful, you know, it's calm, quiet, no noise or fighting going on." Rather than fully writing off the neighborhood as a yuppie haven, Anthony values it for precisely the same reasons its residents do: it is comfortable, safe, and easy to *be* there. This, in sharp contrast to the Fillmore.

San Francisco Map

Fillmore District
theater
movie theater
Major Project Subject
Restaurant
Analysis Center
Liquor Stores
Low income housing
candystores
Do you get it?

Golden gate bridge it's important
the people that live on the rich side
the people have to cross the bridge to get to work

Richmond
Pizza Parlors restaurants and candy stores and homes

Marina District
restaurants and candy stores
one liquor store
Analysis
Restaurants

George Washington
Analysis

In the bottom corner of his map Anthony asks "Do you get it?" I did. Anthony's map not only captures aspects of San Francisco, it captures aspects of himself. In particular, it highlights two key characteristics I have long observed in Anthony. First, he call things as he sees them. Never one to beat around the bush, Anthony speaks his mind, a trait which has gotten him into quite a bit of trouble at school, work, and home. Second, Anthony's map demonstrates his unique perspective on the world. Anthony sees things differently than most people, youth or adults. At the time he drew this map, Anthony was navigating a complex geography of physical, economic, and social disjunctures. His map provides some insight into his experience across a rocky and disparate landscape. Anthony's experience of the Fillmore is inseparable from his experience of the city as a whole. His travels across neighborhoods are constantly shaped by the contrasts among these very places. Each neighborhood is defined only in relationship to others. Suttles (1968) argues that

> The dimensions along which residential areas may differentiate are numerous, but they seem to devolve around a single cultural principle: residential groups are defined in contradistinction to one another. In other words, residential groups gain their identity by their most apparent differences from one another. . . . As counterparts to one another, neighborhoods seem to acquire identity through an ongoing commentary between themselves and outsiders. (pp. 50–51)

This commentary is not limited to residents of the particular neighborhoods involved. Media commentary, the motives and actions of "concerned" individuals, and institutions (e.g., Chambers of Commerce, neighborhood business associations, realtors, and local politicians) all join in the constant dialogue which constructs neighborhood identities.

Although Anthony's understanding of the Fillmore may not overlap completely with that of any other San Francisco resident, the aspects Anthony draws on his map highlight the *public images* of the neighborhoods. These are images Anthony shares with many San Francisco residents. The contrasts Anthony captures on his map are played out in the physical and socioeconomic realities and public perceptions of the Fillmore, Richmond, and Marina. These images are also embedded in the many other maps we have seen. I did not map the commercial establishments of the Richmond and the Marina, but I am reasonably sure that, had I, the maps would overlap with and affirm the patterns Anthony depicted. The Richmond is known as a primarily middle-class residential neighborhood with a range of restaurants at least in part because the area is far more residential than the average San Francisco district. Likewise, the Marina is a virtual zone of wealth in the city: the homes in the Marina and Pacific Heights are far larger than the average dwelling and their owners/renters wealthier than the average San Francisco resident. The Marina's rents are 14% higher than the city average, with Pacific Heights/Cow Hollow an astonishing 33% higher. In contrast, the average rent in the Fillmore is 16% lower than the city median. Finally, though the Western Addition is rapidly gentrifying at its borders, the heart of the Fillmore is still dominated by low-income housing and corner liquor stores with few non-chain restaurants. San Francisco is a geographically, socio-economically, and racially divided city and, though they won't always say it, its residents know it. Jefferson High School students know it.

As I shadowed my participants in their classes, sat with students at assemblies, hung out at lunch or drove around the city, I would frequently ask students about their dominant neighborhood identifications. Ethnic associations abounded in their responses. With the exception of recent migrants to the city, most students could identify the demographic public image of several neighborhoods with ease. At times, I would turn my questions around, asking what neighborhoods were associated with which ethnic groups. The responses were the same. The idea of racially-defined neighborhoods was never questioned and the responses were consistent across almost all students with whom I spoke.[2] With some variations, most youth I asked would could up with a list something like the following.

Primary Demographic Group	Neighborhood(s)
Chinese Americans	Chinatown, Richmond, Sunset
Russian Americans	Richmond[3]
Japanese Americans	Richmond, Japantown[4]
Caucasians	Marina, Pacific Heights, Richmond[5]

---

[2]Some neighborhoods, particularly those that were not dominated by any one group or were extremely heterogeneous were never mentioned. Most of these neighborhoods were also geographically distant from the Richmond and Fillmore. Had I interviewed students living in the eastern part of the city, more of them might have mentioned Bernal Heights, Noe Valley, the Excelsior or Duboce Triangle.

[3]In this case, some students identified streets (e.g., Geary and Clement) rather than a neighborhood (e.g., Richmond).

[4]Few non-Japanese youth identified Japantown with the Western Addition.

[5]Caucasians live throughout the city, as do most ethnic groups. The largest percentage of the City's white population is clustered in the northwest. Most students were not familiar with several smaller enclaves such as Forest Hills, West Portal and St. Francis Wood. According to the 2000 Census, Caucasians make up 80% of San Francisco's Noe Valley, one of the few neighborhoods in the city that is becoming more homogenous. The neighborhood, jokingly referred to by some city residents as "Snowy Valley" is now the most white area of the city. Its residents

African Americans	Western Addition, Fillmore, Potrero Hill (projects) (and Ingleside)[6]
Latinos	Mission (Excelsior and Ingleside)[7]
Vietnamese Americans	Tenderloin, Richmond
Filipino Americans	Ingleside, Daly City

The fact that most Jefferson students with whom I spoke identified the Richmond as a Chinese, Russian, Japanese, and Caucasian neighborhood does not mean that no other groups lived there. It does indicate that Jefferson students shared a particular, racially-defined public image of the neighborhood. Across individuals, numerous variations emerged: some students had no idea if there was a "Vietnamese" neighborhood. Some, like Raisa, knew almost nothing about the Fillmore and thought most Blacks lived in the Bayview. It is the collective understandings that these students did share, the patterns that emerged from their responses, which are most revealing.

The same analysis applies to student maps. Although I have my own ideas about what Raisa, Anthony, and Amanda were "trying to show" in their maps, I have few grounds upon which to base those "guesses." The patterns that emerged from my map analyses do mirror many of the patterns I observed at Jefferson High School. The exclusion of Jefferson High or the Richmond from many of the Fillmore youth maps resonates with the geographic and emotional distance which played out daily on their journeys to and from Jefferson and in the school's hallways and classrooms. The tendency of Fillmore youth to limit their city maps to the area surrounding their neighborhood is a more difficult one to analyze. In his study of Los Angeles residents from a range of neighborhoods, Lynch (1960) found that those from wealthier areas traveled to many parts of the city and were thus familiar with many neighborhoods. Those with more limited economic means tended to live, work, and play in a more geographically confined area, rarely venturing out to other parts of the city. This pattern was particularly acute for recent immigrants who were not yet conversant in English and were intimidated by excursions

---

are also wealthier and older than most in the city. Children make up only 8.6% of the population, compared to a 15% average for all other city neighborhoods.

[6]The Ingleside is home to the largest percentage of San Francisco's middle-class Black population. Only students living in this area, or black students in the Bayview, tended to identify this.

[7]This area, officially known as the OMI (Outer Mission Ingleside) is an old neighborhood that has undergone rapid changes over the last decade. Many lower middle-class families moved there in the 1980s and 1990s, replacing the largely Irish population that had dominated the area since the 1920s. I found this neighborhood to be relatively unknown to most Jefferson students except for those living in or near it.

beyond their ethnic communities. Although a comparison of the city travel patterns of Fillmore and non-Fillmore youth was not a part of my study, during my eight years at Jefferson I have come to know a fair amount about the movement patterns of Jefferson youth. Most students, particularly those from the Fillmore, are extremely familiar with the city's public transportation system. I would often find youth debating which combination of bus routes would get them to their destination most quickly. Strong emotions and self-esteem seem to be tied to one's knowledge of the system and ability to use it to one's best advantage. Sky, Caprisha, and their peers traveled extensively to many parts of the city and beyond (e.g., Oakland, Daly City, and South City). Interestingly, this knowledge was not conveyed in their city maps. The comparative expanse of city areas contained in the maps of Fillmore and non-Fillmore youth could be explained in many ways. One possibility relates to the degree of comfort and ownership youth relate to different parts of the city. Though Fillmore youth traveled throughout the city, most of them spent the majority of their time in a relatively small geographic space center around their residences. Although they visited other parts of the city, that travel does not necessarily mean they felt fully welcome or at ease in those environs. Their maps may convey the extent of their "comfort zone" in various parts of the city.

After asking all 242 students to draw maps of San Francisco, I returned to their classes once again. This time, I asked students to map their communities, first their geographic/residential community, then any other "cognitive" communities to which they belonged. I still remember looking over the piles of community maps that first afternoon after school. Having closely observed as the Institute class worked on their maps, I was already in awe of the physical and social details they had encoded in their maps. Quickly riffling through the other classes' maps, I was immediately struck by the contrast. Whereas the non-Fillmore students had drawn extensive and detailed maps of the entire city (in contrast to the more limited scope of the Fillmore youth), their community maps depicted limited levels of local knowledge. Most of the Richmond and Sunset students sketched two by two block maps with very little detail. They included their own home, row upon row of virtually identical houses, a tree or yard here or there, and the occasional restaurant or corner store. Over 65% of these maps did not include any identifiable acquaintances or neighbors. In contrast, the Fillmore students' maps contained extensive social knowledge about their residential communities. Though the information contained in these maps varied greatly, once again, key patterns emerged. These patterns can be understood as critical characteristics of the Fillmore's local master identity.

Though all neighborhoods are comprised of multiple communities, Suttles (1968) uses the term *master identity* to refer to that identity which a neighborhood takes on as dominant at any given time. The process by which a neighborhood's master identity emerges varies, but Suttles argues that this identity is often based upon comparisons to other areas. Relative rather than absolute differences characterize differentiation among neighborhoods. Thus, a neighborhood's master identity often develops around those few qualities a given neighborhood can clearly claim as both definable and unique. Suttles uses the term *master identity* to refer to those characteristics attributed to an area by a majority of city residents, both within and beyond a particular neighborhood. I employ Lynch's concept of the *public image* (1960) to capture this city-level identity and employ a qualified version of Suttles' term, the *local master identity*, to connote that identity shared and constructed among neighborhood residents. Analysis of the community-level maps youth drew provided me with one of many ways to begin to make sense of this constantly evolving communal identity.

CONSTRUCTING A LOCAL MASTER IDENTITY: INTERSECTING LANDSCAPES IN THE LIVES OF URBAN YOUTH

The local master identity of the Fillmore, like that of any neighborhood, is under constant construction, attack, and re-affirmation. In order to make sense of the socially constructed aspects of this identity, I turned to the community maps drawn by local youth. Drawing upon my extensive work with these youth in their homes, at school, on the streets, and with their peers, I pulled out those characteristics that were most dominant and consistent in the local master identity. Making sense of this identity was like trying to shoot a moving target; this identity only "exists" through the socially determined, embedded, and evolving interactions across all layers of the Fillmore landscape. Nonetheless, key characteristics of this identity did emerge over time as relatively constant (with the emphasis on the *relatively*). These characteristics include: extensive social knowledge and shared histories across peer groups and generations; an expansive faith-based network based in the Fillmore and extending outward (and across the Bay); a conflictual sense of communal belonging and anomie; a perceived sense of chaos concurrent with highly structured social relations; an ambivalent, often combative relationship with the police force; frequent passage *through* the neighborhood by key groups (i.e., locals "cruising," drug buyers, and cops) and avoidance by others (i.e., most other "outsiders"); the dominance of liquor stores on the commercial landscape and low-income housing on the residential landscape; drug dealing and its myriad social, economic, and emotional influences; organized "gangs"; highly organized violence (predominant), a sense of random violence (less common), and a related high frequency of homicides (specifically among young Black males); high unemployment, the "hanging out" (and "outside") that accompanies it and the frequently evolving "street corner" landscape evolving from both. This master identity is characterized not only by these core qualities but also by the area's geographic and social borders. These borders are maintained via physical structures (e.g., gates, streets, underpasses, and inwardly-facing architecture) and social interactions. These borders—defined in socioeconomic, racial, gender and behavioristic terms—are enforced by both residents and outsiders. The social uses of the *ghetto pass*, a social tool which enables access for those who might otherwise be excluded, highlight many of the key borders and their use, maintenance, and contestation.

Angel's map is representative of many of the Fillmore community maps, though his includes more specific details than most. His map is geographically detailed, including trees, cars, stairs, the housing center office, mail boxes, the janitor room, parking lots and garbage collection areas. Angel conveys some of his experience of these physical structures and spaces through his differentiation of the houses along Turk and Scott Streets. Here is a nuanced relational world. His map indicates that the two blocks surrounding his home are populated by (and divided into) family, friends, acquaintances of friends, neighbors, variously identified "strangers," and unknown individuals. Although Angel describes these people as "strangers" his map reveals a far deeper knowledge of them. He reveals his complex relational network through his identification of over half his neighbors by either name (e.g., Elicio and Dingo) or various defining characteristics (e.g., Asian people's house, some White guy with husky dog, dope pheen house, play station dude house, and dangerous premises). Angel depicts a heterogeneous social space, diverse in its racial and social demographics. The Fillmore's local master identity is that of a Black community, but Angel (a Latino) locates Latinos, Asians, Blacks and Whites on his landscape. Two of Caprisha's neighbors are Asian American as well. This diversity runs contrary to the area's public images and master identity. The predominance of African Americans continues to define the neighborhood. When I commented to her one day that her complex was more mixed than many people thought, she laughed and said "yeah right. A bunch of Blacks with a few Asians and Mexicans thrown in. That's mixed? I don't think so."

NEIGHBORS DANGEROU' PREMISSE

NEIGHBORS

NEIGHBORS

COUSIN HOUSE

Neighbors

NEIGHBORS

NEIGHBORS

other Ca

MAIL BOXES

CENTER OFFICE

RANITOR ROOM

ASIAN PEOPLE HOUSE

NEIGHBORS

NEIGHBORS

MY HOME

NEIGHBORS

MY CAR

REILy Lot

MRS OLD HWE LADY

HWE 5

UNCLE's HWE 5

BEAUTY SALON

THRF STREET

SCOTT STREET

TURK ST

TURK ST

PARKING LOT

EVA ane HOUSE

EDDY HOUSE

Harries HOUSE

HOME HOUSE

John HWE

MR HWE

NEIGHBORS

RUSSIAN

PUSSIAN

Japol HWE

Japol Shaul wife

Japol Shaul wife

PUNy HWE

Japhe dragos

Elicious HWE dragos

THRESSA PENN HOUSE HWE5

I asked Angel to describe his community in writing.

"My community"

In my community it smells like a lot of cars because all day everyday cars are
coming up and down the block and I believe Scott and Turk street is cursed because there are at least 2 or 3 accidents there in two weeks. I think my community needs to get those lights fixed I mean by time, because once the light start
going yellow cars are already coming up the hill flying for the green. And sometime to cars connect and ~~make~~ create sparks. My community also needs more
police on patrol because there's a lot of drugs in my community which allow's
hurt dope fiends to come through my neighborhood causing chaos and a big
MESS.

Angel's commentary hints at several of the Fillmore's master identity characteristics. The first thing he mentions is the through traffic, speeding, and accidents. His analysis of this traffic hints at its roots: this traffic is not random.
The timing of the lights (a component of the built landscape) influences Angel's world with disturbing sounds, smells, and accidents. Scott, Turk and
Eddy Streets are not major thoroughfares; Geary, Golden Gate, and Fulton
are the major east–west avenues through the area, with Fillmore and
Divisadero shuttling most of the north–south traffic across. Despite this,
Scott, Turk, and Eddy *are* heavily trafficked. Locals "cruise" the area, seeing,
being seen and "flying for the green." Cops also patrol the area regularly, often in unmarked cars. Outsiders also drive through. Some of these are San
Franciscans crossing the city, some are lost tourists in search of Japantown,
and others are buyers in search of a dealer. Drugs and violence in the Fillmore
are the two descriptors most frequently cited by youth describing the area. As
Angel points out, the two are inextricably related: the drugs in his community are causing chaos and "a big MESS." Angel's call for increased police patrols in the area captures a tension many of his peers seemed to struggle with.
Angel, along with Anthony, Joseph, Alfonzo and others, frequently critiqued
the behavior and presence of cops in the Fillmore. Several police-related
deaths in the neighborhood and a number of midnight raids did little to improve the police force's troubled reputation. Despite their anger toward police, many of these same individuals would cite the limited number of police
patrols or lack of action as proof that "they (the government, politicians, outsiders, and/or the police) don't care about the little man." What appeared at
first to be incongruent if not contradictory attitudes I later came to understand as variations along an individual–structural continuum.

Police and the laws they enforce have shaped the lives of many of my participants in powerful ways. The frequency, quality, and impact of police–resident interactions depends largely on one's proximity and allegiance to the "outside." One of Anthony's closest friends and street peers was Joseph. Joseph's father was arrested and imprisoned for theft and drug dealing. His mother was shot in the head by a neighbor when Joseph was 10. Despite her identification of her attacker and a knowledge of her motivation, Joseph's mother refused to testify to the police. According to Joseph "She felt like, 'what good will it do? The harms been done and why send another black into the police's hands for no reason?' She wanted to just deal with it herself." Throughout his middle and early high school years Anthony had evaded the police on a nightly basis. Although he was never arrested, his frequent encounters with law enforcement were marked with conflicts. Despite the fact that he was actively selling immediately prior to many of these encounters (i.e., he *was* breaking the law) Anthony attributed most of these conflicts to individual police racism. He often cited their focus on sellers rather than buyers. Occasionally, he also complained that he knew of lots of "white collar" sales going on in the Richmond—"out in the Avenue apartments"—but the cops never arrested those people: "They're just out to get the ghetto boys, they don't even mess with them big-time dealers. Shiiitt." When Anthony and others spoke of these interactions, they referred to individual cops, describing them as greedy, stupid, racist, and two-faced. Given that these were face-to-face interactions between humans, youth experienced them as such. As their public- and self-respect were challenged through each interaction, their anger against police as individuals multiplied. When discussing the police force more generally, as a branch of the government responsible for protecting public safety, youth responses occasionally fell toward the more structural end of the continuum. As they understood it, violence was a problem in their communities at least in part because the police were not fulfilling their protective and peace-keeping roles. Few issues fell on any one end of the continuum. In reality, most youth I worked moved back and forth along the continuum within the same discussion, unable to reconcile the contradictions presented to them.

These contradictions were made vividly clear in the aftermath of a police raid on the Marcus Garvey housing complex in the Fillmore on the morning of October 30, 1998. At approximately 5:20 a.m. 90 San Francisco police officers descended on the complex, fully armed. According to official police department statements, the raid was planned after almost twelve months of careful surveillance and documentation of the drug dealing of the "so called

Knock Out Posse," a local gang known to run a major drug dealing operation out of the complex, intimidating many residents in the process. The police department documented dozens of complaints from residents about drug and gang activity in the complex (*San Francisco Chronicle*, 4/29/99). Officers forced their way, unannounced, into thirteen units, making eleven arrests and confiscating seven handguns, $4,000, and several ounces of cocaine. A pit bull owned by one of the residents was shot and killed during the raid, a raid highlight that seemed to intrigue the media more than other aspects of the "event." At a press conference several hours after the morning raid, Assistant Police Chief Earl Sanders explained "The message is we will not tolerate gang behavior. Hopefully, we made a big dent in it. If not, we will continue our efforts until we do." At least one resident, quoted in the *Chronicle* report, thanked the police for finally doing something about the violence. "This is letting people know that they just can't do what they want in the city and just get away with it," said Tommy Price (*San Francisco Chronicle*, 10/31/98). Despite the desire of most residents to live in a safe and peaceful environment, few voices of support emerged for the police action emerged following the raid.

Hoping for an element of surprise, the raid began in the early hours of the morning. Less than four hours later, unaware that the raid had occurred, Randi and I began our second-period class at Jefferson by collecting weekly notebooks. The room was virtually silent. Caprisha sat slouched in her desk, staring at her notebook, and refusing to make eye contact with me when I greeted her with a "Good morning" and a smile. Kneeling down to her eye level, as Randi was concurrently doing three rows down as she spoke with Alfonzo, we quickly realized something, something big, was amiss. Touching Caprisha lightly on the arm, I peered into her downcast eyes, moist with tears. Like most of the students in the Institute, Caprisha had endured her share of hardships and had learned to control her emotions (sometimes to a degree that scared me. Witnessing such external control in the face of such internal pain was both inspiring and difficult). Although Caprisha occasionally cried with me in private, she did so only twice in public. The raid hours before presaged one of those tearful floods.

Over the next 50 minutes Randi and I attempted to understand what had transpired that morning, how our students were feeling about the event, and what we could do to help them work through it. It became immediately clear that no one in the room understood exactly what they were feeling. How could they? Two of our students lived in the raided complex (Caprisha and Sky), four lived across the street, and 23 lived in the Fillmore. Hearing them slowly recount what had happened, I expected to hear anger—deep, unquenched anger. Instead, what I observed were 23 scared young people. Sleeping in their homes, they had been awoken by the sound of breaking wood and glass, gun shots, and an onslaught of armed police officers (some of them wearing full combat gear, complete with gas masks). Small children, some younger than six, were "flex cuffed" with plastic tie wraps. In at least one case, a screaming two-year-old was reportedly separated from his mother for at least half an hour while police searched her unit. According to one *Chronicle* article, the police rationalized this behavior in terms of the children's safety, and their possible gang involvement. "Police insisted that some gang followers were as young as seven years old" (*San Francisco Chronicle*, 10/31/98). It was only as our conversation continued, as the students slowly opened up and allowed themselves to express their fears publicly, that their conflictual emotions came into play. Interpretations and evaluations of the raid ran the gamut from incensed anger to tentative gratitude.

Debriefing with Randi after class, we both expressed our surprise at the concurrent anger, appreciation, and sadness felt by many of the students. It seemed to me, as I looked back on our discussion, that most of them were torn between competing explanations for the violent state of their neighborhood. They were attempting to make sense of what had occurred with the tools before them. These tools included personal experiences, locally-based rationales, and expectations shaped by past histories with the police force *and* local dealers. These tools were hardly enough to make sense of the complex relationship among poverty, drugs, violence, law enforcement, race, and power that was structured into their historic, built and social landscapes. Caprisha and others openly acknowledged that there was gang activity in the complex, while Jacori denied it. (As we soon see, at least half of the students in our class were quite familiar with the "so-called KOP).)" Despite her acknowledgement of the activity, she and others did not identify this activity as necessarily problematic. They had grown up surrounded by such activities. Most of them knew the rules. They knew who was who, where the borders were, and when they changed. Caprisha and Sky had grown up with many of the KOP members, they went to school with them, lived across the street with them; some of them were "almost family." Though Caprisha and her family contained themselves within their own unit most of the time, they were far from afraid of the KOP members. "That's just 'so and so' " Miss Martin would often tell me, "Nobody to be afraid of." Although the public images (presented via the police and media) of the KOP, the Marcus Garvey Complex, and the Fillmore were dominated by visions of ruthless, violent, highly-organized gangs, the residents I knew had constructed a somewhat different version of these images in the own lo-

cal master identity. Yes, drug dealing was a common fact and yes, violence—and death—accompanied it. But these activities did not necessarily
imply the same degree of fear and loathing expressed so often in the mainstream press. On many occasions Sky and Caprisha (alone and with their
peers) would laugh about the low-level status of the KOP. Hanging out at
Caprisha's one afternoon with her grandmother and aunt (Christine), Caprisha recalled a recent break-in up the street. When I asked if it might have
been the KOP, everyone laughed, obviously tickled by the idea of the KOP
carrying out such an activity.

Caprisha: Did I tell you I talked to Jovan (her ex-boyfriend) the other
           day? He called me up, all like wanting to talk and I was . . .

Ingrid: He called you? Did he hear about you and Wesley (breaking up?)

Christine: Oh he called her alright. (We all laugh).

Caprisha: No, but did I tell you about his place, his brother?

Miss Maxey: I can't believe that happened, they have that lock and all.
              Those Turkwood places are . . .

Ingrid: What happened? Is he still living at home? I thought he moved
           out to State?

Caprisha: He's still at home and his little brother, he was like home
           watching videos or something and the doorbell rang and he an-
           swered it and like three guys came in and tied him up and stole
           their TV, video's, PlayStation. They took all their stuff.

Ingrid: Did he know them? Did he . . .

Christine: (to Caprisha) Weren't they wearing masks?

Caprisha: Yeah, he says he couldn't see them. But you know, people are
           saying it's like an inside job. You know, those places up there
           you have to have a code to get inside.

Ingrid: Like over at Anthony's? Like the gate with the . . .

Caprisha: No, to get in the *building* you need a code.

Ingrid: And these guys were already at his door?

Caprisha: Yeah, so they think it was an inside job—and they went right
           to the video games.

Christine: Like they knew right what they came for.

Ingrid: Do they have any idea who it could be? Like could it maybe be
           like the KOP? (Much laughter)

Christine: No way.

Caprisha: There's no way they could pull something like that off. They're scary.

Ingrid: Scary? Or scared?

(more laughter)

Caprisha: Scary . . . (they all laugh) they too scared to do that kinda job. (laughs) Grandma's always saying "which of them got the gun?" cuz they be all acting like they got all these guns and they're all sharing like one for all of them or something. (Laughter). Isn't that right Grandma?

(Miss Martin nods, laughing)

Those guys over on Third Street (Bayview/Hunter's Point)? You don't mess with them. They're the real thing. Over here it's just like, you know, Joseph, Greg . . . what they gonna do?

Caprisha and her family didn't hang out with the KOP; they didn't hang out in general. Nonetheless, based on their 18-plus years sharing housing, school, and a neighborhood, they did know the group and its individual members well and their perceptions of them were a far-cry from those presented in the media.

Sky's connection to the KOP was more intimate. Lacking a stable home life and in search of male companions to play basketball with, Sky was no stranger to the streets. She frequently hung out on Eddy Street, at the corners of Steiner or Fillmore, relaxing with her "buddies" as she called her street acquaintances. Looking back on the raid several days later, Sky told me she had seen it coming. "I told them something was up, something was gonna happen. They didn't believe me, were all like 'get back to your books.' But I knew," she told me, laughing with glee at the accuracy of her prediction. "I told them 'I told you so. What do you expect, those cops be driving around all the time, never saying anything to you, never bothering you for that long? They had to be up to something. It's never quiet like that.' (laughs) I saw it coming, I saw it, I told 'em I saw it, but did they listen? No. Dumb asses (we laugh)." Sky's comment, that they told her to "get back to her books," is telling. Although Sky seemed equally at ease on the basketball court, in the classroom, and hanging out on Eddy Street, her commitment to school and achievements there defined her, at least in their eyes, as a school girl. This identification did not deny her access to the street community: she had a "ghetto pass."

Sky's familiarity with the Knock Out Posse is revealed in her community maps. Both of Sky's maps are dominated by the built landscape, specifically housing complexes. Additionally, she includes such physical landmarks as the bus stop, speed bumps ("it slows the cops down at least") and trees. Combined, the two maps tell us quite a bit about the world around her. Sky's map, like Angel's, also highlights particular aspects of her spatial experience. Unlike Angel, who identifies many spaces and things in terms of specific individuals (including his family and his car), Sky does not name any particular persons or identify places in terms of them. Rather, she sketches the social world in terms of groups and messages.

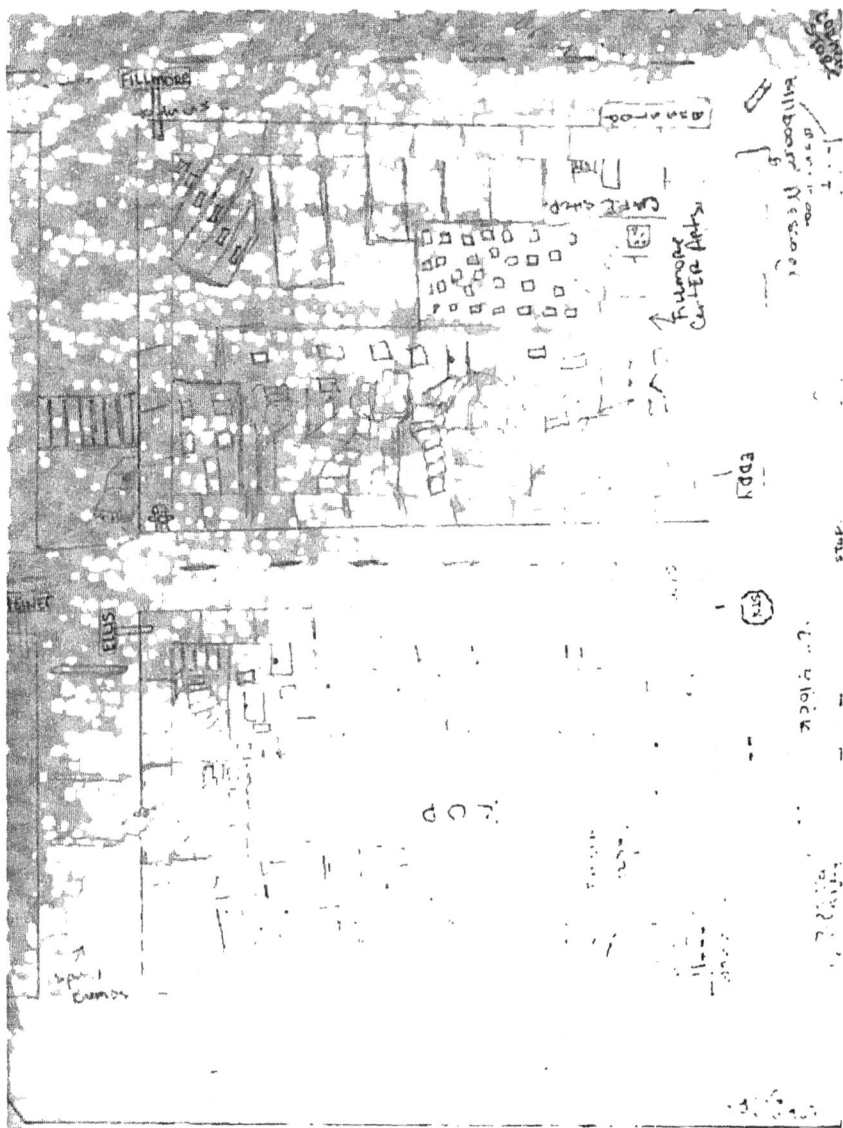

Unlike Angel's map, which reveals some clues as to his relationship with the spaces he portrays, Sky's map tells us little about her connection to the area she has sketched. Her written commentary on the area sheds a glimmer of light.

A community is supposed to have togetherness. My community lacks in that. My community is made up of one big complex of people as while as outsiders. A

place where action and love is lacked for some. It's a place where all should feel
safe and confident but they don't. Instead of tearing away buildings and putting
right back up they should be giving their future doctors, lawyers, accountants,
dentists, etc. a chance by putting a well together Non-Profit Organization
within the community. Because from what I understand who's ever in charge
their tearing up fixed streets just to waste money which is sad. Some need
neighbors that get along. I wish we had a dentist office near and why aren't they
advertising STAY IN SCHOOL on our bill board instead of NEWPORT with
a smile and OLD ENGLISH w/ a thumbs up and they put them right near
schools. And then they say there's no hope for the kids but truth is there's <u>no
hope for the future.</u> (underlined three times)

Several themes connect the community descriptions my Fillmore students
composed. Most of their maps displayed nuanced, highly structured social
worlds—webs of human connections. In contrast, all of but three of their
compositions emphasized, as did Sky, the neighborhood's lack of community,
connection and "togetherness."

In his study of a predominantly black neighborhood in Philadelphia David
Ley (1974) argues that a *frontier mentality* comes to envelope neighborhoods
under constant siege of poverty, drugs, and violence. The constant drive to
fulfill the most basic of wants and needs of residents encourages a "me against
them" mentality. Ley argues that individuals most often direct these feelings
of mistrust at those closest to them: their fellow residents. In the Fillmore,
this sense of anomie is in sharp contrast to the sense of community presented
by Fillmore youth through their proclaimed identification with "the 'Moe."
Ley also develops the concept of *the defended neighborhood*. Many Fillmore residents feel they must defend the image of their neighborhood—and of themselves—to outsiders. This unity against "the other" does not necessarily lead
to unity within. Through my work with Fillmore youth I learned that the
street is governed by an "always cover your back" mentality. Trust is limited
to only the closest of family members and long-term friends. Ley analyzes this
issue in terms of individuals competing against each other for the fulfillment
of their needs. The intensity and pervasiveness of such competition leads to
increased uncertainty among residents, which in turn challenges, and often
breaks down, the very internal cohesion so many outsiders attribute to and
fear in such communities. Of the many youth I have worked with, Sky was
the most wary of trusting others. Abandoned by her father and raised by her
crack-addicted mother (who often stole from her), Sky had learned early on
to protect herself. Although she identifies this area as "her" community, Sky
does not actually place herself in the map or her commentary, leaving it un-

clear if she herself is one of those lacking action, love, safety and confidence, in need of friendly neighbors, and in search of an optimistic future. This personal removal was common with Sky. Although she frequently spoke with passion and eloquence about ideas, she rarely connected these ideas to herself. Over time, I came to learn many things about Sky, a young lady who had been betrayed and hurt by most of the adults and institutions in her life. She opened up slowly, according trust even more cautiously.

In early October, when Sky first drew these maps, I asked her to talk about them with me. Besides goading me to find out about the KOP on my own (a test of sorts, I surmise), our conversation revealed little. As we gradually became closer, I was able to fill in some of the connection-points on her map. Sky knows the "E" street well, having spent many an evening of her middle and high school years hanging out on Eddy or Steiner. Although many women travel along and occasionally hang out on the street, those who are regulars are generally there with a male (often a boyfriend). Sky was one of the few females among her peers who "hung out with the guys" on a regular, purely platonic, basis. As we shall see in the upcoming analysis of gender-defined spaces, networks and access, Sky was an anomaly on the gender-defined landscape of the Fillmore.

Sky's most obvious addition to the maps is her placement of the "KOP" acronym at the center of her housing complex. In the late 1990s, the Knock Out Posse emerged as the Fillmore's most powerful and prominent gang. The group is loosely defined, with most of it activities revolving around drug sales in the central Fillmore. Several aspects of Sky's identification of the KOP stand out. She identifies a group of individuals with one name, in this case the KOP. She does not, however, identify the group by its "full name," the Knock Out Posse, but uses its insider name, the KOP, or "KO" for short. Although the KOP is common parlance among most of the youth I worked with, it is far from common knowledge among all Fillmore residents. Despite the fact that the group was identified openly by the police force and local media, this did not ensure full local knowledge. Knowledge about the group, like knowledge about many other social specifics of the Fillmore, depended on one's own social networks and access to others. These networks and their social consequences are explored in the following sections. Over the course of my time in the Fillmore, the KOP was not mentioned (at least in my presence) very frequently. Anthony was very comfortable talking about his *past* involvement with another group, yet he was far more cautious when talking about the *active* KOP, particularly on tape. A transcript from one of our early walks (when I had asked him to give me a tour, describing things as if I was a complete foreigner to the area) is fairly representative of his "on-tape" responses. Anthony was particularly evasive in this instance as we were walking in public, toward a group of his friends.

Anthony: So that would be like up in the KO area.

Ingrid: So what is the KO area?

Anthony: Marcus Garvey (the housing complex they operate around). Knock out. Knock Out Posse. But with the thing (tape recorder) I don't feel too comfortable with that, people might thing I'm snitching or something (We're walking up Grove Street and see a group of young men ahead).

Ingrid: Should we put the tape recorder away? I think so (I put it away quickly).

Anthony: Yeah, I think so.

Anthony was referring to the borders of the Fillmore when he mentioned "up in the KO area." He was not referring to the Martin Luther King/Marcus Garvey complexes, but to the general area "around" them. Sky's map further highlights the identification of spaces in terms of their social organization.

Sky places the KOP at the center of the apartment complex on her first map, specifying their location more carefully in her second. She locates the group in the central courtyard areas of the complex, and, quite powerfully, in the area by the playground (depicted here as a swing set). Although Sky locates the KOP's control within the apartment complex on one side of Eddy Street, the group's influence extends beyond this area to the streets along Eddy and the complex across the street. She notes the "E" (Eddy) Block or "hang out block," drawing rough stick figures on one map, dots for "people hanging out" on the other. Although a number of the individuals hanging out on Eddy are active in the KOP, many others, Sky included, hang out there as well. She explained to me that this street area is more "open," trafficked by a wide range of neighborhood residents and outsiders on foot and in vehicles. Like Angel, she qualifies her descriptions of the traffic: there is a structure to its composition and movement. Rather than random cars and people moving by, Sky breaks the movement down into social categories.

Driving down Eddy one Saturday afternoon I spied Sky sitting at a bus stop with several others. As I pulled my car up across the street and rolled down the window, she saw me and ran over. Neither of us had eaten, so we decided to go get some pizza and she hopped in, waving goodbye to her buddies.

Ingrid: Who were they? I don't think I've seen them around

Sky: Who them? (laughs) They just my buddies. You know, my pals.

Ingrid: Your friends.

Sky: My buddies. My friends is my sistas

Ingrid: Do your sisters hang out there? Sharonda?

Sky: Naw, not really. Nicole sometimes, but mostly when she's with me.

Ingrid: (Laughing) They looked all surprised when you knew me. They musta been thinking "who is she?"

Sky: (laughs) They know you're not no undercover. They know who all of them is. You can spot them before you see them. And they've seen you around. I think Laron seen you out at Jefferson.

Ingrid: He went to Jeff? Did I have him?

Sky: If you did, (laughing) you wouldn't of known it. He wasn't the school type. He be outside most of the time.

Ingrid: If they hadn't of known me, I mean like known who I was, would you still have come up to the car?

Sky: Oh, yeah. By me walking over they knew you were o.k., you were cool.

Ingrid: And if I hadn't of known you?

Sky: Like what? What would they do?

Ingrid: Yeah

Sky: Leave you be. I don't know.

Ingrid: What if maybe I was looking to buy? What if I wanted to buy something, if I pulled up and waited would they come over?

Sky: (Laughs and looks at me incredulously) I'm sorry, (laughs) I'm sorry, but Ingrid, ain't no way you be buying anything. You don't have the look (laughs).

With some probing on my part, Sky makes several social distinctions of varying sharpness. The contrast between school-goers and those who hang "outside" is a relatively sharp distinction, with little overlap. The distinction between myself and a non-local drug user is equally sharp (although Sky later struggled to explain why she knew this to be so.) My status as a neighborhood "outsider" is less clearly marked. Although I do not "belong," my status as a teacher, residents' knowledge of that role, my friendship with Sky and others, and my frequent presence in the neighborhood all set me apart from the typical "outsider." These characteristics and social knowledge of them also set me apart from the undercover cops I might otherwise be confused with. Less clear is Sky's differentiation between her friends ("sisters") and her street acquaintances ("buddies"). Even more fuzzy is the line between those who sometimes hang outside (e.g., Amanda) and those who rarely if ever do (e.g., Sharonda). Conversations with both Joseph and Anthony confirmed the social knowledge and differentiated status among the many individuals and groups using the Fillmore streets.

> *Joseph:* You know you might see important people coming over here to buy drugs and I even, I have friends who have clientele in the avenues, up by Jefferson, over there in that area, so . . .
>
> *Ingrid:* Do they usually bring it to them, or do some people come down here?
>
> *Joseph:* It just some people be on the streets with their business and some people do it outta their house. I even know people that have other people buy drugs for them.
>
> *Ingrid:* Indirect, so they don't even . . .
>
> *Joseph:* Uh huh
>
> *Ingrid:* It's probably safer if you have a clientele, isn't it, so you don't have to be on the streets?
>
> *Joseph:* Yeah. Yeah You could say that.
>
> *Ingrid:* Unless you run into an undercover (we laugh)
>
> *Joseph:* Uh huh. And they got undercovers but there's more undercovers in the Tenderloin area. You know who the cops is, you know what cops to look out for, you know what cops you can kinda, you know, get by with, and you know what colors, I mean what kind of color of the car, and they you also know the narc cars. I mean, if you hang on the block all day you see them come through and they usually look like tourists, they try to look like tourists and they usually got a camera or something.

In contrast to the "outside," the areas within the walls and gates of apartment complexes are more clearly demarcated, with the gates limiting some car and foot traffic. These buildings themselves protect the area from public (and police) view, making the inner courtyard more easily marked and controlled than the streets just yards away. These inward facing housing complexes are but one of many legacies of the redevelopment efforts that swept across the Fillmore in the 1960s and 1970s. Once dominated by street-facing Victorians, much of the area housing stock has been replaced with one and two-story housing structures oriented away from the street to an inner courtyard, parking, gardens, and/or play areas. These architectural transformations have powerfully altered the social landscape deeded to Sky and her peers. The KOP's ability to "control" key inner courtyards is but one testimony to the social breakdown resulting from such housing changes.

With several exceptions, all of these complexes were modeled on the design movements of the 1960s and 1970s. The first wave of redevelopment housing consisted primarily of high-rise complexes, full of identical units with no internal communal spaces. These large complexes were surrounded by one or two shared parks. The second wave of housing was characterized by horizontal rather than vertical sprawl. Most of these homes employed the classic "inward facing construction." This was initially designed to focus human activity at the central core of each complex. For the most part, this design has worked in counter-productive ways. The streets continue to serve as the primary social space for residents. However, with all units facing their backs to the streets, residences have become more disconnected from the street life. The consequences of this human disconnect are many. Jane Jacobs wrote her now-classic *The Death and Life of Great Cities* (1961) in response to such architectural transformations. Central to Jacobs' general argument about the role and function of cities is her belief that buildings, institutions, and the humans who use them must all interact across the urban landscape. She sharply critiqued the Le Corbusier-inspired notions of separating human beings and urban functions. Residential, commercial and social functions are best served, she argued, when they overlap, pushing up and against each other. Her view on the inward-facing complexes which came to dominate the low-income housing landscape could not be more clear:

> There must be eyes upon the street, eyes belonging to those we might call the natural proprietors of the street. The buildings on a street equipped to handle strangers and to insure the safety of both residents and strangers, *must be oriented to the street. They cannot turn their backs or blank sides to it and leave it blind.* (Jacobs, 1961, p. 35, emphasis mine)

In her discussion on the assimilation of children, Jacobs addresses the need to have spatial designs that encourage regular interaction among adults and children.

> Planners do not seem to realize how high a ratio of adults is needed to rear children at incidental play. Nor do they seem to understand that spaces and equip-

ment do not rear children. These can be useful adjuncts, but only people rear
children and assimilate them into civilized society. (Jacobs, 1961, p. 82)

As Jane Jacobs understood four decades ago, the spatial structuring of residences, parks and commercial areas is highly consequential.

"Outside" Corners

Sky's identification of "E" Street and its hangers resonates with key aspects of
the social landscape I observed in my time in the Fillmore. Eddy Street between Steiner and Pierce is one of a rough dozen key social corners in the Fillmore. When Anthony, Joseph, and Sky talked about the "outside," they were
referring not only to the general space outside the safety and confines of
homes or housing complexes (and the authority figures residing in them) but
more specifically to particular areas "outside." Key blocks, intersection and
corners play a powerful role in shaping the overall social landscape of the Fillmore. Though the majority of residents are not "on the outside" or hanging
out at these corners, they play a central role in the construction of the Fillmore's public images and local master identity. The Fillmore Master Map depicts the distribution of these social spaces. Mapping the built landscape is
relatively easy. Walking and driving the Fillmore, I was able to identify
stores, housing and faith-based institutions quite easily. I drove around with
Anthony, Sky, Joseph, and Caprisha several additional times to confirm information. In some cases, I had to check with local experts to verify specifics
(e.g., Miss Martin regarding an un-named church). Mapping the social corners of the Fillmore was far more challenging. Youth I worked with had varying definitions of what constituted a key "outside" corner. The questions they
asked me in response to my queries about street corners reveals much about
the social construction and definition of these spaces, the range of their definitions, and factors influencing them.

> *Anthony:* You wanna know where people hang out? Or where people be
> selling? At night or in the day?
>
> *Caprisha:* You mean like across from the McDonalds, where that guy got
> shot last month? Where people been killed?
>
> *Sky:* It's not just corners you know. If you wanna know everywhere
> people be hangin it will take us all day. Inside houses, too?
>
> *Anthony:* You wanna know what stores people be hanging out at? Cuz
> that' kinda like the same thing, sometimes. Like over on Bu-
> chanan, and at the Goldlane.

Sky: I know some of the corners have changed. Like once someone
            gets killed there, no one be hanging there for a few weeks,
            sometimes never.

Alfonzo: I know you can find me in front of Turkwood. I don't know
            about anyone else.

Joseph: I don't think "corners" is really it, Ms. Seyer. People be goin' all
            over.

Alfonzo: (responding to Joseph's comment and refuting his earlier one)
            Bullshit "all over." What about Golden Gate? over by Grove?
            And Webster?

These responses to my requests for help in identifying key social spaces highlight the complexities I faced in my endeavor. As Sky and Joseph point out,
people hang out everywhere: outside, inside, on corners, in parks, and in their
homes. I was interested in a particular type of social space and yet, as the youth
figured out, I wasn't very clear on exactly what spaces I in fact meant. This was
partially the result of my evolving understanding of these social spaces and partially a conscious effort to be vague, so as to develop my definition based upon
their understandings, not mine. The fact was, I was interested in a fairly narrow
band of the Fillmore's social spaces. I was interested in these because of their
influence on the neighborhood's public images, master identity, and quality of
life. The street corners I have mapped are those dominated by young, black
males, many of whom are actively dealing. They are the corners outsiders and
locals "walk around" (depending on their ghetto pass). They are the corners
police patrol more often than others. They are the corners, like corners across
the nation, that have come to define the inner-city, the "ghetto," black males
and the urban poor in the minds of many an American.

The key "outside corners" mapped on the Fillmore Master Map are not random. As my "informants" reminded me, they is also not static. At least one of
the corners on this map is now "gone" (i.e., "The Flav" at Webster and Fulton)
and several are temporarily closed down due to recent homicides (i.e., the corners of Buchanan and Hayes and Fillmore and Golden Gate). As these locations are the most concentrated sites of drug sales in the neighborhood, it is not
surprising that drive-bys and face-to-face shootings occur at these sites more often than others. These spaces take on meaning from the individuals and groups
who interact across them, giving them names, assigning them roles and value,
and occasionally pulling them out as personal and group historicizers. Walking
from his house to find Joseph one afternoon over three years after he left the
streets, Anthony offered to take me by his old hangout. As we approached the
corner of Grove and Webster Anthony suddenly stopped. He stood for some

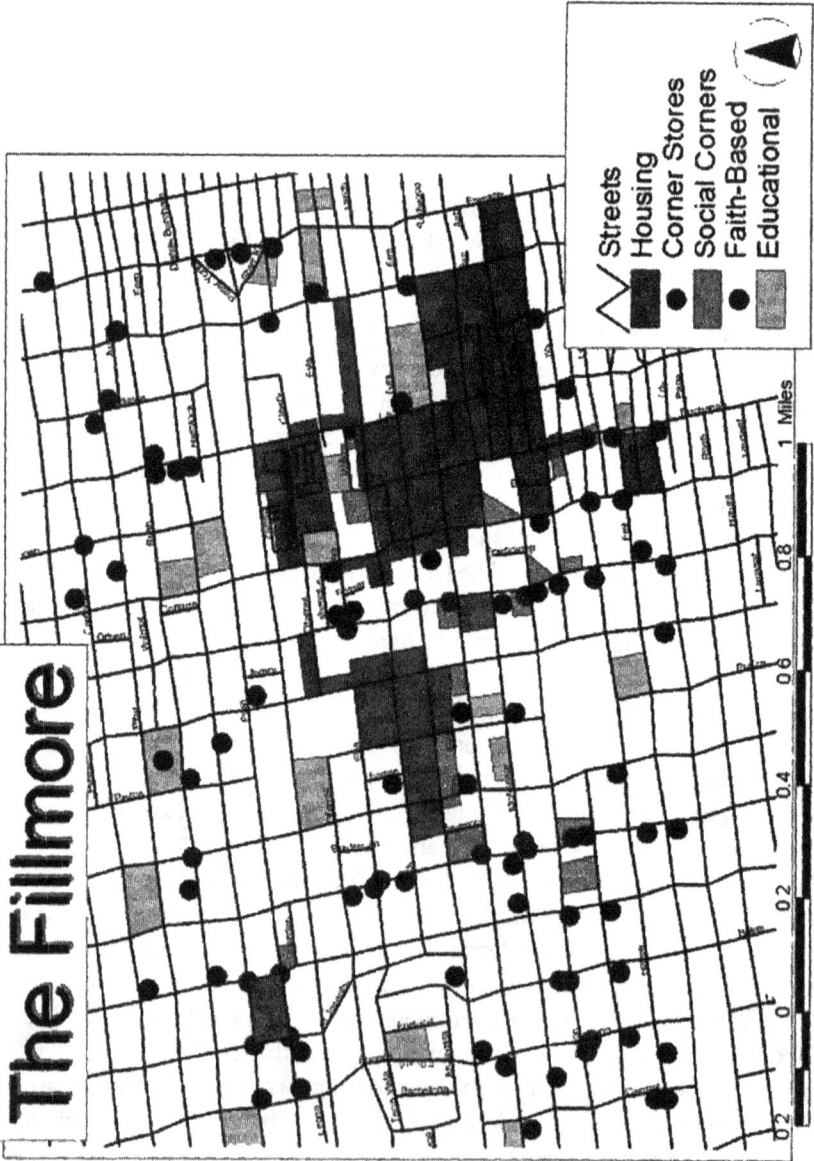

The Fillmore

Legend:
- Streets
- Housing
- Corner Stores
- Social Corners
- Faith-Based
- Educational

0.2 0 0.2 0.4 0.6 0.8 1 Miles

time at the corner, looking around. He started to talk and then stopped, look-ing around once more before stepping back and kneeling beneath the tree be-hind us. As he recalled his favorite place, his voice seemed to go deep within him; his speech slowed and several times he seemed to catch himself from cry-ing (something I have never seen him do).

Anthony: This area was known as the Flav. Used to be their area, but now it's all the Ujamistas.

Ingrid: So they like control it?

Anthony: Kinda, but not really. If you earn yourself a ghetto pass, you can be coming through here anytime. (keeps looking around the area. Walks to a corner under the tree and kneels down). When I was on the outside, this was my favorite place . . . (long pause) cuz this is where I met with my friends at, it's where I made my money at, this is where I had my good times at. (pause) Right here on this block. We shot dice, that's games, you know we talked about things, talked about the future, we got drunk, we got high together, we did everything together, it's like a family.

Ingrid: What do you guys talk about?

Anthony: We talk about the world, we talk about girls, I mean, we don't talk about it in that case, but we talk about 'em, yeah, you know, we talk about girls (laughs), but that's not all we talk about. I would say the main thing we talked about on the block was (pause) . . . was making money, I think. Yeah, how to make it and what you're gonna do with it.

Ingrid: Like lots of us. That's why they call us a capitalist society I guess (we both laugh) And what do most people wanna do with the money?

Anthony: What do most people do? They wanna buy a car, and get a fix, stuff like that, that's what most people do in the ghetto where I live, they just get clothes and cars. Clothes n cars. Yeah. They don't invest in nothing. . . . That's why people say we stupid.

Ingrid: So when you talk about the future, you aren't talking about "I wanna buy a house and get out of here?

Anthony: People think that in the ghetto we're not aware of what goes on in the government . . . we talk about politics, we talk about all that.

Ingrid: Man, I wish I had that tape! Those must have been some con-versations.

Anthony: Yeah, they were. They were (almost melancholic).

Ingrid: But that was a long time ago for you.

Anthony: Yeah, that was a long time ago. My memories aren't as vivid as they used to be.

The Flav no longer physically exists, not for Anthony and not for his friends. I asked Anthony if he came to the Flav often now. "I walk through a lot you know, but come here, to, you know, be? Naw, not too often. It's not the same." When I asked if it made him sad, reminded him of his past, he nodded but said nothing. Anthony chose to leave the "outside" but he has many fond memories from those times. For Anthony, the times he shared, the sense of belonging he felt, and the physical place of the Flav are inseparable. Today, the corner of Fillmore and Grove acts as a lived historicizer for Anthony. The Flav reminds Anthony of lessons, both good and bad. "This is where I had my good times at. . . . Right here on this block . . . we did everything together, it's like a family," he said. Anthony has yet to replace the connection and happiness the Flav enabled. Rasheem is in jail and J.D. lost his ghetto pass. Several young men were killed in the two blocks surrounding the Flav in the spring of 2001. This corner reminds him of this cautionary lesson, recalling the good times past and the life he has thus far saved. Anthony's world has been torn between life on the outside and inside since he was eight or nine. These social corners are critical to his understanding of his neighborhood, his past, his life, and its possibilities. As such they are central to his experience of the Fillmore's master identity. Although few in the Fillmore share such an intimate history with any of the neighborhood's "key social corners," Anthony's reminiscences demonstrate the power of these locales to define images and identities.

Corner Stores

The Fillmore Master Map is made more powerful when analyzed alongside two of the area's built structures, those of low-income housing and corner stores. In several cases, social corners develop a symbiotic relationship with corner stores. The constant movement of customers in and out of the store provides a steady stream of activity, distraction, and potential customers for corner hangers. The normal congregation of regulars around stores also distracts police from possible deals as they go on. In some cases, regular dealers use stores as their main base, conducting deals within and beyond the store. For those without such a relationship, the store provides a welcome space to retreat within when the cops do circle past.

The story of the corner store, crime, death, and controversy surrounding 719 Webster exemplifies the relationship between the built and social landscape. For over four years locals were concerned about the relationship between the King's Super Market, the hang-out in front of the store and skyrocketing crime in the neighborhood. In 1995 the store's liquor license was suspended after state regulators designated it a "disorderly house." The state's investigation resulted from a police report detailing 166 calls over 22 months regarding assaults, fights, robberies, shots fired, and weapons used or viewed. Twenty-four drug related incidents were also cited. Despite a probationary period, few changes were made. In 1997 and 1998 the store was cited for illegal alcohol sales. In 1998 a local community group, the Alamo Square Neighborhood Association, lobbied police, city supervisors, and the Mayor's office to have the store closed down. Joyce Ruger, a 70-year-old woman who lived down the street, spearheaded the lobby. In August of 1998 she was found murdered in her home. It was only after Ruger's murder that the city attorney's office finally took action, filing suit against King's as a "public nuisance that must be shut down to protect the community." The suit went on to allege that King's "for a considerable amount of time has engaged in selling liquor to minors and drunks and allowed drinking, loitering, harassment of citizens and other illegal and annoying activities." Unable to find any "adequate remedy" for these problems, the city demanded Kings' closure. It was to take a second death before change could occur. In 1999 a local drug dealer, Rick Curry, was shot and killed at the store. According to police reports, Curry was a major narcotics dealer and had been using the store as his address for some time. The store finally closed several weeks later. A storefront church has since taken its place.

At least five of the key corners on the Fillmore Master Map are located directly in front of or across from a corner store. Many others are related systematically to local housing structures. With the exception of two corners west of Divisadero, all of the Fillmore's key corners are located across from or between low-income housing projects. Corner "turfs" are claimed by those who live in the housing complexes closest to them. The Flav was one block up from Anthony's home; Joseph and Greg live in the MLK/Marcus Garvey complexes nominally run by the KOP. When I asked Caprisha if Alfonzo was in the KOP she smiled. "No, he runs up in Turkwood. He lives up there." The dominance of low-income housing in the Fillmore influences the social landscape far beyond its impact of drug dealing corners.

Low-Income Housing

To a random outsider driving through the Fillmore, each block of housing might seem much the same: some newer than others, all interconnected complexes with their backs to the street, surrounded by gates. Though much of this housing does fall under the rubric "subsidized," there are key differences between public and subsidized housing. Caprisha, Sky, Anthony and Joseph all lived in privately managed subsidized housing complexes. The only two remaining public housing "projects" in the Fillmore are undergoing renovation with HUD Hope VI funds. Although the *subsidized* Marcus Garvey Homes are nominally run by the KOP, the complex has never carried the same reputation for violence (quantitatively or qualitatively) as the *public* housing projects only three blocks away. One of those, the Hayes Valley project, runs along the southern border of the Fillmore. Long known as one of the more violent projects in the neighborhood, the San Francisco Housing Authority (SFHA) is attempting to create a mixed-income complex. One hundred and seventeen of the 195 new units are set aside for public housing, the remainder are designated for a range of incomes, all of them in the low-income range, many of them Section 8. The Plaza East project due to re-open in 2002 will replace a 276 unit high rise (constructed in 1956 and "plagued with criminal activity") with 193 public housing "Victorian style town houses and flats." Prior to its demolition, the Plaza East was known to local youth as "O.C." or "Outta Control." These two complexes, along with the Pink Palace closed down in the early 80's, have long been known as the most violence-plagued in the Fillmore. Across the city, similar patterns emerge.

Although my participants complained about the quality of life swirling around them, they frequently expressed pride in their homes themselves. Anthony, Sky, and Caprisha often described the Fillmore as a ghetto, but they rarely spoke of their housing complexes in terms of negative qualities or their subsidized nature. When I asked Anthony to give me a guided tour of the Fillmore, speaking as if to a total outsider, he began "We're in Loren Miller Homes, This is where I stay, it's an apartment building. I think it's a pretty nice place. It's pretty safe." Caprisha lived in a cooperatively run complex or "co-op" while Sky and Anthony lived in privately managed complexes. All three housing areas were developed as part of the A-2 redevelopment project. During the initial phases of A-2, priority in allocating housing development sites was given to local non-profit sponsors. HUD Section 8 funding as well as FHA monies were used for all construction, with the sponsoring organization facilitating various aspects of a project's development, unit allocation, and eventual management. Some of these organizations did not enter their redevelopment relationships with management experience and easily fell prey to mismanagement and corruption. Both Caprisha and Sky's complexes faced this problem in the 1970s. After a period of time under government control Caprisha's project became a co-op. Evaluations of the effectiveness of the co-op management vary. By most accounts I heard, the elected management "ran the books okay" but was virtually non-responsive to the many other challenges facing residents. Caprisha's complex was raided by the police twice during my research. Each time, the police commented on the need for greater local control of the area. Few structures were in place to encourage such control. Most of the co-ops in the area are governed by elected committees. A major role of these committees is the hiring and oversight of complex managers. Most of these managers focus on financial governance and play an extremely limited role in terms of social governance or leadership. In 2001, a police raid in the complex aimed at rooting out the KOP focused first on the unit of the co-op manager. According to Caprisha's grandmother, several guns and a large supply of drugs (owned by the manager's son) were found in the unit.

Sky conveys several other interesting characteristics of the built landscape on her map. At the corner of Eddy and Fillmore she marks several advertising billboards, one for cigarettes, one for beer. She also places the "café shop" on the corner, the only coffee shop serving the Fillmore (in contrast to the eight serving five blocks of the Upper Fillmore). She also notes the construction barricade one block up ("That damn hole has been there for months" she comments). Across from the "E" block, noted on her second map as a "drug free zone," is a funeral home, one of five in the Fillmore. "Drug Free Zone" signs are common in the inner-city neighborhoods such as the Fillmore, often placed near housing areas or schools. I initially thought the signs were posted for their (less-than effective) deterrent impact and found their proximity to drug dealing areas ironic if not symbolic. Walking up Golden Gate Street one day Anthony pointed out a drug free zone sign posted at the housing project across the street, clarifying for me the more specific purpose of their location. "It's like if you get caught selling drugs it's like twice the time in a drug free zone. It's like more time added. And it seems like these places over here are all drug-free zones, so if you live around here they setting you up for more time, right up front. Look at this, all a 'drug free zone'" (points ahead to a group of guys at Fillmore and Golden Gate, a known selling corner). Anthony shook his head and we both laughed. Anthony and I are not the only ones to recognize and laugh at this tragedy. In his 1996 show *Bring the Pain* Comedian Chris Rock joked: "That's right, now we got the 'war on drugs.' That's Bullshit. The war on drugs is just another way to get more mothafuckers in jail. That's all it is." The impact of these signs on those arrested is no laughing matter. They influence those who are not arrested as well. Anthony was always quick to spot and speak out against the ways in which "the system" was working against he and his peers. I do not know the intentions of the policy makers who decided to place drug-free signs in key drug-dealing neighborhoods, attaching a higher prison sentence with them. I do know that they most likely did not intend to perpetuate a sense of us versus them among young Black males, nor did they realize that their decision would be one of many to perpetuate Anthony and his peers' sense that they lived in a neighborhood under attack, a neighborhood in need of constant vigilance. A *defended* neighborhood (Ley, 1974).

Though not as common as "Drug Free Zone" signs, funeral homes are an important institution on the Fillmore landscape. The national death rate among African Americans males ages 14–21 is more than five times higher than that for White males. In the first five months of 2001 San Francisco witnessed 25 homicides, six of them gang-related. Most of these homicides involved young Black males. Funerals, then, are a relatively common event. During my formal research period (three years), Anthony and Caprisha attended five funerals each, Sky seven. The resulting banality of these events was not lost on Anthony. I asked him to take me to the informal memorial site that had been erected for a recently murdered 17-year-old.[8] The murderer was still "at large" though he hinted that at least a few people did know the perpetrator. Commenting on the reasons behind their lack of cooperation

---

[8]Primarily Black youth create these shrines to the fallen, including balloons, pictures, liquor bottles, and flowers to mark the murder sites in Bayview-Hunter's Point, Sunnydale, and the Fillmore.

with the police, Anthony vents his frustration with the frequency of funerals
and his community's responses to them.

> *Anthony:* So I guess you could say that it's a fault on the community and
> it's a fault on the police department, too. We allow it to happen
> and we don't say nothing and we just allow things to happen.
> Like after a murder one time, by Virgo's (a gang in the mid-90's),
> a person named T-Call had died and when the police came they
> was laughing and joking like it was just a regular event! But, I
> don't think you can expect them to take it seriously when the
> people in the community don't take it serious. I think if we took
> it more serious then the police would take it more serious so I
> don't put all the fault on them, I put a lot of the fault on the
> community.
>
> *Ingrid:* So you don't think people take death as seriously as they should?
>
> *Anthony:* Yeah.
>
> *Ingrid:* Do you think it's cuz it happens so often, it's like normal?
>
> *Anthony:* Yeah. Not only is it a joke to the police but it's a joke to the
> black community, I think, 'cause people they get dressed up and
> go to these funerals. Some people be trying to look nice and get
> their hair done hoping they'll catch people at a funeral. This is at
> funerals!
>
> *Ingrid:* So it like social event?
>
> *Anthony:* Yeah! And you know, they talk about it, that be the main topic
> of conversation for about a week or two weeks, about the funeral,
> how the person died, who shot him and alla that, and then peo-
> ple go to the funeral and be talking about "we need to stop all
> this, putting on big scenes crying, like they love a person, and
> then two, three weeks later they be right out, doing the same
> thing. So to me, that's a joke. So people would say I'm wrong for
> saying that, but that's what I see.

Anthony is not alone in his frustration with the community's response to such
deaths. The Rev. Amos Brown (a former city supervisor and pastor of the Third
Baptist Church, one of the Western Addition's "Big 3" black churches) spoke
out against memorials such as the one at Buchanan and Hayes. "These memorials show the hopelessness that has engulfed many in our community," Brown
said. "These street rituals show that this generation is intoxicated with death"
(*San Francisco Chronicle*, 7/1/01, A20). Unlike gravestones and official land-

marks, these makeshift memorials remain for only a month or two, temporary historicizers for youth who mark off their 20-odd years in terms of deaths and funerals. Brown's frustration with the memorials expresses not only his concern with the violence and deaths plaguing his neighborhood, but also how the youth process these deaths. In his mind, funerals are appropriate was to memorialize the fallen, street corner memorials are not. These memorials remain, public statements to the world until they are removed. It is possible that these public representations also trouble Brown. The construction of the area's images and master identity are also at stake here.

BORDER CROSSINGS AND SPATIAL ACCESS

People and spaces are defined both by what they are and what they are not. The Fillmore's master identity emerges as much from its contrast with other neighborhoods as it does from its own particular character. That character is only understood in terms of what it is not, making the separation of the Fillmore from its neighbors and larger city impossible. These contrasts of which I speak are often made most visible at borders. It is at these boundary crossings that differences are made notable and meaningful. Moving across any landscape is a process of continual border crossings. Some of these crossings are visible, made relevant via social constructions. Others go unnoticed. The extent to which any crossing is social relevant depends on the persons crossing and their relationship and understanding of the border and spaces being traversed. Driving north on highway 101, a sign notifies the observant driver that they have entered the City and County of San Francisco. For the average driver, this border crossing does not impact their travels. Once within the city, few borders are as clearly marked, though many of them are far more influential. Important borders in Anthony, Caprisha, and Sky's lives include those of their District, neighborhood, community, turf, home, and social corners.

The District

San Francisco is divided into Districts (e.g., the Sunset, Richmond, and Mission). During their high school years my participants spent the majority of their time in the Sunset and the Western Addition Districts. The Western Addition is never clearly delineated in the minds of San Francisco residents, businesses, or planners. One reason for this difficulty is the district's constant evolution. When I asked people to define the district's borders, many older San Franciscans would ask me to for more chronological specificity. "You mean now, or before the war?" asked several Nisei's. "Western Addition now or before redevelopment" was also a common query among Blacks and Japanese Americans. The Western Addition's official boundaries were set in 1865. Those boundaries changed, at least in residents' minds, during or after key historical events: The 1906 fire, WWII and redevelopment being the three most commonly cited. As the district enters the 21st century, gentrification, although less clearly an "historical event," may prove to be the next boundary definer. According to current neighborhood borders used by the city, the Western Addition is bounded in by more surrounding neighborhoods (nine) than any other in the city. If Hayes Valley, Duboce Triangle and Alamo Square are added in, the Fillmore is literally being pushed in upon by upwards of 12 neighborhoods. Several of these neighborhoods lean toward the upscale (i.e., Pacific Heights and Nob Hill) and/or hip and trendy (e.g., Hayes Valley) leading to a fair share of NIMBYism.

Among current African American residents I spoke with, the Western Addition's most commonly shared boundaries are Van Ness, Divisadero, Geary, and Fell. When speaking with Nisei, they would extend the northern border several blocks past Geary to California. Both of these borders create a fairly straightforward box, with the Fillmore placed almost exactly in the center. Other responses included "the area around Japantown," "all around Kaiser and all, that area," "pretty much the Fillmore," "Van Ness to Divis., from Geary to um, hmmm . . . Fell? Oak?" and "Masonic to Van Ness, from the Haight over towards J'town." Whereas individuals varied in the markers they used to define the district (i.e., streets, neighborhoods, and commercial centers), their responses did overlap with some consistency to map a general rectangle in the center of the city.

The Western Addition is a formal San Francisco District and does have official boundaries. Although San Franciscans' perception of these current borders varies depending on their experience in the area and their knowledge of its historical landscape, a relative consensus about these borders does emerge (i.e., Oak, Van Ness, California/Geary, and Divisadero/Masonic). The boundaries at the neighborhood level of the Fillmore are more evasive. These boundaries varied most among residents and non-residents. Most non-residents I spoke with were relatively vague about the borders of the Fillmore, lumping the neighborhood in with the Western Addition more broadly. Once again, historical questions arose. "The Fillmore" fell into four general public images: the predominantly Jewish Fillmore of the 1920s, the primarily Japanese Fillmore of the 1930s and early 1940s, the "Harlem of the West" Fillmore of the 1940s–1960s ("pre-redevelopment") and the ghetto Fillmore of today. San Franciscans' sense of the Fillmore's boundaries today seemed to be most directly tied to their historical relationship with one of those historical periods. Despite the fact that the Fillmore had changed, particular historicizing periods (and their boundaries) overpowered current social landscapes and the borders defining them. Thus, my Nisei in-laws defined the Fillmore as roughly overlapping with the Western Addition whereas my participants mapped a much smaller area within the district.

The Neighborhood

When I asked youth to define the boundaries of their neighborhood, the question always seemed to surprise them. It was as if I were asking about something so assumed it was never discussed. Given the specificity and con-

sistency of the explanations I received, I came to believe that these boundaries were so normalized and assumed that they were never questioned, formally discussed, or "thought about." Although rarely if ever analyzed, these
boundaries do shape the Fillmore's master identity, its social landscapes and
the lives of its residents. Anthony's borders clearly overlap with the "outside"
world, as he uses "the KO area," "where we hanging" and "certain streets" to
mark off the neighborhoods social edges.

> It depends. Like some people think it's a larger area and to us, it's not really, it's
> just like where we hanging. (Which would be what then?) For me? I would say
> like, certain streets, like Oak Street, all the way around KO, I would say that's
> the Fillmore to me. Laguna, Divisadero, Hayes and Eddy. Not really to Geary,
> well, I guess you could say that, too, around the KO area.

He references to the neighborhood's public image, "*some* people think it's a
larger area," qualifying his description with reference to "us." ("You know,
the kids who *live* here," he explained when I asked him to clarify the pronoun.) This contrast between local youth and "others" resonated with an
outsider–insider/us versus them mentality pervasive among many Fillmore
residents. References by locals to neighborhood borders came up when key
interactions and contrasts (often conflicts) with other neighborhoods and
non-locals arose. It is critical that Anthony says "not really to Geary" with no
prompting, seemingly contrasting *his* borders with those of *others*. Geary is a
particularly important border, as it marks the transition from Upper to Lower
Fillmore (and from Pacific Heights to the Fillmore, non-Black to Black, gen-
trified to low-income and wealthy to poor). Caprisha's response qualified the
insider–outsider continuum even further. In her explanation of the Fillmore's
borders she explained the "real" borders with those of "some people," specifically those on the "outside" (i.e., gangs, dealers). Anthony lives toward the
eastern end of the Fillmore. When I asked youth who lived in the more western regions, closer to Divisadero, many extended the Fillmore's boundaries
only as far as Webster or Buchanan.

In contrast to Anthony, Joseph and Sky, Caprisha's movement around the
Fillmore is limited largely to car and bus rides to and from her home, church,
work and the store. She rarely "walks around" or hangs out. Her borders mirrored these experiences, drawing upon streets rather than social spaces.

> *Ingrid:*   What would you say the borders of the Fillmore are, like what
>   are the edges?
> *Caprisha:* The Fillmore? Like where does it go to?

Ingrid: Yeah

Caprisha: (thinks several seconds) I guess that would be like Webster,
            Geary, um Divisadero, I guess and Hayes . . . no, Fell, Fell?
            (looks up, visualizing) . . . no Oak, Oak. (giggles) Yeah, Oak.

Ingrid: (laughing) Were you trying to make sure you got True Be-
            lievers in there?

Caprisha: (laughs) How'd you know?

Ingrid: You're all like "Hayes? No Fell? No Oak . . . No . . . Where
            True Believers? Fell? Oak. Why not. . . ." (laughter)

Miss Martin: (who has been listening to us and laughing) I'd say Haight
            Street, and out by, what is that? Masonic? Mount Zion and
            A.M.E.'s out thataways.

Although I joked with Caprisha about the seemingly random nature of the
boundaries she was describing, they are anything but arbitrary. It was crucial
that Caprisha was moving or extending the boundaries in her mind to include
her church (True Believers) within the Fillmore.

Although the specific streets varied by several blocks, by the time you had
crossed Divisadero (W), Webster (E), Grove (S), or Eddy (N), there was no
doubt you were in the Fillmore. David Ley found similar overlaps among residents' mental maps and those of geography. "Although individual idiosyncrasies rule residents' mental maps of their neighborhood, considerable overlapping and agreement does exist. For the overwhelming majority of residents,
the perceived neighborhood boundary does not exceed the boundaries of
Monroe. . . . Thus, there is close agreement between our boundaries of geographic and analytical convenience, and the residents' boundaries of mind"
(Ley, 1974, p. 79). Sitting at a McDonald's one school day, Joseph, Caprisha,
and I lamented our soggy burgers and agreed we should have gone for pizza.
This inspired a recollection of a Round Table meal several years before.
Rapidly reminding each other of the details, I was soon lost in the flood of
their laughter, only able to gather that Joseph had looked at someone the
wrong way and before they knew it they had to leave that place FAST.
Caprisha delightedly recalled flying down Geary, the other car in hot pursuit.

Caprisha: I was so scared. I was like, oh, oh, I couldn't look, I was freak-
            ing-out.

Joseph: Then we pulled that turn at Divis. (laughs, miming a sharp turn
            of the steering wheel) and swung onto Turk. We hit Steiner
            and he was gone. Gone. That motherfucker was gone!

Caprisha: They weren't coming into the Fillmoe!

Joseph: That motherfucker was out there, out-o-there, heading on home to Potrero. Out-o-there!

Given the antagonist's Potrero Hill connection, it is quite likely that the borders he was unwilling to cross were more turf than neighborhood defined. As Anthony's description attests, turf and neighborhood borders often bleed into one another. In the Fillmore, competition among gangs and competition over turfs has been less conflict ridden than in Los Angeles' Compton or other gang-dominated areas. In contrast to the Bayview/Hunters Point, intra-neighborhood turf conflicts are far less common than intra-neighborhood battles. Whereas Hunters Point youth identify themselves primarily by their housing project and/or turf, Fillmore youth identify first and foremost with their 'hood, "The Fillmoe" or "Moe." For young men on the "outside" gang and/or turf affiliations are secondary. While hanging outside, Anthony was active in the Flav area centered at Webster and Grove. At the same time, Joseph was dealing with the KOP on Eddy and Alfonzo worked the Turkwood area one block west. Joseph and Anthony are close, as are Joseph and Alfonzo. Such cross-affiliation friendships are unheard of in some parts of Hunter's Point.

Within the Fillmore, turf borders are relatively permeable; *socially* permeable but not *commercially* so. Anthony, Joseph, Alfonzo, and others can move fluidly across intra-Fillmore turfs provided they abide by certain rules. Visiting friends in the MLK/Marcus Garvey complexes is allowed, drug dealing by outsiders is not. The borders of the KOP's purview are carefully marked, both on residents' cognitive maps (recall Sky's placement of the KOP on her map) and on the built landscape. KOP affiliates publicize these borders with tags on the housing complexes' gates and walls. Ley (1974) argues that the most contested areas for gangs (and many other groups) are the boundaries of their turf and it is thus these areas which are most frequently marked with graffiti. Various aspects of the group identity are drawn upon in these tags: its name (KOP), its locale (Street *number* and *name*, 1600 Eddy), neighborhood (Fillmoe) and members (Hot Boyz). These tags are most prominent at the physical borders of the KOP turf. I found KOP tags at Jefferson as well: on student papers, blackboards, desktops, book covers, and posters.

The KOP taggers appropriate a range of pre-existing structures and media to claim their space. Given the school's denial of so much that the Fillmore and the KOP represented, it was hard not to interpret the KOP tags at Jefferson as acts of resistance, however cautionary. The group's "claim" of public spaces and structures in the Fillmore was far more blatant, the most obvious

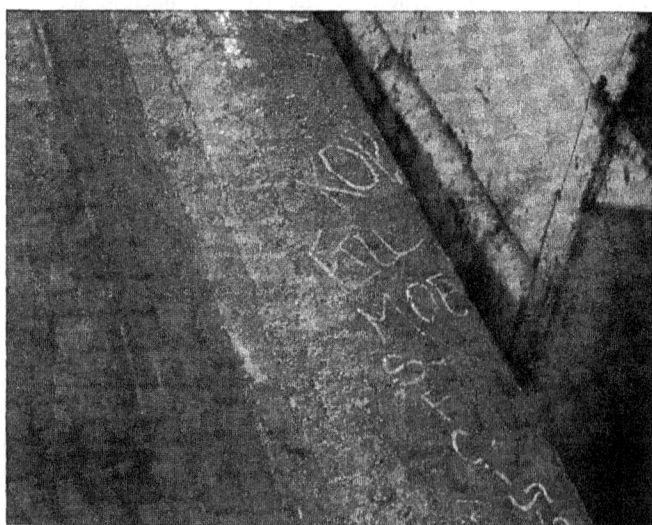

example of the creation and claiming of a *counter space* as I observed in my work. Most of the tags I found were on the gates and walls surrounding the Martin Luther King/Marcus Garvey complexes. These gates functioned as yet another structural and social boundary on the Fillmore landscape. Given their designated purpose, the KOP's appropriation of the gates made their statements ironically powerful.

On her maps Sky locates several gates at the entrance to the MLK complex parking lot. In fact, all of the housing complexes in this area are surrounded by gates, some of them in working condition, others not. Caprisha's housing complex was surrounded by gates that didn't work. "These things haven't worked for years," she would remark almost every time we pushed open the rusting gate. In contrast, Anthony's newer gates were computer controlled and required a scan card or phone code for access. Most of these gates were installed in the last decade in an effort to decrease violence in the area. Describing his housing complex to me as we left his house one day, Anthony commented

> I think it's pretty safe. I don't think it's the gates 'cause the people that get in, the people that use to get in but don't live here? They still get in. So I don't think the gates really help 'cause they know people in here, they get cards from them, stuff like that, they got codes . . . so they still find a way to get in. So that's why I think the gates don't help. But then some areas, you know they got a lot of old people in there and they really check up into you. You try to get in they all like "who are you? Do you live in here?" If you don't they be asking who your folks' name is" and all that. I mean it is violent. There is a lot of violence in here but I don't think that the gates make it no better. 'Cause my feeling is like when they put the gates up, it makes it seem like a jail, like you're locked in the place you live in. And if something was to happen', if there was some situation and you had to run and get away and you couldn't because the gates is there. (We approach Laguna and Grove). I know a couple friends who live over here, folks I went to school with. But I don't really know too much about this place. They got a gate though (grins over at me). They put gates on all these places around here. Supposed to stop the violence (smiles again).

These gates serve to further strengthen the boundaries between the street and housing, not only to protect residents from outsiders, but to keep residents themselves *out* at key moments. Specifically, some residents explained to me that the gates were installed to limit the movement of drug dealers and thieves from the "site of their crimes" (i.e., the street) to the safety of their residences. As Anthony points out numerous times, he himself does not credit any decreases in violence to the gates. Rather, he once again emphasizes his sense of Fillmore residents being misunderstood and mistreated by outsiders with power. The gates don't make him feel safe, they make him feel like a locked-up criminal. His repetition of "supposedly" and "supposed to" highlights the contrast between the planners' intentions and the actual results. Anthony was not a firm believer in the effectiveness of government and the gates were just one more example of "the system's" bad intentions and failure. The useless of the gates was not lost on Anthony, who began to make a joke out of the wasted resources invested in the gates. As we walked, Anthony continued to point out the many gates we passed. He may not know much about the housing project at Laguna and Grove but he *does* know it has a gate. (Anthony pointed out four more gates over the next six minutes, each time we added some joke to the gate's existence. Two we tested didn't work and one was wide open.)

Walking that afternoon with Anthony, we criss-crossed a number of boundaries, far more than I was even aware of. As we turned up Grove toward Buchanan, we entered a social corner nominally controlled by a group of eight to ten young men. As we approached, I slid my tape recorder away (as I would three other times that afternoon). My access to these areas was enabled by my connection to Anthony, but his presence could not always ensure my safety, or his. Whenever I walked around with Anthony, I was cognizant of his constant need to maintain his ghetto pass, his access to the streets that he had formally "left behind." I never knew how *much* my presence pushed the limits of his pass, though I know we pushed those limits several times. Those limits were largely determined by the specifics of the social web stretching across the Fillmore and Anthony's place within it.

Ghetto Passes

Whenever I walked with Fillmore with Anthony or Sky, we moved among a sea of familiar faces. Tapes of our walking conversations are peppered with greetings (most often initiated with a "Whuz up?") and brief conversations, most of them involving a joke and laughter. Both Sky and Anthony have spent much of their childhood and teen years "outside" and are comfortable in these street spaces. Despite his decision to stop selling, Anthony has maintained his "ghetto pass" and this enables him to guide me across numerous social borders, opening up many spaces to which I would otherwise be denied access (or possibly safety). Anthony and Sky's access to these spaces is a byproduct of continual negotiation and relationship maintenance.

The social nature of all borders and spaces is encapsulated in the concept and uses of the ghetto pass. Ghetto passes are extremely nuanced, enabling an individual differential access to social and geographic spaces at particular times. Their nature is revealed in the language surrounding their use. Passes are "earned" and "taken," just as one can get "caught up in" the life of the street that issues most passes.

Anthony: And one of my close friends, he in jail. He can't really hang around here 'cuz he'd get killed.

Ingrid: How come he'd get killed?

Anthony: It's just certain things he was in. So he can't come around here no more. And my other friend, Kenneth, his nickname is J.D., he's kinda in the same thing, he can't come around here no more.

Ingrid: So where does he live?

Anthony: He lived here before but as I said before, his ghetto pass got took.

Ingrid: So how does your ghetto pass get took?

Anthony: If you, I don't know, people see you as a, as what they'd say a "bitch ass niggar?" than you can't come around like, if you's a punk, if you don't stand up for yourself, or you snitch on somebody, or if you um kill somebody, like the wrong person, than you can't come around no more. But if you do, the person knew so many people, you know what I'm saying? so you could get killed pretty easy.

Ingrid: So you stay at home, you can stay where you stay, you just can't go into certain area? So they're not going to come and try to kill you in your place?

Anthony: The best thing is to move. But even then, you know, there's a lot of people in the Fillmore, since the projects got tore down lots of people moved to different areas so even then you could get caught up, still. I've seen fairly respectable people not be able to come around no more. Yeah.

Ingrid: So people move to like Oakland? Richmond?

Anthony: Yeah. Or way out.

Anthony's description of ghetto passes contains several variables governing their use. Rules of behavior govern the outside and are applied to pass access as well. Although Anthony at first struggled to define what rule violations would lead to a ghetto pass getting taken, he does eventually list a fairly specific set. Snitching and weak behavior are not tolerated. Not all killing is wrong: it depends on *who* you kill. (It is important to note that Anthony was not claiming that killing the right person was morally or ethically acceptable, only that this would not lead to a ghetto pass being denied.) These rules are enforced socially. As Anthony explains, if you kill the wrong person, his crew will come and find you. Also notable within Anthony's description is his division of people into (overlapping) types: the bitch ass niggar, the punk, and even "fairly respectable people" can all lose their access depending on the street rules they've violated. Anthony hints that generally those who lose their passes deserve it when he compares them to the anomalies, the "fairly respectable people" who can occasionally be kicked out as well. Though other passes are not named, access is earned, availed and denied based upon a similar set intersecting variables, including individual histories with social groups and the spaces they control, social work invested in maintaining this access, the gender and age of individuals in relation to social groups ad the status of the individual "pass holder" on the insider–outsider continuum.

Access to relationships, spaces, and landscapes is built upon a historic foundation: the personal history of an individual with groups and spaces is the most critical determinant in determining access. Anthony's current ghetto pass is largely the legacy of his long history with the young Black men who control the streets and corners of the Fillmore. He shares a large part of his past with these young men and these shared pasts do not disappear once the conditions of their relationships change. It is especially important that the years Anthony and his street peers shared were their early, formative ones. Anthony, J.D. and Rasheem (his two closest friends) spent much of the years between childhood and young adulthood together. These years, critical to the development of their senses of self, both as individuals and in relation to the larger society, were nurtured in the social milieu of the streets. J.D. lost his ghetto pass and Rasheem was imprisoned. It was around the time of these two events that Anthony decided to leave the street life. Although he shared his adolescent years with this peer group, it is critical that he made a break from them as he approached adulthood.

Sky and Caprisha's histories with various groups in the Fillmore also helps to afford them differential accesses. Both young women grew up with most of the young men known to "control" the streets. Although Joseph and Alfonzo are important dealers in the area, it is the girls' history with them as friends rather than boys' income-generating status that defines their relationships. Caprisha and her family are particularly close to Joseph. One of Caprisha's aunts was involved with Joseph's father for some time and she helped to raise him for several years. A web of similar connections extends across the social landscape of the Fillmore. This network is constantly evolving. J.D. got his ghetto pass taken. Things change. When one relationship changes, many others change as well. Thus, a history of affinity does not imply automatic or continual access.

Access, like the human relationships it is based upon, must be actively maintained. Time must be invested and personal alignments carefully crafted. Both of these require a deep understanding of the norms governing particular groups, spaces, and relational networks. Caprisha is a threat to only a few of the Fillmore's social groups. For the most part, her gender and identification as a "church girl" limit her threat potential and enable a fair degree of social and spatial access. Her gender and social connections provide her and her family with a "complimentary safety pass" of sorts. She and her family maintain these passes via ongoing relationships. Caprisha talks with Joseph, Alfonzo, and Anthony whenever she sees them around, her grandmother occasionally talks to Joseph's "auntie" on the phone. All of these encounters are shared over and over again via social networks, indicating who is aligned with whom. Given her limited threat potential, Caprisha doesn't need to invest much time in these relationships. On the contrary, if she too much time "outside" her presence would increase both the number of relationships requiring maintenance and her threat potential while challenging her status as a "church girl." Over time, her social access at church would also be questioned.

Anthony must work far more carefully to maintain his ghetto pass. Anthony was an effective and committed street member and drug dealer for almost five years. Having quit the life on the outside he must strike a finely tuned balance: hanging out "outside" just enough to convey his continual friendship with and support of his street peers without raising doubts about his true allegiance. If he needed some quick money Anthony could quite easily buy a bag or two of dope and sell them for some quick cash. Such a move would completely change the conditions of his current access.

Anthony: Sometimes I be tempted to uh get a sack and sell that, just so I can have money, but I never be tempted to come and hang out on the block like I used to.

Ingrid: Can you just kinda pick up a bag and sell it, can you come in and out like that?

Anthony: No, not really. If they know you do that, its like if you're gonna be into the streets, then you should be into the streets, but its not good to be in the streets and then be going to school. If you gonna do it, you should be into 100%.

You cannot "kinda" sell. When it comes to selling, you are either in or you're out. It is one thing to have access to spaces and social contacts, it is quite another to have access to the commercial possibilities they enable. As long as Anthony does not sell, spends some but not too much time outside, and maintains the right social alignments, his access is relatively assured.

Social alignments are tricky wherever you go. My most recent experiences on the 150-member faculty of a San Francisco public high school and as a graduate student at Stanford University have proved to me that unwritten but strongly enforced rules, cliques, and social networks are far from the sole purview of the Fillmore streets. There is at least one critical difference between my world and Anthony's: in the Fillmore, a mistake can kill you. Examples of such mistakes are eerily common. Damien Sparks, the cousin of Caprisha's boyfriend, was killed in the fall of 1999. Only 15 years old at the time of his death, Damien had started selling only months before. A verbal altercation with the wrong person appeared to end uneventfully. That "wrong" person returned fifteen minutes later with a loaded gun and shot Damien in the head, in front of at least five witnesses (one of them Damien's twin sister). In the aftermath of his murder, many people explained Damien's death in terms of his mistakes. These "mistakes" were based on his lack of knowledge: he "didn't know who he was messing with," or "hadn't learned the rules." He was a novice to the streets and got in over his head. Though details were unclear, it was also hinted that Damien had sold to his murderer's customer in the days prior to his death. A seller who wants to stay alive has to know who else is selling, where, and to whom.

The young man who killed Damien was reportedly a 22-year-old from the East Bay. Networks and access cross turf, neighborhood and city boundaries (some gang "passes" extend as far south as L.A.). Gang and drug related borders and access are the most dangerous—and therefore most critical in the formation of public images and master identities. It is true that drugs and the violence it engenders dominate the social landscape. They do so not through disproportionate numbers of activities or actors, but via their power to influence, intimidate, and possibly kill. Philippe Bourgois spent three years studying crack dealers in New York's Puerto Rican El Barrio. Like the Fillmore, drugs, poverty and violence dominate El Barrio's social landscape. Bourgois (1996) argues that "Most of El Barrio's residents have nothing to do with drugs. The problem, however, is that this law-abiding majority has lost control of public space." In the Fillmore, losing control of public space has led to a loss of control over the public images and master identities constructed about the neighborhood. The perceived contrast of the drug lifestyle with those of mainstream behaviors and values also heightens their role in the construction of images. The neighborhood's master identity influences path-way options and lifetime opportunities. The desire to earn money, to do so in ways that are readily available and relatively easy, and to fight to maintain ac-cess to these income streams characterizes many, arguably most, workers in our capitalist system. Despite these similarities, most outsiders view the typi-cal street-corner drug dealer with disdain, distrust and fear.

Drugs and violence are one of many determinants of social and spatial ac-cess. Gender, age, and one's outsider–insider status are among the others. Since the late 1970s feminist geographers such as Dorothy Hayden (1996) have been re-mapping public and private spaces in terms of gender relations. In some parts of the country (and San Francisco), women play an active role in organized gangs and drug sales. In the Fillmore, gangs and drug sales are one of several structures which actively work to maintain male-dominated public spaces. Females are integrally connected to these worlds as buyers (of-ten addicts/"dope phiends"), romantic partners (and occasional "covers"), and family members. They are excluded from drug selling, a critical safety border. This exclusion is maintained through the interactions of males and females. The power of males over public spaces is encoded in language and acts. Violence against women, ranging from calls of "bitch" and "hoe," to threats of attack and gang rapes, work to keep females "in their place." An-thony and Joseph frequently spoke of wanting to settle down with a "church girl." This expressed desire for a girl who "stays inside" further sustains spa-tially encoded gender boundaries. (It also hints at the pathway and life to which the two young men aspire.) Exclusion from drug sales excludes females from this income stream. It also excludes them from much of the highly-organized violence.

Females maintain spaces and borders of their own, defined, as are the oth-ers, by histories, relationship networks, time, and alignments. Some of the gender networks I observed in action seemed to be more clearly demarcated than the more amorphous male networks (gang and non-gang). Whereas males often moved between and across groups, female social networks within the Fillmore allowed far less "bleeding" across borders. Many of the most tightly enforced borders were those based around a shared and therefore "fought over" males.

Among Caprisha's circle, females have one set of rules, males another. The standard for females is higher and they are held to that standard more stringently by their fellow females. These rules are known and understood. As a mark of sisterhood, women are expected to follow them. The use of "sisters" to refer to all women conveys this communal idea of all women. During many conversations, Caprisha and her friends conveyed that such sisterhood was necessary because men were so untrustworthy and manipulative. In an "us" against "them" mentality, sisterhood gains relevance and power. Males can be "fought for" and "won." These fights are governed by "rules" as well. Girls can fight each other but one girl cannot fight for another. Sky consistently broke these rules, fighting for her female friends. That these friends did not come from the Fillmore further deepened her offenses, in the eyes of many.

In contrast to the simplistic account shared among Caprisha and her friends, Sky's relationship with males and females were less sharply differentiated and more complex. Sky consistently crossed a wider range of spatial, gender, and ethnic borders than did Caprisha. One afternoon soon after graduation, Sky excitedly recounted her most recent fight with another girl. She reveled not only in her physicality, but in her blatant disregard for gender boundaries as set. Sky was smashing away at these boundaries, through her physical punches, yes, but more consistently and effectively through her platonic friendships with males, her choice of non-Fillmore, non-Black female friends, and her refusal to abide by spatially-enforced gender roles. While Caprisha and her friend continually acted to enforce gender boundaries, Sky was fighting to break them down. It was her refusal to follow the rules and the objections this raised that highlighted the rules for me. When rules are accepted, they are almost invisible. It is contradictions and anomalies that leave the best clues.

Guest Passes

Through her physical defense of several non-Fillmore females, Sky was extending a guest pass of sort to her closest friends. These girls were not the only ones to earn guest passes through their connections to key insiders. My access to the Fillmore was dependent on and thanks to my personal relationship with many residents. Most of my time in the neighborhood was spent with people. I didn't live or work in the neighborhood and had to "create" reasons to be there. In the early stages of my research, before I could just "drop by" Caprisha's or Sky's, I actively worked to "create" reasons for my presence. These activities also served as avenues via which I developed new relationships and learned about the Fillmore. Over time, as I met more people, I began to have reasons to be around: meetings to attend, people to check in with, things to drop off, and acquaintances to hang out with. My increased familiarity with the neighborhood greatly eased my transition with Sky, Caprisha, and Anthony. They became my reason for "being around." The longer I spent there, the more accepted my presence became. Never, however, have I had not needed one of them or their peers to be with me. I could not drive up to Eddy and Steiner today, park and just hang out on the corner without breaking several social norms. It is only with (or on my way to) one or more of them that my presence is normalized and allowed.

Early on, my role as a Jefferson teacher came to the forefront of my Fillmore identity. Jefferson is the primary high school serving the neighborhood. Having worked there in different capacities from 1993 to 1999, many residents between the ages of 14 and 21 had either had me as a teacher or seen me at school. Whenever I met new people with one of my participants, they would invariably introduce me as a teacher, former teacher, and/or Jefferson teacher. This identification came with its share of drawbacks. Despite my connection to an often antagonistic institution, my role as a teacher allowed me to be clearly placed: I was a teacher and I had students and former students in the neighborhood and I was there to see them therefore I had a legitimate and understandable reason to "be around."

The power of my teacher identity was brought home to me one afternoon as I walked along Fillmore Street near Hayes. I had just begun my research and was not very familiar with the area. I had often seen groups of males hanging around the corners at Golden Gate and Hayes and had stayed away from them thus far. Deciding that I needed to push myself and my stereotypes, I continued walking that afternoon past Golden Gate. My hastily written field notes from that afternoon recall my walk.

10/5/98

After lunch with Max I decided to walk around a little. I need to just walk around more, be around, Walked down Fillmore towards Hayes. As I crossed Grove I felt several people walk quickly up behind me. I kept walking, trying to look unconcerned and confident. One young guy came up on my right, one toward my left. "Looking nice to-day. I'm into mixing some colors today, pretty woman. How 'bout you?" I heard just to my right. I tried to laugh confidently and started to cross Grove. Two guys picked up their speed just slightly and eased themselves in front of me, positioned so they were standing in front of me but not quite blocking my way. "Hello, hello" one said. "Heading my way?" he asked. My heart started to pump ever so much faster but I tried to stay calm. I was on Fillmore Street in the broad daylight. What could happen? I also didn't know a soul around and didn't see too many people. As I turned to look him in the eye, his partner took one look at me and his mouth opened into a wide smile. "Ms. Seyer!" he beamed. "Montel, right?" I smiled back. Montel had added a set of gold teeth since I'd last seen him, but the smile was still the same. "How've you been?" he asked. Before I could finish, he quickly told me he was keeping busy, taking classes at City (College) and trying to make something of himself. "That's great." I smiled. "She's a TEACHER?" one of his friends asked, laughing. "Wish I'd had some teachers looked like that." This friend, the most talkative of the four, continued his earlier pick-up lines, asking if I was interested in mixing a little black and white sometime soon. "Not unless I get divorced, and that won't be anytime soon," I replied. Montel and his other friends laughed, but this guy was not giving up easily. Edging closer, he commented that a married woman was fine with him, bring my man along for all he cared. As he continued, I eyed Montel looking down and edging slightly away. He seemed embarrassed but unwilling or able to intervene. As my only contact at the time, I wasn't about to let him go anywhere. "How's Tafari (his little brother) doing?" I asked. As we bantered about this, his family and church, I slowly crossed the street, then back across Fillmore till I was once again heading north—away from the direction they were headed and back toward Max's studio. Each time Montel and I stopped talking, his friend would move in verbally and physically as Montel inched away. Before he got far, I would move myself back toward Montel with yet another follow-up question or two. Finally, as I edged my way down Fillmore, one of the other friends reminded them all of where they were headed and they reluctantly turned around, not without a parting move from their Romeo. "That man of yours treat you bad, just come on back down here" he reminded me with a grin. I told him not to be waiting, laughed and went on my way, breathing a huge sigh of relief and feeling pretty stupid that I wasn't more prepared for that.

Sitting in Max's studio rapidly writing up my recollection of the interaction, several ideas ran through my head. While it was unlikely anything would have happened, Montel's presence and his relationship with me made that even less unlikely, for which I was grateful. The reality was, I didn't and don't know what might have happened. I was in an unfamiliar space governed by unfamiliar rules. I was alone. My teacher identity helped me with Montel, but it was also clear he wasn't willing to extend a clear "guest pass" to me in front of his friends. Montel was one of three Whitfield boys who had quite literally plagued the teachers and administration of Jefferson for the past six years. Montel was the most easy-going and mature, Tafari the most extreme. The Whitfield parents were even more well known among staff than their boys, infamous for showing up at conferences, defending everything their children had done, playing the "race card" when that didn't work, and citing religious freedom when that failed as well. (The Whitfields were members of a small black Hebrew denomination.) Given his frequent run-ins with the administration, I was surprised at how openly excited he was to see me that afternoon. Montel had never been in my class but we knew each other from my work with a student advisory group and from frequent hallway interactions. I had always found Montel very agreeable: he just didn't go to class. He had graduated several years before, just barely. His desire to prove to me that he was still in school and doing well reminded me yet again that even the most troubled students do value school and the values it embodies. Whether or not Montel was actually attending classes at City is a moot point (rumor has it he was not). What was important was that it was important to *him* for *me* to think he *was*: the image of himself as a college student was one he still aspired to. Even a student who had been consistently defined and treated as a failure by the very school I represented accorded me respect. This was to play out again and again in my time in the neighborhood.

The terms of any pass are never written down or carefully delineated. Rather, they are learned via observation and trial and error. As I have never known the actual extent or limits of my access, I began by moving slowly and carefully, rarely pushing boundaries until my participants led me across them. My interaction with Montel and his friends is one example of me crossing a boundary at the wrong time. I was later to learn from Anthony that Grove Street from Fillmore to Laguna was a "ghetto pass" area, one I would need his guidance to visit. I did so many times, but only with him. All of my participants gave me subtle clues along the way as to where, when, and with whom I could travel. As I left his house, Anthony would often casually ask where I was parked. Depending on the time and place (of parking), he would offer to walk me to my car. Caprisha pointedly told me where to park when I came to her complex. Other locals also gave me hints. Sky never took me to her mother's apartment but when I asked Max how to find the address (wondering where it was) he cautioned me not to go alone and offered to have someone walk me there if I really needed to go. In order for any pass to work it must be visible. My identification as a teacher or friend of Anthony's only worked if it was made public. It is the public nature of all aspects of lived landscapes, including passes and spatial access, that heightens their importance and influences the play of relationships in all neighborhoods, the Fillmore included.

Public images, master identities, corner stores, low-income housing patterns, and the borders of district, neighborhood and turf: each is a key determinant of the social organization of the Fillmore and the lives that organization makes possible. As we have seen, the maps drawn by Sky and her peers reflect many of the key *defining* characteristics of the Fillmore. These characteristics define not only the neighborhood, but also the range and specific parameters of the opportunities availed to and appropriated by Fillmore youth. Three low-income housing complexes and two corner stores are within a block of the corner Anthony and his peers called The Flav. This corner took on social and emotional significance for Anthony at a key period in his life. As we have seen, the Flav, as a *place*, is defined in terms of the buildings, people, activities, and borders that intersect there. Although Anthony's experiences at this place during his five-plus years on the outside are important in and of themselves, my interest is in the connection of these experiences to the possibilities they enable or constrain for him. Given the dominance of the "outside," primarily drug-dealing defined aspect of the Fillmore's local master identity, it is not surprising that Anthony, Joseph, Alfonzo, and many other young males participated in that world during their teen years. This participation enabled particular opportunities for them, as Anthony detailed in his heartfelt description of the Flav. It also limited other possibilities, particularly those emerging from participation and success in formal educational and communal institutions. As Anthony so often said "you can either be inside or outside, but you can't be both."

REFERENCES

Bourgois, P. (1996). *In search of respect: Selling crack in El Barrio*. Cambridge, UK: Cambridge University Press.

Hayden, D. (1996). *The power of place: Urban landscapes as public history*. Cambridge, MA: MIT Press.

http://www.census.gov/main/www/cen2000.html

Jacobs, J. (1961). *The death and life of great American cities*. New York: Random House.

Ley, D. (1974). *The black inner city as frontier outpost*. Washington, DC: Association of American Geographers.

Lippard, L. (1997). *The lure of the local: Senses of place in a multicentered society*. New York: The New Press.

Lynch, K. (1960). *The image of the city*. Cambridge, MA: MIT Press.

Lynch, K. (1976). *Managing the sense of a region*. Cambridge, MA: MIT Press.

Rojas, J. T. (1993, Spring). The enacted environment of East Los Angeles. *Places, 8*, 42–53.

San Francisco Chronicle. (2001, July 1). Murder tributes irk black leader. A20.

Suttles, G. D. (1968). *The social order of the slum: Ethnicity and territory in the inner city*. Chicago: University of Chicago Press.

Sward, S. (1999, April 29). Claims against S.F. in police raid case: Cops turned co-op into 'Vietnam' residents say. *San Francisco Chronicle*, A21.

Van Derbeken, J. (1998, October 31). Residents say cops roughed them up during raid. *San Francisco Chronicle*, A17.

II

Studying "Side by Side": Ethnographic Applications to Educational Settings

7

Studying Side By Side: Collaborative Action Ethnography in Educational Research

Frederick Erickson
University of California, Los Angeles

Frederick Erickson is George F. Kneller Professor of Anthropology of Education at the University of California, Los Angeles, where he also is a participant in that university's interdisciplinary Center for Language, Interaction, and Culture. A specialist in the use of video analysis in interactional sociolinguistics, microethnography, and discourse analysis, his research in education has focused especially on the study of social interaction as a learning environment. He also does basic research on the nature of social interaction, focusing especially on timing and rhythm in the social coordination of interaction, relationships of mutual influence between listening and speaking, and the signaling of multiple social identities in talk. His publications include (with Jeffrey J. Shultz) *The Counselor as Gatekeeper: Social Interaction in Interviews* (Academic Press, 1982) and *Talk and Social Theory: Ecologies of Speaking and Listening in Everyday Life* (Polity Press, 2004) and numerous articles and chapters, recently including "Some notes on the musicality of speech" (2003) and "Culture in society and in educational practices" (2004). He has also written extensively on qualitative research methods in education. Erickson is a former president of the Council on Anthropology and Education of the American Anthropological Association and editor of that society's journal *Anthropology and Education Quarterly*, and is a former Vice President for Division G (Social Context of Education) of the American Educational Research Association. In 1998–1999 he was a Spencer Fellow at the Center for Advanced Study in the Behavioral Sciences, Stanford, CA., and in 2000 he was elected a Fellow of the National Academy of Education.

In her classic essay on "studying up" Laura Nader raised issues of power/knowledge for American anthropology before most of us were reading Foucault. The problems of basing disciplinary knowledge on empirical processes of "studying down" persist for anthropology in general and for the anthropology of education in particular. Moreover, the recent NRC report on "science based research in education" shows, by its failure to name and address directly the power/knowledge problems which result from the institutionalization of "studying down" in conventional educational research, a lack of critical awareness of the ways in which educational research tends to silence and misrepresent those who possess the least authority in schools—teachers, students, and parents—at the same time as such research privileges the professional cultural perspectives of administrators and, especially, of policy makers. This silencing and misrepresentation intensifies as the conventional educational research is, in its Western means-ends instrumentalism, increasingly "relevant" to current public discourse on educational policy. Collaborative action ethnography, in which researchers, education professionals, students, and parents inquire together on issues they define mutually, provides an alternative to the elitism of traditional ethnography and to that of the usual "hard science" policy-oriented research in education. This chapter explores the possibilities and difficulties of collaborative action research as an approach to ethnography in education; of studying "side by side."

STUDYING UP

Laura Nader (1969/1974) in an essay in the volume *Reinventing Anthropology* edited by Dell Hymes pointed out that as the practice of ethnography developed among sociocultural anthropologists, the anthropologists had mostly done participant observation among people whose power and social rank was less than that of the visiting anthropologist. By "studying down," the anthropologist was leaving uninvestigated the lifeways of those who exercise power—this was even true in the exotic, primitive societies visited first by anthropologists, and it was even more true when anthropology tried to come home to modern societies. Especially in the anthropologist's own society, Nader urged the anthropologist to "study up"—to visit and document the lives of the privileged and powerful.

Because the anthropology of education in the United States has mostly been done within our own society, Nader's injunction would seem especially apt for us. But, with some notable exceptions, such as Alan Peshkin's recently published study of an elite school (2001) in which he acknowledges the influence of Nader's essay, and Bradley Levinson's recent edited volume of ethnographic studies of educational policy formation (Levinson et al., 2002), the anthropology of education has tended to study down more than up—to visit the lives of impoverished families or those of teachers in low SES schools rather than visiting the lives of more affluent school board members, state and federal politicians, businesspersons whose firms "partner" with schools, test construction and analysis specialists, foundation executives, and textbook publishers, all of whom exercise clout over the conduct of schooling in particular local school communities. There are many potential objects of educational anthropology's "studying up," in Nader's terms. (It should be noted that not only her essay but the whole volume *Reinventing anthropology* reads now as remarkably prescient.)

THE PERCEIVER'S SUBJECTIVE AND MICROPOLITICAL SITUATION IN FIELDWORK

Around the time of publication of Nader's essay a distinct yet related critique of standard anthropology and sociology was made by various feminist authors. They pointed out that not only was the *object* of the fieldworker's attention important to attend to, but also was the mentality/subjectivity of the fieldworker as a perceiving *subject* trying to make sense of others' lives, especially in fieldwork circumstances in which the power relations were asymmetric between the observer and the observed. That line of argument suggests that we need to pay attention not only to the relative location of objects of our inquiry—where the fieldworker shines her flashlight of research attention—up or down the social hierarchy—but also to the social situatedness of perceiving an other—what the fieldworker is able to see and hear through personal/social lenses and filters—through her gendered, classed, age-graded, and raced/ethnicized ways of seeing and feeling in the world, especially as these are in part mutually constructed in the interaction that takes place between the observer and observed—an interaction, which presents itself to the interactional partners as partially pre-constructed by history—weighted with social gravity. At the very least, self-reflection by the observer is required in such a learning situation.

The dirty secret of fieldwork—its inherent partiality and tendency toward self-deception on the part of the fieldworker—was mooted in 1964 by Laura Bohannon, publishing under the name of Eleanore Smith Bowen the book *Return to laughter* (Bowen, 1964), which was not only produced behind the screen of a pseudonym but was also masked by its presentation as a quasi-novel published by a popular press rather than as a "scientific" research report. Her example of self-disclosure, a recounting of the limits of her awareness and understanding while in the field and of the intensity of her feelings about the people she was "studying" was complemented and extended by Jean Briggs in 1970 in a text explicitly published as an ethnography: *Never in anger: Portrait of an Eskimo family.* Two other women anthropologists published self-critically reflective autobiographical accounts of their fieldwork experience within the same time span, Hortense Powdermaker in *Stranger and friend: The way of an anthropologist* (1966) and Rosalie Wax in *Doing fieldwork: Warnings and advice* (1971).

The notion that the researcher always sees from within (and is also blinded by) the power relationships between her and those she studies was further explicated in Dorothy Smith's 1974 essay "Women's perspective as a radical critique of sociology." Later this theme was picked up in the mid-1980s by George Marcus and James Clifford (Clifford, 1988; Clifford & Marcus, 1986)—that the very act of gaze on an Other by the anthropologist in the field was in a Foucaultian sense an exercise of power, and also was a lens warped by particular and ineluctable distortion. But by the time that Clifford and Marcus had articulated it, this was an insight that had already been well mooted in feminist scholarly circles (see also Harding, 1991; Lather, 1991).

In a previous discussion (Erickson, 1996, titled "On the evolution of qualitative approaches in educational research: From Adam's task to Eve's" [keynote address to the 25th anniversary meeting of the Australian Association for Research in Education]) I have identified two aspects of the fieldworker's problem as being analogous to the task of Adam and that of Eve. In the second book of Genesis, the Creator gives Adam the task of naming all the animals. To name something, in the Biblical sense, was to identify its true character. This is akin to the interpretive validity task set for ethnography by Malinowski in *Argonauts* (1922) and elsewhere—to describe events in ways which make contact with "the native's point of view." Eve's task, in contrast (a task which of course is not mentioned in a text produced in the patriarchal society of the ancient Hebrews) is to make visible for herself the power relations between her and those she is trying to name, before she attempts the awesome responsibility entailed in the hermeneutical act of naming anything.

Thus as we think about the processes of knowing that develop through the conduct of fieldwork and of data analysis in ethnography, a sense of the consequentiality of our choice of research object (studying up or down) needs to be accompanied by a sense of the consequentiality of those ways of seeing and not seeing that are entailed in the kinds of social relationships through which we engage our informants. We need, in other words, to combine Eve's task with that of Adam.

STUDYING SIDE BY SIDE

Another way to approach this problem is to try to "study side by side." By this I mean engaging with those we study as a partner in what Kurt Lewin in the late 1930s and early 1940s (see Lewin, 1946) called "action research," and which William Foote Whyte in the 1950s called "participatory action research" (see Whyte et al., 1989) In the 1970s my friends Jay and Steve Schensul called this "involvement in the action" (see Schensul, 1974; Schensul & Schensul, 1992). Today it is sometimes also called "formative evaluation."

Studying side by side changes to some extent the power relations between observer and observed; in Goffman's terms (1981) it shifts the "footing" of the interaction that takes place between them. Because it doesn't change power relations completely, collaborative action research is not a complete solution to the problem of personally political analysis, the critical phenomenology problem I have called "Eve's task." But it does help make power relations more visible and explicit, as observer and observed exchange and share outsider/insider roles—as "participant observer" and as unusually "observant participant." In the self-reflective arm-wrestling that goes on between the research partners there is a corrective to the blindnesses inherent in Adam's attempts to do his task all by himself.

The Schensuls and many others since have claimed that involvement in the action produces a more valid ethnography—when one produces social research knowledge for immediate use the appropriateness of one's data collection and analysis gets rapid, recursive testing in a way that the slower and more distanced process of classic ethnography is able to avoid. (These consequences of action research and the processes of mid-course correction that produce such consequences become possible whenever one takes a more activist stance, as is illustrated by the "cultural therapy" approach in anthropology of education taken by George and Louise Spindler (1994)). The action researcher is forced to learn things in the field that the less fully participating "participant observer" doesn't learn so readily. The problem is that the romantic "lone ethnographer," entering the field with only a toothbrush, hunting knife, and a naïve confidence in realist ethnography can go through the appearance of participation, establish a seeming closeness to "the natives" which is not in fact actual, and get things wrong—perhaps a bit wrong, or close to half wrong, or more than half wrong.

In collaborative action research the "researcher" partner and the "practitioner" partner share not only in data collection and analysis but in problem formulation and research question definition. Letting the practitioner in on the foundational level of the research process—problem formulation—involves a major shift in the relations between the professional researcher (often university based or research center based) and the practitioner, as Cochran-Smith and Lytle note in their pioneering review of issues in teacher research (1993, see also Stenhouse, 1975 on parallel issues in curriculum research). The contrast between minimally and maximally collaborative approaches is illustrated by Fig. 7.1 below:

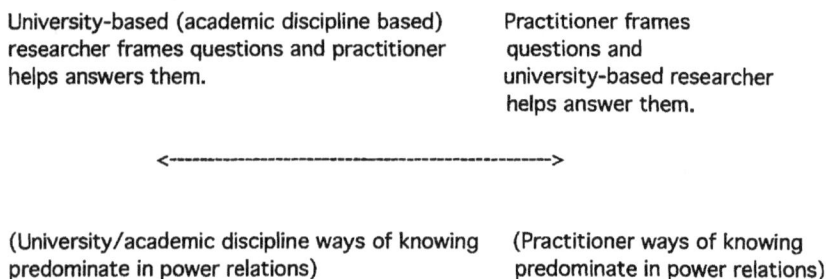

University-based (academic discipline based)   Practitioner frames
researcher frames questions and practitioner   questions and
helps answers them.   university-based researcher
                                                      helps answer them.

<-->

(University/academic discipline ways of knowing   (Practitioner ways of knowing
predominate in power relations)   predominate in power relations)

FIG. 7.1.   A continuum of approaches in collaborative research.

A basic problem with the classic conduct of ethnography is that the so-called "participant observer" doesn't actually participate all that much. In my past presidential address to the Council on Anthropology and Education in 1978, titled "Mere ethnography: Some problems in its use in educational practice" (Erickson, 1979). I used as an organizing device Malinowski's central story from Argonauts of the cutting down of the tree and making a canoe—asking the tree's pardon first, cutting it down, blessing it, carving the wood. (After being blessed again the canoe travels to other islands as part of the Kula ring. It is the canoe story which gives narrative and analytic coherence to the text of Argonauts as a whole.)

I said in my speech that Malinowski's question about the "native's point of view" in building the canoe was a crucially important question, but it was different from the kind of question asked by educational practitioners, which would be more like asking "how can we make this canoe better?" (Such questions are typically the focus of action research.) I said that in order for Malinowski to have gotten a feel for the latter kind of question he would have needed to engage in some of the actual work of building the canoe—he would have had to pick up his end of the log. In so doing he would realize that social action was not gravitationless—he would feel the weight of history.

I then said that for me that kind of classic ethnography still held an appeal for me. It was not that all of those accounts were totally distorted, or lacking in any worth. And they had a certain beauty. But they reminded me of the line in Keats' "Ode on a Grecian Urn": "Heard melodies are sweet but those unheard are sweeter." The incipient tendency in Western academia toward Platonism leads us to privilege the abstract over the concrete and thus to valorize the cleaner-than-life analytic narrative over the messiness of actual, situated practice by human agents. Too much ethnography lacks the contradiction, irony, and nuance of the actual conduct of everyday life—the gritty and grotty stuff that great novels show us. Too often, in a voice of what Rosaldo called "distanced normalizing description" (1989), ethnographic reporting tells its story just a bit too well, a bit too much cleaner than life, with a bit too much coherence.

After the publication of Malinowski's field journal (1967), and especially in the late 1980s through the mid-1990s, a spate of Malinowski-bashing took place. I do not attempt to review all that here nor to repeat it. But a few things must be said about the inadequacy of conventional fieldwork for achieving the very aims of classic ethnography—portraying everyday action narratively "from the native's point of view." And since that was Malinowski's project, claimed by him as distinctive in his own work, a brief discussion of his attempts at achieving those aims is appropriate here.

As Clifford (1988) has noted, Malinowski placed the first two photographs in *Argonauts* the page facing a chronological table in which he listed all the places that he visited as a fieldworker during his 4-year stay in the Trobriands. Those photographs show the ethnographer's tent next to the dwellings of villagers in two of the villages in which he conducted fieldwork. This says to the reader, iconically, "I was really there." It is the warrant for the validity of Malinowski's analysis—the authoritative status of realist ethnography rests on the close presence of the researcher in the field. In the following paragraph Malinowski (1922, p. 51), in his public voice as a realist ethnographer engaged in scientific inquiry, describes his entrance to the village of Kiriwina, which is shown in the second of the two photographs that show his tent:

> It is difficult to convey the feelings of intense interest and suspense with which an ethnographer enters for the first time the district that is to be the future scene of his field work. . . . The appearance of the natives, their manner, their types of behavior, may augur well or ill for the possibilities of rapid and easy research. . . . One suspects many hidden and mysterious ethnographic phenomena behind the commonplace aspect of things. Perhaps that queer looking, intelligent native is a renowned sorcerer. Perhaps between those two groups of men there exists some important rivalry or vendetta, which may throw much light on the customs and character of the people if one can only lay a hand upon it.

In the private voice of the diary entry for Friday, December 14, 1917, Malinowski tells a different story of the process of fieldwork and of his relations with the natives:

> Then to my tent. A few specific tasks: to correct the plan of the village, to copy the ethnographic diary. I did some of this, but though I felt well physically, resistance, the work did not interest me. . . At 12, natives came from two neighboring villages. We talked about crabs, etc. This interview bored me and did not go well. At two, I ordered lunch. Eggs and cocoa. (Malinowski, 1967, p. 151)

On the same day, Malinowski mentions a conversation with a policeman. But in *Argonauts* the police are largely absent—although the presence of the police is a manifestation of the control that colonial powers had on the Trobriand islands, it is not the story of that domination which Malinowski the anthropologist chose to tell. And natives as servants, serving the ethnographer his lunch of eggs and cocoa in his tent? The public scientific voice of the realist ethnographer in *Argonauts* doesn't mention that either. Anticipating Clifford's discussion a decade later, Michael Young, an Australian anthropologist, comments on the conceit of Malinowski's tent (Young, 1979, p. 13): "Thus while the ethnographer's tent seems to have symbolized for him the breakthrough in method which he accomplished . . . the breakthrough in European-Native relationships remained incomplete. A tent, after all, erects and maintains more social distance than any native house." This, on Young's part is an Eve's task-like recognition, and in Nader's terms it shows us the limitations in *studying down*. The asymmetric power relations between Malinowski and those he was studying (with him on top of the asymmetry) got in the way of Malinowski's capacity to see and understand the very "native's point of view" he said he was after as an analyst. Malinowski lived *next door to* the natives—he didn't live *with* them (as Jean Briggs had tried to do [1970]), and he didn't live among them as a fellow native (which even Jean Briggs didn't attempt). This positioning affected the interactional processes of data collection and their subsequent analysis and reporting, as the following observations show us.

Thirty years after Malinowski left the Trobriands, Fr. Baldwin, a Roman Catholic missionary who succeeded him there, reported in a master's thesis in anthropology how the "natives" had remembered Malinowski (Baldwin, n.d., p. 41, as cited in Young, 1979, p. 15): "It was a surprise to me to find that Malinowski was mostly remembered by the natives as a champion ass at asking damn fool questions, like 'You bury the seed tuber root end or sprout end down?' Like asking, 'Do you stand the baby or the coffin on its head or on its feet?' They said of him that he made of his profession a sacred cow. You had to defer though you did not see why."

Baldwin lived on the island of Boyowa longer than Malinowski had done and he learned the local language more thoroughly than Malinowski had learned it. In order to check the validity of Malinowski's portrayal of the "native's point of view," Fr. Baldwin translated large portions of *Argonauts* and read those texts with the Boyowans he knew, some of whom remembered Malinowski's presence among them. It is not that the natives thought Malinowski had gotten things 100% wrong in his reporting:

He seems to have left nothing unexplained and his explanations are enlightening, even to the people who live there. It is curious, then, that this exhaustive research, and patient, wise, and honest explanation, should leave a sense of incompleteness. But it does. I feel that his material is still not properly digested, that Malinowski would be regarded in some ways naive by the people he was studying . . .

I was surprised at the number of times informants helping me with checking Malinowski would bridle. Usually when a passage has been gone over more than once, they would say it was not like that. They did not quarrel with facts or explanations, on with the coloring as it were. The sense expressed was not the sense they had of themselves or of things Boyowan. (Baldwin, n.d., pp. 17–18, as cited in Young, 1979, pp. 15–16)

Of course, ethnography is a rendering—it is not the reality it purports to describe. It is a translation, and all such exercises in interpretation must be partially disappointing. But I think the problem that Baldwin surfaces for us is deeper than just that of the inherent difficulties in doing translation. Rather, it is a problem which arises from the inherent shallowness and incompleteness of the usual so-called "participant observation," which is actually—because of the power relations that obtain between the observer and the observed—a minimally participating kind of observation.

There is a danger in the kind of classic ethnographic description, which arises out of the classic mode of "participant observation," that at best tries to be non-interfering but so often ends up simply being *not very involved but still one-up rather than one-down in the power relations with "informants."* The danger is that, on the basis of such fieldwork the "native's" work of daily social action is described by the ethnographer as if it were effortless, taking place in a universe from which social gravity is absent. What is left out is the weight of history and of immediate material circumstances; the prestructured constraints that people face when they are actually working in the world.

I got this insight, in part from the work of one of my students, Susan Florio. Jeffrey Shultz, Donald Bremme, and Susan Florio—and I began a study in a kindergarten–first-grade classroom that heralded an even more important turning point for me. We had no special funding, but for a postdoctoral grant from the National Institute for Mental Health for Shultz, and for a junior faculty seed grant from the Spencer Foundation. (I had sought funding from the Ford Foundation, but was turned down.) Bremme and Florio donated their research time and got jobs to pay their rent—Bremme working nights as a janitor at Harvard and Florio working afternoons in a gift shop in Copley Square, Boston. Florio's father, who was a video cameraman at CBS in New York, persuaded CBS to donate one hundred slightly used ½ inch reel-to-reel videotapes for our project's use.

This was the first time I was doing ethnographic monitoring of a classroom and it was qualitative research on teaching, as that field was just beginning. We had originally intended to study the classroom for one year, but we stayed for a second year because we were so fascinated with what was going on. (As a result we had a chance to watch the previous year's kindergartners become first graders.) Donald Bremme wrote his thesis about how the children talked in first circle, in sharing time, across the 2 years (Dorr-Bremme, 1982). Susan Florio developed an especially close relationship with a classroom teacher in the second year of the study. I remember one day in about mid-October of that second year when Susan came to my office at the university looking rather anxious. She said, "You know, I'm starting to think that as I write my fieldnotes and I look at the classroom, I'm looking at things more and more as I used to when I was a middle school teacher, and as I interview Marty, we're talking about what to do with Linda! Is there something wrong with that?"

Linda was a new first grader. She was much bigger than the other children, and she was Armenian American, whereas many of the other children were Italian American. How to help Linda fit in, literally and figuratively, was at the front of Marty's concern in early October. As an ethnographic researcher, Susan was taking on Marty's questions of practice as her own. When Susan said in my office, "Is there something wrong with that?" I had the presence of mind to say, "No, that's fine! Keep doing it!" At the time, neither was I entirely sure why Susan was anxious, nor was I fully aware of how important that moment was as a turning point. I sensed it was somehow important, but I didn't understand how or why. Now I realize that Susan and Marty had serendipitously crossed a line defining the power relations between researcher and researched. The traditional definition of the observer's research role defined the researcher's rights and obligations in a very asymmetric way, vis-à-vis the subject of the study. It was a colonialist relationship: "Me frame research question, you act. Me look, you do." Susan was moving from the stance of minimally interfering "participant observer" to that of what we came to call "observant participant."

By adopting some of Marty's research questions, power relations were changed between Susan and Marty. One result of this was a fine doctoral thesis. Another was that Susan and Marty wrote a paper together revealing their experience as collaborators. It was titled "The Teacher as Colleague in Classroom Research," written in 1978 by Susan Florio and Martha Walsh and published in 1980. This chapter was one of the first in print that discussed the kind of collaboration and dialogue that would become more and more characteristic of some kinds of qualitative research in education, and also would be followed by the movement of practitioner research in a next academic generation.

Although by 1978 I had the insight about the "gravitationless" portrayal of social action in conventional ethnography and had published a comment on it, my own fieldwork experience in studying early elementary teachers was such that I didn't sense until 4 years later the palpable weight that is inherent in the everyday work of classroom teaching. By that time (1982) I had spent complete school years of fieldwork in four elementary school classrooms. But, sitting in the back of the room writing fieldnotes and videotaping, I still didn't "get it"—what the work of teaching felt like. Like Malinowski I had pitched my tent next to the houses of the village. But I hadn't been doing the work of daily living in the village. To be sure I was doing "fieldwork," yellow note pad and all—but it did not include sharing in the teacher's daily work.

A VIGNETTE

The morning of March 25, 1982, I was working in a second-grade classroom where I had been visiting frequently since the previous September. A few days earlier the teacher had presented the students with a writing assignment. They were each to study a different animal and then write a few paragraphs about various aspects of the animal's life. The sets of paragraphs would then be put together as an essay with four or five parts.

The lynx was Alex's animal. In a writing conference with Alex that morning the teacher said he should write that day about how his animal got its food. So the question for him became, "How does the lynx get its food?"

Alex was the least fluent reader in the class. He left the teacher's desk and I went with him. Alex walked to the back of the room to a table on which was placed a big encyclopedia of animals, with colored pictures. (The book was too big for the children to use on their desks, so each child took a turn at looking at the book on the table.) Alex sat down at the table and I sat next to him. The book lay closed before him. Beside the book he had placed his notepad and pencils. Alex looked at the book for a few moments. It seemed that he had stopped.

I suggested that Alex look in the index. He appeared to be puzzled. The index, I explained, was in the back of the book. Alex opened the book at the front and turned through its pages all the way back to the index. "The animals are listed in alphabetical order," I said, as I turned the index pages until we came to the "l's." There was an entry for "lynx" with a page number next to it. Alex read the word "lynx" and then stopped.

I said that the word just to the right of the word in the index showed the number of the page in the book on which the information about the lynx could be found. Alex turned slowly back through the pages of the book until we found the page noted in the index. On that page there was a little written text, and nothing in it mentioned the lynx. Most of the page was taken up by a large picture of many animals that were found, as the title of the picture said, in a "Mixed Forest and Prairie Habitat in a Temperate Climate."

The lynx was shown crouched on the limb of a tree near the edge of the forest. Rabbits, grouse, and other small animals were shown on the prairie and on the ground beneath the trees. I pointed out the lynx on the page. Alex looked at it. I said, "The lynx eats meat. Can you think how the lynx might get its food?" Alex said, "Jump?" "That's right," I said, "The lynx could jump off the branch and catch a rabbit or grouse or maybe a squirrel that was on the ground."

Alex closed the book. He went off to his desk to write about what the lynx ate. A few times he went up to the teacher's desk and asked how to spell a particular word. Other children were writing away on their essays, producing paragraphs quite adeptly. But by the end of the morning Alex had still not quite finished his written answer to the question, "How does the lynx get its food?"

Alex was slogging through the mud, step by step. I was reminded of the Boy's Town Orphanage fundraiser poster I had seen when I was young. In the poster, an older boy is carrying on his shoulders a younger boy who is holding a crutch. The older boy is portrayed as speaking to the viewer of the picture. The caption reads: "He ain't heavy, Father, he's my brother." On March 25, 1982 my fieldnotes said: "Boy's town poster. Alex is *heavy*. I feel exhausted."

That morning I had picked up my end of a pedagogical log. Never before as an observer had I felt the kind of weight that a child like Alex must have presented to an elementary school teacher. Nor had I had a way of feeling something like the weight that Alex must have been feeling as he struggled with that kind of a writing task. No wonder many teachers avoid students like Alex—slide by them—and no wonder students like Alex slide by or shut down when faced with the kind of classroom task he encountered. In my experience of engagement in the action with Alex, I gained a sense of the social gravity in such a scene that my earlier fieldwork and descriptive reporting—done from a less participating stance—had not allowed me to learn. (Vignette taken, with slight adaptation, from F. Erickson, 1994/1995)

DISCUSSION

After the existential shift in field experience in 1982, I changed my research approach. I became involved in collaborative action research relationships. Some were with medical school colleagues, for I had an appointment in a department of pediatrics as well as in a school of education. I engaged in a study of the cultural adaptation of foreign medical graduates in a residency program—where I was also an instructor in the residency (see Erickson & Rittenberg, 1987).

In a later medical project, one could say that I was "studying up." I was a co-investigator in a study of the clinical coaching of residents done by experienced physicians—in backroom supervisory conferences that are called "precepting." As in the foreign medical graduate study, we were studying backstage, confidential professional socialization in an elite profession. The precepting physicians made much more money than I did. (On the other hand, I was doing the study in collaboration with the M.D. director of the ambulatory clinic in which the residency teaching program was held, and he and I held nominally equivalent rank as fellow university professors. In that sense I was working with peers (see Ende, Jack, Pomerantz, Anita, & F. Erickson, 1995; Erickson, 1999).

I also began a series of collaborative action projects with elementary school teachers and their principals. Within the Institute for Research on Teaching at Michigan State University I became involved in a collaborative action research project that we called Teacher Development and Organizational Change, in which we worked with three early-grades teachers (see Berkey et al., 1990; Campbell, 1988; Erickson, 2001).

As part of that project, professors from the school of education at Michigan State University came to the classroom at least once a week and spent an entire morning or afternoon. We made a contract with the teachers that each time we came, the visitor and the teacher would write no more than two half-sized pages of recollection of something that we noticed. Then we collected what everyone wrote and each week added copies of the pages to one ring binder in the principal's office at the school and another that went on a file cabinet in our bay in the school of education office building. Everybody got to read what everybody wrote every week. We did this from February to June, and then started again the following fall. One week in early October into that next fall, another turning point happened for me.

ANOTHER VIGNETTE

I had been working that year with Fran Minnick, a second-grade teacher who joined our group after one of the first-grade teachers we had been working with had to go on leave because of an illness. On a very warm October afternoon, Fran and I were sitting with the bottom reading group. We were both very uncomfortable; indeed, that day the bottom reading group was excruciating for all concerned. The students seemed bored. One after another, they read haltingly from the basic basal reading text. Fran looked at me with a pained expression as the least adept reader in the entire room got stuck in his turn at reading aloud. Fran looked at me with a pained expression. For me it was like watching Alex again, three years later, in a different classroom in a different school system. I went home very upset. What would I say in my journal entry? I felt I must write about the bottom reading group, but I didn't want to offend the teacher.

Finally, after waking up at two o'clock in the morning, I wrote my two half pages. I decided to say what I really thought and felt. I took a deep breath and began to write. I said that what was going on in the bottom reading group seemed to contradict what the teacher had told the students on the first day of school was a main aim of hers—that the classroom that year would be a place where it was safe to make mistakes.

At the beginning of the year the teacher told me she had two big concerns: one was what she called the "spread"—she thought there was a wide range in what the kids were able to do in this year's second-grade class, a wider spread than she had had for a long time. She also thought it was very important to make it safe for kids to make mistakes. The fear of mistakes was a serious barrier to learning. Yet 6 weeks later, there we were in ability-ranked reading groups, the whole notion of which contradicted the teacher's aim for safety.

In my journal entry I wrote that such ranking made the bottom group an occasion for "the public display of incompetence." I tried to say this respectfully, as to a colleague, but it was a kind of candor I had never practiced in my previous work as a so-called nonjudgmental participant-observer, who wasn't participating all that much. Having written my entry I went back to bed and slept fitfully.

I drove out to the school in the morning with a sick feeling of unease. I liked Fran. I thought she was a good teacher. Would she think I was just another smart-ass from the university? When Fran read my entry that evening she was at first offended. Then she remembered that she valued my concern about her students and she believed my journal entry reflected that concern. She called Kathy, a first-grade teacher next door, who suggested that she try using the children's own writing as material for all the reading groups.

A day later, when I drove out to the school to face the music and see what Fran thought, she was very forthright with me. She said her first reaction on reading what I wrote was, "Who does he think he is?" But she'd been uncomfortable in the bottom reading group too. By the time I saw her, she had resolved to try to do something different with reading as one way of dealing with this problem of the "spread" that she saw.

In the next few weeks, she totally reorganized her reading program, having the least skilled writers dictate their stories to her and to other children. This was a profound breakthrough for her, in the way she approached reading (Fran's side of this story is told by her in Berkey et al., 1990). It was also a deep breakthrough for me in my relationship with her as a colleague. I broke out of this pattern of classic participant-observer ethnographic stance, in which during interviews the researcher never says what he or she really thinks to the person being interviewed. It's only a kind of Rogerian echo response that you give—you never really communicate your true thoughts and feelings to the "informant" or "research subject." The line I crossed with Fran that day was analogous to the line that Susan Florio had crossed with Martha Walsh some years earlier. I began to realize that, and I decided I wasn't going to do any more of the kind of distanced observing that I had done before, but rather would work more and more collaboratively with teachers.

I then moved to the University of Pennsylvania and became involved in two projects where we worked much more collaboratively with teachers. One of these was called "Taking Stock and Making Change," where we worked with five elementary schools (see Erickson & Christman, 1996). We created with each one a school self-study team, which involved the principal and a group of teachers, some of whom were members of a school governance council. The teams looked around their schools for issues they wanted to address and reflected on what was going on with an idea toward making some kind of change. In one school a research question that developed was, "Where are all the reading books in the school?" It turned out that there were all kinds of instructional materials that had been squirreled away by various teachers over the years, under inner-city school conditions of shortage and hoarding. As a result of beginning to look and make it okay to talk about where the books were, a whole set of relationships around literacy instruction began to change in the school.

In another school, teachers began to look at the issue of kids getting into fights and hollering racial epithets on the playground during lunch. As they began to observe and to take stock, they were initially concerned that the non-professional lunchroom aides who also supervised the kids on the playground were hollering at the kids, and then the kids were hollering at each other. In the course of their inquiry, the teachers began to realize that they never talked to the lunchroom aides. They had never asked the lunchroom aides anything about what *they* knew. What resulted was a joint research project with the lunchroom aides and some of the teachers looking at the way in which the recess was organized and making some deep changes. This very quickly resulted in a sharp drop in the number of kids who got sent to the school nurse with bloody noses, and in the number of kids who got sent to the principal for having hollered a racial slur at someone else. So it seemed that practitioners themselves, with a little bit of outside help, had the capacity to study their own circumstances and come up with insights that made a difference.

The second University of Pennsylvania project was inspired by a teachers' research group, the Teachers' Learning Collaborative. This is a group of teachers in Philadelphia who have been meeting every Thursday after school to talk about their practice and about individual children. The group continues in existence with some change in membership. A few of the original members who are still there were very much influenced by Patricia Carini and her ways of helping teachers look at children's abilities and interests. One of the things that Carini had done in the Prospect School that she founded in Bennington, Vermont, was to keep longitudinal records of children's written work and drawing, across all the grade levels, in what she called "an archive of children's work." From that we came up with the idea of an archive of teachers' work—an interactive archive using digital multimedia, to which teachers would contribute examples of the *how* of their practice and its development. The idea was that other teachers might look at these materials and see some of the backstage details of how they pulled off certain kinds of instruction. Because the teachers were part of the National Writing Project we focused in our pilot work on the teaching of writing in the early grades.

Under the direction of the teachers we videotaped and collected student work, the teachers made comments on the work, and we put everything together into a prototype interactive multimedia archive. This permitted a virtual visit to the classroom. You could click with your mouse on the face of a student and a screen would come up that showed all the information contained in the archive about that particular student. You could then click again and see that student in a small group brainstorming story ideas, then switch to a clip of that student writing the story, and to another in which the student was having a writing conference with the teacher about the first draft of the story. If you wanted to, after looking at the clip of one child brainstorming a story idea you could switch to another child and see her brainstorming a story idea. We set up the archive so that potentially you could approach it to pursue a range of different issues and questions. For example, you could say, "I wonder how the teachers set things up in the first few days of the school year." Clicking with your mouse you could review the teachers' daily journal entries and look at video clips of the first few days of school. The purpose of such an archive was to support richer, more focused conversations among teachers than those which typically occur, as well as to provide primary research materials for university-based researchers. I then left the University of Pennsylvania to go to UCLA and one of my colleagues in that work at Penn, Ralph Ginsberg, died in a tragic automobile accident. In consequence, that effort did not continue in Philadelphia.

I am now involved in a similar project with Lisa Rosenthal Schaeffer, Alejandra Rivera-Santini, and Doris Levy, who are teachers at UCLA's laboratory school, the Corinne A. Seeds University Elementary School (UES). We're developing digital libraries of their practice, under their direction, with similar aims to those I described for the Philadelphia prototype. The school as a whole is interested in developing its web site to include video and other materials that show in detail how we do certain things in instruction at the school—early literacy instruction and project-based science instruction. We want to make this available in limited-access ways on the Internet for continuing professional education relationships with other teachers— dialogic relationships, in firsthand contact and also in virtual contact—relationships that respect what the teachers know to start with and then try to build on that foundation toward further growth of insight and practice.

A particular current effort has been to show how early grades teachers teach basic concepts in science ,thematically across entire school years, in ways out of which precipitates a long term project that lasts for the final quarter of the school year. In one recent year, a team of three kindergarten-first grade teachers taught the physics of matter, energy, and motion in two adjoining classrooms of students. My job, at the teacher's direction, was to help document, through videotaping and observation, the year-long evolution of instruction in physics and the children's participation in the full range of kinds of learning activities that occurred across the year.

As in the Philadelphia Teachers Learning Collaborative, the UES teachers were working in an intensely local way with unique groups of students, and they were also inspired by thinking that had come from far away. In the

UES case, this influence came from the early childhood education approach that has been developed since World War II in a pre-school at Reggio Emilia, a village in Northern Italy. In this approach to curriculum and pedagogy "less is more": children explore and learn a limited set of basic concepts in great depth. Their learning is facilitated by the children's experiencing relevant scientific phenomena in a variety of sensory modalities—looking, handling, tasting, listening, talking, moving in space. After these experiential encounters with basic ideas the children represent their developing understanding in a variety of semiotic ways—drawing, using mathematical symbols, modeling in clay using found objects, talking, writing, dancing.

For example, as the children learned how matter changes state from solid to liquid to gas, the teachers introduced the metaphor of "dancing" as a way of characterizing the movement of molecules more rapidly across wider spans of space as more and more heat was added to a substance. The children drew analytic diagrams of the increasing motion and dispersal of molecules, they modeled this in clay, they wrote about it and they also danced as a representation of this idea, dancing as if they were molecules themselves.

By the last quarter of the school year the long-term project had developed. Its purpose was to "make work easier." Toward this end the students and the teachers built two classroom sized roller coasters that linked the two adjoining classrooms, allowing messages to be placed inside a ball which was then rolled back and forth through the roller coasters so the messages could be sent between the two rooms. (Because this school is in southern California the classroom doors opened onto the outside world rather than onto an internal hallway, and the roller coasters were built on the outside walls of the two classrooms.)

The basic physics concept demonstrated by a system such as a roller coaster is a distinction in the dynamics of motion and force—a distinction between to kinds of energy; kinetic and potential. At differing regions in a roller coaster kinetic energy is maximized (as speed increases along down slopes to highest velocity), while at other regions potential energy is maximized (as speed decreases along up slopes to lowest velocity).

The construction, testing, and analysis of the roller coaster and what it shows about energy and motion has been documented by video footage, written commentary by the teachers (together with commentary written by myself and graduate student assistants), voice-over commentary by the teachers, still photographs of examples of children's work in various representational media, photographs and charts showing features of the physical and social environment of the classroom together with instructional materials—all these information sources are archived in the digital library, analogous to a Web site, which is being assembled mainly by one of the three teachers during a year's leave of absence from classroom teaching responsibilities.

In this digital multimedia information-space we are designing, a story is being told that is akin to that found in a classic ethnographic monograph (as in the typical chapter on the "annual cycle" of activity in a "village," which in our case is a "classroom village"). But a multimedia assemblage of information goes beyond the bounds of the conventional ethnographic monograph in at least two ways. First, the information is assembled not only to "tell a story"—with a linear order determined by the story's authors—but also to be available for engagement in non-linear ways by users who are *virtual visitors* rather than *readers*. The users can visit certain points in the school year intensely and visit other moments in the year less intensely. They can compare the work of individual students or focus mainly on what the information materials arrayed show about the teachers' planning. The virtual visitor, in other words, is potentially more active than is the reader of a written text. Even taking account of what "reader-response" theory tells us about how readers "construct" the texts they read rather than simply being passive recipients of what a text presents, a virtual visitor to a digital information space of the kind we are designing is even more of a constructor of the information site as a representation of teaching practice. The visitor to the site, by engaging it in non-linear ways, co-constructs the site with the site's designers, and this is a position of greater agency in relation to the "text" than is that of a reader of a written document. It is much more a position of agency than that of the viewer of an ethnographic film, in which the linear sequence of information is entirely fixed in advance and the viewer cannot "fast-forward" or reverse in viewing, in ways analogous to those of a reader flipping back and forth across sets of pages in a book.

We hope that our virtual visitors will make use of their agency to become more than just tourists at our information site. We hope, in other words, that the visitors will develop an ethnographic analytic eye through the processes of their visiting. But we cannot control completely what our visitors make of the information we have made available, if we are to create an information space that can be accessed interactively. We are sacrificing the very executive authorial control over representation that has been recently criticized in the conventional ethnographic texts of written monographs and edited documentary films.

A second difference from the conventional ethnographic monograph is that the digital information space itself was produced not by a single ethnographer operating alone as a scholar but by a collaborative research team in which the teachers, as "observant participants," had primary control of the process of defining, collecting, and reporting the "data." As the "ethnographer" in this collaboration I was a partner, and substantively I was a junior one. "The natives" (the teachers and students) were not fixing my lunch, nor simply letting me watch them, nor simply answering the questions I chose to ask them. I did have considerable influence in our partnership—I was by no means a passive partner. But my influence was exercised through dialogue, within the reciprocal relations of mutual influence that are inherent in collaborative action research.

CONCLUSION

It must be noted that although my research relationships have changed profoundly as I began to share power and work responsibility with those I was studying, the relationship is not that of total parity of power. This is manifested vividly in an embodied way—whenever I visit the early grades' teachers' classrooms, even in the role of fellow researcher/colleague, I can leave the room to go to the bathroom whenever I wish—but the classroom teacher can't.

The action research relationship doesn't remove issues of power difference from the research process—but it makes them more visible within it. There is greater candor now in my exchanges with those I study.

A disadvantage is that the action research situation can blur my critical sense—I tend to ally with teachers now, and perhaps in so doing I come to share in some of their professionally situated false consciousness. It is easier to do "critical ethnography" from a slightly more distanced stance. (On the other hand, critical ethnography presents special ethical problems. How do I get informed consent from a teacher to enter his or her classroom for a long term stay to "unmask the underlying racist/classist bias in her practice as a witless tool of the capitalist mentality and power structure." In my role as action researcher I may be tempted to render a more celebratory account of teaching practice than I might otherwise do, but at least I don't risk blindsiding the teacher with a published, scathing critique after leaving her classroom. The tensions between being overly celebratory and overly critical in ethnography are paradoxical and thus can never be entirely resolved.)

Studying side by side may have a useful place, along with *studying up*, as we try to achieve a more realistic and complete account than we've had in the past of the workings of educational institutions in modern societies. It is worth recalling that the point of Eve's task—the insight that we can only know in and through the particular circumstances of our work, including its power circumstances—is not a new insight. Even before feminism, Marx had noted it. His realization that the processes of working shape not only the body but mentalities and senses of horizon as well, has informed students of human social life for a century and a half. And the workers are not entirely unaware of their circumstances—false consciousness or "hegemony" is not total, as June Nash points out in her ethnography of Bolivian tin miners titled "We eat the mines and the mines eat us" (1979) and as James Scott points out in *Weapons of the weak* (1985) and *Domination and the arts of resistance* (1990).

In studying side by side it is possible to develop honest accounts of social and cultural production and reproduction, which do not make the work of workers look weightless, but which do not portray them as totally determined either. Social gravity is present in teachers' and students' work in schools. It does not make inevitable the immediate and long term consequences of that work. We need ethnography of education which can show us both the social gravity in the daily practices of teaching and learning in classrooms and the opportunities for socially progressive or regressive choice that resides in it, opportunities for accomplishing social justice or injustice locally. These are opportunities and challenges which present themselves continually to teachers and students in the course of their everyday work together.

REFERENCES

Baldwin, B. (n.d.). Traditional and cultural aspects of Trobriand Island chiefs. Unpublished M.S. thesis. Canberra: Anthropology Dept., Royal Society of Pacific Studies, Australia National University.

Berkey, R., Curtis, T., Minnick, F., Zietlow, K., Campbell, D., & Kirschner, B. (1990). Collaborating for reflective practice: Voices of teachers, administrators, and researchers. *Education and Urban Society, 22*(2), 204–232.

Bowen, E. (1964). *Return to laughter.* Garden City, NY: Doubleday.

Briggs, J. L. (1970). *Never in anger: Portrait of an Eskimo family.* Cambridge, MA: Harvard University Press.

Campbell, D. (1988). Collaboration and contradiction in a research and development project. *Teachers College Record, 90,* 99–121.

Clifford, J. (1988). *The predicament of culture: Twentieth century ethnography, literature, and art.* Cambridge, MA: Harvard University Press.

Clifford, J., & Marcus, G. (1986). *Writing culture: The poetics and politics of ethnography.* Berkeley: University of California Press.

Cochran-Smith, M., & Lytle, S. L. (1993). *Inside/Outside: Teacher research and knowledge.* New York: Teachers College Press.

Dorr-Bremme, D. (1982). *Behaving and making sense: Creating social organization in the classroom.* Cambridge, MA: Harvard University, Unpublished dissertation.

Ende, J., Pomerantz, A., & Erickson, F. (1995). Preceptors' strategies for correcting residents in an ambulatory care medicine setting: A qualitative analysis. *Academic Medicine, 70*(3), 224–229.

Erickson, F. (1979). Mere ethnography: Some problems in its use in educational practice. *Anthropology and Education Quarterly*, *10*(3), 182–188.

Erickson, F. (1994/1995). Where the action is: On collaborative action research in education. *Bulletin of the Council for Research in Music Education*, *123*, 10–25.

Erickson, F. (1996). On the evolution of qualitative approaches in educational research: From Adam's task to Eve's. *Australian Educational Researcher*, *23*(2), 1–15.

Erickson, F. (2001). From research "on" teaching to research "in" teaching: How I have been learning to collaborate with teachers in the portrayal of their work. 25th Annual Charles DeGarmo Lecture. (Delivered at American Educational Research Association, April 11, 2001. Published by the Society for Professors of Education.)

Erickson, F., & Rittenberg, W. (1987). Topic control and person control: A thorny problem for foreign physicians in interaction with American patients. *Discourse Processes*, *10*(4), 401–415.

Erickson, F., & Christman, J. (1996). Taking stock/making change: Stories of collaboration in local school reform. *Theory into Practice*, *35*(3), 149–157.

Florio, S., & Walsh, M. (1980). The teacher as colleague in classroom research. In H. Trueba, G. Guthrie, & K. Au (Eds.), *Culture in the bilingual classroom: Studies in classroom ethnography*. Rowley, MA: Newbury House.

Goffman, E. (1981). *Forms of talk*. Philadelphia, PA: University of Pennsylvania Press.

Harding, S. (1991). *Whose science? Whose knowledge?: Thinking from women's lives*. Ithaca, NY: Cornell University Press.

Lather, P. (1991). *Getting smart: Feminist research and pedagogy with/in the postmodern*. New York: Routledge.

Levinson, B., Cade, S., Padawer, A., & Elvir, A. (Eds.). (2002). *Ethnography and education policy across the Americas*. Westport, CT & London: Praeger.

Lewin, K. (1946). Action research and minority problems. *Journal of Social Issues*, *24*(1), 34–46.

Malinowski, B. (1922). *Argonauts of the Western Pacific: An account of native enterprise and adventure in the archipelagoes of Melanesian New Guinea*. London & New York: G. Routledge & E. P. Dutton.

Malinowski, B. (1967). *A diary in the strict sense of the term*. New York: Harcourt Brace.

Nader, L. (1969/1974). Up the anthropologist: Perspectives gained from studying up. In D. Hymes (Ed.), *Reinventing anthropology*. New York: Random House/Vintage Books.

Nash, J. (1979). *We eat the mines and the mines eat us*. New York: Columbia University Press.

Peshkin, A. (2001). *Permissible advantage?: The moral consequences of elite schooling*. Mahwah, NJ: Lawrence Erlbaum Associates.

Powdermaker, H. (1966). *Stranger and friend: The way of an anthropologist*. New York: W. W. Norton.

Rosaldo, R. (1989). *Culture and truth: The remaking of social analysis*. Boston: Beacon Press.

Schensul, S. (1974). Skills needed in action anthropology: Lessons learned from El Centro de la Causa. *Human Organization*, *33*, 203–209.

Schensul, J., & Schensul, S. (1992). Collaborative research: Methods of inquiry for social change. In M. LeCompte, W. Milroy, & J. Preissle (Eds.), *The handbook of qualitative research in education*. San Diego & New York: Academic Press.

Scott, J. (1985). *Weapons of the weak: Everyday forms of peasant resistance*. New Haven, CT: Yale University Press.

Scott, J. (1990). *Domination and the arts of resistance*. New Haven, CT: Yale University Press.

Smith, D. (1974). Women's perspective as a radical critique of sociology. *Sociological Inquiry*, *44*, 7–13.

Spindler, G., & Spindler, L. (1994). *Pathways to cultural awareness: Cultural therapy with teachers and students*. Thousand Oaks, CA: Corwin Press.

Stenhouse, L. (1975). *An introduction to curriculum research and development*. London: Routledge & Kegan Paul.

Wax, R. (1971). *Doing fieldwork: Warnings and advice*. Chicago: University of Chicago Press.

Whyte, W. F., Greenwood, D. J., & Lazes, P. (1989). Participatory action research: Through practice to science in social research. *American Behavioral Scientist, 32*(5), 513–551.

Young, M. (1979). *The ethnography of Malinowski: The Trobriand Islands 1915–18*. London: Routledge & Kegan Paul.

8

Toward Teacher Education that Takes the Study of Culture as Foundational: Building Bridges Between Teacher Knowledge Research and Educational Ethnography

Jerry Rosiek
University of Alabama

Jerry Rosiek is an Associate Professor of Educational Research at the University of Alabama. His scholarship examines the way culture mediates teachers' understanding of their work and the implications of this mediation for teacher education practice and policy. His work has been published in *Curriculum Inquiry, The Journal of Teacher Education, Educational Theory,* and *Harvard Educational Review.*

This chapter explores the similarities between recent developments in the fields of teacher education and cultural anthropology. It makes the case that teacher education scholarship, specifically research on teacher knowledge, could benefit by a greater articulation with the fields of cultural anthropology and educational ethnography. The chapter opens with an excerpt from a case study of cultural conflict in a high school biology lesson. Both this example and the process by which the case study was produced are used as illustrations of the need for an appropriation of cultural anthropological theory and ethnographic methods in teacher education scholarship. The essay ends with an explication of what such an appropriation might look like.

> *So the question is not the presence or absence of critical reflexivity of the sort that has been fetishized in the academy on the 1980's, but rather its precise locale and articulation. Indeed, the future of critical ethnography itself depends on our abilities to understand its affinities with critical sensibilities in other*

> power/knowledge domains. Far from taking the distanced perspective on the
> "other" that has traditionally been ethnography's stance, ethnographers in-
> volved in such new locations are differently poised altogether. Today, the fact
> of intellectual or cultural affinity between observer and observed is indeed use-
> ful knowledge, guiding us in new terrains and pointing up the need to modify
> standard fieldwork assumptions and settings.
>
> George E. Marcus, 1999
> Critical Anthropology Now

What practical insights enable good teaching? Who can legitimately represent those insights? Who is the appropriate audience for research on teaching? Can teachers produce research on their own teaching and have that constitute scholarship? What is the place of collaboration for such research?
What is the appropriate mode of representation for this research? These and
other similar questions have been at the heart of a profound rethinking of research on teacher education since the 1980s.

Very similar questions have also been at the heart of a complex of theoretical and methodological innovations in the field of cultural anthropology.
Who can legitimately represent the culture of another? Who is the appropriate audience for such representations? What is the place of collaboration in
that research? What is their appropriate mode of representation for this research? Cultural anthropologists have recognized that there is no way to represent the culture of others that is not shaped by the cultural norms in which
that representation is being produced. Consequently these representations
cannot claim some final transcendental authority, but instead need to be understood at least in part as expressions of the interests encoded in the culture
from which the representation originates. Anthropologists have led the social sciences in developing modes of analysis that reflexively interrogate the
cultural contingency of academic representations of "other" cultures.

Although there has been some articulation between these recent developments in teacher education scholarship and cultural anthropology
(Ladson-Billings, 1995; Spindler & Spindler, 2000), far more could be done
in this regard. In this chapter, I make an effort to further this articulation by
focusing on a specific area of teacher education scholarship known as
teacher knowledge research. I begin by examining an episode of teaching
that became the focus of a teacher knowledge research analysis. Using this
example, I make the case that teacher knowledge research focused on addressing cultural difference in the classroom could benefit by appropriating
some of the reflexive approaches to analysis that have been developed by
contemporary anthropologists and educational anthropologists. I also offer,
conversely, that the practical focus of teachers' studies of their own practice

can serves as a tonic for the tendency to narcissism and over-abstraction in some reflexive ethnography.

ANTI-COLONIALIST ANTINOMIES
IN A BIOLOGY LESSON: AN EPISODE

The following episode is a condensed and slightly modified excerpt from a case study published originally as "Anticolonialist Antinomies: A Case Study of Cultural Conflict in a Biology Lesson" in *Curriculum Inquiry* (Chang & Rosiek, 2003). This case study was part of a larger research project involving 15 experienced science teachers in which the teachers were asked to examine the practical knowledge that enabled them to provide challenging science curriculum to cultural minority students.

This excerpt is based on Paokong John Chang's experience teaching a lesson on cellular biology to a class of southeast Asian, predominantly Hmong, immigrants. His immediate challenge was how to teach a concept of disease that contradicted his Hmong students' traditional beliefs about health and the natural world. Chang wanted to teach science, but he did not want to contribute to a colonialist/assimilationist erasure of Hmong culture. The challenge we faced as researchers attempting to describe this teaching moment was twofold: (a) to report accurately on this moment of teaching, while critically tracking the way various cultural discourses shaped the conception of appropriate science curriculum, and (b) to critically track the way our own representation of the teaching moment was being influenced by various professional and cultural discourses.

Paokong John Chang was grading papers at his desk. It was the last few minutes of the last day of the 6-week grading period. The bell rang. He could hear the students pour like a torrent of bodies and shouts into the hallway. The few students who were working on their test reluctantly turned it in and left as well. Only Lia Xiong was left. "Take your time" Paokong assured her, "I will be here for a while." He said it distractedly, barely looking up from the grading he was doing.

The test was on cellular division. Since Paokong's class was for ESL students (English as a Second Language), he required them to do a lot of drawings on the test. Draw the cell. Draw the process of mitosis. The last day of the unit, however, had dealt with mutation of cells and the cellular basis for some diseases like cancer. He hadn't been able to figure out how to use diagrams with that part of the test, so he had students write a paragraph using diagrams to explain mutation and cellular diseases. Some of the students really struggled to express themselves in English and he struggled with how to grade them. It was their science knowledge he wanted to assess, not their mastery of written English.

A few seconds passed and Lia quietly approached his desk. She placed her test in basket marked for this purpose and waited. Paokong looked up and said, perfunctorily, Finished? "Yes. I think I did well." He was sure that she had. Lia was a disciplined student and bright. He was surprised she had taken so long with the test. Lia lingered and repeated "I think I did well." "I am sure you did," Paokong seconded her confidence. "You should not worry about it any longer and go have a fun weekend." Lia nodded, but did not leave. He thought for a moment that she wanted him to grade her paper immediately, something he made a policy of not doing. "I have a question, Mr. Chang," she announced. He was already preparing his answer in his mind—no, you'll have to wait till Monday.

Instead she asked, "You do not really believe these things about 'cancer,' do you?" She seemed to have forced the question out with some effort. After a pause she continued, "I mean, you are Hmong. You know that a person gets sick because they have lost their pleng and that you must get the shaman to do the proper rituals if you are to be reunited with your pleng and become well." Paokong was caught off guard. This was not the question he had expected. He put down his pencil and considered Lia carefully.

Paokong's first impulse was to politely and authoritatively reply that, yes, he does believe in cellular biology and in what he has taught her about cancer. He felt an impetus to free her from a world filled with superstitions and align her with a more "civilized" way of thinking about the world. He hesitated, however, and leaned back in his chair, looking at the jumble of tests and biology texts on his desk. He knew Lia's question was not just about DNA and cells. Traditional Hmong beliefs about diseases are connected to other Hmong beliefs about the world. Those beliefs are connected to people's commitments to family, community, and themselves. This fabric of beliefs brings people together and enables them to live and love and support one another.

Paokong felt the weight of Lia's gaze on him as he thought about her question. Maintaining a supportive community is especially high stakes for Hmong immigrants in the United States. In many families the Hmong fabric of belief is being worn thin. Young children are losing their connection to traditional practices; they do not understand the stories their parents tell them and their parents often do not understand the experiences their children are having. The frequent result is a lack of respect for parents and a rejection of their guidance. Sometimes this rejection is for the better; some traditional beliefs need to be reconsidered, Paokong believed. The problem is that very little of substance is replacing the traditional beliefs. The growing vacuum of meaning in Hmong life is being filled, not by another healthy set of cultural values, but by a thin ethic of consumerism. More than four thousand years of communal Hmong wisdom and solidarity is being eroded and replaced with vulgar individualism, hyper-sexualized images from music videos, and a craving for expensive clothes and tennis shoes (Thao, 1999).

Paokong knew that most Hmong are not conforming to the "model-minority" stereotype of Asians in America. The Hmong community in the United States shows all the signs of a community in distress—high rates of poverty and unemployment, high rates of high school and middle school drop-outs, high rates health problems including psychological depression, substance abuse, and suicide (Fadiman, 1997; Walker-Moffat, 1995). This was part of why he had chosen to be a teacher. He knew that the assault on Hmong cultural values is not an abstract issue. It affects people's health, their bodies, their minds, and their families.

He looked again at Lia and felt at risk of doing something terribly wrong, of losing something very important. He thought it was as if he was being presented with a game of jingo-stix—that game where sticks are stacked one upon the other and players take turns pulling individual sticks out of the stack without disturbing the larger structure. The loser is the one who pulls the stick out that finally causes the structure to collapse. Paokong could have contradicted Lia's belief about the "pleng" and cancer. He could have suggested her beliefs were superstitious and told her the scientific view is a more accurate account of reality. And maybe that would not have affected her overall identity at all. Maybe she would have found a way, by herself, to integrate those unfamiliar ideas into her sense of being Hmong. But there was always the chance, he thought, that this would be the one thing that finally sent her whole Hmong identity into collapse, and with it her health, her family bonds, her overall well-being. The risk of contributing to that gripped Paokong with concern.

After what seemed like a long time, Paokong drew a breath and told Lia that he needed to think more about her question. I don't want to answer such an important question too hastily, he explained in his imperfect Hmong. Let's talk about this again after class on Monday. She seemed pleased with his response. "O.K. Mr. Chang. Thank you!" she responded cheerily, and turned for the door, where she offered another "Thank you!" before leaving. He listened to the receding voices of her and her friends who had been waiting in the hall, but they were speaking Hmong too fast for him to understand what they were saying.

A TEACHER'S PRACTICAL KNOWLEDGE ABOUT CULTURAL DIFFERENCE

In much of the contemporary teacher research and research on teachers' practical knowledge, inquiries focus on the pedagogical approaches teachers use to deliver a taken-for-granted curriculum. The curriculum itself rarely becomes the topic of inquiry. In the previous episode, however, Chang's encounter with Lia required more than reflection on his pedagogical techniques. Chang found himself caught between two systems of value, two cultural discourses that provided conflicting reads on what should be taught in that moment. Each cultural system had unique features that gave it some claim to authority in the situation. Each also had built in blindnesses which weakened those claims to authority.

On the one hand, Chang felt bound by the authority of the professional discourses in which he worked. These professional discourses were expressions of a larger cultural system in which Chang himself had been socialized. Trained in biology, Chang was persuaded that cellular mutations *do* result in diseases collectively referred to as "cancer." And he felt it was his responsibility as a public school teacher employed by the State of California to effectively teach the curriculum he was assigned. More poignantly, Chang's mother was a cancer survivor. His family's traditional beliefs had caused them to delay in getting modern medical care for his mother. As of the writing of this chapter, his mother was fully recovered and in good health. Nonetheless Chang bore some resentment toward the way his family's traditional beliefs had put his mother's health at risk. He felt strongly that Lia needed to understand her own body accurately enough to make sound decisions about her own health. He believed his biology curriculum provided such understanding.

On the other hand stood the authority of Hmong traditional beliefs about health and healing. Although Chang was ambivalent about certain specific aspects of traditional Hmong culture, overall he held traditional Hmong culture in high respect. He believed that Lia's beliefs about disease, although not literally true, were part of a unique cultural fabric of values, identity, and practices that had sustained Hmong people through two millennia of persecution and hardship. The Hmong had suffered a thousand years of attacks and pressure to assimilate from the Chinese. When threat of genocide finally forced them to flee China, they found temporary safety in Laos and Vietnam. Eventually the majority cultures there sought to forcibly assimilate the Hmong and, when that did not work, to eliminate them.

Today Hmong refugees in the United States are facing pressure to assimilate from yet another majority culture. Instead of direct threats aimed at adults in their community, the pressure to assimilate in the United States is focused primarily on children and is delivered through schools, health service agencies, and mass media. Although less violent than the pressure they faced in Southeast Asia, the consequences are still profound for Hmong quality of life. Communication between generations is becoming difficult in many families. Commitment to ancient communal rituals and values is waning among the young and is being replaced by little more than a thin ethic of consumerism. Although the Hmong are not facing physical extinction in the United

States, they are facing cultural extinction. Chang's concern about this loss was not born of nostalgia. He saw the material effects of this cultural erosion in his students' lives. Hmong families were fracturing. Local social work professionals reported declines in the mental and physical health of the Hmong population in the area. Depression, substance abuse, suicide, gang participation, and drop out rates are higher for Hmong than for almost any other demographic group in Southern California (Chang & Rosiek, 2003; Fadiman, 1997; Walker-Moffat, 1995).

It is against this backdrop that Hmong traditional beliefs command a moral, if not scientific, authority. The tradition of Western science may have a more accurate accounting of physical diseases, but it places no value on the well-being of the Hmong people—collectively or individually. Hmong traditions, despite their limitations, place Hmong well-being at the center of its values. They keep people connected and by so doing keep them healthier than they would be otherwise. When Lia approached Paokong Chang, he did not see simply a learner of Western science. He also saw someone whose sense of family, community, and emotional health was potentially at risk. He saw a young woman in the midst of a conflict between two broad cultural systems, and both of those cultural systems could lay claim to what and how he was teaching.

His was a dilemma between competing cultural imperatives. The professional discourses that constitute his role as a science teacher (and the broader Western cultural discourses that rationalize the profession) were in conflict with a Hmong cultural discourse that framed him as a trusted teacher for Hmong students. As a teacher conducting research on his own teaching practice, it was not enough in this situation for Chang to examine the pedagogical challenge of teaching his biology curriculum well. He also needed to recognize and critically analyze the cultural presuppositions underlying his curricular objectives.

The case study from which the above excerpt was taken was the outcome of a process of inquiry on the practical knowledge that enabled Chang's teaching of science in a culturally diverse classroom. The research was conducted in collaboration with me and a team of experienced science teachers. The project was grounded in the scholarship of teaching and teacher inquiry literature. The unit of analysis for studies in this literature is most often the teacher's experience of practical classroom challenges. And the concepts used for analysis are most often appropriated from the disciplines of cognitive psychology and/or social psychology. The analysis of Chang's encounter with Lia, however, required an analytical lens that frames schooling and curriculum as a cultural activity. It required a conceptual framework and a unit of analysis that could track the consequences of practical teaching decisions beyond the individual child's competencies, and beyond the classroom, to the larger social, cultural, and historical context in which children—in which we all—live.

One obvious place to reach for such conceptual tools is the field of educational ethnography. As was mentioned earlier, there are some teacher knowledge researchers who are influenced by and explicitly build on the educational ethnography literature (Ladson-Billings, 1995; Liston & Zeichner, 1996). But there has been no systematic effort to articulate between the theoretical and methodological presuppositions underlying these two fields of study. In what remains of this chapter I undertake to begin such an articulation by examining some of the limitations of contemporary teacher knowledge theory. I then describe how building closer ties to the field of educational ethnography could help in transcending those limitations, and the implications that would have for the preparation of teachers, teacher education scholars, and teacher education departments.

TEACHER KNOWLEDGE RESEARCH

Teacher knowledge research takes as its project bridging the gap between general educational theory and the practical work of teaching. Researchers in this area illuminate what happens in that gap by encouraging teachers to systematically reflect and report on their practice (Clandinin & Connelly, 1996, 2000; Cochran-Smith & Lytle, 1993, 1999; Grossman, 1990; Liston & Zeichner, 1996; Noffke, 1992, 1997; Richardson, 1994; Rosiek, 2002, 2003; Shulman, 1987, 2000; Wilson, Shulman, & Richert, 1987). Stepping back and looking at this process of reflection, these scholars ask: what is the nature and the content of the knowledge that enables sound practice in those situations where teacher behavior cannot be reasonably prescribed? Based on their answers to this question, recommendations are made for improvements to teacher education policy and curriculum.

One of the issues on which teacher practical knowledge researchers are most significantly divided concerns the end products or goals of teacher practical knowledge research. Some scholars wish to see teachers' practical knowledge documented—usually in the form of case studies—so that a general knowledge base of practical insights can be established for use in teacher education programs (Rosiek, 2003; Sconiers & Rosiek, 2000; Shulman, 1987, 2000). Others, citing the radically context-dependent nature of teachers' practice, are skeptical about the possibility of establishing such a general knowledge base. They recommend instead preparing teachers to conduct research on their own practice (Clandinin & Connelly, 2000; Cochran-Smith & Lytle, 1993, 1999; Noffke, 1997).

These differences of opinion about the ends of teacher practical knowledge research are relevant to our discussion because they frame current discussions about the appropriate means of teacher knowledge research. Perhaps the most pointed of these differences concerns the role university academics should have in documenting teacher's practical knowledge. Those most interested in examining the practical dimension of teaching specific subject matter concepts often envision this research happening in collaboration with university trained researchers. Their conception of the research process is modeled after university based scholarship, including peer review, publication of findings, and the establishment of a codified practical knowledge base for teaching. Those who consider the process of teacher inquiry more important than its product often see university researchers as unnecessary or as a source of unwanted distortion of teachers' inquiries (Cochran-Smith & Lytle, 1993, 1999). According to this view, teachers' practical concerns are significantly different than the questions that drive university-based research. The product of a teacher's inquiry is seen as being intended first and sometimes exclusively for the teacher inquirer herself.

What we see here is an insider/outsider opposition set up between practicing teachers and university based teacher education scholars. Teachers are outsiders to high status academic discourses grounded in traditional social scientific disciplines. But university researchers are outsiders to the local discourses that shape and sustain teachers' practical understanding of their classrooms. This insider/outsider conception of teacher practical knowledge research gives rise to two basic conceptions of how to address the gap between academic social science and teachers' practice. On the one side are attempts to broaden the scope of what we call "educational research" to include space for documentation and analysis of teachers' practical insights, while still retaining basic academic norms. On the other side is the notion that academic discourse norms are themselves the problem, and a call to set up a separate sphere of institutional support in which teacher inquiries can develop according to their own logic. This particular division within the field has been sustained long enough to warrant naming the respective sides of the debate. The phrase "the scholarship of teaching" (Shulman, 2000) is used to refer to the former type of research, while the term "teacher inquiry" or "inquiry-as-stance" (Cochran-Smith & Lytle, 1999) is used to describe the latter approach.

Many studies, of course, do not fall easily into either of these two extremes, and the actual research can be thought of as falling onto continuum between

Scholarship of Teaching
Focus on collaboration between university academics and teachers. Goal is to produce a peer reviewed written product modeled after academic publications.

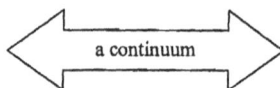

a continuum

Teacher Inquiry
Focus on teachers working individually or in collaboration with other teachers. The process of inquiry is the most important product.

FIG. 8.1. Teacher research continuum.

these two approaches (see Fig. 8.1). The point here, however, is not to reify this distinction, but to call it into question. This dichotomized conception of research on the practical dimension of teaching has generated a profound and salutary rethinking of teacher education practice. I offer, however, that neither of these positions provide adequate conceptual tools for examining cultural difference in the classroom. A more pluralistic conception of the discourses that influence/support/distort teacher inquiries is needed.

MORE THAN TWO DISCOURSES

The dichotomy just described is a natural consequence of discussing teacher knowledge on the premise that it is formed primarily by professional discourses. The discourse of professional academics is contrasted to that of teachers. The concern is raised that academic discourses, which privilege general/theoretic knowledge, overshadow and silence the discourses of teachers, whose insights are more local/practical. The result is that teachers' practical insights are lost to a broader community.

I offer that this conception of teachers' insights being caught in the shadow of a single *professional* discourse—that of academic researchers—artificially limits the scope of teacher practical knowledge research. What is missed is the way teachers are often caught in a liminal space between different *cultural* discourses that claim authority over their teaching. I use the term *discourse* here in its Foucauldian sense that refers, not just to language in a narrow sense, but also to extensive networks of signification and subjectively experienced meaning that include gestures, institutions, architecture, cosmology, common sense beliefs, and identity (Foucault, 1965, 1980; Spivak, 1988; Sullivan, 2001). "Discourse," used in this way, refers to the way systems of meaning provide people not just beliefs about the world, but also their identity, desires, and the criteria by which such beliefs are evaluated.

Looking at teachers' work through this lens, we can see how the cultural systems that supply teachers' curricular philosophies and personal values are multiple, and may be contradictory or even incommensurable. Certainly, some practical classroom challenges do emerge out of disconnects between teachers' training in the academy and local circumstances. However, other practical challenges emerge out of disconnects between general systems of cultural meaning. When this is the case, teacher inquirers cannot avoid negotiating these conflicting discourses. University based collaborators in teacher knowledge research face similar conflicts between the discourses of their professional training and the discourses of the non-academic communities in which they live and work. This discursive conception of teacher knowledge research requires a rethinking of conditions under which this research takes place. The following diagram provides the simplest possible illustration of the conceptual expansion I am trying to describe.

In Fig. 8.2, the work of teaching is framed by a teacher's professional discourse communities, which are in turn a part of the broader cultural discourse communities that frame her life. But the meanings constituted in the broader cultural discourses exceed the bounds of the professional discourses, providing additional meaning to teaching practice, meaning that may conflict with that provided by their professional discourses. Similarly, university researchers live and work within both cultural and professional discourses, with similar excesses and potential conflicts. Additionally, the professional and cultural discourses of the university collaborator in such research is often not identical to that of the teacher. Finally, both of the researchers in this dy-

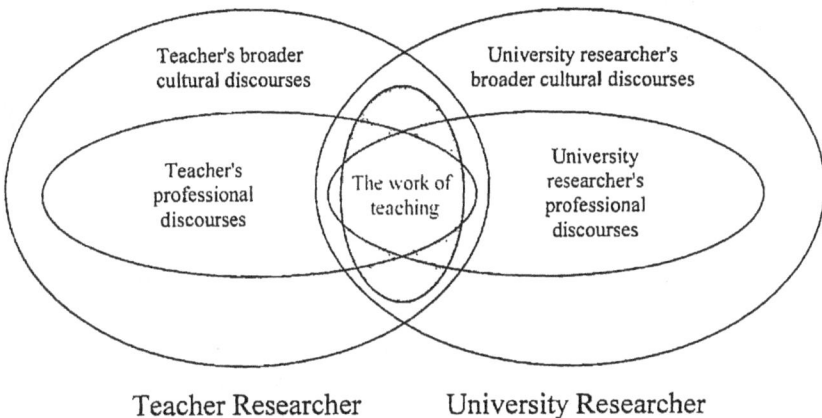

Teacher Researcher   University Researcher

FIG. 8.2. A discursive conception of teacher knowledge research.

namic may be examining the behavior and experience of students whose culture differs from their own (not pictured in the diagram). The potential interactions between different discursive lenses multiply very quickly.

If we take into consideration that conflicts between cultural, as well as professional, discourses are sources of practical challenges for teachers, then certain methodological questions come immediately to the fore. Perhaps the most serious of these concerns the unit of analysis for teacher practical knowledge research. Teacher practical knowledge research—both scholarship of teaching and teacher inquiry style studies—relies almost exclusively on individual teacher reflection as a source of data. Although there is a great deal to be learned from listening to what teachers have to say about the practical realities of teaching, the reflective powers of individual teachers do have limits. This is an especially salient consideration when looking at the ways teachers deal with cultural difference in the classroom. Culture is constituted precisely by those taken-for-granted beliefs, values, and categories of thought that shape conscious reflection. Practical challenges to teaching that arise out of encounters with cultural difference, therefore, would not lend themselves to reflective inquiry by individuals or groups who share a culture of origin. In these cases the very epistemic and moral values that guide teachers' reflection would be part of the cultural systems that are in conflict. When reflective inquiry is undertaken in these conditions, the most frequent result is a focus on the culture of the Other as a "problem" and responses that reinscribe the taken-for-granted normality of the majority culture (Delpit, 1995; Liston & Zeichner, 1996; Valencia, 1997; Varenne & McDermott, 1998). An analysis is needed that respects the insights that teachers reflection on their own practice can produce and that simultaneously critically tracks the limitations that culture puts on that reflection.

BEYOND THE CRITICAL FEEDBACK OF PEERS

It should be noted here that existing teacher knowledge theories are not naive about the trustworthiness of teachers' self-analysis of their practice. They do make provisions for the limitations of practitioners' own reflective capacities (Fenstermacher, 1994). In the inquiry-as-stance tradition, for example, it is often suggested that teachers work in communities of inquiry with other teachers, who can provide critical feedback on their analysis (Cochran-Smith, 1999; Noffke, 1997). This would provide some check on individual teachers' biases. However, it does not proved a sufficient check against cultural provincialism when the members of the communities of teacher-inquirers all share similar cultural frameworks (Noffke, 1997).

In the scholarship of teaching tradition, an attempt to account for the limitations of practitioners own reflective capacities is made by building a peer review process into the conception of teacher research. A blind peer review process modeled on that of academic research journals has the benefit of avoiding local provincialisms. However, academic communities are often subject to their own disciplinary provincialism. Additionally, "peer review" can only be a check on the discourse limitations of a teacher's inquiry if the reviewers are not themselves unconsciously inscribed into the same system of cultural values as those whose manuscript they are reviewing. Because many such reviewers would be members of the same linguistic, class, cultural, and even racial communities as those they review, this is an important consideration. Academic review processes have not historically proven to be a sufficient check against many forms of collective bias and myopia.

In both major approaches to teacher knowledge research, scholars have looked to the presence of another teacher or scholar to check the limitations of their analysis. They have not, however, specified the conditions under which such critical feedback can be effectively provided. If it is only personal bias with which we are concerned, then any other person not sharing our personal history could, in principle, be an effective assistant in this regard. On the other hand, when we adopt a discursive conception of research on teacher knowledge, both the scope of teacher inquiries and the awareness of possible sources of error are increased. Having other persons provide feedback on the research is not enough to insure that the taken for granted cultural viewpoints from which our analysis emerges will be recognized and critically examined. Something additional is needed.

The research process that produced the case study about Paokong Chang's biology lesson provides an illustration of this point. Chang was the primary teacher researcher for the previously mentioned case study. It was his experience that was being examined. I was a university trained researcher who collaborated with him in the development and writing of that case study. In other words, I was a person who might be expected to provide Chang with a critical check on the limitations of his own reflective capacities.

At some level this did happen. Simply by creating a research project that examined the way cultural difference influenced science teaching, certain taken for granted attitudes about science education were called into question. For most of the participating teachers, including Chang, the improvement of his teaching was seen as something accomplished by inquiry based science curriculum or constructivist teaching approaches that were assumed to benefit all students equally, and thus cultural difference was a minor consideration, if it was considered at all. Chang's knowledge of cultural difference in the classroom was assumed to assist his delivery of these improvements. That knowledge was not thought to be a source insight that could call into question the substance of science curriculum. My status as a university researcher, and my knowledge of a research literature that examines on the significance of cultural difference for educational practice, enabled me to leverage a deeper conversation about relation between culture, colonialism, and science curriculum in the official space of a district sponsored professional development seminar. Sharing with teachers examples of the research that critically examined the cultural foundations of science education theory and practice had a multiplying effect. Once the limits of science reform discourse had been questioned, members of the teacher-research group were inclined to critically challenge one another and the ideal of science teaching practice promoted within their district.

This was a salutary and anticipated effect of inviting teachers to consider questions outside the bounds of the traditional science education reform conversation. It was not, however, a sufficient inoculation against the danger of my own cultural myopia. This was revealed to me much later in the process, when Paokong Chang and I were exchanging drafts of the case study we wrote together. It was perhaps our third exchange. The focus and basic outline of the narrative was in place. We were crafting particular passages and scenes for readability. In my most recent draft I had edited and elaborated (based on what I thought I had heard in our interviews and discussions) his reflections on Lia's state of mind the day she approached him. I had framed Lia as a confused young woman, caught in the cross currents of Hmong and U.S. culture. She was approaching Mr. Chang for guidance, for help in dealing with competing cultural discourses.

We were sitting at a picnic table, and Paokong was silent as he looked at the section. Eventually he sighed. "I don't think you are hearing me correctly," he offered. "Lia wasn't confused or worried in that story," he explained. She wasn't? "No, she wasn't worried about herself at all. She was worried about me." Worried about you? Slowly, the nature and scope of my presumption began to dawn on me. "Yes, see . . . she knew she was correct in her belief about the *pleng*. She was concerned about how far I had strayed from being Hmong. She was concerned that I had become lost."

Two years of working with Chang on this case study, and still I had not heard this part of the story that Chang took for granted. Had I been left to write the case study alone based on interviews and journal entries, or had Chang not been an insider to Hmong culture, I would have overwritten Lia and John's story with a distinctly Euro-centric narrative—the poor little im-

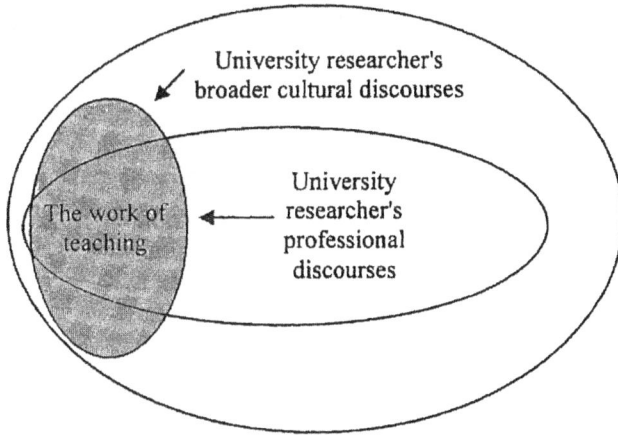

FIG. 8.3.   Discursive influences on university researchers.

migrant girl trying to find a way to integrate her traditional beliefs into a new culture. It had not occurred to me that Lia was confident that U.S. culture was inferior, confident that the Hmong would successfully resist assimilation, and that Paokong Chang was at risk to succumbing to an inferior culture. Despite the fact that my professional training had included the study of critical multiculturalism, post-colonialism, and the way social science research had been historically complicit with imperialism, my taken-for-granted presumption of the natural and inevitable supremacy of my own culture was still shaping my analysis.

This lapse on my part is less idiosyncratic, I think, than it is an indication of the extent to which these cultural narratives are deeply ingrained in our taken-for-granted relations to the world. The wider cultural discourses of which we are a part inevitably contribute to, and compete with the professional research discourses that frame our research. This is illustrated in the section of the above diagram that focuses on the contribution of university trained academics to teacher knowledge research (see Fig. 8.3).

UNIVERSITY RESEARCHER

In my initial representation of Lia's motivations for approaching Chang, the broader cultural discourses in which I had been socialized got the better of the more critical discourses that I was initiated into in my professional training as an academic. What this reveals is that the simple presence of others—be they other teachers or university academics—in the teacher knowledge research process is not enough to secure this research against cultural blind spots.

The field of teacher knowledge research has given considerable attention to the potential conflicts and tensions between teachers' professional discourses and university researchers' professional discourses. What the previously mentioned example highlights is that there are other discourse conflicts that can hinder teacher knowledge research. The question arises for university based teacher knowledge researchers, what can we do to more systematically guard against our broad cultural discourses overwriting either our professional training or the culturally inflected understanding of the teachers whose knowledge we are trying to document?

My ability to appreciate the import of Chang's objection was due in part to my education in cultural anthropology, where the necessity of cultural reflexiveness was first introduced to me as a research issue. More than a general awareness will be needed, however, if such reflexivity is to become a general feature of teacher knowledge research practice. This chapter now turns to some specific ways to make that reflexivity more pervasive.

Building Bridges between Educational Ethnography and Teacher Knowledge Research

To the extent that classrooms are characterized by cultural diversity, teachers face challenges that require them to think about cultural difference everyday. Even in culturally homogenous classrooms, teachers see students and their practice through lenses provided by their culture. Although our cultural lenses are our most basic tool for working through classroom challenges, sometimes these lenses themselves constitute a source of difficulty. Culture blinds us as well as enables us. Teacher knowledge research, if it is to respond to the full range of practical challenges faced by teachers, will therefore need to find ways to document, analyze, and represent, not just the culture of students, but the way culture mediates teachers' understanding of their classrooms.

The field of educational ethnography offers a variety of conceptual and methodological tools that would enable teacher researchers to undertake this kind of analysis. Among these tools are: a language for discussing research on and through culture, modes of data collection, a literature from which to draw references and models, and modes of representation that honor the complexity of cultural—not just professional—insider/outsider relationships.

I also believe teacher knowledge research can make a reciprocal contribution to the field of educational ethnography. We would not expect that a teachers' practical understanding of their teaching practice would be identical to an ethnographer's more distant relation to their subject. Where the ethnographer's first task is to understand the relationship between schooling processes and broader cultural dynamics, a teacher researchers' task is to understand their own actions in a cultural context. To use the language of cultural anthropology, ethnography produces analysis from an etic perspective, teacher knowledge research produces analysis from an emic perspective.

For the scholar that sees ethnography's only project as the naturalistic description of the operation of culture, then teacher knowledge research may seem little more than a source of data. Teachers provide emic insights that can inform educational ethnographers' etic analysis of the operation of culture in schools. However, for ethnographers who see their writing not only as descriptive, but also as productive of the cultural processes they document, and who are committed to changing that culture, then it would seem teachers should be considered much more than sources of data.

This more reflexive and activist ethnography requires an audience whose attitudes and actions can be transformed by ethnographic writing. One of the possible audiences for critical ethnography is policy makers. But recent years have illustrated that educational researchers, even the most stringently positivistic among us, cannot be sanguine about their ability to influence highly politicized educational policy debates at federal, state, or local levels. Another possible audience, however, is educational practitioners themselves—administrators and, most importantly, teachers. If critical ethnography is to inform teaching practice, then at some point the etic analysis of cultural influences on teaching will need to be encountered by teachers and transformed into emic understanding of the classroom scene.

It would be naive to think such transformation could be straightforward; that it would happen simply as the result of teachers reading ethnographies. Ethnographies offer richly textured, but still general insights. A teacher reader of this literature has to determine the extent to which the situations he or she reads about are parallel to his or her own specific context. A teacher's greater proximity to practice will require him or her to extend, and even challenge, some ethnographic insights.

This additive and transformative process need not be idiosyncratic. It could and should be conducted professionally and collaboratively, in dialogue with other teachers and with university researchers, so that the bridge to practice is constantly being refined and improved. Teacher knowledge research is uniquely positioned to do this work.

Details of an Articulation

So what would this articulation between the fields of educational ethnography and teacher knowledge research actually look like? In what follows, I lay out four resources/practices that teacher knowledge researchers could constructively appropriate from the field of educational ethnography, and which could serve to further an articulation between these two fields of inquiry.

1. A literature Base About Culture and Schooling.   There is no need for teacher knowledge researchers to reinvent the wheel when it comes to the analysis of the influence of culture on educational practices. There is an extensive literature on these processes that has already been generated by half a century of educational ethnography which teacher knowledge researchers could build on, critique, and refine. There are already many examples of teacher education scholarship grounded in this literature (Chang & Rosiek, 2003; Cochran-Smith, 1991; Delpit, 1995, 2003; Ladson-Billings, 1995; Liston & Zeichner, 1996; Sconiers & Rosiek, 2000). So models exist upon which new teacher knowledge researchers can draw.

To encourage this use of educational ethnographic literature by teacher knowledge researchers, two things would need to happen. First, teacher education programs that emphasize "action research" and "teacher inquiry" would need to build the study of this educational ethnography literature into their curriculum. Teacher researchers cannot draw upon this literature if they do not know it exists. Second, in PhD programs where university based teacher knowledge researchers are prepared, a teacher's responsibility to engage in reflexive analysis of the cultural influences on their practice needs to be emphasized. And the contemporary educational ethnographic literature needs to be presented as an important resource to such analysis, a foundational literature to teacher knowledge research equal in significance to the research literature in educational and developmental psychology.

2. The Importance of Fieldwork That Involves Cultural Immersion.
One of the most basic premises of ethnographic research is the belief that in order to understand a culture, you must spend time immersed in that culture. Fieldwork, in which the ethnographer leaves the security of their culture of origin and spends months, even years, living and interacting daily with persons in their home community, is part of what gives an ethnographer the authority to make reports about other cultures. Although the imperialistic aspects of these claims to authority have been rightly questioned in recent decades, fieldwork that involves immersion experiences retains its ability to

deepen our understanding of other communities and to increase the warrant of ethnographic descriptions.

If teachers are to comment on and analyze cultural difference in their classroom, I offer they will need to seek out such immersion experiences with the cultures they seek to understand. At one level teacher researchers, if not their university collaborators, are always doing immersive fieldwork in the classroom. The classroom in many cases, however, provides a very limited form of immersion. Schools and their norms are created by majority communities. The cultures of smaller or less politically powerful communities in a school district are not available at the school sight for immersion experiences. A teacher would need to travel off the school site to have these immersion experiences.

Again this would have implications for the way we teach teachers and doctoral students about teacher knowledge research. The often taken-for-granted unit of analysis in teacher knowledge research is the classroom. This would need to be broadened. And opportunities for extensive off-campus experiences in students' communities of origin would need to be built into the design of teacher knowledge research projects. This would also place a premium on working with teachers who grew up or live in the communities in which they teach.

3. Innovative Modes of Representation. Teacher knowledge researchers have given considerable attention to critiquing the power relationships between university academic discourses and the discourses of teachers. Teacher knowledge researchers have been at the fore-front of exploring ways of representing teacher knowledge that negotiates the often fraught power dynamics between these two communities. Sometimes this involves excluding the university researcher from the research process altogether (Cochran-Smith & Lytle, 1993, 1999; Noffke, 1997). Sometimes this involves teachers writing narratives in the first person, with the help of a university editor (Clandinin & Connelly, 1996; Connelly & Clandinin, 1999). At other times it involves university researchers writing clinical case studies of teachers' practice in the third person, with copious cross-checks with the teachers themselves. And on still other occasions it involves intensive collaborative approaches to writing, where every sentence is co-crafted by a teacher researcher and a university collaborator (Chang & Rosiek, 2003; Sconiers & Rosiek, 2000).

However, as was pointed out early in this chapter, the tension between the professional discourses of teachers and university academics is not the only discourse conflict that merits the attention of teacher knowledge researchers.

There are also broader cultural discourses shaping the analysis of both university academics and teachers that need to be critically tracked and carefully represented. Contemporary ethnographic theory has explored the methodological implications of the way culture mediates knowledge production more than any other branch of the social sciences. In particular, ethnographic theorists have experimented with a variety of reflexive representational practices that can help researchers deal with the cultural contingency of their analysis.

A full exploration of these representational practices is beyond the scope of this essay. However, I will examine three recent innovations in ethnographic writing that could be especially useful to teacher knowledge researchers: auto-ethnographic, polyvocal, and performative approaches to ethnographic writing.

Auto-ethnography is a blending of the genres of auto-biography and ethnography (Behar, 1997; Reed-Danahay, 1997; Ellis & Bochner, 2000; Holt, 2003; Mykhalovskiy, 1996; Sparkes, 2000; Spry, 2001). Like many teacher knowledge research texts (and unlike traditional ethnographic texts), auto-ethnography is written in a first person voice. It does so, however, not to highlight the expertise of the author about their local circumstance, but instead to highlight the limitations of the perspective of the author and to stand down from the claims to totalizing epistemic authority implied in the disembodied third-person voice of traditional ethnographic writing. As such, auto-ethnographers spend more time reflecting self-consciously on the limitations of the cultural lenses they bring to the situation they describe. Although the first person writing is common in teacher knowledge researchers, the acute cultural self-consciousness demonstrated in most auto-ethnographic texts will be less familiar. This self-conscious style could be a useful tool for teacher knowledge researchers attempting to describe their experience of cultural difference without over-writing that cultural difference in a manner that I almost did with Chang's story.

Polyvocal approaches to ethnographic writing refers to using representations of multiple voices, speaking from different perspectives with different priorities, often in different registers (tone), in an ethnography (Behar, 1993; Lather, 1997; Tobin & Davidson, 1990; Tsing, 1993). This does not simply mean the liberal use of inset quotes that are then encapsulated by analysis provided in an academic voice. This refers to the fragmentation of the text such that each of the voices represented is able to provide their own analysis of the other voices and subject positions in the text, such that no one narrative unity emerges in the writing. Such textual fragmentation could be employed by teacher knowledge researchers to represent the multiple and often conflicting cultural discourses that shape classroom experience, as well as the tensions and conflicts between academic and classroom teacher discourses. It would be particularly useful for representing the collaborative process between teachers and university researchers.

Performative approaches to ethnographic writing refers to approaching ethnographic texts less as literal representations of the scenes they describe, than as rhetorical acts that produce and reproduce our phenomenological relations to those scenes (Angrossino, 2002; Bagley & Cancienne, 2002; Barone, 2000; Barone, & Eisner, 1997; Butler, J., 1990; Clifford & Marcus, 1986; Conquergood, 1985, 1989; Denzin, 2003; Dimitriadis, 2001; Spry, 2001). This area of innovation often involves the most radical departures from traditional ethnographic writing, so much so that it may not be recognized by some as even belonging in the ethnographic tradition. Without being drawn into disputes about disciplinary boundaries, suffice it to say here that this approach to ethnographic reportage often employs artistic modes of representation, including, but not limited to literary stylization, theatrical stagings, and the use of visual art mediums.

Teacher knowledge researchers have experimented with a variety of narrative modes of representing teacher knowledge, including artistically crafted and fictionalized stories (Chang & Rosiek, 2003; Sconiers & Rosiek, 2000). The literature on performative approaches to ethnography can enrich these experimentations, and help tailor them to the purpose of communicating teachers' lived experience of cultural dynamics in the classroom.

The general purpose of these innovative modes of representation has been to move away from descriptive prose that implies the researcher has access to some privileged perspective outside of cultural discourses, from which they can give a totalizing account of the operations of culture. Whether or not teacher knowledge researchers adopt any of these specific modes of representation, dealing critically with the way culture frames all views including the researchers' will require that the culturally contingency of teacher knowledge representations be signified in some manner.

4. Theoretical Frameworks. Finally, if teacher knowledge researchers are to explore the cultural dimension of their own knowledge production, then they will need theoretical frameworks that can make connections between the epistemological, ideological, and practical features of their claims. The cognitive scientific theories most widely used by teacher practical knowledge theorists, or the loose sampling from Kurt Lewin's theories used by some action researchers, do not provide sufficient conceptual vocabularies for describing the relation between teacher knowledge and culture. Many theories have been deployed by ethnographers to describe the relation between knowledge and culture generally, for example, marxism, functionalism, phenomenology, symbolic interactionism, structuralism, post-structuralist and pragmatic semiotics, Freudian and Lacanian psychoanalysis, practice theory, post-colonialism, feminism, orientalism, and so on. Whereas any and all of these may prove useful in a given teaching situation, I mention two of these, because they seem have obvious affinities to the work of teacher knowledge researchers.

Practice Theory.   Practice theories are one of the most obvious places to look for frameworks suitable to teacher knowledge research. These theories acknowledge that people's lives are shaped by macro-social dynamics—both symbolic and material—of which they have little awareness and over which they have even less control. Practice theorists point out, however, that these cultural and material structures do not completely determine human activity. Pierre Bourdieu (1992, 1998) has forwarded the concept of "habitus" to describe the local adjustments, innovations, and accommodations worked out by local communities within larger cultural structures. This parallels much of the writing that calls for research on teachers' practical knowledge, insights that enable teachers to extend and modify general knowledge about teaching to fit their local circumstances. Also working in this tradition, Anthony Giddens (1986) has offered what he calls *structuration theory*, which highlights micro-social processes by which larger macro-social structures are reproduced and maintained. Giddens is concerned to identify the location and limits of human agency within large cultural and social systems. And he finds that agency in the reflective capacities of individuals and local communities, when they are able to question the naturalness of the institutional arrangements in which they find themselves. This parallels much of the writing about teachers' taking an inquiry-as-stance or action research approach to their work. What Bourdieu's and Gidden's theories can add to contemporary teacher knowledge research is a greater contextualization of that local practical, knowledge in larger cultural dynamics.

Semiotics.   Practice theories provide a framework for thinking about the relation between local epistemic practice and larger cultural discourses. However, they do not focus extensively on the cultural contingency of the researcher's own view of the teaching scene. The most obvious place to look for theories about this kind of researcher reflexivity is post-structuralist semiotics, which has been used in sociology and anthropology to carry out the most extensive interrogations of the cultural positionality of the social science researcher (Clifford & Marcus, 1986; Foucault, 1980; Lather, 1997; Marcus, 1998). These theories highlight how all social science representations are composed of conventional cultural signs assembled within discourses defined by certain norms of expression. The content of these representations, therefore, are always determined within the bounds of the taken-granted-meanings encoded in cultural discourses. Post-structuralist literary criticism has provided very effective analytical tools for exposing and critiquing these encoded meanings.

Post-structuralism, however, has features that will limit its utility for teacher knowledge researchers. Its emphasis on the arbitrary nature of the relationship between signs and their referents, and by extension between disciplinary discourses and their objects of inquiry, leads to a nominalism that reduces individual experience to only what macro-social discourses make of it. Although many aspects of teaching experience may, in fact, be conditioned by professional and cultural discourses, the stronger claim that this accounts for *all* that is significant in teacher experience makes post-structuralist theory ill-suited for teacher knowledge research. Although less developed by contemporary social scientists, pragmatism may provide a semiotic theory better suited to the projects of teacher knowledge researchers (Rosiek & Atkinson, forthcoming). Pragmatic semiotics has been employed by social scientists looking for ways to investigate the intersection of individual experience with broad cultural dynamics (Haraway, 1991; Joas, 1997; Morales, 1995; Mutaawe, 1998; Pihlstrom, 1998; Shank, 1995; Stringer, 1997) In any case, a semiotics of teacher knowledge is needed, if any detailed reflexive analysis of the discourses that frame teacher knowledge research is to be undertaken.

Conclusion: Teacher Education in Which the Study of Cultural Is Foundational

In the preceding section, I described at length the conceptual and methodological tools that teacher knowledge researchers might appropriate from educational ethnography, as a way of enabling a greater articulation between these two fields. I have done so as part of an effort to make the case that teacher knowledge researchers both can, and should, make the examination of cultural influences on teaching central to their work. I have further argued that this requires teacher knowledge researchers to reflexively examine the cultural influences on their own research practices. I have pointed to the resources in educational ethnography, and cultural anthropology more generally, that could be of use to teacher education scholars in this regard.

I want to be clear, however, that I do not see this articulation between teacher knowledge research and educational ethnography happening in one direction. I believe educational ethnography needs teacher knowledge research as much as teacher knowledge research needs educational ethnography. Policy makers are simply not listening to educational researchers these days, let alone to educational ethnographers with strong social justice oriented views and lacking quantifiable research conclusions. Although educational scholars of all stripes need to continue to "speak the truth to power," and bear witness to the policy travesties being carried out at state and federal levels, to limit our sphere of action to decision-makers at these levels is, I offer, to cede the struggle for educational improvement to reactionary forces. Educational ethnographers need to take their message to the practitioners of the teaching craft. Delivering this message will require dialogue, a willingness on the part of educational anthropologists to listen and have their practice transformed by teachers' experience at least as much as teachers will be transformed by a serious engagement with educational ethnography.

If disciplinary divides, and the over-simplified accusations of impracticality and false consciousness that come with them, can be set aside in favor of a detailed examination of the possibilities and limitations for cultural analysis conducted from within teaching practice, I believe we can create a new kind of teacher education practice. This will mean doing the hard work necessary to build bridges between educational ethnographic theory and the practical experiences of teaching. The eventual pay-off could be the creation of teacher education curriculum that treats learning as a cultural practice, as opposed to an exclusively or even primarily psychological one. We could see teacher education programs that are built around teachers having immersion experiences in the communities in which they teach; that takes as a central goal preparing teachers to critically interrogate their own taken-for-granted cultural assumptions about schooling and learning; that provides teachers with the information and understanding they need to make connections with the various communities from which their students come. And we could educate of teacher researchers to produce a local literature on the cultural habitus of schooling in their communities that extends, complements, and critiques the more macro-social analyses produced by university based educational ethnographers. This literature could, in turn, be used in local teacher education curriculum, and as a source of data for university based researchers.

This possibility of a teacher education in which the study of culture is genuinely foundational seems worth the effort to me.

REFERENCES

Angrossino, M. V. (2002). Babaji and me: Reflections on a fictional ethnography. In A. P. Bochner & C. Ellis (Eds.), *Ethnographically speaking: Autoethnography, literature and aesthetics* (pp. 327–335). Walnut Creek, CA: Altamira Press.

Bagley, C., & Cancienne, M. B. (Eds.). (2002). *Dancing the data*. New York: Peter Lang.

Barone, T. (2000). *Aesthetics, politics, educational inquiries: Essays and examples*. New York: Peter Lang.

Barone, T., & Eisner, E. (1997). Arts-based education research. In R. Jaeger (Ed.), *Complementary methods for research in education*. Washington, DC: American Educational Research Association.

Behar, R. (1997). *The vulnerable observer: Anthropology that breaks your heart*. Boston: Beacon Press.

Bourdieu, P. (1992). *The logic of practice*. Stanford, CA: Stanford University Press.

Bourdieu, P. (1998). *Practical reason: On the theory of action*. Stanford, CA: Stanford University Press.

Butler, J. (1990). Performative act and gender constitution. In S. E. Case (Ed.), *Performing feminisms, feminist critical theory and theatre* (pp. 270–283). Baltimore, MD: Johns Hopkins University Press.

Chang, P. J., & Rosiek, J. (2003). Anti-colonialist antinomies in a biology lesson: A case study of cultural conflict in a science classroom. *Curriculum Inquiry*.

Clandinin, D. J., & Connelly, M. F. (1996). Teachers' professional knowledge landscapes: Teacher stories. *Educational Researcher, 25*(3), 24–31.

Clandinin, D. J., & Connelly, M. F. (2000). *Narrative inquiry*. San Francisco, CA: Jossey-Bass.

Clifford, J., & Marcus, G. (Eds.). (1986). *Writing culture. The poetics and politics of ethnography*. Berkeley: University of California Press.

Cochran-Smith, M. (1991). Learning to teach against the grain. *Harvard Educational Review, 51*(3), 279–310.

Cochran-Smith, M., & Lytle, S. (1993). *Inside outside: Teacher research and knowledge*. New York: Teachers College Press.

Cochran-Smith, M., & Lytle, S. L. (1999). Relationships of knowledge and practice: Teacher learning in communities. *Review of Research in Education, 24*, 249–305. Washington, DC: American Education Research Association.

Connelly, M. F., & Clandinin, D. J. (1999). *Shaping a professional identity*. New York: Teachers College Press.

Conquergood, D. (1985). Performing as a moral act: Ethical dimensions of the ethnography of performance. *Literature in Performance, 5*, 1–13.

Conquergood, D. (1989, January). Poetics, play, process, and power: The performative turn in anthropology. *Text and Performance Quarterly, 9*, 82–95.

Delpit, L. (1995). *Other people's children*. New York: The New Press.

Delpit, L. (2003). *The skin that we speak: Thoughts on language and culture in the classroom*. New York: W. W. Norton.

Denzin, N. K. (2003). *Performance ethnography critical pedagogy and the politics of culture*. Thousand Oaks: Sage.

Dimitriadis, G. (2001). *Performing identity/performing culture: Hip hop as text, pedagogy, and lived practice*. New York: Peter Lang.

Ellis, C., & Bochner, A. (2000). Autoethnography, personal narrative, reflexivity: Researcher as subject. In N. K. Denzin & Y. S. Lincoln (Eds.), *Handbook of qualitative research* (2nd ed., pp. 733–768). Thousand Oaks, CA: Sage.

Fadiman, A. (1997). *The spirit catches you and you fall down*. New York: Farrar, Straus & Giroux.

Fenstermacher, G. (1994). The knower and the known. In L. Darling-Hammond (Ed.), *Review of research in education* (pp. 3–56). Washington, DC: American Education Research Association.

Foucault, M. (1965). *Madness and civilization*. New York: Vintage Books.

Foucault, M. (1980). *Power/knowledge: Selected interviews and other writings 1972–1977.* Colin Gordon (Ed.). New York: Pantheon Books.

Giddens, A. (1986). *The constitution of society: Outline of the theory of structuration.* Berkeley: University of California Press.

Grossman, P. (1990). *The making of a teacher: Teacher knowledge and teacher education.* New York: Teachers College Press.

Haraway, D. (1991). *Simians, cyborgs, and women: the reinvention of nature.* New York: Routledge.

Holt, N. L. (2003). Representation, legitimation, and autoethnography: An autoethnographic writing story. *International Journal of Qualitative Methods, 2*(1).

Joas, H. (1997). *The creativity of action.* Chicago: University of Chicago Press.

Ladson-Billings, G. (1995). Toward a theory of culturally relevant pedagogy. *American Educational Research Journal, 32*(3), 465–493.

Lather, P. A. (1997). *Troubling the angels: Women living with HIV/AIDS.* Boulder, CO: Westview Press.

Liston, D., & Zeichner, K. (1996). *Culture and teaching.* Mahwah, NJ: Lawrence Erlbaum Associates.

Marcus, G. E. (1998). *Ethnography through thick and thin.* Princeton, NJ: Princeton University Press.

Marcus, G. E. (1999). *Critical anthropology now: Unexpected contexts, shifting constituencies, changing agendas.* Santa Fe, NM: School of American Research Press.

Morales, A. (1995). *Renascent pragmatism: studies in law and social science.* Burlington, VT: Ashgate Publishing.

Mutaawe, K. F. (1998). *Self and social reality in a philosophical anthropology: Inquiring into George Herbert Mead's socio-philosophical anthropology.* New York: Peter Lang.

Mykhalovskiy, E. (1996). Reconsidering table talk: Critical thoughts on the relationship between sociology, autobiography, and self-indulgence. *Qualitative Sociology, 19,* 131–151.

Noffke, S. (1992). The work and workplace of teachers in action research. *Teaching and Teacher Education, 8*(1), 15–29.

Noffke, S. (1997). Professional, personal, and political dimensions of action research. *Review of Research and Education,* 305–343.

Pihlstrom, S. (1998). *Pragmatism and philosophical anthropology: Understanding our human life in a human world.* New York: Peter Lang.

Reed-Danahay, D. E. (Ed.). (1997). *Auto/Ethnography: Rewriting the self and the social.* Gordonsville: Berg Publishing.

Richardson, V. (1994). Conducting research on practice. *Educational Researcher, 23*(5), 5–11.

Rosiek, J. (2002). Pragmatism's unfinished project: What William James has to offer teacher knowledge researchers. In J. Garrison (Ed.), *William James and education.* New York: Teachers College Press.

Rosiek, J. (2003). Emotional scaffolding: An exploration of teacher knowledge at the intersection of student emotion and subject matter content. *The Journal of Teacher Education, 54*(5), 399–412.

Rosiek, J., & Atkinson, B. (in press). The need for a semiotics of teacher knowledge research: What Charles Sanders Peirce has to say to teacher education scholars. *Educational Theory.*

Sconiers, Z., & Rosiek, J. (2000). Historical perspective as an important element of teacher knowledge: A sonata-form case study of equity issues in a chemistry classroom. *Harvard Educational Review, 70*(3), 370–404.

Shank, G. (1995). Semiotics and qualitative research in education: The third crossroad. *The Qualitative Report, 2,* 3, http://www.nova.edu/ssss/QR/QR2-3/shank.html

Shulman, L. (1987). Knowledge and teaching: Foundations of the new reform. *Harvard Education Review, 57,* 1–22.

Shulman, L. (2000). From Minsk to Pinsk: Why a scholarship of teaching and learning? *The Journal of Scholarship of Teaching and Learning, 1*(1), 48–52.

Spindler, G. D., & Spindler, L. S. (Eds.). (2000). *Pathways to cultural awareness: Cultural therapy with teachers and students.* New York: Corwin Press.

Spivak, G. C. (1988). Can the subaltern speak. In C. Nelson, & L. Grossberg (Eds.), *Marxism and the interpretation of culture* (pp. 271–313). Urbana, IL: University of Illinois Press.

Spry, T. (2001). Performing autoethnography: An embodied methodological praxis. *Qualitative Inquiry, 7*(6), 706–732.

Sullivan, S. (2001). *Living across and through skins: Transactional bodies, pragmatism, and feminism.* Bloomington: Indiana University Press.

Stringer, E. (1997). *Community-based ethnography.* Mahwah, NJ: Lawrence Erlbaum Associates.

Thao, P. (1999). *Mong education at the crossroads.* Lanham, MD: University Press of America.

Tobin, J., & Davidson, D. (1990). Ethics of polyvocal ethnography. *International Journal of Qualitative Studies in Education, 3*(3), 271–283.

Valencia, R. (1997). *The evolution of deficit thinking.* Washington, DC: Falmer Press.

Varenne, H., & McDermott, R. (1998). *Successful failure.* Oxford: Westview.

Walker-Moffat, W. (1995). *The other side of the Asian American success story.* San Francisco, CA: Jossey-Bass.

Wilson, S., Shulman, L., & Richert, A. (1987). "150 different ways" of knowing: Representations of knowledge in teaching. In J. Calderhead (Ed.), *Exploring teachers' thinking* (pp. 104–124). London: Cassell.

9

Digging Deeper: Using Reflective Dialogue to Illuminate the Cultural Processes Inherent in Science Education

Lorie Hammond
California State University at Sacramento

Lorie Hammond is a teacher educator at California State University at Sacramento, who works with pre-service teachers and teacher colleagues in Professional Development Schools which serve immigrant and low income students from Mexico, Southeast Asia and a variety of American roots. Her research interest is in creating community based science settings, such as school community gardens and family science nights, where immigrant parents, teachers, pre-service teachers, children, and researchers can operate as communities of learners, teaching and learning together and sharing their rich "funds of knowledge." "Digging deeper" evolved from this setting, as an attempt to use narrative and ethnographic techniques to capture the dialogues which evolved between diverse pre-service teachers as they struggle to develop identities as teachers of children who, like themselves, are caught in profound cultural transitions.

"Multicultural" education reforms, in science education and other topics, often provide pre-service teachers with alternative theories, pedagogies, and curricula for working with diverse populations, but rarely explore the ways in which the pre-service teachers' own cultural heritage and position affect their teaching. This omission is particularly important when pre-service teachers come from a variety of minority and majority backgrounds themselves, and experience dynamic relationships to these backgrounds. In this chapter, we attempt to "dig deeper" into the way diverse pre-service teachers understand and teach about the natural world, through co-creating reflective cultural dialogues. These dialogues address ways in which pre-service teachers experienced schooling themselves, as well as how they perceive "standard" curricula as

adults who identity with two or more cultural traditions. The cultural dialogues presented are used as examples of how "cultural therapy" can be incorporated into teacher education.

A SNAPSHOT OF FAMILY SCIENCE NIGHT

The school cafeteria is brightly lit and crowded on this family science night. The theme of the evening is plants. Each table is manned by two pre-service teachers who have prepared a hands-on experience for kids and parents to do together. One table is spread with butcher paper, and covered with aromatic herbs, filling the room with scents of peppermint and hierba buena, rosemary, lavender, green and purple basil, ruda, cilantro, and more. Each family writes, in their language, the name of the herb and how they use it. Children help to translate their parents' words into English. A Hmong and a Spanish speaking pre-service teacher help two mothers to communicate about their herbs. The parents are surprised that although their countries of origin were across the world from each other, they both use cilantro and mint. For the Mexican parent, mint (hierba buena) is used as a tea to help the stomach. For the Hmong mother, it is used with meat. An Afghani parent joins in, speaking of mixing mint with black tea. Soon the butcher paper is filled with labels for herbs in Spanish, Hmong, Arabic, Urdu, and Hindi, along with English translations and descriptions of how they are used. Later, in the classroom, pre-service teachers will work with children to create a simple book which shares this information with their peers. Two teachers from the school join the conversation, and tell parents that they are considering creating an international herb garden in the school-community garden. The parents agree to bring cuttings of their own herbs to contribute.

At another table, pre-service teachers are helping children to plant seeds, which have been shared by the parents. One Iu Mienh grandmother who has donated mustard green seeds which she has collected, tells the story of how mustard greens saved the lives of Mienh people, since they grow naturally and can be eaten when other crops fail. She says that she feels obligated to propagate mustard in appreciation. Others begin to talk about how mustard seeds appear in the Bible, and how universal this plant is. Families who generally do not communicate across cultural and linguistic barriers share stories at this event, assisted by pre-service teachers, themselves immigrants, who help to translate.

At a third table, pre-service teachers demonstrate on graph paper how to plan a garden as a way to teach fractions, a skill which many students struggle with in school. To our surprise, we learn that Hmong people do not have fractions in their number system. How, then, we ask, do they measure? Parents describe various measurement strategies, such as using string. As an instructor of science and math methods, I note that this will be a good springboard for a discussion of ethno-mathematics. Pre-service teachers might survey immigrant children and parents about different techniques for measuring, thus demonstrating how to build community "funds of knowledge" (Moll et al., 1992) into the standard school curriculum on fractions.

INTRODUCTION

Family science nights like the one described here are part of the science methods class in a bilingual, multicultural elementary teacher education program focused on enabling pre-service teachers to teach effectively in low income, diverse communities. This article describes one aspect of this program, in which ethnographic techniques are applied to a science methods course. Although the specific context is science education, we believe that the approach described in this article could apply to any subject area, as an "anthropological approach" to teacher education in and for diverse communities. Furthermore, it is our purpose to illustrate that while anthropological perspectives on teaching and learning are often relegated to social foundations and multicultural education courses, contextualized teacher education courses such as science methods provide rich and often overlooked contexts in which applications of sociocultural theory to practice can be enacted and critically examined.

The authors of this chapter are educators, and include the teacher educator/researcher and the pre-service teachers enrolled in a multicultural elementary science methods class. The participants are themselves diverse, five of the eight being immigrants from either third world Southeast Asian countries or hill tribe (fourth world) minorities within these countries. The course centered around several experiences: an ethnographic study of the natural and social "funds of knowledge" (Moll et al., 1992) in one urban, diverse community; community service learning experiences, such as family science nights, which incorporated these "funds of knowledge" in science lessons; and reflective dialogues about these experiences.

In this course, family science, garden, and cooking events, which incorporated community strengths, needs and interests, become vehicles for bridging the gap between immigrant families and their schools. A major pedagogical challenge faced by pre-service teachers was how to link the experiences which community families share to state standards in science. The author has written about this challenge in other publications, which focus on pedagogical reform of science for immigrant, urban students (Hammond, 2001) and on Community Service Learning (Hammond & Heredia, 2002). However, the purpose of this chapter is to "dig deeper" into the identity issues that diverse teachers face in learning to teach in public schools guided by "standard," mainstream content and pedagogy, yet situated in non-mainstream communities. The focus of this chapter is on narrative analysis of a series of reflective dialogues among pre-service teachers. These dialogues emerged in response to both readings and shared teaching experiences with K–6 urban students. Their purpose is to illustrate, by example, how an "anthropological" perspective might transform the process of learning to teach.

WHAT IS AN "ANTHROPOLOGICAL" APPROACH TO SCIENCE EDUCATION?

The increased diversity in the United States and other first world countries, coupled with the globalization which connects all peoples and schooling endeavors, have transformed most educational situations into intercultural spaces. This has led many science educators, as well as educators in other subjects, to rethink their work, including their concept of science, their pedagogy, and their research approaches. Many science educators have looked to anthropology, the discipline expert at cultural and cross-cultural matters, for direction in reframing their work. Although anthropologists may not recognize all of the research which deals with sociocultural issues in education to be "anthropological," the influence which anthropological thinking, especially from the field of Anthropology of Education, is having on education in science and other fields is enormous. One might assume that this work represents one of the new directions in anthropology and ethnography, although much of the work is not being done by anthropologists, but rather by educational researchers, teacher researchers, and learning communities of various sorts.

In the science methods course, two key criteria define our approach as "anthropological." The first is an awareness of both science and education as cultural processes. The second is the use of ethnographic techniques as a tool for understanding communities in which we work and in analyzing and reflecting on our work in these communities. These two criteria guide the work in this article, which is one of many examples of ethnographic work now occurring in the context of science education reform.

EPISTEMOLOGY AND SCIENCE EDUCATION

How do anthropological concepts, such as the understanding that cultures hold differing world views, influence science education? If science is viewed as a cultural activity, which, like any other human endeavor, is situated in a socio-historic context, then traditional assumptions about science as an "objective" process separated from culture must be re-evaluated. The struggle to position Western science culturally while acknowledging the importance of its quest for objectivity and rigor has become the subject of much equity oriented work in science education research (Aikenhead, 1996; Barton & Osborne, 2001; Cobern, 1996; Lee & Fradd, 1998; Ogawa, 1995; Rodriguez, 1998; Turnbull, 1997). Some researchers of culture and science are concerned with the collision between multiple world views, derivative from Western science and from other cultural perspectives, which confront many non-Western students (and teachers). In the cases which follow, even third and fourth grade science standards raise issues related to differing world views. How can these views be negotiated? For Ogawa (1995), the key lies in redefining science more broadly as "multiscience," a study of the natural world, in which Western science, traditional science, and personal science perspectives each play a part. For Aikenhead (1996), who works with indigenous people in Canada, it is important that educators understand teaching as a kind of "border crossing" for non-Western students, and reform their pedagogy to make this crossing possible. Turnbull (1997) suggests that science see itself as performative, rather than representational, so that it can be constantly re-negotiated, ideally in "third spaces" in which the contributions of Western science and of other world views can be negotiated and re-formed.

For Barton and Osborne (2001) and Rodriguez (1998), science has traditionally been defined in order to privilege the cultural knowledge of those in power. Science reforms must therefore not only enable minority students to access Western science, but also expand science itself to include minority voices and to address environmental and social justice issues. Moll et al. (1992) suggest that if school curricula integrate community "funds of knowledge," which in the case of science would be Ogawa's traditional knowledge, as well as standardized knowledge, then education becomes more relevant to minority students.

The family science and garden projects on which this chapter is based build on the research previously cited. Pre-service teachers study the physical and cultural resources of the community before designing science curricula, then design lessons around themes, such as nutrition and gardening, which are important to this community. Within the curricula designed, standard Western science content and process is taught, as one of several ways in which the physical world can be approached and understood, and as a set of understandings that educated world citizens must have. However, the conception that science is cultural rather than "neutral" is central to this work, in that pre-service teachers from diverse backgrounds are encouraged to explore their cultural and personal views of how the world works, as well as to learn to teach the "standard" assumptions and processes of Western science. In addition, immigrant parents are encouraged to share their "funds of knowledge" in a manner which privileges this knowledge as valuable and relevant to school science. The assumption is that both Western science and traditional understandings about the world are socio-historical realities, which can be discussed as part of the process of evolving a new, mediated science relevant to diverse communities.

PEDAGOGY AND SCIENCE EDUCATION

Other researchers challenge the **pedagogy** of science as a cultural process which must be re-examined in cross-cultural settings. "Constructivism," a much used term for a pedagogy in which students "construct" their own knowledge through experimentation, is commonly taught to pre-service teachers as an effective, essential aspect of good science education. Several aspects of "constructivism" lend themselves to ethnographic extensions. The first is the initial stage of the lesson, in which students are encouraged to reflect upon their prior knowledge of a subject as a springboard for launching an hypothesis. This stage can be extended into a setting in which various kinds of cultural knowledge can be shared, by students, parents, or community members. For example, when asked what they know about the rainforest, immigrant students from Southeast Asia were encouraged to gather stories from their families about what it is like to live, hunt, and raise crops in a rainforest. In this case, children, pre-service teachers, teachers, and parents worked together to do mini ethnographic studies of their own community. These studies formed the background upon which science lessons are based.

A second aspect of constructivist teaching that can be extended to include ethnographic techniques is the reflective dialogue, which occurs after the lesson. Rodriguez (1998) defines an approach to science reform, Socio-transformative Constructivism (STC), which blends constructivism with a social justice agenda. One aspect of this reform is the use of reflective socio-cultural dialogue among students. Gilbert's work (2002) applies STC, using personal reflective dialogues about health science issues in their own lives to engage diverse middle school students who were not traditionally interested in science. In Brandt's research (2004), an ethno-botany course is reformed through the addition of field experiences in a rural, Native American community and reflective discussion and essays about these experiences. In all of these cases, the researchers' students engage in deep socio-cultural dialogues about issues of culture, equity, and/or environmental justice, in addition to issues of content and pedagogy, as part of their science education. This chapter follows the STC tradition, because the research centers on dialogue with and among pre-service teachers about cultural and political, as well as content and pedagogical issues.

DIALOGUE AS CULTURAL THERAPY

In this chapter, the authors have attempted to "dig deeper" into their own complex identities, as simultaneous members of diverse communities, novice teachers, and evolving individuals. Together, the researcher and the pre-service teachers used reflective dialogue about science as a way to access cultural dilemmas, applying the notion of dialogue as "cultural therapy" (Spindler & Spindler, 1994). In cultural therapy, socio-historical patterns which guide our teaching perspectives are identified, analyzed, and potentially overcome by being redefined as cultural rather than personal dilemmas. Cultural therapy emphasizes how individuals can de-construct the contradictory identities they experience so that they can work toward the creation of more conscious and integrated identities.

This work also draws from practice theory (Eisenhart, 1995, 2000; Levinson, Foley, & Holland, 1996), which merges socio-cultural and individual approaches to human development. Proponents of practice theory argue that while individuals react to both their socio-histories and the constraints of their present environments, they are not completely determined by these constraints. Rather, Eisenhart (1995) argues that the individual, through conscious reflection, can create her own story within societal boundaries.

> (Individuals) are neither simply soaking up, like a fax, what is presented to them, nor are they simply playing whatever tunes come to them for the pure enjoyment of it, like a jazz player. The stories they use are mediational devices that enable certain kinds of newcomer experiences and disable others; they affect how the newcomers are treated by others, and they anticipate the kinds of identities available to them within the organization. (p. 20)

The purpose of this article is to share the stories of a diverse group of pre-service teachers, attempting to reconcile their own cultural values with the pre-scripted identity of becoming a teacher in an urban, public school.

HISTORY OF THIS STUDY

During the past 4 years, I have been teaching science methods courses using Community Service Learning (CSL) at Professional Development School (PDS) sites. This work is done within a Title II supported Equity Network[1] of teacher education programs experimenting with effective ways of preparing teachers for diverse, urban schools. In our PDS science methods course, pre-service teachers work directly with language minority children and families in the context of a school-community garden and family science and literacy nights, while simultaneously studying culturally relevant, critical pedagogies in science.

We believe that this work is transformative, in that it creates a **learning community** of minority and mainstream people, and of children, adults, and pre-service teachers, who participate in science inquiry projects together. Participants exchange knowledge as teachers and learners, using standards as guidelines, rather than transmit a body of pre-planned knowledge in a hierarchical teacher–student relationship. The following five principles guide the design of lessons taught by pre-service teachers:

- Inquiry-based, social constructivist science
- Conscious teaching of academic English through science and incorporation of home languages when possible
- Incorporating local issues into standards-based lessons
- Incorporating minority community funds of knowledge into lessons
- Active learning in cooperative, cross-age groups

After each lesson is taught, both pedagogical and socio-cultural reflective dialogues are held to discuss the success of the lesson and its cultural implications. Transcripts from the socio-cultural dialogues became the data collected for this article.

Pre-service teachers who experience learning communities commonly make statements like the following:

Family science nights give us an experience not only with subject matter, but with the community. They do not translate into my teaching, they have reformed it. I was forced to deal with real-life situations in which my lesson plans were not successful with a group of children, and was faced with the challenge of helping these students to learn. I had to share languages with my peers. In one case, we used both Hmong and Spanish to communicate with the families who came. I do not think that the same kind of confidence can be gained through study in an isolated environment where teachers

[1]The Equity Network is a 5 year, Federal Title II grant supported project, running from 2000–2005. It is coordinated through the College of Education at California State University at Sacramento, and involves six school districts and a community college district, along with CSUS, in creating teacher education for diverse, low income schools.

are learning to teach through a textbook or by watching simulations of situations. (A
Spanish bilingual pre-service teacher)

I have taught science methods to several groups of pre-service teachers each
year. I have elicited pre- and post-reflections on attitudes toward science and
science teaching, as well as ongoing reflections about teaching in a diverse
community context. However, I have had little time to explore the changes
which have occurred in individual pre-service teachers as a result of this class
experience.

The semester of this study, a unique opportunity presented itself: a small
group of pre-service teachers ($n = 7$) in a science methods class enabled me to
do in-depth research on individual reactions to the course. Five of the pre-
service student teachers in this class are from Asian immigrant families (2
Hmong, 2 Filipino, 1 Cambodian). The other two are mainstream Americans, although their childhood experiences with poverty ($n = 1$) and with life
on a small family farm ($n = 1$) provide a socio-historical context which links
their experience to our work in equity and/or science. These two students
have self-selected to join a bilingual/multicultural cohort in which 90% of
their peers are language minority students. This choice suggests a deep commitment to multicultural and equity issues previous to their experience in the
program. It is both an enrichment and a limitation of this study that the participants are unusual among groups of pre-service teachers in their pre-
existing deep commitment to minority populations.

Participating in small group, reflective conversations over a 15-week semester has enabled my students and me to "dig deeper" into the cultural development of science teachers than ever before. These conversations were
made possible by the willingness of the class to co-research their own actions
and reactions, with the intention of contributing to this article as a group.

CHALLENGES INHERENT
IN THE METHODOLOGY

Using dialogue in a classroom setting as a method of ethnographic data collection poses a variety of challenges and questions. The first is that meaningful dialogue can only be built in a context of trust. Pre-service teachers involved in this project shared the following information about the conditions
they felt were necessary for such an honest dialogue.

The Asian pre-service teachers stated that they generally do not volunteer
personal information in classes, even within their "multicultural" teacher ed-

ucation program. This is because they are only comfortable talking to the other Asian students, with whom they share the most common ground. Even discussions with Latino students can be threatening, partially because Latino students constitute a majority in this teacher education program. Although their program is centered on learning to teach in diverse communities, pre-service teachers within it often identify themselves by ethnic group, along similar lines as children in K–12 schools, and are reluctant to share openly in cross-cultural settings.

Asian students also say that they tend to write the answers they believe the professors want, even in classes on multicultural education which are focused on the expression of various points of view. This comment illustrates how difficult it is to create a truly critical, open dialogue. Asian students share that they have been trained by their families to maintain "two worlds," school and home, and to share personal experience only in the latter. This attitude is particularly true for Cambodian and Hmong students, whose parents are refugees from a war in which their group was persecuted. Students from refugee families say that their families direct them not to divulge personal or cultural information outside of their own ethnic community.

It is also important to note that many students have complex identities within their own countries of origin, as well as within the United States. For example, both the Cambodian student, who is Chinese Cambodian, and the Hmong students, who are from Laos, grew up as members of insular minority groups within their home country, before becoming immigrants within the United States. For them, it is a big jump out of their initial culture to join the Pan-Asian culture within the university. This small group of pre-service teachers includes Hmong, Cambodian, Filipino, and other Southeast Asian students who have never before been in intimate contact with members of each other's groups. It is important to note that such complex layers of cultural positioning affect the possibility of gathering honest information from minority students as children or as adults.

BUILDING TRUST

Given these factors, how can trust be built? In this case, because Asian students admit that they are most comfortable talking honestly among themselves, the small class made up of almost all Asian students assisted them in feeling comfortable. The students were also willing to talk with me, and with the two white students in the cohort, because the group is small and because they sense that we are truly interested in what they have to say. In the case of this particular research project, the dual circumstance of 1) working all semester in a small group and 2) working on hands-on, physical projects in the garden, has broken down barriers. It is difficult to create situations in regular university classes in which students can honestly share their personal identity struggles.

The pre-service teachers also explained that many of the experiences that they have with mainstream people outside of school, such as in workplaces (stores, restaurants, offices) where they have been employed while going to school, do not encourage openness. A Persian student reported a pervasive anti-Arab sentiment in a department store where many co-workers take her for Latina and hence express their honest opinions. Similarly, a Cambodian student stated that her co-workers in a store say that they do not like Asian immigrants but that she is "an exception." They describe themselves as "loving her to death" just "like another daughter," but the message she receives is that they will accept her as long as she acts "white." Once again, she has tailored her skill at living in two worlds.

It is also important to remember that most student teachers, in a state university, which serves mostly working class students, do not have the luxury of living in dormitories away from home, with a diversity of people. Their experiences outside of class are almost entirely within their own ethnic communities. Almost all live at home or are married and have families. Most live with three or four generations of family members, in an environment where their original language is still spoken. Even commerce is often experienced within their communities, as in the Pan-Asian commercial district which has developed in our community and is complete with large Asian grocery stores, travel agencies, medical offices, and lawyers. Minority pre-service teachers often mention their conscious commitment to helping students from their own group, yet many have little personal experience with either suburban children or other minorities within their urban community, and are no more prepared to teach "other people's children" than are mainstream pre-service teachers.

Just as any ethnographer must develop trust in a culture of entry, other researchers who would institute dialogic research with their students need to consider the importance and complexity of gaining the kind of trust which leads to honest rather than superficial discussion.

MATCHING THE METHODOLOGY TO THE CULTURE OF THE PARTICIPANTS

Cultural and linguistic factors led us to use dialogue rather than, for example, reflective writings, as a way to gather data about minority pre-service teachers. Asian students, like Latinos, come from relational cultures where the social construction of knowledge is a given. These students, like Southeast Asian parents interviewed in another setting (Hammond, 2001), expressed anxiety when "put on the spot" to answer cultural questions in individual interviews or in writing. They asked if we could share this information in a group setting, where they can reinforce each other. Secondly, although our pre-service teachers have learned proficiency in written English, it is not a comfortable medium for many of them, especially when they want to express personal thoughts. Hmong students, for example, come from an oral, storytelling culture, and are most comfortable expressing themselves orally rather than in writing.

THE ROLE OF THE RESEARCHER

The researcher/professor played several roles that should be clarified. First, she organized the science methods class, punctuated by service learning events that were planned with mentor teachers at professional development schools. Second, she mentored student teachers in planning for these events, observed them teaching, and assessed their performance. Third, she operated as a researcher, observing the learning community and guiding and recording the reflective discussions, which followed each teaching experience. In this action research setting, the researcher was a participant and can make no claims to objectivity. One potential challenge to trust building is the fact that the researcher was also professor, grading students on their performance. Such a role seems to contradict that of collaborator and member of a co-research team. However, this complex role serves a necessary function in that it enables the researcher to make pedagogical reforms in the context of her science methods class, thus providing pre-service teachers with an action-research experience as well as with experiences working in diverse communities. By combining the role of professor, community organizer, and action researcher, the researcher was able to expose her students to similar roles which they might play as teachers, instructing, advocating for, and organizing the communities in which they find themselves, and hopefully researching the effectiveness of their own experiments.

In addition, it should be noted that the role of professor as judge was diffused to some degree by the purpose of the course, which focused on learning together how to teach a diverse community rather than on individual achievement by pre-service teachers. Most projects were group efforts, with the one exception of reflective writings, which were not graded. The purpose of a cohorted teacher education program is to help everyone achieve competence, rather than to grade students competitively. In this setting, everyone can succeed, and the individual skills—cultural, social, and academic—which students bring to the table can be celebrated. Unfortunately, the K–12 schools in which we worked do not operate under the same assumptions.

While the researcher initially wanted to create a full blown research collaboration (such as that described by Erickson, chapter 7, this volume), in which the pre-service teachers participated in creating research questions and participated through the writing stage of the project, this was not feasible for both conceptual and practical reasons. Conceptually, the action research was spearheaded by the professor as a way to create science methods class which would better enable pre-service teachers to work in diverse communities. The course was not conceived by the pre-service teachers, who participated in this course as one of many pre-teaching experiences. For practical reasons, the pre-service teachers did not therefore participate in writing this research, since the course had ended when this writing occurred. Although the researcher is an advocate of co-research, and has participated in co-teacher-research projects, it also seems important to state that not all players operate in settings with the same roles and motivations. The researcher has an ongoing interest in the intersection of science and culture in the context of teacher education. The pre-service teachers are novices who must learn many aspects of teaching, including how to teach science, while simultaneously grappling with their own identity struggles as diverse new teachers. Our hope was that the dialogic approach taken in this methods class helped us all to understand how science, culture, and the roles we play intersect in complex ways as teachers, both in the classroom and at the university. The third case study below discusses what we learned. It is also our hope that reflective dialogue could become a part of our permanent tool kit in dealing with the cultural issues faced within classrooms and at the university, as a way of acknowledging that everything we are teaching and learning is part of a cultural process with deep identity implications for all involved.

DATA COLLECTED

The following paragraphs give short portraits of the pre-service teachers involved in the project. All names are changed, by request of the co-authors.

Bobby is a Filipino male whose parents have become middle class and educated. He is a highly creative pre-service teacher who likes to write stories and poetry. He uses stories as a way into science, and tends to universalize from his experience.

Stories develop who we are. If you have a story of ancestors in a rice field with bare feet, these stories will develop the character of the children that follow. For many Americans, these stories are several generations back. For us, they are our parents' and grandparents' stories. It's the story that makes the people.

Jenny is a Chinese Cambodian female who is a realist. In response to Bobby's comments, she said,

But we are also made by our experience. For example, I am changing as my experience changes. When I came to the USA, I had nothing, so I was not picky about clothes or food. Now I am picky, because I can afford to be.

Jenny's family were refugees from the devastating war in Cambodia in the 1970s. They are protective of their family and identity, and encourage Jenny, who lives at home, not to rely on friends outside the family, but to stay within it. They also encourage her not to share with outsiders, but to be successful and maintain two identities. Jenny feels like she lives in two worlds. With Americans she calls herself "Chinese" and "Cambodian," within her group, she is "Jen" and "Khmer."

Cherrylyn is a quiet Filipino female who considers her major values to be family, celebration, and education. She considers herself to be a cultural hybrid between Eastern (Asian) and Western (Catholic, Spanish) traditions.

Cho is a Hmong male in his mid-twenties, who has four children, having married in high school in accordance with traditional expectations. He identifies deeply with Hmong culture, and is eager to talk about cultural matters. I have observed Cho in both math and science methods classes, creating innovative solutions to problems which combine his background knowledge (e.g., applying Hmong paper folding to geometry) and an understanding of Western concepts. Cho makes the following comments about science:

Many of the things I learned in science in school are really new, which makes these concepts very hard for the immigrant student. But some things, like the garden, are so obvious to me that I would not even have taught them in school. Hmong don't look at the process of the garden, or question it, it is just there, and everyone understands it. All kids grow up knowing things about the natural world without studying them. I would not have thought of teaching these things in school. When I came to this program, I had a view of school from Asia. Just reading and writing, and that's all. No science, social studies. It was a privilege to go to school at all, but we learned everything else outside. But here I have noticed that kids don't even know that the apple has seeds, and why. Maybe it's because their parents peel it, and take out the seeds, so they don't even know what an apple is. Now I know that I should teach these things, and my background will help me because I know them.

Lu is a young Hmong woman with a baby at home. She is eager to have a profession, having started the credential program this year 3 weeks after her baby was born. She and her husband live with his mother, who cares for the baby. Lu described school as "where she always wanted to go, to get away from home, and be with her friends." She has ambivalence toward her Hmong culture, and some of its traditions. Lu, like Cho, is surprised at all the things that are taught to young children in school here.

We didn't have science in school, or especially not art! No one would teach you motor skills, like how to cut with scissors. Either you figured things out or you dropped out. There, kids want to go to school. Here they are forced to. If you showed an Asian parent two classrooms, one with learning in groups, the other with the teacher in the front, they would choose the one with the teacher in front every time. We have really had to rethink the role of the teacher (in this program). For example, it would never have occurred to us to have the kids learn from each other. The teacher would be the only one who knows something. (Jenny added here that her father, who was a teacher in Cambodia, did not want her to be a teacher in the USA for quite a while because he feels that teachers are not respected here.) Now I share a lot of the things I am learning with my father. Things like young children need to move around, and talk, if they are to learn. He is very interested. It is changing him too.

Anita is a young American woman who grew up on a small family farm. Everyone in the family helped grow crops and sell them at the farmers' market. They also led school tours of their farm. Anita has brought in boxes of science resources that her family developed for these tours, and is very interested in teaching kids principles of horticulture.

Working with farmers, whom I view as "real" people, and managing farmers' markets, I think science teaching should first come from real life examples before going to texts.

Haley is a young American woman who had a mixed childhood, partly with a mother who, although educated, became poor due to mental illness, and partly with a father who is a college professor and researcher. She experienced a lot of instability, and sometimes poverty, moving from place to place, and is highly articulate, questioning, and politically conscious.

I'm very sensitive to kids who come from poverty. I am aware that kids don't have control over where they live or how much money they have. So I would teach with an

*understanding that every child is different and brings different ideas and perspectives
into the class.*

Three Dialogues: Several types of experiences can become the springboard
for reflective cultural dialogues. In this paper, case studies of three dialogues
are presented. The first emerged from an evocative reading.

DIALOGUE #1: CHICKEN AND RICE:
FOOD AND CULTURE

The following excerpt is from a dialogue which occurred after student teachers read a case study, "How do we grow rice?" (Hammond & Charmbury,
2002). The article was written about our community, and describes how a
teacher wrote culturally appropriate lessons for Southeast Asian children
which focused on growing rice as a link to family heritage knowledge.

> **Cho:**   *The rice article was interesting because I remember learning about the
> food pyramid at school. I learned about food groups we didn't eat at
> home. I felt we ate the wrong foods. It made me feel that my food at
> home was bad. I wondered if we couldn't afford the right foods, or if
> my family was too stupid to eat them.*

> **Bobby:**   *I never realized how American my packed meals at school were. I had
> a sandwich and fruit. The other Asian kids had chicken and rice. My
> older brother was spoiled and got what he wanted. I wonder what role
> he played in getting us American food for our lunches. He got us cere-
> als—high sugar ones—because he asked for them.*

> **Anita:**   *I'm happy to see school lunches involved with the agricultural commu-
> nity. Some are buying fresh, organic foods.*

> **Lu:**   *When I was in first grade, my friend and I did not want to stand in line
> and have a free hot lunch at school. We wanted to bring a cold lunch
> and just sit down. So we arranged to bring our own lunch. But it was
> embarrassing to bring rice and chicken. My friend brought just a big
> bag of KIX—it was the only American thing she could find, and she
> didn't want to be embarrassed. It was an awful lunch, so after that we
> went back to a hot lunch.*

Many important topics emerge from this short dialogue. Both Cho and Lu
were prompted to remember their own feelings at school as minority children.
Cho's comment, that he felt his family was either "too stupid" or "too poor" to

eat the foods prescribed on the food pyramid taught at school, expresses one of many instances in which he straddled contradictory values from school and home. The food pyramid is a standard artifact taught in science classes, where a large triangle is divided into sections according to what kinds of food should be served many times a day (breads and cereals are at the base), several times a day (meat, dairy, eggs, fruits and vegetables), and infrequently (fats and sugars). This lesson would almost certainly appear value neutral to the teacher presenting it, yet was internalized by a minority child, Cho, as a judgment on his (different) home experience. It is interesting that Cho mentioned the food pyramid, because this particular lesson is an explicitly culturally rather than "scientifically" derived artifact, which represents an exemplary American diet and is often reproduced for free by commercial food producers, such as the American Dairy Association, to educate children about their need for milk. "Ethnic" alternatives to this pyramid, which might feature beans and tortillas or fish, vegetables, and rice, are currently endorsed by multicultural educators. My point is not to espouse one "politically correct" food pyramid over another, but to point out how many cultural assumptions are embedded in a seemingly simple science lesson, designed for third graders.

Both Bobby and Lu allude to how embarrassing it was to bring an "Asian" lunch to school when they were children. Bobby realizes through this conversation that a demanding older brother served as a cultural broker, enabling him to bring the acceptable "American" sandwich and fruit to school for lunch. Lu was not so lucky. Her attempt to bring her own lunch, but avoid an Asian lunch, resulted in such an abysmal meal, consisting only of dry cereal, that she and her friend were forced to return to the "free lunch line" in the cafeteria.

Anita brings her organic farm experience to the discussion, applauding more healthful trends in school lunches, and raises an important nutritional question. If "sugar cereals" (Bobby) and other packaged foods are socially superior to chicken and rice at American schools, what responsibility do these schools actually have to nutrition education? Often immigrant populations change from good traditional diet to "junk food" diets when coming to the United States, with disastrous results in youth obesity and diabetes. Many schools contribute to this trend by selling baked goods, chips, sodas, and other "treats" in snack bars and fundraisers, and by giving unhealthful food prizes for good behavior or academic work.

In this short discussion, the positioning of each of the four speakers reflects their backgrounds, backgrounds which in turn will affect the perspectives which these new teachers bring to their teaching. It is clear that no simple stereotypes, based on ethnic groups, can be used to predict each student's perspective. Bobby is Asian, but was well assimilated to school food, and perhaps to school in general, because he followed an aggressive older brother who brokered his entry into American culture. For Lu and Cho, school was an environment where being Asian was embarrassing or where family habits felt judged as stupid or wrong.

The rest of the same day's discussion soon went beyond food into a consideration of whether the alienation between home and school, which many children experience can lead to school failure. Cho responded as follows:

> **Cho:** *Yes, gangs come in . . . when culture falls apart. I just saw a video on a Hmong rapper. He talks about feeling caught between cultures. He talks about feeling alienated in school, looking for others to relate to, hanging out with others like himself and then being called a gang. When you are alone, and can't speak the language, you want to attach to your group. Sometimes you join a gang to do so.*

When minority students experience a curriculum which contradicts the messages they get at home, they are put in an alienated position which can lead them into resistant behaviors. The example of the food pyramid is a small one, insignificant in itself. However, it demonstrates how teachers inadvertently deliver messages that belittle home values. This occurs because "standardized" curricula are assumed to be value neutral rather than to represent majority perspectives which need to be critically examined in a diverse society. An easy solution to the food pyramid problem would be simply to ask children what foods they eat, and enable them to build their own pyramids, based on nutritional principles. However, for such a lesson adaptation to occur, teachers need to be aware that subjects like science are cultural and require "border crossing" (Aikenhead, 1996) on the part of their students. Jenny's comments during this dialogue illustrate the importance of curricula which take students' cultural worlds into account.

> **Jenny:** *It is important to connect the curriculum to home. When I was growing up, there was home and school. I was one way at home and one way at school. My clothes didn't feel right. I got donations from the church, and I was embarrassed by them. I soon learned that there were two worlds. If the teacher brought my stuff into the classroom, it would have let me be one person.*

In addition to illuminating pedagogy changes that might occur if schools were aware of the cultural nature of their curricula, this dialogue sheds light on the "hidden agendas," which are transmitted during the non-educational parts of the school day and may be as important as those in the classroom. Informal activities, such as lunch, may place minority students in the position of "fitting in" by eating American foods or feeling alienated and embarrassed by eating their family's (often more healthful) foods. In addition to the social pressures created by these situations, ignoring the educational impact of "non-teaching" moments makes us lose opportunities for knowledge exchange. The nutritional impact of assimilation from an Asian diet, rich in vegetables and low in fat, to an American diet is not always positive. Cafeterias and schools in general often model poor nutritional habits while teaching nutrition in the science classroom. One function of reflective dialogues is to unearth the ways in which overt and hidden agendas contradict each other. In Project FIELD,[2] the cafeteria became an educational site through "ethnic food days" in which parents cooked foods from the garden in traditional ways and served them on special days. In addition to providing improved nutrition, these events empowered minority communities by 1) displaying community foods as exemplary, 2) allowing minority parents to demonstrate their expertise as gardeners and cooks, and hopefully 3) enabling minority students to feel like "one person" who can sometimes experience the culture of home at school.

DIALOGUE #2: A DIALOGUE ABOUT LIFE AND DEATH WHICH EVOLVED FROM A LESSON ON LIFE CYCLES

As an introduction to a lesson on the life cycle of the strawberry, Bobby attempted to make a plant life cycle comprehensible to fourth graders by comparing it to a human life cycle.[3] His version of the human life cycle was illustrated by a posterboard with a picture of a baby, then a child, then an adult, and finally an aging Buddha. After displaying each picture, Bobby commented that like the strawberry, humans go through this cycle and are then reincarnated. This introduction took Bobby's audience by surprise, in a school made up predominantly of Mexican Catholic students and teachers. Most interesting to the class was the fact that he had no idea it would be an

---

[2]FIELD, Food Security through Economic Literacy Development, was a USDA funded Food Security Grant that supported the school-community garden projects in our community from 2000–2003 as sites of economic and educational development.

[3]From a science perspective, this is a misleading comparison, but that is not the subject of this chapter.

unusual presentation. This lesson led to a discussion of how the pre-service teachers view the human life cycle, a concept which is in the fourth grade science standards.

Lu: *My aunt is dying of cancer. I said that the disease is killing her, so the shaman can't help. We don't need to waste money on the shaman. She's been dying for 2 years. You can see all her ribs. The shaman can't help.*

Anita: *But there is a link between spirituality and health. Is there a point when the shaman realizes that it is beyond his help, and starts preparing her for death?*

Cho: *No. Shamans believe that each person has a piece of paper from heaven that says how long he will live. The shaman wants to negotiate, to extend the person's fate.*

Anita: *Priests prepare people for the other world. Doesn't the shaman do that?*

Cho: *There is no preparing for death. Only trying to extend life. You prepare for death after the life is over.*

Lu: *Yes, the shaman wants to argue that the person's contract is not over.*

Bobby: *I don't know if the shaman is right or not, but I don't deny it. I think of religion as like language transfers—like people mean the same things in different religions, but they use different words.*

When this discussion began, we all realized that the topic of life cycles was rich in cultural material. Lu is clearly concerned about her dying aunt and about her own position between Hmong and American culture. Anita joins the conversation, attempting to make sense of the Hmong perspective in terms of her own experience with the Catholic religion. Both Cho and Lu then take the role of defining Hmong traditions in relation to life and death, although Lu is ambivalent about these traditions. Anita's attempts to draw a parallel with her own experience fail. This leads Bobby, often the mediator, to assert that in different religions, people really are using different words to talk about the same thing. However, both Cho and Lu's words assert that they are not talking about the same thing: that the Catholic priest embraces death as redemption, and prepares people for it, whereas the Hmong shaman sees life and death as part of a contractual arrangement in which his job is to negotiate for a longer life for his client, rather than to help her accept or embrace her death.

Lu continues the conversation, obviously interested in sharing her culture and her own dilemmas with it.

Lu: *In our culture (Hmong), we prepare for life after death after people die. A person comes to the house to say poems and take the person who died back to where he originated. We put on shoes so he can walk a long way through the forest. My dad was born in Laos, so he had to be taken all the way back, as he had come, through Merced, then Utah, then Thailand, in the camps, then Laos. If this doesn't happen, his spirit won't find its way home. Sometimes the spirit doesn't make it all the way back. Then he will stay around, and appear in our dreams and beg for money. This happened with my dad. Then my mom had to take food to his grave, to make him happy. My mom is half and half. We were converted to be Mormons, but we do the Shaman part too.*

Everyone was fascinated by Lu's description of Hmong death rituals, especially in the case of immigrants, who must retrace their international journey before finding peace. Then Jenny joined in, with a parallel story from Cambodian life.

Jenny: *When my boyfriend's father died, they packed up a suitcase to put at his bedside, with clothes, spirit money, everything he would need on his journey.*

Lu continued, in a kind of monologue.

Lu: *When you die, you must wear traditional clothes, because you will be reborn as what you are. We used to just put on a Hmong traditional costume, with a death robe over it. But now my mom put a Hmong costume, then a business suit, then the death robe on my father, because she wasn't sure what he would become in the next life.*

The poignant position that Lu sustains, as a first generation immigrant caught between cultures, seems metaphorically similar to her father's confused identity in death, symbolized by the need to wear both a Western business suit and a Hmong costume, because no on knows in what form he will reincarnate. The Hmong are a hill tribe which lived in isolation in the mountains for several hundred years before the Secret War in Laos in the 1970s, which caused Lu's family and other hill tribe people to flee for their lives and begin a long journey, often of 15 or 20 years, between refugee camps, countries, and finally cities in the United States. The tradition of dressing for your next incarnation in a Hmong robe, a costume traditionally worn by all Hmong, would have made sense for centuries, but is now called into question. No wonder Hmong people believe that there are many restless souls, who travel around and create anxiety in living people. Lu continues:

> When you get married, a girl is given a death robe. And kids buy parents death robes as gifts. They are very expensive. When I got mine, I said: "I don't want to be Hmong again in the next life. It is too hard."

Lu's statement stunned us all. She is a daughter-in-law in a traditional Hmong household, a member of her mother's part Hmong, part Mormon family, and a modern American college student learning Western science and other subjects. Her confused identity, at least at present, is too much for her to bear. In contrast, Bobby, who experienced American culture through the eyes of a Filipino whose parents gave him an American school lunch, once again asserts his own comfort with cultural hybridism.

> **Bobby:**   Filipinos like me are Catholic, but we didn't feel that religion was really ours, so we added our superstitions. Before we bury our dead, we have a rosary with them. We place a set of rosary beads in the hands of the person being buried, but before we do that, we break the chain. If it isn't broken, we believe that the dead person can come back and pull his favorites with him, using the chain to hook them. He will want us with him in the afterlife. The rosary is a circle of life, but the other part came from our religion, before the Catholics.

Cherrylyn joins him.

> **Cherrylyn:** We prepare food for the dead, about two weeks after they die. This is like the Chinese. I can see both the Chinese and the Spanish traditions in our culture.

In this dialogue, the variable positioning of pre-service teachers in relation to their culture is evident. Whereas Cho is comfortable with Hmong culture, and is a traditional Hmong rather than a convert to Christianity, Lu is caught in a dilemma with her own culture, and sometimes feels she does not want to be part of it. As she gets educated, she rejects some of the beliefs of her family, and is put in conflict. Yet she still lives in a traditional situation where her new opinions are not accepted. Her position may be influenced by her identity as a woman, since Hmong culture is a patriarchy in which young women must live with their in-laws. This situation often puts these women under a lot of pressure, especially if, as in Lu's case, both her mother's conversion to Mormonism and her own education place her in conflict with the traditional household in which she lives.

Bobby and Cherrylyn, on the other hand, are comfortable with the hybrid elements that formed Filipino culture, and which make up their own identities, and are able to look from a distance at the cultural elements which have formed them. Bobby, who was reared middle class, takes a universalist view of culture, perhaps because his family exerts less traditional pressure than those of his peers. Arellano et al. (2001) discuss how Filipinos commonly act out several belief systems which seem contradictory, "just in case." For example, if a person is sick, he or she will simultaneously visit the Western doctor at the health clinic, use a traditional herbal remedy from the garden, and go to the Catholic Church to pray. Perhaps the Filipino history of cultural blending over hundreds of years leads to comfort with multiple identities which is not present in immigrants such as Hmong, who have recently stepped out of cultural isolation into a multicultural reality including Christianity, Western science, media culture, and more.

Obviously, the discussion about life cycles did not resolve the deep identity struggles that Lu and others face in their daily lives and in their lives as teachers. However, this discussion facilitated the unpacking of cultural assumptions generally ignored in science education settings. Because we encouraged pre-service teachers to write lessons which expressed their point of view, we discovered Bobby's belief in reincarnation, which deviated markedly from the Western convention of presenting the life cycle as a one-way journey, with no spiritual dimension. This revelation in turn prompted a discussion about "life cycles" in a broader sense, including both physical and spiritual aspects, and a description of Hmong practices, previously not known to the other pre-service teachers. The traditional separation of church and state, acted out as religion versus science, was ignored, being a convention with which these immigrant pre-service teachers were hardly familiar. Because spiritual beliefs were discussed in the context of science, the conversation became much deeper and broader than intended in the science standards studied. The study of the life cycle became truly that: a consideration of deeper questions of life, death, and afterlife.

Ogawa's (1995) notion of "multi-science," which includes Western, traditional, and personal science, applies to this situation. If the life cycle is taught from a multi-science perspective, then it becomes a broad theme relevant to all people's life experience. Western science plays an important part within this theme, as it did within a lesson on the strawberry life cycle, in which students went in the garden and identified its four stages after they experienced Bobby's discussion of reincarnation. Yet non-Western points of view were introduced as well, then discussed dialogically. Certainly Ogawa's third category, personal science, could be incorporated, if children were to share their own views on the matter. A similar set of lessons on the life cycle was once enacted by two teacher researchers, Mendez and Placencia (1996), who collaborated with others at their school site to teach Western science concepts, including the anatomy of the skeleton and the life cycle of pumpkins, within a broader cultural celebration of *día de los muertos*, or Day of the Dead, in which an altar is created to honor the ancestors. This holiday was also culturally internationalized beyond its original roots in Catholicism, through the creation of an Ancestors' Day in which Asian, American, and Mexican children came together to commemorate their ancestors and to honor the cycle of the seasons.

Although this dialogue suggests new pedagogies, its main importance is as a tool for cross-cultural awareness. In this case, the discussion illuminated the comfort or discomfort which pre-service teachers were experiencing leading lives caught between cultures. Lu's pain, which drove her not to want to be reborn as a Hmong, parallels her mother's confusion about whether to dress her father in a business suit or traditional Hmong costume in preparation for his next incarnation. It is clear that Lu has much to resolve in deciding what to present to her students, who are often immigrants like herself, when she teaches science. It was important that the class could see Lu's confusion and pain, since many of the children and families they teach will be caught in similar cultural dilemmas.

DIALOGUE #3: FOOD AND FAMILY
ARE ALL WE NEED TO KNOW

On the final day of class, we held a discussion about what it is important to teach, and how. Perhaps because of our context, in the garden, the topic of food emerged once more.

> **Cho:** *We Asians don't eat to live, we live to eat. But knowing things about where food comes from is just something I assumed. It never occurred to me before that we need to teach this in school, because it is so much a part of our culture.*

Jenny: *Maybe it is because we were deprived of food. We had to spend all our time getting it.*

Cho continues a theme which was introduced earlier—that although he knew many things from his background, it would not have occurred to him to teach them in school had he not been a part of this teacher education program. It is clear that he had considered school a highly bounded activity, in which certain skills like reading and writing were taught, but other kinds of knowledge, such as an understanding of the natural world, were excluded and assumed to be taught at home. Participating in the garden project informed Cho that many urban kids do not know about the natural world, and that even Hmong kids no longer grow up farming and gardening with their parents. For Jenny, the garden project is a reminder that food used to be hard to get. As in earlier cases, these two Asian student teachers assume different postures toward the same experience, farming, one seeing it as fundamental to understanding life, the other, as a hardship imposed by deprivation. For Bobby, the purpose of giving children concrete experiences is to create an identity story, which then builds character in the child.

Bobby: *I think our stories develop who we are. If we have the story of our ancestors in rice fields with bare feet, these stories develop the character of the children that follow. Americans are far from these kinds of stories now. It's the story that makes the people.*

Jenny: *But it is also your experience. When I came here, I had nothing. I was not picky about food or clothes. Now I'm picky. I can afford to be.*

Bobby and Jenny's perspectives reveal an age-old philosophical debate. Are we formed by our stories or by our experience? Both Cho and Jenny associate being "picky" with being privileged in the United States, but with different moral implications. For Jenny, being "picky" is a privilege that one cannot have until it is affordable. For Cho, a traditional Hmong, being "picky" is a wasteful trait exemplified by American culture, a trait that should be resisted.

Cho: *People waste things here. My parents say, "don't marry an American girl because she will take one bite of a chicken and throw the rest away." My students don't even know that there are seeds in an apple, because by the time they get it, the seeds and skin are gone. They don't even know what an apple really is. When you go to a fancy restaurant, they throw even more away, just to make a decoration. In Asia, all of the chicken is there. Here, the more you pay, the less you get. I'd rather pay less and get more.*

In this conversation, Cho's value system is consciously at odds with his perception of American values, which he sees as wasteful and superficial. The notion that people do not know what an apple "really is" implies that the separation from subsistence farming which people experience when they come to the United States is a separation from land and from an appropriate sense of appreciation that a chicken is a whole entity, all of which is valuable and should not be discarded, just for status and "decoration." Bobby's words build on Cho's.

> **Bobby:** *I noticed that growing up. When I ate at friends' houses, their parents would throw food away after dinner. My mother would put it in the sauce for the next meal. Really, food and family are all we need to know.*

Bobby, the storyteller, is clearly discussing more than food. His assertion that "food and family are all we need to know" is a value judgment on the importance of keeping one's priorities straight, and remembering the things that truly sustain us. Many of these, in his view, come from family values as transmitted by modeling (as in his mother making sauce) and stories (as in his telling about it).

As course instructor, I felt compelled to interject a question about whether what we have learned through service learning and reflective dialogue prepared the pre-service teachers to teach standards based science, which covers more than "food and family."

> **Lorie:** *Sometimes I fear that because we spend so much time on community work, we don't spend enough time learning about a range of science lessons. What do you think?*

Anita and Haley reinforced that our emphasis on experience and process, rather than content, was workable for them.

> **Anita:** *What is important is to model and practice. We create models, then we practice them with kids, then we reflect and re-apply what we know.*
>
> **Haley:** *We have been learning tools. It's our job to find the lesson ideas.*

> Anita: *There are lots of ideas on the web. The trick is knowing how to imple-*
> *ment them, and why.*
>
> Jenny: *I'm an independent learner. When we invented the lessons together,*
> *and reflected on them, it opened my mind to other people's ways of*
> *thinking.*
>
> Cho: *Yes, it is hard to create one thing together. But it worked. It is good for*
> *us, and for the kids. But you have to get used to it.*

I was interested in the responses of Jenny and Cho, who spoke of their difficulties working on teams to create and teach lessons. Given that Asian cultures are thought to be collective, I surmised that the contrast they felt was
between our cooperative learning activities and previous individual activities
at school or university.

My final question was about whether or how the pre-service teachers
would use reflective cultural dialogue in their own classroom teaching.

> Lorie: *Do you think you would have the same kind of dialogue in a K–6*
> *classroom as we have in class?*
>
> Haley: *It depends on the age group. Some subjects, like death, wouldn't be*
> *appropriate.*
>
> Anita: *I think that you could have the same kind of dialogue. Like you guide*
> *us, but the conversation can meander. This will happen in a classroom*
> *too. The kids will let you know what it is appropriate for them to talk*
> *about.*

It is interesting to note that Haley felt death to be an inappropriate subject
with young children, but that Anita considered it a question of how the
teacher guided the discussion. Kids, in her opinion, will know what they are
ready to talk about. For Bobby, always the cultural broker, the key is to use
such dialogue to enable students to understand that their cultural dilemmas
are like those of others, across cultural boundaries.

> Bobby: *I think that if you share cultural comparisons, like we do, the kids will*
> *feel more comfortable about what they do at home. Like if a kid is*
> *Punjabi and doesn't eat meat, I could tell him that Catholics do the*
> *same thing at Lent.*

For Haley, it comes back to where we began, with the question of trust.

Haley: *What is most important is that people feel comfortable, so they can be honest.*

Lessons Learned

Although reflective dialogue about the cycle of planning, teaching, and assessing is common to teacher education, reflection about the cultural nature of the subjects taught, the way in which they are taught, and the identity of the teacher and his or her students is rare. However, in an increasingly globalized world, questions about the sociocultural nature and position of subjects like science cannot be overlooked at either the university or K–12 levels of teaching. Reflective dialogue represents a promising tool for introducing cultural awareness into the lives of pre-service teachers, especially in subjects such as science, which are generally assumed to be a-cultural.

As a teacher educator, I learned a great deal from "digging deeper" through reflective, cultural dialogues with my students. One lesson was that each student is engaged in a unique journey, discovering which elements to carry from his or her past life into the role of teacher. This journey is complex for mainstream American students, and much more so for minority students, whose individual trajectories cannot be predicted through either ignoring culture as a factor in teacher development nor through applying stereotypes based on ethnic backgrounds. Strategies that enable students to understand their own cultural positions, and to challenge them through dialogue with others, are an essential part of a teacher education program.

Cho's case makes clear that extensive cultural knowledge, even coupled with comfort within a cultural position, does not necessarily lead to the sharing of this knowledge as a teacher. Urban schools appear so standardized, and sometimes restricted to reading and mathematics instruction, that a teacher like Cho needs affirmation that he can bring the rich resources which his background provides into the classroom. In his case, he needed to understand that to study the natural world is important to his students, and is anything but obvious to those who are reared in urban environments. Knowing what an apple "really is" and how to respect rather than waste resources: these are insights that Cho's Hmong background puts him in a powerful position to teach, because, as he says himself, he knows these things.

Lu is also Hmong, but is a female in her mother-in-law's house, and is caught between Christian, Western scientific, and traditional Hmong beliefs. Lu seeks a career outside the family, despite the pull of a new baby, because the university and her career represent a "place where she always wanted to go, to get away from home, and be with her friends." These background factors, coupled with her individual perspective on them, create a profound identity dilemma in daily life and in deciding what to teach. Many of her students will share Lu's dilemma, in their own unique way. They too, will need opportunities to dialogue about their lives, and to separate their cultural dilemmas from personal idiosyncrasies. While my own perspective makes me hope that Lu will eventually see the positive aspects of her own culture, as well as its challenges, her teaching perspective is hers to form.

Jenny, rather like Lu, struggles with her double or triple identity, as Cambodian and Khmer, Chinese and Jen, and now in part American. Until now, she states that she has played a role at work and at the university, being what she thought Americans wanted her to be. It is interesting that even as a child, Jenny "was one way at home and one way at school." The statement that her clothes, donated from the church, "did not feel right," provides a powerful metaphor for how she felt in general. "If the teacher had brought my stuff into the classroom, it would have let me be one person," she states. How will Jenny do this for the students she teaches? Our hope is that the dialogue we began will continue, so that Jenny, who has thus far conformed to outside expectations, will feel empowered in bringing her own experience into the classroom, so that students like herself can also "be one person."

Bobby has gained a level of sophistication, partly due to the middle class context of his upbringing and the cultural brokering of his older brother, which enables him to identify cultural patterns and to compare and contrast his own cultural experience with that of others. Bobby's comfort level with integrating a variety of cultural influences is paralleled in Cherrylyn, another Filipino. Perhaps the historic Filipino experience of integrating Asian and Western, native, Christian, and Buddhist elements, has taught them to integrate American culture as one more variable. It is interesting to note, however, that Bobby continues to assert that "it is the story that makes the person." Spindler and Spindler (2000) talk about three kinds of selves which people in cultural transition experience. One of these is the "enduring" self, which is well exemplified in Bobby's use of the story. The enduring self reflects past realities nostalgically, through stories and other re-enactments, and gains deep identity gratification by doing so, even if the reality reflected in the story is not his or her life today. A second self, the "instrumental" self, copes with present realities, and learns to be effective. Obviously, a combination of both these selves is essential for well-being. Bobby is highly conscious of his need for both, and has created a role for himself as a teacher storyteller and poet, which enables him to express his own heritage, cope with his present role as teacher, and model a relativistic attitude for his students. Bobby's ability to integrate his roles may have been generated by his own family's ability to adapt and be successful in American life when he was a child. This ability enabled him to feel comfortable in school, because he had brought the right lunch.

The Spindlers' third category of self, the "endangered" self, emerges when the other two are in such conflict that they cannot be integrated, causing extreme identity distress. Lu appears to be in such distress, caught between cultural forces. Many public school students experience similar identity gaps, especially at adolescence, when the chasm between the traditional values of their parents and the American values of school and peer group reaches its extreme. Reflective cultural dialogues might serve as "cultural therapy," in both K–12 and university classrooms, enabling students caught between cultures to express their confusion and gain insight from the similar experience of others. We need teachers like Lu, who understand what their students are experiencing. We also need to create schools where time and validation are given to the discussion of cultural issues. The pressure that standards and testing currently places on urban schools allows no time for dialogue or community building, and distracts teachers from the role they play as human developers, rather than simply transmitters of information. This situation invalidates both teachers' own experience and that of their students.

We did not delve deeply into the identity issues of Haley and Anita, who were fascinated with finding out about the ideas shared by their Southeast Asian counterparts—ideas which they had not previously encountered. Anita's family identity as an organic farmer continues to guide her story, and creates a message about nutrition, science, and environment that she feels confident to carry into her teaching. Haley's deep concern for social justice comes from her mixed experience growing up in both a university household and a household gripped by poverty and mental illness. Haley is able to leverage her own experience to be sympathetic to children in poverty, partly because her background in a university family gives her a sophisticated set of analytic tools. The instructor/researcher, who herself grew up in a single parent family in a lower middle class neighborhood, felt a kinship with Haley and her struggle to create opportunities for children in need, a struggle that has led them both to cross borders into minority communities also organized around issues of social justice. The question of class as culture is profound, and hard to grasp, in American society, where everyone pretends to be middle class. The experience of students like Haley, who are white but come from poverty, would be a good subject for another case study on reflective cultural dialogue, since this study dealt primarily with the Southeast Asian identity experience.

REFLECTIONS ON NEW RESEARCH DIRECTIONS

This case study represents one part of a long term experiment with applying anthropological perspectives to science teacher education. This engagement occurs in the context of a larger initiative, the Equity Network, in which teacher educators at twelve diverse, urban, low income professional development schools in the Sacramento area grapple with how to educate teachers to work effectively in these schools. This case study emerges from my attempt to link equity work to the understandings which have emerged from the application of anthropology to education over the past 50 years. Teacher educators are hybrids, straddling the research community and the community of practice. Although many of the reforms in teacher education are oriented toward multicultural education or equity/anti-racist education, not all of these efforts are grounded in an understanding of schools as cultural institutions and of subject areas, such as science, as socio-culturally situated.

How does an anthropological approach change equity oriented science education? And what do stories from practice, such as these case studies, add to the field of Anthropology of Education? These are big questions, which this case study brushes against.

Fundamentally, an anthropological approach to science education challenges the underpinnings of science itself, rather than simply attempting to create more equitable access to it in its present form. How doe it change science teaching? In a complex of ways, acted out on a daily basis by individual teachers. Cho, who understands what an "apple really is" and how to conserve resources, in the profound way that only a member of a subsistence culture can, has new insights to bring to the teaching profession, as do all the pre-service teachers in this study. How Anita's understanding of organic agriculture, and Bobby's understanding of how stories "create who we are," will affect their roles as teachers remains to be seen. However, it is clear that if teacher education programs and schools do not validate the unique cultural and scientific knowledge which these new teachers bring to the profession, they will be unlikely to apply their knowledge to their work. As Cho and Jenny stated, it would never have occurred to them that they could or should share their cultural knowledge in school, because they had never seen this done in their own schooling experience.

Turnbull (1997) states that it is useful to reconsider science as performative, rather than representational, as a set of inquiries which are constantly being re-created. This approach is generally accepted in scientific communities, who are committed to evidence-based inquiry and to the notion that present theories are just that, and are subject to refinement and change. However, science in the elementary school, like other subjects, is generally treated as a set of "standards," or facts, which need to be memorized and mastered. Textbook and test driven science too often teaches students to parrot the findings of past scientists, while providing students with few opportunities to do science for themselves. A parallel problem exists in all subject areas. An ethnographic approach to school reform is useful in this situation. How can teachers, schools, and communities recenter their curricula on their own lives, past, present, and future? One way is to re-envision school reform as performative, being created in specific cultural settings and environmental contexts which are each, by definition, local and unique. Of course, broad standards and skills can be applied in all settings, but meaningful educational research can emerge through tapping the personal and cultural resources of each teacher and school community, working in partnership with university and community partners, to make sense of the social and natural world in which they and their students are situated. Such as community development view of education is by definition ethnographic, in that local resources cannot be tapped unless they are first understood. If Cho, a highly intelligent fifth year university student, did not realize that his knowledge of horticulture was relevant to teaching science, then how rare it would be for an immigrant parent with a similar cache of knowledge to step forward to share it in school. And how rich would a school become if this were to happen.

In addressing what practice can add to Anthropology of Education research, one might echo Erickson (chapter 7) in asserting that shared research between teachers and ethnographic researchers can benefit both. The cultural dialogues shared in this chapter could not have occurred without the context upon which they were reflective. This context is a set of partnership schools, in which teacher education occurs as part of long term partnerships with individual mentor teachers and with teacher research and community based projects. For example, garden projects at several school sites are organized through the school–university–community partnerships, supported by grants from agencies such as USDA and Toyota. University researchers assist teachers in writing grants which focus on integrating science and language development, curricula and parent and community involvement. Project CULTURES,[4] an ethnobotany garden project currently forwarded by two

---

[4]CULTURES is a one-year Toyota Tapestry science grant received by a science specialist and a language development specialist at Westfield School, Washington Unified School District, West Sacramento, in conjunction with UC Davis, CSUS and Yolo County Office of Education partners. Its focus is on using ethnobotany to draw immigrant parents' funds of knowledge into the school science and language curriculum during the 2004–2005 school year.

teacher specialists, fourth grade teachers and students, an ethnobotanist from UC Davis, a teacher educator from CSUS, and a county science coordinator, is one such project. CULTURES takes an ethnographic approach to life science in the fourth grade, basing it on Mexican and international horticulture traditions, and creating an oral history project which shares the knowledge of immigrant parents through community books, created by children as ethnographers. It is within the context of projects like these that reflective cultural dialogues among pre-service and in-service teachers can occur. Although Anita's sentiment, that "science teaching should come first from real life examples before going to texts," is axiomatic to many science educators, the creation of "real life examples" in immigrant communities sometimes requires projects that bridge home and school in new ways. Teaching pre-service teachers, teachers, and K–12 students themselves to be ethnographers, unearthing the cultural knowledge inherent in their communities, is a first step which can then create a context in which cultural dialogue might occur.

Ethnographers are expert at studying communities, including schools, but are not always familiar with the political and practical concerns necessary to launch reform programs. Working in partnership with teachers, parents, and administrators is necessary for such reforms to occur. Educational researchers and reformers, on the other hand, often invent curricula and other reforms out of context, applying the notion that school reform is not useful if it cannot "go to scale." Our experience suggests that we should rethink our notions of school reform as a contextualized process that is most effective at the local level, and results from a sensitive blend of outside expertise and community knowledge. In such an "ethnographic" notion of school reform, reflective cultural dialogue becomes a necessity, as people from various positions come together to negotiate a rich and meaningful story to pass on to their children.

REFERENCES

Aikenhead, G. S. (1996). Science education: Border crossing into the subculture of science. *Studies in Science Education, 27,* 1–52.

Arellano, E. L., Barcenal, B. L., Bilbao, P. P., Castellano, M. A., Nichols, S., & Tippins, D. J. (2001). Case-based pedagogy as a context for collaborative inquiry in the Philippines. *Journal of Research in Science Teaching, 38*(5), 502–528.

Barton, A. C., & Osborne, M. D. (Eds.). (2001). *Teaching science in diverse settings: Marginalized discourses and classroom practice.* New York: Peter Lang.

Cobern, W. W. (1996). Worldview theory and conceptual change in science education. *Science Education, 80*(5), 579–610.

Eisenhart, M. (1995). The fax, the jazz player, and the self-story teller: How do people organize culture? *Anthropology & Education Quarterly, 26*(1), 3–26.

Eisenhart, M. (2000). Boundaries and selves in the making of "science." *Research in Science Education, 30*(1), 43–55.

Gilbert, A. (2002). *How transformative is sociotransformative constructivism? Utilizing critical ethnography to investigate a discourse of transformation*. Presented in the multimedia symposium at the National Association for Research in Science Teaching Annual Conference, New Orleans.

Hammond, L. (2001). Notes from California: An anthropological approach to urban science education for language minority families. *Journal of Research in Science Teaching, 38*(9), 983–999.

Hammond, L., & Charmbury, D. (2002). How do you grow rice? In Tippins, Koballa, & Payne (Eds.), *Learning from cases: Unraveling the complexity of elementary science teaching* (pp. 78–85). Boston: Allyn & Bacon.

Hammond, L., & Heredia, S. (2002). Fostering diversity through community service learning. *Network, 9*(1).

Lee, & Fradd. (1998). Science for all, including students from non-English language backgrounds. *Educational Researcher, 27*(4), 12–21.

Levinson, B., Foley, D., & Holland, D. (Eds.). (1996). *The cultural production of the educated person: Critical ethnographies of schooling and local practice*. Albany: State University of New York Press.

Mendez, A., & Placencia, N. (1996). Dia de los muertos: An integrated curriculum. Distributed by the Bilingual Integrated Curriculum Project (1986–1997), West Sacramento, CA: Washington Unified School District, Categorical Projects Office.

Moll, L. C., Amanti, C., Neff, D., & Gonzalez, N. (1992). Funds of knowledge in teaching: Using a qualitative approach to connect homes and classrooms. *Theory Into Practice, 31*(2), 132–141.

Ogawa, M. (1995). Science education in a multiscience perspective. *Science Education, 79*(5), 583–593.

Rodriguez, A. J. (1998). Strategies for counterresistance: Toward sociotransformative constructivism and learning to teach science for diversity and for understanding. *Journal of Research in Science Teaching, 35*(6), 589–622.

Spindler, G. D., & Spindler, L. (Eds.). (1994). *Pathways to cultural awareness: Cultural therapy with teachers and students*. London: Sage.

Spindler, G. D., & Spindler, L. (2000). *Fifty years of anthropology and education: 1950–2000*. Mahwah, NJ: Lawrence Erlbaum Associates.

Turnbull, D. (1997). Reframing science and other local knowledge traditions. *Futures, 29*(6), 551–562.

10

Narratives of Location: Epistemology and Place in Higher Education

Carol B. Brandt

University of New Mexico

Carol B. Brandt is a postdoctoral researcher at the Center for Informal Learning and Schools at the University of California, Santa Cruz. She received her Ph.D. in Educational Thought & Sociocultural Studies at the University of New Mexico. Her dissertation research focused on school science identities and scientific discourse among Native American women in higher education. Prior to her research in higher education, Carol was an archaeologist and ethnobotanist for the Pueblo of Zuni Cultural Resources Program. Carol's long-term interests bring together crosscutting studies that link language, geography, and anthropology to bring more democratic practices of engaging in science.

This chapter chronicles how senior-level college students in my ethnobotany seminar explored the nature of place, those locations in which we construct knowledge in science, and how place is linked to epistemology—the origin, nature, and limits of knowledge. Ethnobotany, the study of plants used by human cultures, is one way for students to examine traditional knowledge from indigenous communities, while reflecting upon the epistemology of Western science as taught in the university. Here, I recount how a critical place-based approach is an ethnographic tool for analyzing the narratives of the students in my class, and also provides a novel pedagogical approach to higher education. In this seminar I integrate ethnographic methods into our classroom activities as students and I examine the cultural activities that surround local knowledge about the use of plants. By using an anthropological approach, I argue that faculty can arrive at a new awareness of their practice, and students can come to a critical understanding of our construction of science in the university setting.

PLACITAS, NEW MEXICO

Together, the students and I walked slowly downhill through the orchard, winding our way through the tall grasses, ditches, and brush piles. On this July morning, a light rain had fallen, and the trees were filled with the watery songs of warblers. We matched our pace to the measured strides of Patrociño,[1] an elder in the village, who was leading our fieldtrip through the farm. Patrociño and the students had just finished studying a large map of *acequias*, the community ditches that direct water from the springs to agricultural fields in Placitas. Together we followed the path of water from the mountainside through the ditches to the shareholdings of the *acequia* community. As we walked, Diego, one of the students in my class, caught up with me, and said in quiet voice, "Did you hear how Patrociño talked about the difference between being "educated" and being knowledgeable? I know what he means by knowledgeable—it's here. It's the farm, *la tierra*." Diego flashed a smile from behind his mirrored, wrap-around sunglasses and then stepped forward quickly to join students in front of us.

Escaping the university classroom and walking in the orchard made possible a gentle shifting of worlds, a new perspective, and a fresh location in which to understand academic science. Our fieldtrip to Placitas offered students in my ethnobotany class an opportunity to recognize how epistemology in science—the origin, nature, and limits of knowledge—is intimately linked to place. In this chapter, I recount how a critical, place-based approach is an ethnographic tool for analyzing the narratives of the students in my class, and also provides a novel pedagogical approach to higher education. In this seminar I integrate ethnographic methods into our classroom activities as students and I examine the cultural practices that surround local knowledge about the use of plants. I argue that by using an anthropological approach to science, faculty can arrive at a new awareness of their practice, and students can come to a critical understanding of epistemology and our construction of science in the university setting.

This ethnographic research explores: How do students experience a curriculum that encourages them to gain an awareness of "place" and the cultural process of academic science? How do students respond to an invitation to traverse epistemological borders? After a semester-long course in ethnobotany at a university in the southwestern United States, I asked students to help me evaluate the effectiveness of this seminar. I was interested in understanding

---

[1]All names presented in this analysis are pseudonyms.

their experiences in our class, and how our discussion, readings, activities, and fieldtrips affected their relationship with academic science.

THE UNIVERSITY CLASSROOM
AND THE "CANON" OF SCIENCE

My 9 years of experience as a staff employee within science in higher education corroborates the observations of Wellington and Osborne (2001, p. 79) on science pedagogy: "School science is still dominated by the transmission of information." Lectures or laboratory exercises are still standard fare in our science education classrooms at the university. In this setting, students have few opportunities to examine the epistemological underpinnings of science, and to question how knowledge is generated within our institutions. Instead, courses in academic science typically focus on students becoming familiar with scientific information and the range of knowledge produced within the discipline of science. For example, students in a genetics class learn the details of molecular transcription and translation, but rarely do they look at the sociopolitical context of molecular technology, the historical development of knowledge, nor do they critique the texts or published articles that are used in their classes. In much of university learning, science is non-historical and without context, and proceeds uncritically.

Our educational system socializes students at an early age to accept the canons of science and the "official knowledge" (Apple, 1999) of scientific research. Students at the university level are taught to comply by carefully taking notes at lectures, to write rigidly using scientific discourse, and to anticipate professors' questions on multiple-choice exams. Even laboratory experiments, where one might expect inquiry to be practiced are cookbook, step-by-step exercises. Blades (2002) portrays this pedagogy as a destructive pathology, and indicts science education as "a bulimia of information" (p. 72). And so, in these contexts, students may master the content of scientific knowledge and understand the process of scientific inquiry, but they are sadly lacking in understanding the complex ways in which science contributes to our rapidly changing world. When speaking about the current state of science education, Blades (2002, p. 70) observes that: "students rarely, if ever experience *science*, but certainly do receive an education." He contends that students are held captive in a system where schools substitute contrived experience for students' own exploration of the natural world.

DEFAMILIARIZING SCIENCE—
MAKING THE FAMILIAR STRANGE

I designed this course to teach science in a way that encourages students to evaluate "knowledge," negotiate diverse points of view, and understand the social and political consequences of academic research. Frankly, I wanted students to understand science as a cultural process, complete with its own language, social structure, rules, and rituals. However, critically examining one's own culture and being able to describe the norms in which we are immersed is extremely difficult. Spindler and Spindler (1982) argue that to study education, one must make the familiar strange. Through ethnographic techniques that bring a new stance or perspective, researchers can use this distance to make "the cultural translation from familiar to strange and back to familiar" (p. 21). Similarly, Kaomea (2003) suggests ways of defamiliarizing and "making strange" the every day practices of schooling by analyzing the many silences, absences, and erasures in curriculum.

Rather than directly studying our own academic culture in higher education, I designed a seminar on the cultural construction of science through ethnobotany—the cultural use of plants for medicine, agriculture, and material culture. In our class together, I emphasized traditional knowledge and a "sense of place" within communities of the rural Southwest. Many of these communities are suffering from economic depression: a collapsed agricultural economy, privatization of communal resources such as water and timber, and gentrification—the conversion of old adobe homes and farmland to affluent housing. Using methods of defamiliarization provide one way to understand the situated knowledge in these communities and offers anti-oppressive (Kumashiro, 2001) and decolonizing methodologies (Gruenewald, 2003a; Smith, 1999). By giving voice to local knowledge and local experts who have been historically excluded from academic discourse, a curriculum in ethnobotany looks at the political and social context of knowledge.

Ethnobotany as Cultural Therapy

Spindler and Spindler (1993) describe strategies for teachers and students to see their own schooling in a new light and appreciate diverse lifeways. Through the technique of "cultural therapy" Spindler and Spindler focus their students' attention on the cultural processes of education in other contexts of schooling and use ethnography as a vehicle to understand their own beliefs about teaching, learning, and education. Likewise, ethnobotany is a form of "cultural therapy" and becomes a foil for discussing our own academic culture in science. This indirect approach involves using ethnographic methods for understanding the context and culture of traditional knowledge systems, while constantly providing opportunities for students to reflect on and juxtapose their own experiences in academic science to our observations in the "field."

As cultural therapy, my approach to ethnobotany emphasizes that students recognize and explicate the unequal political and social relationships they observed among local communities, regional government, and larger institutions. In this way, the ethnobotany seminar also becomes a critical pedagogy of place. The ethnobotany of "place" explores the ecological, sociocultural, political, economic, and environmental relationships enmeshed in a specific locale. It explores the knowledge generated at a geographic location, and in turn, allows students to talk about the knowledge generated within the university campus and to explore similar or contrasting relationships in their learning.

Ethnobotany and a "Sense of Place" in Science

With its focus on location, the ethnobotany seminar emphasizes those places where science is generated, highlights those who are included/excluded in the construction of knowledge, and explores how knowledge is valued and wielded in the expression of power relationships. Gruenewald (2003a, 2003b) advocates place-based education that serves as a "counter-discourse" to normative trends in school systems. A place-based approach challenges the goals of schooling that emphasize accountability, standards, and testing that prepares students as consumers in an ever-increasingly global economy.

> Place, in other words, foregrounds a narrative of local and regional politics that is attuned to the particularities of where people actually live, and that is connected to global development trends that impact local places. Articulating a critical pedagogy of place is thus a response against educational reform policies and practices that disregard places, and that leave assumptions about the relationship between education and the politics of economics unexamined. (Gruenewald, 2003a, p. 3)

This place-conscious approach (Gruenewald, 2003b) looks at science in its physical locale, and positions that science in relation to larger sociocultural and economic frameworks. By building an intimacy with place, this type of education reveals the complex web of interdependencies: biological, physical, social, economic, political, and spiritual. Through place, I hoped that students would be able to examine the borders of their knowledge. In creating a sense of place with science, I wanted students to question: Where is knowledge constructed? Who is doing science in these places? Whose knowledge is valued? How does knowledge affect the quality of life and the sustainability of the environment in these places?

Ethnobotany as an Academic Discipline

Ethnobotany is a multidisciplinary field bringing together anthropology and the study of plants for medicine, agriculture, and human material culture (shelter, tools, or art). Harshberger (1896), a botanist, coined the term *ethnobotany* after studying plant materials excavated from archaeological sites in southwestern Colorado and realizing their value in understanding prehistoric life of the "cliff dwellers" in the southwestern canyons. Finding evidence of maize and beans among the archaeological materials, Harshberger grasped that ancient people possessed sophisticated knowledge to cultivate crops in a high-elevation, arid environment.

Although ethnobotany recognized indigenous knowledge and wisdom, like other academic research, it has a long history of domination and exploitation of indigenous people. In the early-20th century, ethnobotany was couched in the romanticism of "primitive" culture, and like anthropology, was motivated by the academic infatuation with the exotic "Other." Ethnobotany was also undertaken by the U.S. government to document plant knowledge that was rapidly being lost as entire Native communities succumbed to disease, forced relocation, and federal policies of assimilation. As the federal government moved to erase indigenous communities, the Bureau of American Ethnography was instituted to document "dying" cultures and make collections for the national museums.

Ethnobotanical research completed in the late-19th and the first half of the 20th century was a colonial endeavor; researchers took possession of traditional knowledge with little consideration for the communities that had maintained this information for generations. Anthropologists like Mathilda Coxe Stevenson wedged their way into communities and demanded access to traditional plant knowledge, while touting "a moral responsibility to elevate the Indian" (Parezo, 1993, p. 46). Others, understanding the scientific value of traditional plant knowledge, were dedicated to learning about economic uses of plants, but with the intent of commercial profit, or in the name of publishing "academic science."

Academics now regard ethnobotanical knowledge as a reflection of complex evolutionary relationships between indigenous communities and their environment (Bohrer, 1986; Rea, 1997; Schultes & Raffauf, 1990). Today, ethnobotanists employ research methods from the social sciences and diverse disciplines within the biological research, including biochemistry, ecology, agronomy, and plant genetics. In many ways, the economic and academic imperialism in ethnobotanical research is still played out. For example, anthropologists are actively working to document useful medicinal plants and their preparations for introduction into the pharmaceutical industry (Balick & Cox, 1996). And yet, ethnobotany has grown to include academic activists (Nabhan et al., 2002; Posey et al., 1984; Turner et al., 2000) who collaborate with indigenous people to preserve language, understand traditional ecological knowledge, and safeguard traditional lands against the threats of globalization: deforestation, mining, gas and oil extraction, urbanization, and industrial agriculture.

In light of this academic history, teaching ethnobotany with a place-based approach takes on a decolonizing agenda. Smith (1999, p. 5) argues that academic research "is not an innocent or distant academic exercise but an activity that has something at stake and that occurs in a set of political and social conditions." Smith contends that spaces are needed for a dialogue that gives the local and indigenous a presence in research, and thereby offers a process in which Western science and notions of scientific research can be decentered. By understanding the relationships of place, students participate in cultural de-colonization—identifying, extracting, and dislodging dominant ideas about education, research, and knowledge (Gruenewald, 2003a).

THEORETICAL FRAMEWORKS

My theoretical approach draws from an eclectic synthesis of social constructivism, critical theory, social studies of science, feminism, critical geography, and ethnography. In designing this course, and the evaluative research that followed, I blend a diverse set of theoretical perspectives.

At the heart of place-based education is social constructivism, an understanding of how students construct knowledge and the importance of the social context in which learning occurs. Place-based education is rich with sensory stimulation and depends upon cultural mediation for cognitive development. This "intersubjectivity," as theorized by Vygotsky (1986), is the dialogic conversation, between teacher and student, or students and their peers. The interaction of people and environment is mediated by language and is narrative in nature. Whereas social psychologists like Vygotsky have focused on language and narrative, little in educational theory has included the importance of physical space, location, and the relationship of our bodies to space in teaching. Place-based education acknowledges that in teaching, the kinetics of our bodies and place are connected to our minds and emotions. As students are immersed in the context of community, they construct scaffolding, important meanings, and critical understandings through interaction with that location (Theobald & Curtiss, 2000).

In my teaching and research, I rely on critical literacy and pedagogy that carries scientific literacy into a more sociopolitical realm. Scientific literacy means that students are able to understand the political and social context of scientific "texts" (written word, talk, and action) and understand how these texts are generated. Equally important, as students read, they bring their own experiences, their linguistic proficiency, and cultural experiences to the process of making meaning. Freire and Macedo (1987) elaborate on this type of literacy as a source of power, as rooted in the possibility of people to understand and transform their society. By being able to "read the world," Freire and Macedo redefine canonical notions of educational texts to include other ways of representing knowledge. Like Freire (1970) I am interested that students are able to reflect on their "place" and understand social, political, and economic contradictions. Reading the world is the first step toward transforming oppressive structures in education and society.

Sociological studies of science, like that of Gieryn (1999), offer useful metaphors of cartography to understand epistemology in Western science. He looks at the cultural space in which knowledge is constructed and considers the boundaries or borders of what constitutes Western science and nonscience through time, and how epistemic authority is reproduced by reference to these boundaries. And while Gieryn was speaking metaphorically, I argue that these epistemic arguments are expressed materially, are spatially segregated, controlled, and represent real conflicts acted out in the classroom, as well as in homes and in the market place.

Pedagogy of place also draws on critical spatial theory and feminist theory in education. Critical spatial theory (critical geography) developed by Foucault (1977), Lefebvre (1991), and Sibley (1995) argues that power and knowledge are exercised spatially, in both a metaphorical and physical sense. Sibley (1995) looks at the geography of exclusion and how boundaries are erected as the result of economic, political, and social ideologies. Sibley, by looking at socio-spatial structuring, examines exclusionary processes in the home, in the locality, and at the national level, and how the production of knowledge is segregated at each location. Feminist science pedagogy (Barton, 1998) studies how students position themselves in relation to science, and their location in the construction of knowledge. Feminist theory asks epistemological and ontological questions about scientific research and challenges its stance as value-free, objective, valid, and rigorous (Harding, 1991).

Underlying these varied theoretical approaches is ethnography and a desire to understand how actors within education are culturally produced, the ways that these participants generate cultural forms, and the cultural products that result from these relationships (Levinson & Holland, 1996). For educational anthropologists, ethnography is a way of "experiencing, enquiring, examining" (Wolcott, 1999) and is the primary method for observing and understanding these processes. Educational ethnography as defined by Spindler (1955) provides the groundwork of contemporary approaches to study culture in schooling. Despite the dynamic nature of schooling in the 21st century with new patterns of economy, migration, and technology, Eisenhart (2001) argues that there is no substitute for first-hand participant observation. "Only by watching carefully what people do and say, following their example, and slowly becoming a part of their groups, activities, conversations, and connections do we stand some chance of grasping what is meaningful to them" (p. 23).

METHODS

Case Study Research

This ethnographic research uses case study methodology as described by Merriam (1998). A case study is: "an intensive, holistic description and analysis of a bounded phenomenon such as a program, an institution, a person, a process, or a social unit" (Merriam, 1998, p. xiii). The case examined in this research includes those students who participated in the ethnobotany course I taught in the summer and fall of 2001, and the summer of 2002. My intent is to present a rich description of the participants and the multiple variables that may hold potential importance in understanding the cultural processes in this educational context (p. 41). Case studies are anchored in every day conversations, activities, and local context; case studies provide a dynamic and holistic account of cultural phenomena.

Having taught the class three times, this study could be seen as a multiple case study, or a collective case study. However, my attempts at systematic observation, journaling, and study did not occur until I was teaching the class the third time. Although the majority of my observation data are collected from the third class, I also invited students from the other classes to come to our discussion, to be guest speakers at our third class, and to offer their reflections and autobiographies for my analysis. My analysis and subsequent presentation looks at the students and my practice as a whole, instead of using each course as a way to organize my data, as an analytical framework, or a way to present my findings.

I also turned to practioner research methodology described by Anderson, Herr, and Nihlen (1994), whereby the teacher and her students (in this case, university level students) collaborate on research that evaluates the effectiveness of pedagogy and students' experiences in the classroom. Practioner research offered me guidance on how I might negotiate my dual "positions" as instructor and researcher (see the following discussion). Also, practioner research provided me a way to make the familiar, taken-for-granted aspects of teaching and look at them in a new light, from an outsider's perspective.

The Academic Setting

My research takes place at a large research university in the southwestern United States, situated in an urban population of 600,000. The campus has more than 24,000 students attending graduate and undergraduate classes, with an enrollment that is largely students from underrepresented ethnic groups (52%): Hispanic, Latina/o, and Native American. As a "commuter" campus, few students live in the university dormitories, and instead are embedded within the nearby urban neighborhoods, rural towns, and Native American reservations.

Although the ethnobotany course was housed within the Department of Biology, I advertised the class to departments across the College of Arts and Sciences; I required students to have an introductory biology class as the only prerequisite. I taught the course three times between fall 2001 and the summer of 2002. Sixteen to twenty undergraduate students enrolled in each class, with a total of 50 students completing the course. In the summer sessions, we met Monday through Saturday for 3 hours each day over a 4-week period. The course format in the fall semester was a 2.5-hour weekly seminar that lasted for 16 weeks. The syllabus alternated between paper discussions, group activities, guest lecturers and fieldtrips. The course emphasized both current academic research in ethnobotany and traditional knowledge systems from non-Western cultures.

In designing the seminar, I wanted to "disrupt" the typical format of a seminar and expand the notion of spaces for learning by taking students out of the classroom to new locations. I also wanted to challenge the perception of who is an expert by bringing a range of guest speakers that included members of the local Native American and Hispanic communities—who lacked the validation of academic degrees. We integrated science content into the course with my own "mini-lectures," short research reports given by students, and articles published in academic journals. Topics included: diabetes in Native American populations, the biodiversity of traditional cultivars of maize in the Southwest, the ecology of *acequia* (traditional irrigation) systems in Hispanic communities, and the biochemistry of traditional plants used for medicine.

The third time I taught the class, in the summer of 2002, the fieldtrips were focused on one place, the village of Placitas, located 20 miles north of Albuquerque, New Mexico. Established in the 1850s, Placitas still maintains traditional farming, orchards, and an *acequia* system, but is being heavily impacted by gentrification and the conversion of farmland to large estates for a newly arrived affluent population.

As part of the fieldtrips, I encouraged students to use ethnographic methods to document their observations. Through the use of their field notes, I encouraged students to pay attention to the physical contexts of our interactions with members of the community, the language each participant used, the movements of all participants, and the tools each person used in their work and teaching with us. In the last of our fieldtrips to Placitas, I brought along digital cameras for still shots and movies, and asked students to document their experience, and the traditional knowledge we learned.

Students enrolled in the class represent a diverse cross-section of the campus population: Native American, Hispanic, Asian, and Caucasian students with ages ranging from 20 to 61, from diverse socio-economic backgrounds. Most students are in their third or fourth year of undergraduate study; five students were non-degree or in a masters program. Sixteen out of the 50 students who took the course agreed to participate in the evaluation.

The Locations from Which I Conduct Research

Recognizing the range of positions from which I undertake this study is a critical starting point in my analysis: I come to the ethnobotany class as an instructor, a staff advisor within the university, and a graduate student. These "positionings," or subjective locations shape my approach in the design of the ethnobotany course, and also influence my listening and choice of narratives that I hear among the students in my class. I am a White, middle-class woman born and raised in a homogenous, midwestern rural community. Nevertheless, I have many years of experience living and working in cross-cultural settings; I came to the university after spending 10 years as a peripatetic archaeologist, traveling from one archaeological excavation to another throughout Alaska and the Southwest. As an archaeologist, I worked within indigenous communities and for tribal programs, gaining a sense of knowledge systems dissimilar to my own "white bread" education in Middle America. These years of working in diverse communities do not accord me any special status or authorization to conduct research with "minorities." Rather, these experiences lend me some awareness about the unequal relationships in research, and the long history among traditional communities of forced assimilation through compulsory education.

Due to my graduate degree in science and my background working in culturally diverse communities, I was hired by the university to work with underrepresented students (largely Hispanic, Latino/a, and Native American) in the sciences. Eventually, I became the staff advisor for the largest undergraduate unit on campus with more than 800 undergraduate majors. In the course of one semester I worked with hundreds of students, helping them to plan their courses, to complete their paperwork for graduating, or to talk with them about careers. From these many conversations I came to recognize that students have rich narratives and lives very different from my own. I wondered, how do they connect to the abstractions of scientific knowledge at the university?

As a doctoral candidate in education, I brought ideas from academic readings, research in education, and conversations with other graduate students in my program. My graduate degree emphasizes the sociocultural context of language in education with a critical and postmodern stance. Admittedly, this chapter does not portray the slow convergence of ideas and experiences that now form my foundation for ethnobotany as a place-based approach. When I first proposed teaching this class, I was motivated by my love of ecology, along with vague notions of creating a different kind of conversation about science with students. I could not have predicted what would emerge through the three incarnations of teaching this class. Not until I had finished teaching the course the second time did I realize the role that epistemology played in this course; it was teaching the course the third time that I truly became engaged with the notion of "place" and began systematically examining my own practice and students' experience in this seminar.

Data Analysis

Data for this research include: course evaluations written by the students; research papers, field trip reflections, and autobiographies written for the course by the participants; focus group discussions; and, the researcher's reflective journal. Data were analyzed using the constant comparative method (LeCompte, 2000; Strauss & Corbin, 1990) of successive and iterative readings of data and artifacts, locating patterns of themes in texts and transcripts, and aggregating these themes into larger categories. After I had reduced the categories, I presented my findings to students through member checking via electronic correspondence (e-mail).

I completed this first round of analysis and presented my findings at academic conferences. However, I was unhappy with the constant comparative method of analysis that, as a graduate student, was the only way I knew how to approach data. Widely promoted as part of qualitative research in my graduate program, this form of analysis places emphasis on commonalities and dominant patterns, reducing texts and settings to central ideas. As I began to write this chapter, I decided to look at my data again—and this time use narrative inquiry (Clandinin & Connelly, 2000). I was particularly interested in understanding those narratives that conserve the complexities of students' stories and highlight their awareness of epistemology and standpoint in science. Rather than reducing data to simplistic themes, ethnography should capture the nuance, ambiguities, and internal contradictions as participants strive to make coherence out of their lives. The three dimensional inquiry space discussed by Clandinin and Connelly was especially helpful. Going back to students reflections and autobiographies, I looked at their narratives in terms of three dimensions: temporal—extensions into the future or past; spatial—the physical context of the narrative; and the personal—those relationships highlighted in their narrative.

FINDINGS

The following narratives portray the ways in which places have shaped our lives *and* our construction of knowledge in science. I have selected three narrative themes that offer insight into students' experiences in a placed-based science curriculum, and their increasing sense of science as culture: embodiment and epistemology; shifting scales; and sense of self in place. Although I present these key narratives separately, they connect, overlap, and intersect in many ways.

Embodiment and Epistemology

In their fieldtrip reflections and focus group discussions, a common theme that emerged was the importance of experiencing place first hand, and spending an entire day learning about one location in our fieldtrip. Some wrote about new insights that local experts brought to the fieldtrip—seeing place through the eyes of the "Other" and understanding another construction of knowledge. Other students wrote about slow, embodied experience of a place as we spent the day in one location. Next, Jonah writes about our trip to Poshuwingüe, the ruins of a 15th-century pueblo on the Chama River in my second semester of teaching ethnobotany. On the mesa above the ruin is a piñon and juniper woodland and remnants of a vast agricultural field system that becomes obvious only after several hours of hiking and observation.

> The ground was where the action was. As we traveled and learned more about the ancient agricultural systems, I began to get a real feel for the place, and needed to imagine what it would have been like so long ago, just doing what humans do—modifying their environment. The basic agricultural manipulations undertaken to feed a small population still shape the land five centuries later. This is amazing to me, got me thinking about what my own home and city would be like if abandoned to nature for that amount of time. Somewhere along the drive back, these thoughts collapsed inward, and I went from pondering the road construction we passed through to trying to imagine what the Albuquerque area would have looked like had the city never existed at all. All of our readings felt pretty meaningless standing there at the ruins. I guess it was interesting to walk out there with some knowledge of the scientific methods that tell us about the place, how we know what we know from studying scattered remains of fires or garbage, the descendents of plants the people used, and comparisons with similar ancient and modern groups. But none of that crud really entered my mind while at the site—none of it could tell me what it would have felt like to be standing there back in prehistory better than actually standing there hundreds of years later. After the fieldtrip, I was left with a sense of integration. The pueblo ruins by themselves make little sense, but seeing the entire site as a place where human endeavor and natural ecosystems came together brings an entirely new context to littered stones and broken pottery. A community emerges, one where half a millennia ago a group of people clung tightly to the natural world just as they felt the need to control it. You can feel ancient hands on the rocks, in the dirt, wrapped around the weeds. You can feel people and the lives they once led. (Jonah, fieldtrip reflection)

This is just a portion of a long reflection from Jonah about our fieldtrip to the archaeological site with the remainder dedicated to his love of geology. His opening "the ground was where the action was" referred to his inability to look up and take in the rest of the landscape—he was so "fixed" upon the rocks. Finally, when we climbed a hill above the ruins and looked at the placement of the ancient village in the landscape that he began to sense integration. I was also struck by how Jonah moved between scales of time and

space, between the ancient past and the future to look at the landscape differently. It was through his physical experience with place, and the process of
walking that he gained a new perspective on the scientific knowledge from
his geology classes. And yet, the abstraction of school science could not ap-
proximate the same meaning that Jonah found through embodied experience
of landscape.

In contrast to Jonah, in our focus group discussion Brenda could talk only
about her *disorientation* of being in a new place and realizing that she lacked
an informal knowledge system to negotiate the landscape. Her strongly embodied experience had a reaction opposite to Jonah. After the fieldtrip,
Brenda confessed to me that this was her first "hike" in the desert, ever—despite her upbringing in a rural community. Her numerous questions about
shoes, insects, maps, and clothing before the fieldtrip came flooding back to
me as she recounted her fear and struggle to keep up with the group. For
Brenda, the level of her disorientation dominated her ability to make sense of
it all. The intensity of the sensory experience for her was overwhelming and
she had little context in which to place the fieldtrip. For Brenda, wandering
in the landscape seemed pointless, much like her approach to science; she
looked for external authority, a guide to lead the way.

Shifting Scales—From Local to Global and Back Again

Students also related local knowledge to science in the global arena. It
seemed that the more we tried to focus on a local place, the more our discussions opened into discussions of wider geographic significance. As one student put it: "Someone is always upstream and somebody else is downstream,"
when referring to the legal battles for water in Western states and the trickle
of the Rio Grande we send downstream to Mexico. Being so close to Mexico,
border issues found their way into many of our discussions and students' writing. Several students recognized that the plants identified with Native New
Mexican identity (e.g., chile and maize), had migrated with people from
Mexico, Central, and South America. In many ways, students noted the "fluidity" of knowledge, plants, and people, acknowledging their historical movements across oceans to new continents. But students realized that these
movements where often accompanied by violence and extreme human suffering that academic science often erases or chooses to ignore.

The ethnobotany class in the fall of 2001 took on a special significance
and many of our discussions surrounding local issues connected to the events

of 9/11, the subsequent invasion of Afghanistan, and the on-going colonization of third world countries. Margaret wrote in her reflection:

> Today's guests are two doctors from the School of Medicine who do research in Africa. While waiting for their appointed arrival, we go over assigned readings and end up in a biochemical discussion on diabetes and nutrition. We don't always discuss biochemistry in ethnobotany, I muse, as the conversation becomes a debate as to why body cells become non-receptive to insulin and are unable to uptake blood sugars. The program moves on, the doctors alternating to tell their pieces of the story. They describe their adventures looking for traditional foods and medicines in an over-grazed and over-used arid landscape. The slide show and the program continue. We see a smiling young girl with her grandmother. "She may not live beyond the age of twenty," the good doctor tells us as he explains she has sickle-cell anemia. "She may not even be alive right now," the unspoken words haunt the classroom. One tragedy lies heavily upon another. Later, the doctors have struggled through their stories. The class discussion is sensitive and thoughtful. One student asks: "Have there been social disruptions, have people had to move around a lot, and have they lost 'traditional ecological knowledge' that thousands of generations might have established when settled in one region?" The answer is complicated. In this age of Texan presidents, everything is compared to Texas. So in an area the size of Texas and Oklahoma combined, there are over 200 different—radically different—ethnic groups. Poverty is the culprit. The land will not support everyone, so ethnic hate becomes the catalyst to population control. "Poor countries are messy," the doctor shakes his head, "they are very complicated." The esoteric "ethnobotany" question goes unanswered. Did I miss the point of tonight's lecture? Was I supposed to be left with a focus on using traditional food plants to battle malnutrition? Or was the true message tonight one of coping in an angry world? (Margaret, speaker reflection)

The "angry world" in Margaret's reflection acknowledged the conflicts over place and identity that we rarely hear about in the media, or in our science classes at the university. In their research for the ethnobotany seminar, students related evidence of the globally "northern" nations control over manufactured goods, food, and biotechnology, with southern countries being exploited for their rich natural resources. Margaret cited the imbalance, the extremes of having and not having, as complicit in the creation of the "angry world." Later in her extensive writing in this reflection, she described the imbalances in her own world, the unfathomable sadness of losing her own child and a friend's battle with ovarian cancer—all a part of her ambiguous relationship with science. Margaret points out that the guest speakers for our class could have easily omitted the emotionally charged stories of their data collection in Africa. As difficult as these stories are to hear, the doctors from the medical school offered students a way to shift scales from the local to global and back again, and to present the sociopolitical context of their academic research.

When students can express their ability to connect science, local knowledge, and their experiences to a larger geopolitical framework, education then has the *scope and force* that Cobern (1996) speaks about as lessons with relevance to students' lives. Seeing science move from the local to global and extend over a wide range of contexts gave science *scope*. The emotional impact of realizing the personal nature of science in our lives can become enduring *force*, as Margaret previously illustrates, bringing science concepts central to students' thinking.

A Sense of Self in Place

Our final session for each ethnobotany class involved a potluck where students bring foods from a cultural traditions—either their own or another's tradition. Our table included an assortment of foods from a spectrum of cultures: English trifle, posolé, roasted mutton, spoon bread and black-eyed peas, tamales, German dumplings, and olives with hummus. In this relaxed and celebratory gathering, students offered insights and experiences in the class.

In our potluck, I noted how often students talked about their sense of self in the context of academic science and the multiple subjectivities in their life, much like the changing landscapes they experienced. In one energetic discussion, a Vietnamese American, two Chicanos who grew up in migrant farming families, and a Native American student engaged in an animated discussion about living across borders, and the difficulty they experience "going home." They spoke about how being a college student, how being "educated," had impacted their sense of identity and heightened their sense of alienation with their communities. Articulating their experience in a public forum was powerful for these students, but I also noted how forcefully it impacted mainstream students whose entrance into the academy required less effort, or fewer challenges. Again, the conversation was another opportunity for us to recognize the many locations from which we construct science.

In the excerpt from his autobiography next, José talks about ethnobotany in the context of his life. His writing, like his comments in our class, was presented in the style of a *testimonio*, a style of speech wherein the individual speaks collectively for his community and recounts a history of painful events (Smith, 1999).

> *My heritage is made up of two cultures that through time—Xicana and Puebloan, and my family developed an intimate relationship with the natural world. This is evident in*

our traditions and customs. My ancestors had no choice but to learn the uses of such plants for survival. It is no wonder they were masters at the use of such plants. Given this fact, it is amazing to me how in modern times, we have lost so much of this traditional knowledge in a matter of only a few generations. I cringe when I think of what could happen if we do not start to actively preserve this knowledge. I have shared the importance of corn in my culture as well as many other crops that have sustained people in the South since our beginnings. Plants are not only used as food and medicine but also ceremonial, crafts and utilitarian purposes. All life is very much respected in my family and this is evident in how we see our place in the world and how we relate to those around us. (José, Autobiography)

Students from ethnic backgrounds like José were eager to share with their classmates their personal experiences and their struggles to maintain traditional knowledge in their communities while also feeling pressured to get a college degree. Thirty-eight of the 50 students who participated in the ethnobotany class spent a formative portion of their youth and adolescence in New Mexico or Arizona. By using a local perspective and valuing local knowledge, students felt supported in offering their personal experiences in using traditional medicine, in practicing farming or gardening, and in collecting plants for basketry or other material uses—developing theory from their own lives. Their experience became an influential part of the class, and a way to offer their own "funds of knowledge" (Moll et al., 1992). Two students (both Native American) expressed how the ethnobotany class was their first time to contribute a cultural perspective in a science class at the university.

And yet, by focusing on place, students also came to question the use of *one* place to represent their relationship with science, or *one* place from which to describe their relationship to knowledge. One of the assignments in the course was for students to write their own "ethnobotanical autobiography." One re-occurring theme in the autobiographies was the changing landscape of the students' lives. Many students reflected on how the countryside of their childhood home was now suburban housing, the loss of local woodlands and natural areas, or the changing landscape that came with being in a migrant farming family. Some students struggled with the idea of being attached to one place or location from which they developed their sense of self. And, I noted how students carried these place-based identities far away to a new location. For example, Patricia writes:

In my heart, I am a forest person still. I love the smell of the Northern woods. Mostly pine—Norwegian pine, white pine. Pine is ubiquitous. I grew up thinking pine paneling was beautiful. I did not make the connection between paneling and lumbering issues at the time. Lumbering took out Michigan's old growth forests. Most of the pines today are second growth. They are scraggly and often growing in very even rows and columns. There is a small stand of virgin white pines near Grayling, Michigan. This is known as the "Hartwick Pines." The Monarch white pine, tallest in the park, stands 155 feet 45 inches tall and is over 300 years old. I have yet to visit this area, but I drive through it on the way to visit my father. It is near the town of Grayling, which is named after a fish no longer swimming in the rivers. Lumbering did them in, too. It's hard to imagine that most of the trees are gone. The school district I attended was named after the Warren woods. Warren is where General Motors put its Tech Center. The Community College—a couple of miles in the other direction "preserved" the last remaining woods in Warren. They use it for research. (Patricia, autobiography)

CONCLUSIONS: NARRATIVES OF LOCATION

In the opening of this chapter, Diego indicated to me a breakthrough in his thinking about being "educated," the privilege accorded to academic science, and the "knowledgeable" people beyond the university walls. In our conversation about the *acequias*, Patrociño recounted to us how the state water engineers dismissed his abilities and those of the elders within the community. Without assistance from the "educated" professionals, Patrociño and members of the water board capped the spring, constructed a reservoir, and built a system that distributes drinking water to the village, and water via ditches for irrigation. In this way, Patrociño and his community had preserved a fundamental right within their community: access to, and continued use of water for households and agriculture. Had they listened to the state water engineer—who told them that the flow of the spring was too low and geologically improbable, Placitas might have lost their water rights through disuse, and with it, its agricultural identity.

For many students, this was their first opportunity to look critically at the social and political context of knowledge about the landscape, plants, and agriculture in traditional communities and in science. Bringing social and political issues to the forefront of discussions about knowledge was new to many students. Chase (2002) notes that middleclass, mainstream students in environmental science classes have little knowledge of social oppression, political economy, or the history of people's movements in this or other countries. Unfortunately, critical social consciousness about the history of westward expansion tends to be couched in grand narratives (e.g., Lewis and Clark, the railroad, the Gold Rush), rather than a focus on the piecemeal erosion of the West, the progressive ecological and economic devastation in small communities that Marc Reisner (1986) describes in *Cadillac Desert* or the local dis-

place-ment of traditional knowledge that Devon Peña (1998, 2002) documents in northern New Mexico.

As Peña (1998) advocates, we became "subversive kin" through emphasis of local knowledge; we challenged the dominant ideologies and underlying assumptions of conventional academic research. As we spoke of our relationship with places and knowledge, students spoke their identities, their sense of self in the context of science. Through this research experience I became aware of how a unitary concept of identity fails to capture the multiple forms of self-identification and the many locations through which students move. Another way to think about identity is in terms of "narratives of location" proposed by Anthias (2002). In answer to the question—Where do I belong?—Anthias argues that we should be seeking narratives of location from students as they interpret their place in the world. "The narrative is both a story about who and what we identify with . . . and is also a wider story about our practices and the practices of others, including wider social practices and how we experience them" (Anthias, 2002, p. 498).

The course revealed how students' identities or "narratives of location" are linked to physical places whose geography and community are rapidly changing. Our class provided opportunities for them to re-establish relationships and "re-inhabit" locations. Compelling lessons emerged as students shared their own cultural experiences with traditional knowledge. Similarly, Barton (2002) says she values "a sense of place" in her research and education because of the need for students "*to have their places in the world recognized as rich and powerful places of living and learning*" (p. 25, emphasis in the original).

In our discussions, students offered examples of their ability to appraise the landscape of Western science in this uncertain post-9/11 world. The expansion of the classroom to include farms, kitchens, urban markets, and riparian systems created a forum for students to analyze, envision, and construct new ways to understand the meaning of "place" and its relationship to science. Students welcomed the opportunity to raise cultural, social, and political issues—although these conversations were demanding and complex for all of us. The ethnobotany class created what Turnbull (1997) calls a third space: "An interstitial space, a space in which local knowledge traditions can be reframed, decentred and the social organization of trust can be negotiated" (p. 560). The ethnobotany seminar offered a space in which students were able to construct new hybrid knowledge, blending local information, their experiences, and Western science. And, students were able to reflect on and compose new narratives of themselves within science.

Place is a physical construct, but too, place is imbued with symbolism connecting knowledge, memories, and identities. And while increasing mobility has been used to characterize these technological, fast-paced times we live in, we nevertheless have local attachments. We all have daily spaces that we move through and occupy, that remain significant in our lives. These places reflect our relationship with larger institutions that structure our activities, ways of living, and ways of thinking. Likewise, the places in which education occurs are not neutral spaces. Our schools are imbued with rules and regulations that reflect and reinforce authority, structure our relationships with students, influence our pedagogy, and frame our ways of knowing.

> Indeed, the central struggle . . . is creating new spaces of interacting, knowing, and being teachers and students to engage in epistemological and ontological critiques that will help to transform their understandings of the place and practice in creating a more just world. (Barton, 2002, p. 18)

The ethnobotany class was a dynamic experience for the students, our guest speakers, and myself as instructor. These three semesters have reassured me that a transformative curriculum emerges when radically shifting science to be placed-based. Using an ethnographic approach to teaching science that incorporates diverse cultural perspectives supports students in their cultural and cognitive "border-crossing" into Western science.

For me, as a fledgling instructor, the challenges confronted in this class were many, and emphasized skills that reminded me of anthropological fieldwork rather than teaching in the classroom. The logistics of planning fieldtrips and inviting speakers meant constant improvisation. When inviting guest speakers to the classroom, I found that I had to build trust among community members who had every reason to be suspicious of the university. Learning how to moderate tensions in discussion required me to hone my listening skills for nuances in students' language and meaning, and required me to draw stories from students that helped clarify their meaning-making. I learned that a co-instructor is ideal in this setting to assist in moving the dialogue toward mutual understanding and to provide a perspective from another academic discipline. In many ways, this article fails to capture the excitement and the unpredictability of a place-based class session where the students took on the responsibility of authoring knowledge. When we mixed our lives, place, and science together, we are rewarded with the alchemy of education—a transformation that is expansive and unbounded.

Science should never be presented as objective, abstract, or detached, but has a place in students' lives and in the daily lives of people beyond the university walls. By examining knowledge that emerges from place and emphasizing the local through anthropological methods, we can recreate science that is sustaining and moves the university towards social justice.

ACKNOWLEDGMENTS

I would like to thank the students in my classes for graciously sharing their lives and insights with me, and with one another. My writing and research for this study was enriched through many conversations with my colleagues. I thank Jenella Loye, Vickie Peck, Melanie Moses, David Gruenewald, Lorie Hammond, Richard Fraiser, Sharon Nichols, and Deborah Tippins who each shared with me their "sense of place" and new theoretical approaches to science and cultural studies in education.

REFERENCES

Anderson, G. L., Herr, K., & Nihlen, A. S. (1994). *Studying your own school: An educator's guide to qualitative practitioner research.* Thousand Oaks, CA: Corwin Press.

Anthias, F. (2002). Where do I belong? Narrating collective identity and translocational positionality. *Ethnicities, 2*(4), 491–514.

Apple, M. W. (1999). *Power, meaning, and identity: Essays in critical educational studies.* New York: Peter Lang.

Balick, M. J., & Cox, P. A. (1996). *Plants, people, and culture: The science of ethnobotany.* New York: Scientific American Library.

Barton, A. C. (1998). *Feminist science education.* New York: Teachers College Press.

Barton, A. C. (2002). Urban science education studies: A commitment to equity, social justice and a sense of place. *Studies in Science Education, 38,* 1–38.

Blades, D. W. (2002). The simulacra of science education. In J. A. Weaver, M. Morris, & P. Appelbaum (Eds.), *(Post) modern science (education): Propositions and alternatives paths* (pp. 57–94). New York: Peter Lang.

Bohrer, V. L. (1986). Guideposts in ethnobotany. *Journal of Ethnobiology, 6*(1), 27–43.

Chase, S. (2002). Changing the nature of environmental studies: Teaching environmental justice to "mainstream" students. In J. Adamson, M. M. Evans, & R. Stein (Eds.), *The environmental justice reader: Politics, poetics, and pedagogy* (pp. 350–367). Tucson: University of Arizona Press.

Clandinin, D. J., & Connelly, F. M. (2000). *Narrative inquiry: Experience and story in qualitative research.* San Francisco: Jossey-Bass.

Cobern, W. W. (1996). Worldview theory and conceptual change in science education. *Science Education, 80*(5), 579–610.

Eisenhart, M. (2001). Educational ethnography past, present, and future: Ideas to think with. *Educational Researcher, 30*(8), 16–27.

Freire, P. (1970). *Pedagogy of the oppressed.* New York: Continuum.

Freire, P., & Macedo, D. P. (1987). *Literacy: Reading the word and the world.* Westport, CT: Bergin & Garvey.

Foucault, M. (1977). *Discipline and punish: The birth of the prison.* New York: Vintage Books.

Gieryn, T. F. (1999). *Cultural boundaries of science: Credibility on the line.* Chicago, IL: University of Chicago Press.

Gruenewald, D. A. (2003a). The best of both worlds: A critical pedagogy of place. *Educational Researcher, 32*(4), 3–12.

Gruenewald, D. A. (2003b). Foundations of place: A multidisciplinary framework for place-conscious education. *American Educational Research Journal, 40*(3), 619–654.

Harding, S. (1991). *Whose science? Whose knowledge? Thinking from women's lives.* Ithaca, NY: Cornell University Press.

Harshberger, J. W. (1896). The purposes of ethno-botany. *Botanical Gazette, 21*(3), 146–154.

Kaomea, J. (2003). Reading erasures and making the familiar strange: Defamiliarizing methods for research in formerly colonized and historically oppressed communities. *Educational Researcher, 32*(2), 14–25.

Kumashiro, K. K. (2001). "Posts" perspectives on anti-oppressive education in social studies, english, mathematics, and science classrooms. *Educational Researcher, 30*(3), 3–12.

LeCompte, M. D. (2000). Analyzing qualitative data. *Theory into Practice, 39*(3), 146–154.

Lefebvre, H. (1991). *The production of space.* Oxford: Blackwell Publishers.

Levinson, B. A., & Holland, D. C. (1996). The cultural production of the educated person: An introduction. In *The cultural production of the educated person: Critical ethnographies of schooling and local practices* (pp. 1–54). Albany: State of New York Press.

Merriam, S. B. (1998). *Qualitative research and case study applications in education.* Revised and expanded. San Francisco: Jossey-Bass.

Moll, L. C., Amanti, C., Neff, D., & Gonzalez, N. (1992). Funds of knowledge for teaching: Using a qualitative approach to connect homes and classrooms. *Theory into Practice, 31*(2), 132–141.

Nabhan, G. P., Pynes, P., & Joe, T. (2002). Safeguarding species, languages, and cultures in the time of diversity loss: From the Colorado plateau to global hotspots. *Annals of the Missouri Botanical Gardens, 89*(2), 164–175.

Parezo, N. J. (1993). Mathilda Coxe Stevenson: Pioneer ethnologist. In N. J. Parezo (Ed.), *Hidden scholars: Women anthropologists and the Native American Southwest* (pp. 38–62). Albuquerque: University of New Mexico Press.

Peña, D. G. (1998). Los animalitos: Culture, ecology, and the politics of place in the upper Rio Grande. In D. G. Peña (Ed.), *Chicano culture, ecology, and politics: subversive kin* (pp. 25–57). Tucson: University of Arizona Press.

Peña, D. G. (2002). Endangered landscapes and disappearing peoples? Identity, place, and community in ecological politics. In J. Adamson, M. M. Evans, & R. Stein (Eds.), *The environmental justice reader: Politics, poetics, and pedagogy* (pp. 58–81). Tucson: University of Arizona Press.

Posey, D. A., Frechione, J., & Eddins, J. (1984). Ethnoecology as applied anthropology in Amazonian development. *Human Organization, 43*, 95–107.

Rea, A. (1997). *At the desert's green edge: An ethnobotany of the Gila River Pima.* Tucson: University of Arizona Press.

Reisner, M. (1986). *Cadillac desert: The American West and its disappearing water.* New York: Penguin Books.

Schultes, R. E., & Raffauf, R. F. (1990). *The healing forest: Medicinal and toxic plants of the northwest Amazonia.* Portland, OR: Dioscorides Press.

Sibley, D. (1995). *The geographies of exclusion: Society and exclusion in the west.* London: Routledge.

Smith, L. T. (1999). *Decolonizing methodologies: Research and indigenous peoples.* London: Zed Books.

Spindler, G. D. (1955). *Education and anthropology.* Stanford, CA: Stanford University Press.

Spindler, G. D., & Spindler, L. (1982). Roger Harker and Schoenhausen: From familiar to strange and back again. In G. Spindler (Ed.), *Doing the ethnography of schooling: Educational Anthropology in Action* (pp. 20–46). New York: Holt, Rinehart, and Winston.

Spindler, G. D., & Spindler, L. (1993). The processes of culture and person: Cultural therapy and culturally diverse schools. In P. Phelan & A. L. Davidson (Eds.), *Renegotiating cultural diversity in American schools* (pp. 27–51). New York: Teachers College Press.

Strauss, A. L., & Corbin, J. M. (1990). *Basics of qualitative research: Grounded theory procedures and techniques*. Newbury Park, CA: Sage.

Theobald, P., & Curtiss, J. (2000). Communities as curricula. *Forum for Applied Research and Public Policy, 15*(1), 106–111.

Turnbull, D. (1997). Reframing science and other local knowledge traditions. *Futures, 29*(6), 551–562.

Turner, N. J., Ignace, M. B., & Ignace, R. (2000). Traditional ecological knowledge and wisdom of aboriginal peoples in British Columbia. *Ecological Applications, 10*(5), 1275–1287.

Wellington, J., & Osborne, J. (2001). *Language and literacy in science education*. Buckingham, UK: Open University Press.

Wolcott, H. (1999). *Ethnography: A way of seeing*. Walnut Creek, CA: AltaMira Press.

Vygotsky, L. S. (1986). *Thought and language*. Cambridge, MA: MIT Press.

11

Community-Based Science Education Research: Narratives From a Filipino Barangay

Sharon E. Nichols
University of Alabama

Deborah J. Tippins
University of Georgia

Lourdes Morano
Purita Bilbao
Tessie Barcenal
West Visayas State University

Sharon ("Sherry") E. Nichols is an Associate Professor at the University of Alabama in Tuscaloosa, Alabama. In 1998, she and Deborah Tippins initiated collaborative research with colleagues at WVSU in the Philippines. She teaches elementary and secondary science teacher "methods," technology, sociocultural issues in teaching, and qualitative research courses for undergraduate and graduate students. Her research interests include culturally relevant pedagogy, reflective "tools" for science teacher learning, narrative inquiry, and post-structuralist feminist pedagogy and research. She is currently exploring ways to extend notions of community-based science education developed from her work in the Philippines, in a local re-segregated school community of Alabama. Her family nickname, "the yard child," is fitting as she is most likely to be found gardening or swimming when not working at the university campus.

Deborah J. Tippins is a Professor of Science Education at the University of Georgia at Athens, Georgia, where she serves as program head for Elementary Science. During the 2001–2 academic year she was a Fulbright Scholar in the Philippines, attached to the Regional Science Teaching Center of West Visayas State University in Iloilo City, Philippines. She currently serves as co-director of a Fulbright Partnership Project in the Philippines centered on the transformation of science teacher preparation. Her research interests include case-based teaching and learning and sociocultural dimensions of science teaching and learning. In her spare time she likes to play tennis, travel, and take her dog, Samantha, for long walks in the woods.

Purita P. Bilbao is a Professor of Science Education at West Visayas State University in Iloilo City, the Philippines. She currently serves as the WVWU Vice-President for Research and Planning. From 1996–2001, she was the Dean for the College of Education at WVSU. She teachers elementary physics and biology methods courses and graduate level research courses. Purita served as the Director of the *Third Elementary Project* in the Philippines and is immediate Past-President of the Philippine Association for Teacher Education. Her research interests include assessment of teacher and student learning, case-based pedagogy, and action research in teacher education. Many will attest to her exceptional eloquence as a writer, speaker, and ballroom dancer.

Lourdes Morano is a Professor of Science Education at West Visayas State University at Iloilo City, the Philippines. She currently serves as Director of the Regional Science Teaching Center for West Visayas and teaches undergraduate and graduate biology and environmental education. She is responsible for coordinating professional development workshops for teachers across the West Visayas region, often traveling herself to perform workshops such as *Skywatch Night* and *Re-use/Re-new*. Her research interests focus on ways teachers' traditional ecological knowledge influences science teaching and learning, and community-based science education. Lourdes is a native of Antique, the province in which this study took place. WVSU's campus features a number of lovely goldfish pond areas, evidence of her aquaculture expertise.

Tessie Barcenal is an Associate Professor in the College of Education Division of Early Childhood and Special Education at West Visayas State University in Iloilo City, the Philippines. For 5 years, she served as Principal of the WVSU Elementary Integrated Laboratory School. She has taught elementary science for a number of years and encourages the teaching of science in outdoor learning environments. Presently, she is the Project Coordinator of the Graduate Diploma Courses in Special Education. Her research interests include second and third language science learning, and community-based immersion science teacher preparation. During school holidays, she eagerly travels to nearby islands in search of occupants for the butterfly "palace" located at the entrance to the WVSU Laboratory School.

This study uses a narrative inquiry approach to explore the sociocultural context of science teaching and learning in a rural barangay community of the Philippines. Specifically, the study examines the use of memory banking as a mediational tool for understanding science education as a cultural practice. Memory banking was initially developed as a botanical preservation tool to complement conventional practices of gene banking with respect to collection and documentation of knowledge, social practices and technologies associated with the cultivation, harvesting and uses of traditional "heirloom seeds." In this study, we adapted the concept of memory banking to fit our interests in creating a community-based approach to science teaching and learning. Specific and schematic narrative templates are used to represent three emergent themes: The Place of Place, Out of Balance, and Return to Our Roots. This study holds implications for practitioners and science teacher educators contemplating a vision of science teaching and learning which challenges a narrative of standardized science education reform.

INTRODUCTION: SOCIOCULTURAL RESEARCH IN SCIENCE EDUCATION

Much of the research in science education has focused on psychological analyses of learning, specifically attending to issues of conceptual understanding by individual students. More recently, researchers have begun to explore learning as a socially-mediated phenomenon (Greeno, Collins, & Resnick, 1996; Rogoff & Lave, 1984; Salomon, 1993; Vygotsky, 1978), thus taking into account the ways learning may be influenced by social means (Cobb, 1994; Lemke, 2001). Accordingly, sociocultural research strives "to explicate the relationships between human action, on the one hand, and the cultural, institutional, and historical situations in which this action occurs, on the other" (Wertsch, Río, & Alvarez, 1995, p. 11). Framed in terms of science education, Jay Lemke asserts:

> The unit of analysis in research on science learning should not be limited to studies of the Cartesian mind of individual students, rather science education needs to be examined as symbolic activity enacted in a material context and a socioculturally specific community. (2001, p. 307)

For the most part, studies in science education have focused on creating "science communities" wherein the goals and practices of science education are intended to reproduce canonical science knowledge and/or scientific practices. What happens, however, when students leave the science classroom community wherein the discursive practices and knowledge of science may not be central to making sense of everyday knowledge and actions? What is *meaningful* science education in relation to a student's lifeworld beyond the classroom? Who has the knowledge and agency to determine what is regarded as meaningful practices of science education?

Researchers undertaking sociocultural analyses of science education have ventured into students' lifeworlds beyond science classrooms—becoming involved in places such as lunchrooms (Seiler, 2001), their homes and neighborhoods (Aikenhead, 1996; Hammond, 2001), and after-school science programs (Barton, 1998; Fusco, 2001). Angela Barton's (1998) reference to creating "cultural practices" of science teaching and learning, in our view, captures the sociocultural perspective we have brought to this study of science education in the Philippines. Drawing upon critical and feminist theoretical perspectives, Dana Fusco describes the following as tensions associated with viewing science education as a cultural practice:

1. Science is a paradigm that includes a set of practices for describing, explaining, and understanding the physical and social world. Science is not the only paradigm for understanding the world nor is it so fossilized a practice that it cannot include multiple perspectives and understandings.
2. Scientific discoveries (the big ideas) are the products of science, not the totality of science.
3. It is not what students learn, but how they learn that is fundamental to a relevant and quality education.
4. In a practicing culture of science learning, the production of science (and science like) performances is a creative extension of students' lives, cultures, and communities. (2001, p. 862–863).

Our work in the Philippines has similarly focused on envisioning "community-based science education" such that the basis for practicing science education would extend from the knowledge, practices, history, and needs of a rural community.

CONTEXT OF THE STUDY

This study is part of a 3-year collaborative project in which university science teacher educators, from the United States and the Philippines, have worked together to enhance our practices of science teacher education and research. In July 2000, West Visayas State University created a remote student teacher placement site in the barangay of Casay. Six elementary teachers and one high school teacher from Casay joined the university research team to explore ways to build community in science teacher professional development and classroom science teaching practices. The Casay Environmental Education and Indigenous Studies Center was established as an offshoot of this research endeavor.

The research took place in Casay, a barangay (small town) on the island of Panay in the Philippines. The road to Casay is rough and dusty and oftentimes bridges made of wood are destroyed or wiped out whenever strong winds, heavy rains and typhoons visit the place. Casay has a total population of 1,278 whose local citizens are predominantly Catholic. The majority of residents in the barangay are fishermen and rice farmers, with other professionals such as teachers, seamen (those working on foreign boats), and engineers.

In this collaborative research project, Casay Elementary School has served as a nexus for understanding science education as it is practiced by teachers in the barangay. The school is situated on a bluff overlooking the Sulu Sea, surrounded by rice fields and directly adjacent to the Catholic Church; the church oversees the operation of a private high school, and one teacher participated in the project from this site.

Casay Elementary School began as a one-room school building, but was subsequently destroyed during World War II. Following the Japanese occupation, community members worked to reconstruct Casay by hosting beauty and popularity contests and soliciting funds needed to build new facilities, including Casay Elementary. Today, Casay Elementary School is home to more than 400 pupils and 14 teachers. In this context, triple linguistic conventions involving interactions of the local Kiniraya dialect, the national Filipino language (Tagalog), and English create unique dilemmas for science teachers. Furthermore, teachers in this community wrestle with tensions of preserving indigenous knowledge and practices as economic, social, and cultural changes are being incorporated into the daily lifeworld of Casaynons. Casay, like that of many rural barangays across the Philippines, is in transition as traditional values are continually being challenged by new ideas brought about by modernization and the complexity of today's world.

In this study, memory banking served as a tool to enable our team to collaboratively learn about science teaching as a sociocultural practice in Casay. We refer to tool not as an intrusive device, but rather as Wertsch (1998) describes tools as serving a *mediational function*. Memory banking served as a way for teachers to generate accounts that represented sociohistorical referents they deemed important to life in their community. Several key questions guided our thinking as our team explored memory banking as a research approach and as a means for envisioning community-based science teaching and learning: 1) How might memory banking help us learn about life in the community of Casay? 2) In what ways could memory banking contribute to the generation of a community-based approach to science teacher professional development? Given the cultural diversity of the research team, we also wanted to explore a way to write about our research "findings" in ways that would avoid narratives that privilege conceptions of science education generated from outside the Philippines (e.g., the United States). Lastly, throughout our work, we continued to reflect on the ways this study held implications for our thinking about our practices of science education beyond the Philippines.

MEMORY BANKING AS A RESEARCH TOOL: THEORETICAL PERSPECTIVES

Virginia Nazarea (1998), a Filipino and cultural anthropologist, developed "memory banking" as a botanical preservation tool to complement conventional practices of gene banking. Memory banking involves the collection and documentation of knowledge, social practices, and technologies associated with the cultivation, harvesting and uses of traditional "heirloom" seeds. In addition to Nazarea's conception of memory banking as a tool for historical preservation, we drew on the work of Sergiovanni (2000) to understand memory as a dimension of community building. Sergiovanni frames learning communities in terms of relationships involving a sense of place, mind and heart, kinship and memory. For Sergiovanni memory provides community members with enduring images of school, learning and life and "sustains parents, teachers and students when times are tough, connects them when they are not physically present, and provides them with a history for creating sense and meaning" (1994, p. 67). Thus, the work of both Nazarea and Sergiovanni helped us envision memory banking as a tool for understanding a community-based approach to science teaching and as a relationship-enabling tool to encourage a participatory approach (Green et al., 1995) to professional development. In this sense, our use of memory banking, as described in the methods section that follows, stands in stark contrast to the colonizing practices which have characterized educational reform in the Philippines since the early 1900s (see Bilbao et al., 2002).

METHODS OF THE STUDY

Traditionally, research in the social sciences has sought to describe, analyze, and explain the phenomena of interest. In the earlier phases of this longitudinal study, we used case-based pedagogy and photoessay to characterize and understand the relationship of school science to community knowledge and beliefs. In the process, we became aware of pressing environmental dilemmas that were impacting the quality of life in Casay. The group wanted to take action to deal with these issues, but what sort of action was needed? And what assumptions would influence our decisions about action-taking? We were conscious that Filipino education had been colonized by Western outsiders in the past, and that present-day practices of everyday life were subject to the consumerist influences of the global marketplace. Thus our concern was to engage in action research with the intent to practice science education as a community-mediated activity. We began to envision our work as participatory action research—social inquiry inspired by ideas of trust, autonomy, and social responsibility, and characterized by the need to plan, implement and enact change. Green and colleagues describe participatory action research as "a systematic investigation with the collaboration of those affected by the issues being studied for the purposes of education and taking action or effecting social change" (1995, p. 12). Thus, in the third year of this study, as we embraced a more participatory form of research, our roles as researchers became that of co-participants in the development of the Casay Environmental Education Center.

Study Background and Participants

The Casay Research Team was comprised of six elementary teachers, one high school teacher, three student teachers, the barangay captain, and six science teacher educators—four from the Philippines, and two from the United States.[1] Beginning in July 2001, student teachers and teachers engaged in writing cases about cultural dilemmas they perceived relevant to their science teaching. A number of the teacher-generated cases highlighted serious economic struggles, the depletion and destruction of natural resources, and respect for practices of elders in the community. Many of these cases represented disconnections between science teaching and the practices of Casaynons outside of school. Group discussion and reflection on the teachers' cases provided insight into various cultural practices and the stance of science education in Casay's classrooms (Nichols et al., 2001).

To further explore dilemmas portrayed through the cases, the student teachers and teachers developed photoessays around the theme of "science education and our community" (Nichols et al., 2001). Consistent with results of the case writing and reflection, many of the images and stories teachers represented in their photoessay entries highlighted tensions between environmental and technological changes, and economic impacts. The photo-

---

[1]Pseudonyms are used in references to all persons quoted in this study with the exception of the Casay Research Team members.

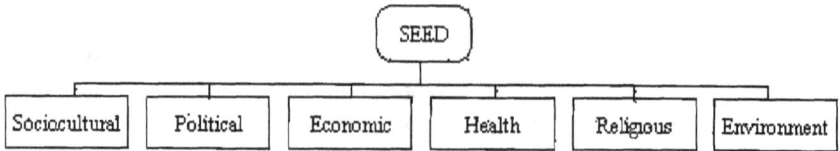

FIG. 11.1. Memory bank chart template.

essays provided a means for us to learn about relationships teachers' perceived between science education and indigenous practices of their community.

The case writing and photoessay activities served as the beginnings for developing our collaborative relationship, and provided contextual insights about science education with respect to life in Casay. Memory banking extended our research, enabling us to explore in-depth practices that have historically influenced life in the community, while at the same time raising questions with implications relevant to the future of science education in Casay.

Data Generation Through Memory Banking

When the Research Team initially learned about Virginia Nazarea's (1998) work with memory banking, we brainstormed how this tool might be adapted to our interests in creating a community-based approach science teaching. Although heirloom seeds were central to Nazarea's (1998) study, we used "seed" in a metaphorical sense to represent and describe places, practices, artifacts, and ways of thinking that characterized life in Casay—in the past and/ or present. Drawing on Beyer and Apple's (1988) conception of curricular interests,[2] the team created a template (see Fig. 11.1) to explore various dimensions of community seeds: Political, Sociocultural, Economic, Religious, Health, and Environment.

The group initially selected the seed of *panu-ob tuob* (the burning of rubbish to drive away evil spirits associated with health problems) to practice data construction. Through group conversations, we referred to dimensions of the seed template to construct a memory bank chart about this practice (see Fig. 11.2). This sample activity subsequently encouraged the identification of additional seeds. After practicing data generation techniques (e.g. development of interview protocols, interviewing skills, audiotape recording

---

[2]These categories were inspired by Beyer and Apple's (1988) conception of curriculum critique as framed within eight questions about decision-making: which included: epistemology, politics, economics, ideology, technical, aesthetics, ethics, and historical concerns.

Panu-ob Tuob and Paaluba-ob Practices performed to cleanse and drive away evil spirits					
Sociocultural	Political	Economic	Health	Religious	Environment
New-born babies, nursing and lactating mothers, adults and anybody who feels the need for such can request	Well-known popular practice People being served treat their services as debt of gratitude	Spends less-don't need to buy the materials to be used Hilot/palteras are paid less compared to medical practitioners	Traditional way of steaming for rapid healing of lacerations Steam drives away mosquito-carriers of dengue fever and malaria Heat from the Paal-ob creates sweating, making one feel "suwabe" or clean fresh	Use incense, holy water and candles because we believe "Light" produced by Panu-ob/ Paaluba-ob is God himself During mass the incense symbolizes Jesus as a true Priest	Continuous preservation of materials, specifically plants because of their need Example: Neem tree drives away mosquitoes within the area

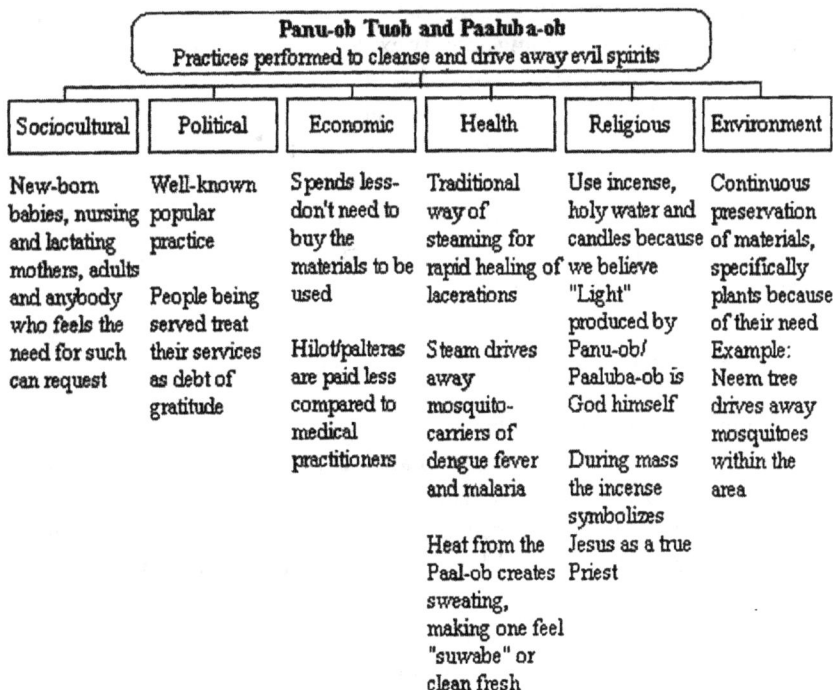

FIG. 11.2.   Panu-ob tuob and paaluba-ob memory bank chart.

techniques), team members divided into pairs to conduct community interviews and gather artifacts that would help them learn more about a seed of their choice. After spending several weeks gathering information about seeds, the Research Team re-assembled to share results of their Memory banking. Team members presented Memory Banks, which included: memory bank charts, artifacts (e.g., fishing net, coconut ladle), and performance of actions (e.g., songs, dances) that were important to understanding the seeds. As the team members discussed the memory banks and related issues, an awareness of environmental tensions in the community moved to the forefront. Team members asked questions and shared understandings of scientific concepts underlying environmental condition in the community. At this point, the intersection of historical insights and environmental consciousness became a centerpiece for understanding community-based science education as a socioculturally constituted practice.

It is important to note that during this phase of our study, team members were engaged in various data-generating activities, while collaborating with community members to develop the Casay Environmental Education Center.

This larger scope of activities yielded data sources that informed our work, including: a community mapping activity exploring the "place of Casay," development of environmental cases linked to Memory Bank charts and the design of classroom pedagogical approaches using the memory banking process. In summary, primary data sources for this phase of the study included: memory bank charts, transcripts of research team discussions, teacher generated cases and narratives, and team member field notes. Secondary data sources included: Casay community map drawings, transcripts of community interviews, and curriculum artifacts such as lesson plans.

Data Analysis Across Narratives

After completing the memory bank presentations, the research team engaged in coding of transcripts to introduce team members to this standard practice of qualitative analysis. With appreciation for the complexity and richness of the data, we used selective or *focused coding* (Charmaz, 2002) to sort, synthesize, and conceptualize the still-large volumes of data by adopting frequently appearing initial codes. Independently at first and then together as a group we color coded data sets with respect to our larger research questions. The coding process lead to the identification of 120 repeating codes, most of which were merged under 12 categories such as environmental awareness, environmental change, environmental practices, legal ordinances, and supernatural beliefs. At this point, it seemed several categories could be drawn together under one theme, however questions were raised about data that might be used to justify a particular category or theme but which could also convey interpretations under another theme. We also felt it was inaccurate to represent the data analyses as if the group shared a singular interpretation, for sometimes it seemed important to convey moments of deliberation that had emerged during group discussions and in the course of data analysis.

We recognize that all data are incomplete and partial versions of life, and that through our data collection and analysis, "we produce only versions of the social world," note Atkinson and Coffey (1996, p. 15). Even through triangulation, data cannot be aggregated to form a complete picture. In fact, coding and categorization, the usual tools of qualitative data analysis, have been associated with a culture of fragmentation that, while necessary to handle large volumes of data, imply a mechanistic process that does not adequately reflect the holistic, contextual nature of the data. To address this concern, Coffey and Atkinson recommend analyzing data from several viewpoints using different methods, which serve to affirm, rather than deny, the diversity of social phenomena.

We turned to narrative analysis to provide an alternative means for our team to recount stories embedded in the memory banks, and our group discussions. Narrative provides a mode of communication resonant with human experience as storied form allows for re-presentation of the dynamic and fluid wholeness of events as these are felt and ordered in the researcher's consciousness (Hellmann, 1981; Zeller, 1995). Thus, narrative analysis enabled our team to look between and beyond the data itself to the ways in which storied accounts reflexively informed our understandings about life in Casay, environmental practices, and our notions about science education as a cultural practice. Ultimately, our intent was not to establish a causal relationship between local narratives and science education, but rather to understand science education as a practice mediated by community narratives. Identifying our research methodology as a narrative endeavor recognized the varied ideologies and experiences voiced in our group discussions. After multiple re-readings of our meeting transcripts, memory banks, and personal journals, the team worked to reconstruct narratives salient to the guiding questions of this study. Some narratives were drawn from data as stories told by participants, whereas others were developed from events composed in storied form by team members.

At this point, we could see two different types of narratives had emerged from our analysis. One set of narratives portrayed community life, while others explored intersecting ideas generated through our group discussions. Wertsch's categories of *specific narratives* and *schematic narrative templates* provided a useful means for rethinking how we might re-present interpretations produced through both our formalistic and narrative approaches to data analysis. Wertsch (2002) characterizes *specific narratives* as featuring specific settings, characters, and events, whereas *schematic narrative templates* explore generalized, abstract forms which underpin a range of specific narratives. Thus, in the section which follows, we have used Wertsch's narrative categories to organize our presentation of results for this study—beginning with portraitures of local life then shifting to our contemplations about practicing community-based science education.

INSIGHTS GAINED: CULTURAL NARRATIVES MEDIATING SCIENCE EDUCATION IN CASAY

Memory Bank Narrative 1: A Fisherman's Story

The research team regularly visited the shoreline of Casay and spent several nights at a beach cottage. During these excursions, the team had opportunities to observe local residents at work and enjoy leisure time along the shore.

Because the natural resources of the sea are central to the lives of Casaynons, the narratives of fishermen seemed an appropriate beginning place to explore practices perhaps relevant to science education.

BLESSINGS FROM THE SEA

Two research team members, both teachers of Casay Elementary, walked toward a small *nipa* (bamboo) hut on the shore. A fisherman appeared to be working with a fishing net under the shade of a *kamalig* (small A-framed shelter made of bamboo). Team members greeted the man, who quickly returned a smile. With brief introductions, the team members informed the fisherman that they were from Casay Elementary School and were interviewing community members about their various livelihoods. The fisherman eagerly agreed to answer their questions, saying: "Although I do not have any children of my own at the school, I am ready to help whenever the school calls with a need." With a few prompts, the fisherman talked about his life by the sea . . .

My name is Mario Abuso. I'm repairing my *buldos* (fishing net). You can see my wife, Celia, over there in the *maría loca* (the inter-tidal zone) among the rocks searching for *panginhason* (mollusks). The best time to do *pankinhason* (mollusk searching) is during full moon and at *hunasan* (low tide) when the seashore is wide and the panginhason are abundant. We use the panginhason for so many purposes. If my wife can find panginhason, we might eat them for dinner with rice. Mostly, my wife hopes to find shells which she can burn and pound to make *mamâ* (a lime-based food preservative made from shells). If she finds beautiful shells, she might carve those into earrings to sell at the market. I doubt she will find so many—these days the mollusks are harder to find. In the past, we could find many shells near the sandy shore, around the coral reefs and among the rocks. My *ugangan* (mother-in-law) has said that when the Japanese were here during the wartime, women chewed betel nut, tobacco, and mamâ as this combination would create a red mixture in the mouth. According to community folk, this protected women from physical abuse by Japanese soldiers as the red spit was mistaken for blood, a sign of tuberculosis. At one time, we used shells for bartering; we can still do this today, but only among my friends on the shore and at the Hermie *Tiange* (a small road-side store) on the road nearby. Anyway, if my wife gets frustrated doing panginhas, she can help me with my buldos net once I return it to the water.

The buldos is an easy net one can use alone to catch milkfish fry. A blue, lightweight net is wrapped across the large "V" made of bamboo arms. You can see here that I need to re-wrap a part of the net onto the bamboo frame. There is a pail placed where the bamboo arms come together. I push the net from the narrow end across the top of the water and milkfish swimming near the surface are caught up in the net. I simply lift up the net and the fish fall down into the pail. If Celia is nearby, I can call for her to bring me an empty pail when mine is full of milkfish. In this area, there are many coral reefs which are natural homes for fish. Also, there is a meeting place where water from the river joins water from the sea, and that is the very place where milkfish live well.

I have another net, the *sahid* which I will use if we see many fish swimming. The sahid is much larger than the buldos. It requires that I use the boat and call for others to help spread out the sahid and to pull it through the water. If I should make a call for help—rich, poor, old and young will come to pull the net and sort the catch. It is tradition that anyone who helps to work the sahid is given a portion of the catch—at least 10% of the fish, or maybe all, are divided for free. The sharing and cooperative work is a good way to maintained and renewed friendships! The sahid does not belong to me—it is owned by Mr. Pelayo, a former mayor of Anini-y. The fish from this place are considered the most fresh. I can sell them for a high price in Iloilo! These days, however, we have great competition for fish as the larger motorized boats off-shore can take a larger catch each day. Our catches near shore tend to have many fingerlings, which are worth very little at the marketplace. Although fishing from the shore is getting harder as the fish are becoming less abundant, we know God will continue to provide for our needs!

Memory Bank Narrative 2: Rich Impressions from the Marketplace

Within a 5 minute walk from any home or workplace in Casay, one is likely to find a tiange stocked with items to meet the sundry needs of local residents. The tiange might be a small booth extended from a home, or a shop with grocer's shelves, and a glass display case. The tiange owner will stock items at the request of regular customers; the tiange also becomes the gateway for new products to reach the community. The adage: "You can find the world in the tiange" aptly describes these small barangay stores. Our exploration of a memory bank about "Tiange," documented and shared by a teacher who owned and operated a tiange near Casay Elementary School, simultaneously portrayed continuity and change in the community, and provided a context to envision relevant science inquiry teaching.

THE TIANGE STORE— A SMALL WORLD OF CHANGE

As the school day draws to a close, my grade four pupil's gather up their book bags and find their younger siblings to begin their journey home. As they walk along the beach, or balance on the terraces of the rice fields, they take their time, knowing that many chores probably await them at home! I, too, quickly gather my teaching aides and walk down the road towards the family tiange. The *tiange*, a small store, is where I work every day after school to earn money to supplement my teaching salary. As a single mother of five, I find that my net monthly 3000 peso teaching salary is barely enough to put food on the table. By the way, I am Maribel Elana Cordova, a resident of Casay and grade four teacher at Casay Elementary School.

Today, as I approach the tiange, I see it in a new light. I'm beginning to think about different ways that the tiange might serve as a place for teaching science. Our action research team has adopted the motto "we make the strange familiar and the familiar strange." Even though I work in the tiange everyday, somehow, today it appears strange! I'm sure it's because of the memory banking process we have been using in our research team meetings. In one of our meetings the tiange was identified as an important place or seed of our barangay. At first glance, the tiange appears to be just a small store that sells a few daily necessities. However, as our team began to discuss the tiange in terms of political, economic, religious, sociocultural and environmental/health issues, I began to recognize the many opportunities it held for involving students in science inquiry. Take, for example, issues related to community health. It seems that the demand for junk food increases every day. In the past, we sold natural foods such as fresh mangoes, finger bananas, rice cakes, *tuba* (fermented drink made from the young coconut), and basic staples such as rice, salt, sugar, soaps, and various medicinal herbs. The rice cakes and other foods used to be wrapped in banana leaves. Recently, young and old alike are asking us to sell chips, candy, and soft drinks. These new foods are changing the nutritional practices of the community, and their plastic wrappers, containers, and aluminum cans are contributing to problems of waste disposal. Likewise, the tiange, always a source of medicinal herbs, now also carries a supply of antibiotics. Since the majority of barangay members can not afford the money or time to visit Western-trained doctors in the city, these antibiotics are sold without prescription.

As I enter the tiange I immediately see the Santa Niño (Christ Child), dressed in green, standing watch over our store. I am reminded that the tiange is much more than a place to buy daily necessities. It is really a part of the life-blood of our community—a gathering place where people seek out the news of the day, and a site to carry out political campaigns. The image of Buddha, displayed in all tianges for good luck, is a symbol of the tiange's Chinese origins. Like many things in the Philippines, the concept of the tiange was introduced by the Chinese in previous centuries and quickly taken up by the Filipino people. I guess nothing stays the same forever. It used to be popular for barangay folks to sit outside the tiange at the *pahuway-pahuway* (small sheltered bench area) sharing the news of the day. However, now friends often sit quietly watching television at the tiange. As people are introduced to the principles and practices of modern marketplaces, the traditional barter system which had a central role in the tiange for many years, is gradually being replaced by other means of carrying out business. For the most part, people can no longer obtain credit lines or trade personal goods at the tiange.

As evening approaches, I gather up the boxes of pins and needles from their storage place below the counter and place them on display. The pins and needles were removed from display during the afternoon, so as not to bring bad luck to the customers. All the while I am thinking about teaching my lessons for the next week. Perhaps the tiange can be a starting place for my students to investigate the nutritional value of foods. Or maybe we can examine the packaging of food products and recycling challenges of natural versus synthetic materials. I am excited about sharing these ideas with the other teachers. Perhaps they will want to join in planning some school-wide science investigations of the tiange.

Memory Bank Narrative 3: Intersecting Narratives of Home and School

Changes are taking place rapidly across the Philippines, particularly with respect to telecommunication technologies. In the span of merely 3 years, we saw cyber-cafés spring up along the streets of Iloilo (approximately a 2-hour drive from Casay). Although internet capabilities have not yet been established in Casay, it has become more common for residents to be seen texting on their cellular phones. Amidst such technological innovations, indigenous health practices such as panu-ob tuob and paalubu-ob are highly respected and sustained by citizens young and old as traditional health treatments which most members of the research team enact regularly at their homes with family members. One teacher shared a memory bank chart about panu-ob tuob and paalubu-ob, which described tensions she perceives between traditional health treatments and her classroom science instruction which debunks these indigenous practices.

PANU-OB TUOB: TRADITIONS IN TRANSITION

It is dusk on a warm, humid evening in Casay. I help my mother gather dried leaves, nine different plants and blessed palm leaves. We mix them together with rubbish and charcoal in an earthen jar. Soon we will set fire to this mixture to create a thick, incense-like smoke, being sure to place it where the smoke can escape through the thatched nipa roof. We will take my youngest boy, still an infant, and pass him through this smoke to drive away evil spirits and help him sleep soundly. This practice, known as panu-ob tuob, is the memory banking "seed" I identified as an important aspect of everyday life in our barangay. It is a popular practice performed on newborn babies every evening. Variations of this practice, known as *paalubu-ob*, are used with nursing and lactating mothers, newly miscarried or aborted mothers, or any adult who feels the need for this ritual. The individual being treated owes a debt of gratitude (*utang nga kabaraslan* in the dialect) to anyone assisting with the ritual. It is also a practice which is intricately linked to the Catholic beliefs of our community. When we carry out panu-ob tuob, we surround the child or adult with incense, holy water, and candles because we believe that the fire that is produced through this practice is God himself.

I'm Josie Legaso, a grade three teacher in our school barrio. I grew up in this barangay so I am aware of the beliefs and traditions of each family living in this community. I have experienced paobra and papukaw, some of the common rituals initiated by quack doctors. The truth is, I perform these rituals and others such as panu-ob tuob firsthand. Over the years, as I have observed the practices of the quack doctors, I have come to believe that there are many things that happen in this world that science can not explain in a rational way. In my university science teacher preparation program I have encountered the notion that all ideas must be proven through empirical evidence and theories before they can be accepted and believed as truth. These conflicting beliefs often create puzzles in my mind. I personally feel that if we only open our eyes and imagination we will see that some of the rituals introduced by our ancestors are based on truth. At other times, however, especially when I'm teaching science, I'm not sure what to believe or what to do in the classroom.

I have practiced panu-ob tuob and paalubu-ob all of my adult life, so it is a ritual that I have always just taken for granted. Now, however, the sharing that took place during our memory banking experiences opened my eyes to consider some unfamiliar aspects of this practice and how this seed might serve as a basis for creating a more relevant science curriculum. Perhaps this practice has survived over the years because of some intrinsic scientific merit. The heat and smoke associated with panu-ob tuob cause the body to sweat and may help to cleanse or rid the body of impurities. Here in our barangay where Dengue Fever is a persistent problem, the evening smoke may be a significant factor in drawing away mosquitoes. Since panu-ob tuob requires a variety of herbs, the importance of preserving these plants can not be overlooked—this is something I had never considered until our memory banking discussions.

In my grade three classroom we have been studying the effects of smoking on respiration. We used an aquarium and cigarettes to explore the effect of smoke on fish respiration. Students are now developing other investigatory projects to study this issue further. Yet there are many students like Mary Rose, who exclaimed "Ma'am, I have observed my mother performing tuob on my baby sister. And it is true, the smoke helps the baby sleep!" I just smiled and told her that there are some things we can't explain through science because they are out of control of man's world. I advised her not to inhale smoke during the practice of tuob. And I pointed out to her that the contents of cigarette smoke may be different than the smoke produced through panu-ob tuob. Even so, I know that I will go home again tomorrow night and help my mother perform tuob on my baby. I will respect her knowledge when she testifies to the fact that past experiences with tuob have been effective in driving away evil spirits. As a science teacher, I can't help but feel a bit of hypocrisy. On the one hand, I am trying to demonstrate to students through experimentation and inquiry the harmful effects of smoke. On the other hand, something deep within me wants to believe that the smoke from tuob really does have some benefit in driving away the evil spirits.

CULTURAL NARRATIVE TEMPLATES MEDIATING ENVIRONMENTAL PRACTICES AND EDUCATION

In the previous section, our analysis of *specific narratives* focused on the storied experiences of individuals as they are situated in the sociocultural lifeworld of Casay. In the next section, we move from specific analysis to an interpretation of *schematic narrative templates* that involve a more reflexive interpretation of datum to take account of the non-verbal and "invisible" aspects of tone, emotion, and diverse personal histories that the researchers brought to the study (Altheide & Johnson, 1998). The analysis of schematic narrative templates enabled us to take a more holistic and critical look at underlying tensions in our research. Accordingly, the research team generated narrative schematic templates salient to envisioning a community-based practice of science education in Casay, which are expressed as three narrative themes: *Place of Place*, *Out of Balance*, and *Return to Our Roots*.

Theme 1: "Casay—A Place of *Place*"

In this phase of the study, teachers and community members, prompted by a national mandate calling for the development of curricula to preserve indigenous knowledge and practices, drew maps to consider "what makes Casay, Casay." For the most part, the community maps depicted memories of childhood play areas, locations of natural resources (e.g., mango groves, fishing areas, river bed rocks) and sites important to barangay events (e.g., a community stage, schools, the market, a bougainvillea tree where elders sit and talk). The maps reinforce the idea that land is inextricably linked to culture, society, the human body and spirit as a pervasive expression of continuity

(McLuhn, 1994). Casay, a community which is sandwiched in between the Sulu Sea and nearby mountain ranges, has a very narrow strip of land on which to live and grow rice and other staple foods. This land is essential for growing traditional foods of the barangay. The amount of fertile land for growing rice has continued to shrink as the export demands for natural resources, especially for hardwoods and fibers such as coconut, mahogany, or buri, has facilitated erosion. The loss of land hectares, even in recent times, disrupts people's relationships with the land, an issue we discuss further under the theme—"Out of Balance."

Connections to the land are perceived to be spiritual and physical, embracing belongingness, gratitude, reciprocity, and generativity. The identities of Casaynons and their well-being are intricately linked to their land. As Lourdes explained, ". . . you plant trees on your land because it is part of your inheritance." Tess elaborated, saying: "In fact, you may plant a tree for every child of your family on your land." Like education, land is the primary inheritance parents pass down to their children. Intergenerational identity is embodied in the landscape as family ownership is signified within "the bones of the land." According to Tess, land ownership and responsibility is an individualistic practice known as the "kanya-kanya" system, whereby individuals are viewed as holding responsibility for the care of their land. However, social pressure comes into play when the land is not being used as it should to benefit the community. Thus, it was not surprising to hear that one landowner had regularly dumped trash outside the fence that secured his property, thinking that the refuse was no longer his problem. Soon, however, subtle tactics of social pressure led the landowner to rethink those actions and to change his practices.

The narrative template "place of place" also concerns an increasing trend for Casaynons to find employment long distances away from the barangay; however, they tend to maintain strong ties with their home and community. Many families have members who have relocated to the larger cities of the Philippines, or have obtained employment outside of the country due to economic necessity and/or limited career opportunities for professionals. Several teachers on the research team shared stories about moving to and from Casay to Manila as their parents found work there, and oftentimes, they recounted childhood days living with relatives in or near Casay while their parents worked far away. Interestingly, many community events and projects are regularly funded by Casaynons working abroad—many employed as seamen and housemaids—for several months or even years. The investment of people in their places is profound, notes Basso (1996), who stated "senses of place partake of cultures, of shared bodies of 'local knowledge' with which persons and whole communities render their places meaningful and endow them with so-cial importance" (p. xiv).

Casaynons' sense of place reaches deeply into other cultural spheres, including their conceptions of education, spirituality, and respect. Education has historically played an important role toward sustaining the Casaynon community, however the knowledge valued is expressed in a common phrase of Antiqueños', as Lourdes shared: "Gone to school but not truly educated." Lourdes went on to describe how this phrase highlights the importance of moral character education in the school curriculum. While going to school, obtaining a job and improving the status of the family is important, a person is perceived to be truly educated when they have a well developed sense of morality, which includes civic responsibility. Tess, clarifying the importance of education, noted: "Education was originally intended to meet the basic needs of food, shelter, and family solidarity; however, availability of resources is redefining what is considered to be a basic need." She added, "the boundaries between school and home used to be blurred, but we are told now that school and home have separate purposes—this is pushed by the curriculum and policymakers. Thus, in terms of science teaching, "hands-on" is something that should be done in the home and not so much in school. "However," Fe noted "the decision-makers are perceived as out of touch with people in the far away barangays." Carla, a parent of children attending Casay Elementary School, shared her beliefs concerning the purpose of education during a memory banking interview: "The purpose of education is to get knowledge in order to preserve humanity. Our world is almost destroyed and even the morality of the people is almost destroyed. And for this reason, we have to do something to make this a better place to live in." In another community interview, the barangay captain explained that, "Education is a process of educating, teaching, or training in order to learn and develop in all aspects, in order to have moral and social development." The focus on the moral dimension of place was a recurrent message among every community member interviewed. Mrs. Sablajon, the PTCA president, stated: "Education should aim to produce builders of a just, humane, and peaceful community. . . ." Mrs. Mediobane added that education is intended to "teach students the knowledge that they must develop in order to become responsible members of the family, community, and country. Members of the research team also discussed the importance of education to Casaynons' sense of place. Mary Jane, the high school teacher, emphasized that education should "draw out systematic development, cultivation of the mind and other supernatural power through continuous learning, reading, training and nurturing." Esperanza, expressing the belief that education was for the purpose of "creating a just and equal society" recalled the words of her father: "My father would always say 'this education is the only inheritance to you that I will give, but no one can take that away from you.' "

A common feature on the maps was illustrations of *Saint Theresa Catholic Church*, the heart of the community, established when Spanish colonists first landed on Casay's shores. The place of the Catholic church in the Casaynon lifeworld was also represented on a large mural of Casay painted at the Environmental Education Center—an image of the Saint Theresa Catholic church was painted in the center of the mural and was the largest image depicted. According to Lourdes, a meeting place or "sentro" would be important in creating a vision for the Environmental Education Center. "It's a place to come together. Catholics need a symbol—it can't be an abstract idea." Teachers and community members recommended that the Environmental Education Center should be inaugurated with a blessing given by the Saint Teresa Catholic parish priest. Accordingly, the Center was officially opened in May 2002, with an "Inaugural Blessing" which featured a candle-lit prayer and sprinkling of Holy water around the interior and outer perimeter of the Center by Father Paul. The blessing was followed by a *composo*, a musical drama about the history of Casay, a sharing of the mission and vision for the Center, a pig roast and the celebratory release of bubbles by young and old alike. Citizens describe Casay as having a unique reputation because of its friendliness, unity and strong faith, which Casaynons attribute to the central role of the Catholic Church. Purita pointed out: "In terms of religion [Casay is] a closed community—anybody who is not a Catholic tends to be an outcast. . . . An indicator of [being] Casaynon is to be Roman Catholic." The central place of Catholic faith is significant toward understanding Casaynons' perspectives regarding their use of natural resources. There is a Filipino saying: "As the sun rises, God's graces flow." Natural resources are viewed as "blessings from God," thus Casaynons freely consume what is provided. An unfortunate consequence of this faithful sense of place is that it has evoked little concern for adopting environmental conservation practices—"God will always provide."

Theme 2: "Out of Balance"

"Communities of memory," said Sergiovanni (1994), are rare ones in which members share a sense of belonging, of common identity, of history and shared goals and values along with an enduring understanding of the intrinsic meaning of these things. In such communities, the sources of authority for leadership are found in shared ideas, communicated and reinforced by the connections of people to each other because this, in itself, has meaning and importance for the community's well-being. "Balance" is a concept which embraces physical, spiritual, emotional and mental dimensions, continually providing evidence for interconnectedness. Casay, a barangay characterized by values of peace, cooperation and unity (Arellano et al., 2001), is typically depicted as a community uniquely in balance. However, with expanding interest in participating in the global marketplace, and the contractual agreements these entail, there is evidence to suggest that Casaynons are experiencing disharmony in their physical environment, and by extension in their personal lives.

The stories of "out of balance" shared by research team members and community members exhibited characteristics of disorder, fragmentation, and/or uncontrollability. Specific stories of out of balance center on themes such as: lack of respect for food, the loss of ground water, "water/air/food is not pure," the disappearance of buri plants, and lacking respect for the environment. Throughout the stories there is evidence that rapid change is taking place as needs exceed available resources. Imelda, a grade two teacher at Casay Elementary School, underscored this point noting:

> Here in Casay are some cases why it is that the number of coconut trees is decreasing. One reason is, land where it used to be planted by coconuts, was converted into rice fields. The other reason is that areas with coconut trees were also converted into residential lots due to increasing number of people. Because of these conversions, people are not even able to replant those trees that they have cut.

Casay has depended on resources from both the land and sea; however as the finite amount of land available for cultivation disappears, increasingly people are looking to the ocean as a ready supply of food and materials. The practice among fishermen is to take the fish and "ask to be even more blessed" in the catch. It is a greater affirmation of one's faith to make this request of God; however, it has not been conducive towards developing an environmental ethic of conservation. "People on the coast don't worry to store resources or save money because the catch is always there. Farmers, however, have to plan—to be more methodological" (8/2/01, Casay Research Team). Purita noted that the belief that God will always provide is anchored in the expression, "Basi pa lang—we have a strong faith that our maker will cause good things to happen."

There is evidence to suggest that values are shifting from a view of community as sacred and grounded in kinship responsibilities to a more technically rational orientation based on social contracts. Teresa spoke of the ordinances that now govern actions in the barangay: "It used to be that the gathering of bamboo shoots was not enforced. But now we have ordinances. Why do we need ordinances?" Modern technologies have brought economic gains and conveniences, but these have often introduced new environmental problems. Consequently, as Fe suggested, responses to such problems are being addressed by instituting rules for environmental practices enforced by *official* authorities:

> Fe: I remember when I was in elementary grades the tiange used to use "jars" which are made of bottles and the caps are made of tin. Today they use plastic jars. And when I was in elementary I remember the *ginamos* (shrimp paste) are wrapped in the gabi leaves or banana leaves. Now they are wrapped in plastics too. When we had our general assembly last week, some of the store owners throw their garbage in the lublub so the issue came up again during the assembly and it's already reached the attention of the people or store owners.
>
> Deb: So do they have an alternative or do they do that because they don't have any alternatives? What do they do if they don't put it in the lublub?
>
> Tess: They are advised to make a hole or a compost pit and then throw it there or burn it. But some of the store owners just throw it in the lublub without making a compost pit.
>
> Fe: The decision we had during our general assembly is that each house should make a compost pit . . . the barangay officials will go around to check on compost pits. Next, they will check on the toilets because it was identified that some families don't have toilets—they just use the beach.

In discussing the tiange in terms of waste disposal issues, several community members were also concerned with the growing preference for non-traditional foods, particularly convenience foods. They attributed dietary changes to enticing advertisements for "junk foods" posted in stores and on television which targeted consumers of all ages. They also noted that Casaynons returning from work abroad introduced non-traditional foods such as spaghetti. Such foods, which replace the traditional dietary staple of rice, are very desirable among community members, as they signify a higher social and economic status because they come from abroad. Several community members noted that it takes a "strong mind" to recognize and resist such temptations. The "out of balance" narratives that were shared by participants reflected a sense of sadness or loss. A comment by Lourdes attributes the "out of balance" metaphor to the adoption of Western capitalist practices whereby people become disconnected from the origins of ideas and living things, which in turn enables lack of consciousness and haphazard actions:

> It will take a lot of efforts to debunk the idea or disturb the idea [of colonialism] because if you look at how we learned, we seem to have abandoned many of those things that made us comfortable in favor of a Western world—a "throw-away" society. In fact, people do not even know the sources of materials that we eat—like some never have seen the pineapple plant bear its fruit.

Research team members wondered why the teachers of Casay had not previously taken notice of, much less acted on, the effects of environmental degradation. One explanation was that loss of environmental awareness comes with the familiarity and comfort of living in one's daily surroundings, as Tess reflected:

> Probably these people [in Casay] have not experienced having no water, unlike here in the city. We value [water] very much because there are times when we don't have water. Probably [Casaynons] are thinking they will always have these things, such as water, around them. They could not foresee the future that later on these things could not be there anymore.

There was also recognition that long range environmental planning and maintenance is challenging when the immediate living needs of families must be met. Lourdes explained:

> I think the reason is that they only see things which are directly affecting their lives, for example, the basic need for food . . . they do not see environment as something that would directly affect their lives . . . you're focus is simply your stomach, your shelter.

The memory banking experience helped the research team reflect on physical needs and changes in the community, and Casaynons' sense of indigeneity. The narratives of place of place and out of balance point to the need for a more authentic science education which revolves around the past and present lives of learners. In this sense, the very idea of environmental education as a Western construct poses paradoxes for barangays such as Casay, which are experiencing rapid economic and social growth.

Theme 3: "Return to Our Roots"

Lourdes' reference to Filipino science education as colonized by Western ideology was not an isolated view; other members of the research team also provided historical accounts of science education as a practice imported from the United States (Bilbao et al., 2002). Following World War II, Filipino educational reform featured the introduction of curriculum texts and pedagogy developed and published by the United States, Australia, and Great Britain. Curricular resources were devoid of Filipino contexts for learning science, and formal classroom pedagogy promoted didactic instruction of abstract modern science concepts. Today, Filipino education reflects conceptions of modern schooling steeped in the individualistic, competitive culture associated with industrialist societies. The disenfranchisement of local contexts and ways of knowing through practices of science education based on conceptions of education purported to modernize (i.e., improve) life, has threatened everyday practices of community in "developing countries" (Gray, 1999; Tavana, Hite, & Randall, 1997; Waldrip & Taylor, 1999). Bill Kyle, who has worked with South African science educators for over 15 years, describes the hegemonic ways western science and science education reform uproot indigenous non-western knowledge:

> Western science promotes a hierarchical and linear form of knowledge production, dismissing questions of context that provide information with meaning and potential application . . . while the history and nature of science can be viewed from the perspective of being detached, impersonal, and 'objective' . . . there is also the human side that links the observed with the object of the observations. . . . The success of modern science is its ability to depict its findings as universal knowledge. Thus, a particular way of knowing has been legitimized, while other ways of knowing have been de-legitimated. By defining civilization and reality, the imperialism of modernity has characterized indigenous knowledge systems as subaltern. (Kyle, 1999, pp. 2–3)

The narrative template of "Return to Our Roots" resonates with David Gruenewald's (2003) conception of a *critical pedagogy of place* that he describes as serving two objectives—the *decolonization* and *re-inhabitation* of curriculum. Modernist conceptions of curriculum emphasize teaching and learning devoid of grounding within local contexts of meaning-making and a locally-generated purpose for education (Bowers, 2001). Tess explained that "to be a *Department of Education, Culture and Sports* (DECS) approved textbook it must be acultural." In other words, Filipino textbooks must avoid using culturally relevant examples, so as not to offend the Muslim population of Mindanao. For example, *lechon* (roasted pig) is a food typically eaten throughout the Visayas, but it should not be mentioned in a national textbook because it is taboo in the Muslim culture. Textbooks are supposed to identify a single, common culture contribution to a one-size-fits-all curriculum.

The memory banking experience provided an opportunity for team members to generate an alternative view of science education as a cultural practice framed within a *community-based* perspective. In the process, teachers developed a critical consciousness that encouraged them to question connections between their cultural roots and their changing environment. Memory bank discussions raised questions among participants about the environment—causes and effects of environmental conditions, sociopolitical tensions, economic and geophysical constraints related to environmental practices, and approaches taken in the past, present and future to deal with environmental dilemmas. The following conversation concerning the decline of milkfish reflects the teachers' heightened awareness of complex interactions contributing to environmental dilemmas in their community:

Fe: I think one of the reasons for the scarcity of fingerlings is the catching of the mother milkfish. Some fishermen are violating the law.

Deb: So, the catching of the mother fish by the big-time fishing operators causes the scarcity of fry because of illegal fishing.

Tess: Another one would be because of the over-collection of the milkfish fry—only very few go back to the sea and become mature. So, there will be less mother milkfish which could reproduce fry.

Espy: For those who catch the mother "bangus" in the seashore, maybe they have no knowledge about what they are doing. When I was in high school, I was able to read that once you catch a mother bangus you have to return it back to the seashore. But the problem is, are the fishermen aware that they are catching a mother bangus?

Fe: Is it only the mother bangus which should not be caught? What about the male bangus? Because we know that a female bangus cannot reproduce without a male bangus.

Espy: For me, the female bangus reproduces many eggs.

Fe: But the egg cell of the female bangus will not be fertilized without the sperm of the male bangus. So both are needed to produce an egg.

Lourdes: Have you ever discussed the life cycle of the milkfish in your class? There is a topic of the life cycle of animals in grade 4, I think? The typical example is a butterfly.

Fe: We realize that now. We discussed about the life cycle of the frog, mosquitoes, but not the bangus.

Lourdes: Then it's now the time to buy a poster of the life cycle of milkfish at SEAFDEC [Southeast Asian Fisheries Development Center]!

Although teachers began to envision local contexts for teaching science, they needed ways to develop their understanding of science concepts associated with environmental phenomena such as the life cycle of the milkfish. In the case of the milkfish, a WVSU graduate student volunteered to obtain information about the milkfish life cycle from the university library. Several teachers consulted local fishermen concerning additional questions about milkfish. The discussion above represents our notion of re-inhabitation as an important dimension of building a science teacher learning community wherein teachers take up positions as active generators of knowledge. Furthermore, this kind of learning community draws on the expertise of others having localized scientific knowledge—both formal and informal in nature.

Teachers realized even colleagues in their midst could be sources for reliable science content information. The memory banking discussions provided Jane, a participating high school biology teacher, opportunities to share background science information about the life cycle of the buri plant:

Jane: This is buri. This one reaches the age of 30 or more. It will take two years for the seed to germinate under natural conditions because of the hard cover. However, when removed from the hard cover, the seed will germinate in about a month. When we get the seed coat [off], it will germinate faster. . . . The plant usually lasts for 30 years or more. When the plant bears flowers, it dies.

Team members also began to critically reflect on social and economic factors associated with the life cycle of the buri plant:

Lourdes: Have you ever asked anyone in the community whether they are planting buri or understood something about the life cycle of buri?

Espy: When we ask our older people of how to plant buri they would tell us that buri grows by themselves. So we considered buri as a wild plant. . .

Tess: What causes the absence of the buri now? Did they cut it and replace it with other plants? I think they planted other plants aside from the buri?

Fe: Because the area now was converted into an agricultural land.

Sherry: Does buri just grow in certain soil types?

Jane: [I read] buri grows in a soil that is sandy-loam. Then it grows in clusters.

Lourdes: Could it be that an environmental issue [is that] because buri bears flowers once and after that they die, is that an environmental issue? Why?

Espy: It is an issue because when you will eat all the fruits [of buri] then there will be no buri left . . .

Lourdes: But take note on your memory bank that buri is used as sources of things like that. And I know in parts of Anini-y down here, we used to buy buri bags, mats and hats from this place. And it was a cottage industry in Anini-y. So now what happens?

The teachers had long accepted the assumption that buri only grows wild; however, the research team discussion created possibilities for science inquiry as participants considered how soil types, and seed production and dispersal might influence the reproduction of buri. Additionally, the discussion lead teachers to question the decontextualized and ahistorical portrayal of science concepts reflected in science textbooks.

Mapping out the relationships of science concepts to the broader array of social, economic, religious, cultural, and other contextual dimensions of life among Casaynons was the beginning of creating "community-based" science education. In the words of one teacher, Fe, teachers have felt "tied down," accountable to teaching national elementary curriculum standards—the *Philippine Elementary Learning Competencies* [PELC] (*Department of Education, Culture and Sports, 1998*). The teachers indicated, however, that they felt compelled to teach beyond the PELC, as Merlinda shared: "Not all that we are teaching is in the PELC—we have to consider the situations of the children that we have in the community." Espy further explained the nature of such "situations" in terms of looking beyond the decontextualized curriculum topics of the PELC to address the cultural background students bring to the classroom:

In our science book, I remember when we have an objective based from the PELC—the practice of first-aid in a poisoning case. If we look at the book, the ideas are very limited. So in order to have more knowledge or ideas to be shared to my students, I gathered materials or information which I found in our house and discussed it [with] my pupils. I also used some of the materials which were brought by my pupils. . . . We discussed about what to do if a person got poisoned. I haven't yet finished my explanations but my pupils are already shouting—"Ma'am, let the victim drink coconut milk". . . . I observed that most of their answers were all based from their practices at home. So their own personal knowledge about first aid was more enriched by some of the concepts that they learned from the book, and you can also learn from them.

The theme of seeing our roots does not simply imply a romantic sense of nostalgia; we recognize that there are tensions between our past, present, and future science and community narratives. Ironies, ambiguities, and relationships between ideas, values, and people are central to the lifeworld of what it means to be a community. The ability to enact science teaching which addresses community needs stands in stark contrast to a curriculum designed for the purposes of *banking* abstract concepts (Freire, 1970). Diverging from a decontextualized notion of curriculum, Casay teachers are beginning to envision a science education that goes beyond the science walls. Not only are they generating a culturally relevant curriculum, they are aspiring to enact practices of science education that centrally value the community lifeworld.

IMPLICATIONS FOR RETHINKING SCIENCE EDUCATION PRACTICES AND RESEARCH

In this study, memory banking served as a tool that supported our learning about science education as a sociocultural practice in the Filipino barangay, Casay. We refer to *tool* not as an intrusive device, but rather in the way that Wertsch (1998) describes tools—as serving a *mediational function*. Memory banking served as a way for teachers to generate accounts which represented sociohistorical referents important to the community lifeworld of Casaynons. The composition of specific narratives by the research team provided a means for exploring our individual interpretations of "community" in Casay; whereas, schematic narrative templates reflected a critical turn within the study as team members examined relationships between the community narratives and our ways of thinking about environmental actions and science education. In this concluding discussion, we want to explore insights and lingering questions concerning our vision for practicing community-based science education.

Reframing Teacher Professional Development and Research as a Community-Based Practice

This study demonstrates the possibilities afforded when science teacher professional development and research is conceptualized in terms of a postcolonial perspective. Since 1898, Filipino classrooms have been occupied by imported teaching strategies and resources (for a detailed discussion, see Bilbao et al., 2001) thus promoting decontextualized, and often culturally irrelevant, practices of science teaching. Approaches to science professional development have followed a similar trend as outside experts have often been used to administer training programs for teachers, thus disregarding teachers' professional knowledge as a legitimate resource for teacher learning. In this study, memory banking served as a tool for enabling teacher educators, teachers, and local citizens to recognize and value knowledge *of* and *for* community. The narratives provided team members a means to explore not only aspects of *what* science knowledge might be seen as relevant, but also to understand ways of knowing in relation to their sense of *being* Casaynons. The notion of *re-inhabitation* of science teaching and learning conflicts with the decontextualized narrative of "standardized" science education reform—a curricular vision devoid of a *sense of place*, as described by David Orr:

> a great deal of what passes for knowledge is little more than abstraction piled upon abstraction, disconnected from tangible experience, real problems, and the places where we live and work. In this sense it is utopian, which literally means "nowhere". . . . Place is nebulous to educators because to a great extent we are a deplaced people for whom our immediate places are no longer sources of food, water, livelihood, energy, materials, friends, recreation, or sacred inspiration. (1992, p. 126)

In our work, we have questioned our own assumptions of what constitutes meaningful science education. Thus in our planning for the study, we avoided placing science education in the foreground—as *the* focal point of our inquiry, rather we used memory-banking to establish a sense of place and to generate a practice of science that embodied the community narratives in which Casaynons find meaning for life.

Moving Beyond Culturally Relevant to Community-Based Science Teacher Education and Research

Our focus on the place of sociocultural and historical perspectives in developing ways to connect science education to the local lifeworld of a community might be described as creating a "culturally relevant" (Ladson-Billings, 1994, 1995) or "culturally responsive" (Gay, 2000) curriculum. However, as Keane and Malcolm (2003) have questioned, these curricular frameworks presume education to be relevant or responsive—*to what?* Within the framework of culturally relevant and responsive science education pedagogy, the science (of the traditional Western variety) remains the same, placing emphasis on helping learners cross borders to become participants in science learning. We see such pedagogy as problematic because of the underlying assumption that there is a deficit in the present state of learners, and that they need they need to relocate to a better lifeworld; in science education learners are beckoned to crossover to become participants in an insular world of science. The promise of such reified curricular landscapes not only enables irrelevant instruction, it also reproduces schools as sites disconnected from the social world of learners. In our view of what it means to be community-based, it is critically important to give central place to the complex lifeworlds students bring as learners, and to explore ways science—and other ways of knowing—might draw on complex intersections of everyday life to produce new and useful insights of benefit to the local community.

Our experiences in Casay provided an opportunity for us to initiate a community-based practice of science education. The conversations that have emerged have challenged us to rethink what, how, and why we teach science. Ultimately, the construction of the Casay Environmental Education Center signified the creation of a Casaynon vision for science education. To begin with, the notion to create a large outdoor structure diverged from the design of Western-style schools which feature classrooms to contain teaching and learning. The location of the Center was significant as it was built on top of a concrete slab—all that remained of a former school structure destroyed during World War II. Community members felt it was an ideal site as it overlooked the meeting of a river and the sea; while still quite beautiful, there was evidence of much erosion along the river's edge and pollution from a pig farm carried directly into the ocean. The construction of the Center began with large speakers playing music to signal that everyone in the community should come to participate in the building process in the Filipino spirit of *dagiyaw*, which translated means "bring what you can to help for all." The architectural design of the Center spoke volumes of a Casaynon vision for community-based science education. The Center had a thatched roof of woven nipa supported by concrete columns; the idea was "to have a wall-less place which could hold as many people as possible." Examples of science learning activities at the Center have included: a skywatch night attended by parents, teachers, students hosted by WVSU university faculty and students, an *Environmental Camp* hosted by the Casay teachers involving an overnight stay for students followed by a community-wide clean up the next day. These science education actions were beyond relevant, they were constitutive of community.

Building Community-Based Visions
Through Critical Conversations

Talking and writing about the intersections of narratives of community and science education in this study poised tensions that have challenged us to think more deeply about our purposes and practices as science educators and researchers. And whereas our conversations have been meaningful, they have often led us into places of uncertainty—a direction antithetical to rhetoric calling a more "scientifically based" approaches to science teacher education and classroom learning. Science education researchers have become critical of national reform strategies which promote use of standardized curricula, high stakes testing and accountability policies have disenfranchised teachers, students, and community members from negotiating purposes and practices of science teaching and learning (Barton & Tobin, 2002). Michelle Fine and Lois Weis identify this absence of dialogue as a hegemonic condition:

> in contexts of systemic silencing, there is no vacuum. Instead, the persistent and uninterrupted echoes of damaging voices of privilege populate the halls and the classrooms. Silence is not simply the absence of exported marginalized voices; it is the simultaneous and parasitic invitation to voices that dominate and "other." (2003, p. 7)

In an analysis of the U.S. *National Science Education Standards* [NSES] (National Research Council, 1996), Alberto Rodriguez (1997) described the *NSES* as having an "invisible discourse" as the text promotes the rhetoric of teaching "science for all," yet is silent in terms identifying and recommending ways to address inequities related to students' ethnic, socioeconomic, and gendered identities. In this study, memory banking prompted remembrances of wartime occupation, beliefs in the supernatural, loss of natural resources, and uncertainties about maintaining traditional practices. Although these identities may seem remote to the interests of science education, as our study illustrates, these are the sorts of narratives of community that challenge what knowledge and ways of knowing citizens may find meaningful. Instead of privileging the grand narratives of scientific research used to reinforce the architecture of modern education—what Dan Lortie (1975) characterized as "eggcrate" structures, we should encourage research approaches that enable communities to generate alternative visions for education like that of Casay's de-walled classroom offering a view of the world.

REFERENCES

Aikenhead, G. S. (1996). Science education: Border crossing into the subculture of science. *Studies in Science Education, 27*, 1–52.

Altheide, D. L., & Johnson, J. M. (1998). Criteria for assessing interpretive validity in qualitative research. In M. K. Denzin & Y. S. Lincoln (Eds.), *Collecting and interpreting qualitative materials* (pp. 283–312). Thousand Oaks, CA: Sage.

Arellano, E. L., Barcenal, T. L., Bilbao, P. P., Castellano, M. A., Nichols, S. E., & Tippins, D. J. (2001). Case-based pedagogy as a context for collaborative inquiry in the Philippines. *Journal of Research in Science Teaching, 38*(4), 1–27.

Atkinson, P. A., & Coffey, J., A. (1996). *Making sense of qualitative data: Complementary research strategies.* Thousand Oaks, CA: Sage.

Barton, A. C. (1998). Teaching science with homeless children: Pedagogy, representation, and identity. *Journal of Research in Science Teaching, 35*(4), 379–394.

Barton, A. C. (2003). *Teaching science for social justice.* New York: Teachers College Press.

Barton, A. C., & Tobin, K. (2002). Learning about transformative research through others' stories: What Does it mean to involve "others" in science education reform? *Journal of Research in Science Teaching, 39*(2), 110–113.

Basso, K. H. (1996). *Wisdom sits in places: Landscape and language among the Apache.* Albuquerque: University of New Mexico Press.

Beyer, L. E., & Apple, M. W. (1988). Values and politics in the curriculum. In L. E. Beyer & M. W. Apple (Eds.), *The curriculum: Problems, politics, and possibilities* (pp. 3–18). Albany: State University of New York.

Bilbao, P., Morano, L. N., Barcenal, T., Castellano, M. A., Nichols, S., & Tippins, D. J. (2002). In P. Fraser-Abder (Ed.), *Professional development of science teachers: Local insights with lessons for the global community* (pp. 70–87). New York: RoutledgeFalmer.

Bowers, C. A. (2001). *Educating for eco-justice and community.* Athens: The University of Georgia Press.

Cobb, P. (1994). Where is the mind? Constructivist and sociocultural perspectives on mathematical development. *Educational Researcher, 23*(7), 13–19.

Charmaz, K. (2002). Qualitative interviewing and grounded theory analysis. In J. A. Holstein & J. F. Gubrium (Eds.), *Handbook of interview research: Context and method* (pp. 675–694). Thousand Oaks, CA: Sage.

Department of Education, Culture and Sports, Bureau of Elementary Education. (1998). *Philippine elementary learning competencies.* Pasig City: Department of Education, Culture and Sports.

Fine, M., & Weis, L. (2003). *Silenced voices and extraordinary conversations: Reimagining schools.* New York: Teachers College Press.

Freire, P. (1970). *Pedagogy of the oppressed.* New York: Continuum Publishing.

Fusco, D. (2001). Creating relevant science through urban planning and gardening. *Journal of Research in Science Teaching, 38*(8), 860–877.

Gray, B. V. (1999). Science education in the developing world: Issues and considerations. *Journal of Research in Science Teaching, 36*(3), 261–268.

Green, L. W., George, M. A., Frankish, C. J., Daniel, M., Herbert, C. J., Bowie, W. R., & Evans, M. J. (1995). *Study of participatory research in health promotion: Review and recommendations for the development of participatory action research in Canada.* Vancouver, British Columbia: Royal Society of Canada Institute of Health Promotion.

Greeno, J. G., Collins, A. M., & Resnick, L. (1996). Cognition and learning. In D. C. Berliner & R. C. Calfee (Eds.), *Handbook of educational psychology* (pp. 15–46). New York: Macmillan.

Gruenewald, D. (2003). The best of both worlds: A critical pedagogy of place. *Educational Researcher, 32*(4), 3–12.

Hammond, L. (2001). Notes from California: An anthropological approach to urban science education for language minority families. *Journal of Research in Science Teaching, 38*(9), 983–999.

Hellmann, J. (1981). *Fables of fact: The new journalism as a new fiction*. Urbana, IL: University of Chicago Press.

Keane, M., & Malcolm, C. (2003). Relevant science education, but relevant to what? *LabTalk*, 47(2), 4–9.

Kyle, W. C., Jr. (1999). Science education in developing countries: Access, equity, and ethical responsibility. *Journal of the southern African Association for Research in Mathematics and Science Education*, 3(1), 1–13.

Lemke, J. (2001). Articulating communities: Sociocultural perspectives on science education. *Journal of Research in Science Teaching*, 38(3), 296–316.

Lortie, D. C. (1975). *Schoolteacher: A sociological study*. Chicago, IL: University of Chicago Press.

Nazarea, V. D. (1998). *Cultural memory and biodiversity*. Tuscon: University of Arizona Press.

Nichols, S., Tippins, D. J., Bilbao, P., Barcenal, T., Castellano, M., & Morano, L. (2001, April). *A narrative study of community, change, and science education through case-based pedagogy and research*. Paper presented at the annual meeting of the American Education Research Association, Seattle, WA.

Orr, D. W. (1992). *Ecological literacy: Education and the transition to a postmodern world*. New York: State University of New York Press.

Rodriguez, A. (1997). The dangerous discourse of invisibility: A critique of the national research council's national science education standards. *Journal of Research in Science Teaching*, 34(1), 19–37.

Rogoff, B., & Lave, J. (1984). *Everyday cognition: Its development in social context*. Cambridge, MA: Harvard University Press.

Salomon, G. (1993). *Distributed cognitions: Psychological and educational considerations*. New York: Cambridge University Press.

Seiler, G. (2001). Reversing the standard direction: Science emerging from the lives of African American students. *Journal of Research in Science Teaching*, 38(9), 1000–1014.

Sergiovanni, T. J. (1994). *Building community in schools*. San Francisco, CA: Jossey-Bass.

Sergiovanni, T. J. (2000). *The lifeworld of leadership: Creating culture, community, and personal meaning in our schools*. San Francisco, CA: Jossey-Bass.

Tavana, G. V., Hite, S. J., & Vance. R. E. (1997). Cultural values and education in Western Samoa: Tensions between colonial roots and influences and contemporary indigenous needs. *International Journal of Educational Reform*, 6, 11–19.

Vygotsky, L. S. (1978). *Mind in society*. Cambridge, MA: Harvard University Press.

Waldrip, B. G., & Taylor, P. C. (1999). Permeability of students' worldview to their school views in a non-Western developing country. *Journal of Research in Science Teaching*, 36(3), 289–303.

Wertsch, J. V. (1998). *Mind as action*. New York: Oxford University Press.

Wertsch, J. V. (2002). *Voices of collective remembering*. New York: Cambridge University Press.

Wertsch, J. V., Río, P., & Alvarez, A. (1995). Sociocultural studies: History, action, and mediation. In. J. V. Wertsch, P. Río, & A. Alvarez (Eds.), *Sociocultural studies of mind* (pp. 1–36). New York: University of Cambridge Press.

Zeller, N. (1995). Narrative strategies for case report. *International Journal of Qualitative Studies in Education*, 8(1), 75–88.

Author Index

Subject Index

For Product Safety Concerns and Information please contact our EU
representative GPSR@taylorandfrancis.com
Taylor & Francis Verlag GmbH, Kaufingerstraße 24, 80331 München, Germany